Aristocrats and Servitors

THE BOYAR ELITE IN RUSSIA, 1613-1689

Aristocrats and Servitors

THE BOYAR ELITE IN RUSSIA, 1613-1689

Robert O. Crummey

PRINCETON UNIVERSITY PRESS
PRINCETON, NEW JERSEY

Publication of this book has been aided by a grant
from the Paul Mellon Fund of Princeton University Press

This book has been composed in Linotron Caledonia
Clothbound editions of Princeton University Press books
are printed on acid-free paper, and binding materials are
chosen for strength and durability. Paperbacks, although satisfactory
for personal collections, are not usually suitable for library rebinding.

Printed in the United States of America by
Princeton University Press, Princeton, New Jersey

to Nancy

*without whom
there would be no book*

ACKNOWLEDGMENTS

Rarely has an author owed so great a debt to so many people and institutions. Yale University and the University of California, Davis, provided sabbatical leaves for research and writing. As a consequence, I was able to spend two extended periods in Moscow, first, in 1968-1969, in the History Faculty of Moscow University as a participant in the University of Toronto's exchange with the Ministry of Higher and Specialized Secondary Education of the USSR, and, subsequently, in 1974, as a visiting fellow of the Institute of the History of the USSR on the IREX exchange with the Academy of Sciences of the USSR. The Yale University Concilium on Foreign Area Studies provided financial support for my first stay in Moscow, the American Council of Learned Societies for the second. In addition, the ACLS generously gave me a fellowship which I used in this country for research, writing, and learning to live with computers.

Many colleagues have helped me along the way. The idea of writing this book emerged from conversations with Gustave Alef, and he has given me encouragement and constructive criticism at every step. I doubt that I would have finished this book without his support. Brenda Meehan-Waters has been a true friend and helpful critic, Joan Afferica contributed valuable advice on archival research and problems of interpretation, Ann M. Kleimola provided insights on the boyars in the sixteenth century, and Daniel C. Waugh helped with bibliographical references and by his incomparable command of the techniques of analyzing manuscripts. I am also grateful to my younger colleagues, particularly Nancy Shields-Kollmann, Peter B. Brown, and Brian Davies, for taking the risk of sharing with me work that has not yet been published.

This book is a collective venture in an even broader sense, since I have learned a great deal from my colleagues who took part in the conferences on the history of Russian officialdom organized by Walter M. Pintner and Don K. Rowney. Moreover, I have profited greatly from the comments of other participants in the international conferences on medieval Russian history that have met, over the years, in Claremont, Oxford, and Berlin. In their very different ways, Hans-Joachim Torke, Carsten Goehrke, and Walter Leitsch have made me think seriously about the basic assumptions on which I have built this study.

For a book of this kind, the support and cooperation of Soviet scholars and institutions are indispensable. I am particularly grateful to the Institute of the History of the USSR and for the diligence and help of the staff of TsGADA, particularly archivist E. M. Dobrushin, who prepared materials for my use. I owe a profound debt to colleagues in Moscow—in particular, S. M. Kashtanov, M. E. Bychkova, S. O. Shmidt, V. I. Koretskii, V. I. Buganov, my "chief" at the Institute, and, above all, the late A. A. Zimin, whose passionate enthusiasm for historical study and love of life and people put the rest of us to shame.

All of these people have contributed something positive to this book; the shortcomings are mine alone. In addition, I have received help from many, many others whose names only they themselves and God know.

Closer to home, I wish to thank my colleagues in the History Departments of Yale and UC Davis for their helpful comments and, far more important, their moral support. My family has lived patiently with the boyars for many years; I owe them more than I can express, particularly my wife, to whom this book is dedicated.

ROC
Davis, California
August 1, 1982

CONTENTS

LIST OF ILLUSTRATIONS
Following page 134

TABLES AND DIAGRAM

* From *Russian Officialdom: The Bureaucratization of Russian Society from the Seventeenth to the Twentieth Century,* edited by Walter M. Pintner and Don Karl Rowney. Copyright 1980 The University of North Carolina Press.

ABBREVIATIONS

AAE   *Akty, sobrannye v bibliotekakh i arkhivakh Rossiiskoi imperii Arkheograficheskoiu ekspeditsieiu.* 4 vols. St. Petersburg, 1836.

AI   *Akty istoricheskie, sobrannye i izdannye Arkheograficheskoiu komissieiu.* 5 vols. St. Petersburg, 1841-1842.

AMG   *Akty moskovskago gosudarstva.* 3 vols. St. Petersburg, 1890-1901.

BK   TsGADA. Fund 210 (Razriadnyi prikaz). Boiarskie knigi.

BS   TsGADA. Fund 210. Boiarskie spiski.

ChOIDR   *Chteniia v Imperatorskom obshchestve istorii i drevnostei rossiiskikh pri Moskovskom universitete.* 264 vols. Moscow, 1846-1918.

DAI   *Dopolneniia k Aktam istoricheskim, sobrannym i izdannym Arkheograficheskoiu komissieiu.* 12 vols. St. Petersburg, 1846-1875.

DR   *Dvortsovye razriady.* 4 vols. St. Petersburg, 1850-1855.

DRV   *Drevniaia rossiiskaia vivliofika.* 20 vols. St. Petersburg, 1788-1791.

ES   *Entsiklopedicheskii slovar'.* Published by F. A. Brockhaus and I. A. Efron. 84 vols. and 4 vols. supplement. St. Petersburg, 1890-1907.

FzOG   *Forschungen zur osteuropäischen Geschichte.* Berlin, 1954-

Izvestiia RGO   *Izvestiia Russkago genealogicheskago obshchestva.* 4 vols. in 3. St. Petersburg, 1900-1911.

JfGO   *Jahrbücher für Geschichte Osteuropas.* Breslau, 1936- Munich,

KR   *Knigi razriadnye.* 2 vols. St. Petersburg, 1853-1855.

LIRO   *Letopis' Istoriko-rodoslovnago obshchestva.* 44 fasc. in 11 vols. Moscow, 1905-1915.

Mosk. nekropol'	Nikolai Mikhailovich, Vel. Kn. *Moskovskii nekropol'*. 3 vols. St. Petersburg, 1907-1908.
PDS	*Pamiatniki diplomaticheskikh snoshenii drevnei Rossii s derzhavami inostrannymi.* 10 vols. St. Petersburg, 1851-1871.
PRP	*Pamiatniki russkogo prava.* 8 vols. Moscow, 1952-1963.
PSRL	*Polnoe sobranie russkikh letopisei.* St. Petersburg, 1841-Moscow, .
PSZ	*Polnoe sobranie zakonov Rossiiskoi imperii.* Sobranie pervoe. 45 vols. St. Petersburg, 1830-1843.
RBS	*Russkii biograficheskii slovar'.* 25 vols. St. Petersburg, 1896-1918.
RIB	*Russkaia istoricheskaia biblioteka.* 39 vols. St. Petersburg-Leningrad, 1872-1927.
RK	*Rodoslovnaia kniga kniazei i dvorian rossiiskikh.* 2 vols. Moscow, 1787.
RK 1475	Buganov, V. I., ed. *Razriadnaia kniga 1475-1598 gg.* Moscow, 1966.
RK 1550	*Razriadnaia kniga 1550-1636.* 2 vols. Moscow, 1976.
Rus. pr. nekropol'	Sheremetevskii, V. *Russkii provintsial'nyi nekropol'.* Vol. 1. Moscow, 1914.
Sb. mosk. st.	TsGADA. Fund 210. Stolbtsy moskovskogo stola.
SGGD	*Sobranie gosudarstvennykh gramot i dogovorov.* 5 vols. Moscow, 1813-1828.
TsGADA	Tsentral'nyi gosudarstvennyi arkhiv drevnikh aktov. Moscow.
Vremennik OIDR	*Vremennik Imperatorskago obshchestva istorii i drevnostei rossiiskikh pri Moskovskom universitete.* 25 vols. Moscow, 1849-1857.
Zap. kn. mosk. st.	TsGADA. Fund 210. Zapisnye knigi moskovskogo stola.
ZhMNP	*Zhurnal Ministerstva narodnago prosveshcheniia.* 434 vols. in 2 series. St. Petersburg, 1834-1917.

Aristocrats and Servitors

THE BOYAR ELITE IN RUSSIA, 1613-1689

"A bear in the woods is like a boyar in town."

"The tsar is gracious and his mercy passes
through the boyars' sieve."

"At a wedding, everyone is a boyar."

RUSSIAN PROVERBS

INTRODUCTION

This book is a study of an elite group, the members of the Boyar Duma or royal council of seventeenth-century Russia. In the seventeenth century, the Boyar Duma was the "highest consultative body" in the Muscovite political system and the focal point of the royal administration and the judicial system.[1] In essence, it was an informal group of prominent advisers and officials of the tsar. When so inclined, the ruler consulted the members of the council on a wide variety of important matters of state. On many occasions in the seventeenth century, they collectively heard judicial appeals, advised the staffs of the bureaucratic chanceries on the handling of difficult cases, and consulted with the tsar on important questions of domestic policy and foreign affairs. A more detailed discussion of the Duma's prerogatives and procedures would take us into an area of intense historical controversy that lies outside the present study. Because it was a customary advisory body, sources of the time do not describe its precise role in the Muscovite system of government nor spell out the ways in which it functioned. We have no protocols of its sessions or summaries of the discussions that must have taken place at its meetings. Understandably, then, historians have debated many features of its constitutional role and inner workings and what their conclusions on these detailed issues imply about the nature of the Muscovite political system.[2]

From their passionate arguments, we can draw a few general conclusions about the changing role and significance of the Duma in the seventeenth century. To begin with, just as in earlier times, the members of the council served the tsar. They gave advice and made decisions on legal and administrative matters when he asked them to.[3] Moreover, the Duma was only one part of a complex network of institutions and informal personal relationships through which the tsar consulted his leading subjects on matters of state or gained their tacit support for decisions that he and his advisers had already made. In the seventeenth century, for example, the tsar also met with the leaders of the Eastern Orthodox

Church, the *zemskii sobor*, or national estates, and with representatives of social groups such as the merchants. On many occasions, the ruler issued decrees entirely on his own authority.

As a body, the Duma stood between the person of the tsar and the growing network of administrative chanceries (*prikazy*). Acting on the ruler's authority, its members decided cases which the chancery officials could not resolve for lack of appropriate legal stipulations or precedents. At the same time, it was the prikazy, not the Duma, which kept records of the decisions and carried them out.

Moreover, in broader terms, the Duma as a body probably took no initiative in setting the course of Russia's foreign and domestic policy. Seventeenth-century sources give us very little information about the process by which political decisions were made. Nevertheless, it seems reasonable to assume that the initiative in establishing national policy came from a small number of the tsar's closest advisers and from the most outstanding chancery officials.

Finally, the Duma's role in the Muscovite system of government was by no means static. By its very nature, its significance inevitably changed somewhat from one reign to the next, depending on the personality and political style and needs of each tsar in turn. Moreover, earlier historians are in rare agreement on the general direction of the Duma's evolution in the seventeenth century. By the late 1670s, the council as a body was beginning to lose its position as the focal point of the governmental system. Its meetings took on a largely ceremonial character, and, even more than before, smaller groups of royal advisers and officials made the decisions that set the course of the state day by day.

In the final analysis, after more than a century of study, we still know far too little about the Duma. Perhaps a brave young scholar will undertake a modern comparative study of the Muscovite system of government unencumbered by the constitutionalist yearnings or defensiveness of the giants of nineteenth-century historiography.

The present work approaches the members of the Duma, not as a body, but as a group of important individuals. For our purposes, the fact that they reached its ranks sets them apart as men of exceptional power, prestige, or good fortune; long before the seventeenth century, the rulers of Muscovy rewarded their leading courtiers and officials with the ranks denoting membership in the Duma—boyar (*boiarin*), *okol'nichii*, *dumnyi dvorianin* and *dumnyi d'iak*. The men who bore these ranks had a special importance in the eyes of the tsar and his closest advisers, either because of an outstanding record of service or through close personal ties to the throne. This study, then, proceeds on the assumption that, to use somewhat dated language, the Duma's ranks included the "power elite" of Muscovy.[4] To what extent, however, is such an assumption justified?

As in all complex societies, power in Muscovy took a variety of forms and was exercised in a variety of ways. In Russia in the seventeenth century just as later, the ability to influence and command other people loomed larger than control of natural and economic resources. The most powerful men were the ones who established and carried out governmental policy. As we have suggested, the tsars and their advisers set the main lines of national policy, often with the assent of the Duma. The officials and clerks of the bureaucratic chanceries recorded their decisions and saw to it that the rest of the population obeyed them. In this, the bureaucracy had the support of the police officials and organs of the state—the military governors of the provinces and their staffs and the army units that guarded the security of the realm. The army and its commanders, of course, also fought against foreign enemies, with distinctly mixed success. In their official capacities, moreover, the generals, governors, and chancery officials all commanded the obedience of large numbers of subordinates. In addition, as we shall see later, power and influence also flowed through channels of less formal personal relationships such as factional alliances, family ties through marriage, and patronage networks. Finally, in seventeenth-century Russia, men and women of the upper classes often had considerable economic power, almost always in the form of landed estates. In this case, as well, control over people was crucial, for ownership of land meant nothing without peasants whose labor the landlord could control.

By these criteria, the most powerful men in seventeenth-century Muscovy reached one of the Duma's ranks at some point in their careers. We find there almost all of the leading bureaucrats and generals of the realm. By and large, its members also included the wealthiest landlords in Russia.

To be sure, a list of the Duma's members does not match the "power elite" of Muscovy precisely. On one hand, some men of considerable power, wealth, or standing never received Duma rank. In particular, the Duma probably contained fewer chancery officials than their real significance warranted, and few of Russia's small group of wealthy merchants became members in our period. Moreover, a small number of noble courtiers who served with distinction in the army or owned vast estates never reached its ranks.

On the other hand, not all Duma members enjoyed extraordinary power or influence. Particularly after the 1670s, as we shall see, a number of comparatively obscure or insignificant men were promoted to its ranks.

On balance, however, the Duma members as a group are well worth studying. Their rank makes them easy to identify, and their number includes almost all of the wealthiest and most powerful laymen of the realm. In particular, the tsar's closest advisers and favorites and the heads of the most important chanceries—precisely the men who, along with the tsar, established national policy—invariably received Duma rank. Indeed, for the historian in search of the Muscovite "power elite," the Duma members are almost too good to be true; for, in Muscovite Russia, political power, high office, wealth, and social standing usually went hand in hand.

As a group, the members of the Duma were by no means homogeneous. Within its ranks we find great differences in personal and family background, patterns of official service, and the related acquisition of wealth and prestige. To mention the most obvious example, the outstanding chancery officials of the time received their training, worked, and lived in conditions that, in some ways, differed dramatically from those governing the lives of their fellow Duma members from the high nobility.

Within Duma ranks, then, there were, in effect, two distinct elites, the bureaucratic and the traditional noble military groups which corresponded roughly to the French noblesse de robe and noblesse d'épée respectively. Moreover, within the latter, as we shall show, there were a number of important subdivisions; royal in-laws, for example, danced to their own special tune. Finally, it should be noted that this study ignores several powerful groups in Muscovy, most obviously the church hierarchy, a few of whose representatives had great personal influence over the ruler and his government and the benefits of leadership of a large and very wealthy institution. Despite their importance, the outline of their careers and the pattern of their lives are so different from those of prominent laymen that it made no sense to include them in the present study.[5]

In examining these interrelated groups, we depend primarily on the methods of collective biography, or prosopography, as it is grandly called.[6] Over the years, I have tried to find out everything about all of the men who held a Duma rank at any time between 1613 and 1689. In the early days of the study, nothing was too obscure for me and my long-suffering research assistants.[7] We dutifully noted every fact we could find in the hope of revealing all facets of the lives of seventeenth-century officials and courtiers—the sources and extent of their power and wealth, their family ties, their social contacts and influence, their thoughts and ideals, their tastes in food, drink, and entertainment, sexual or otherwise. Before long, however, the reality of seventeenth-century Russian sources caught up with us. Court registers and other official documents carefully record the formal service assignments of leading officials and preserve, in stupefying detail, the memory of courtiers' participation in the endless round of ceremonies and banquets that made up the formal social life of the Muscovite court and presented the government's image to the rest of society.[8] Published and easily accessible archival sources give general indications of the relative landed wealth of the members of the Duma, and the few surviving family archives of the period provide interesting details on ways in which prominent Muscovites managed their landed properties and fortunes. To make a thorough study of the economic life of our group, however, would require years of taxing archival work on the surviving land cadasters of the seventeenth century, a task beyond my means and ambitions.

The private lives and the values of the members of the Duma are even more difficult to investigate. We have few private letters from the period, most remarkably unrevealing, and almost no memoirs in which sensitive observers explain and evaluate the actions of prominent contemporaries. Even here, however, the situation of the historian is not hopeless. What the Duma members did, of course, sometimes gives us clues to their attitudes and values. Moreover, some sources, notably the voluminous records of precedence disputes at court, indicate in a more direct manner how they thought about themselves and their families. Still, the surviving sources restrict us mainly to the official career and public image of the Duma members and exclude us from their private lives and thoughts. That, I think, is how they would want it.

Why go to the trouble of reconstructing and comparing the lives of men who lived in a distant country over three hundred years ago? To begin with, I have proceeded on several general assumptions; that Russia was and is an extremely important and interesting country and that sensitive examination of any society past or present tells us much, by implication, about our own society and thus about ourselves. On a more concrete level, there are also good reasons for studying the Duma members, or the boyar elite, as I prefer, for the sake of brevity, to call them. The members of this group included the wealthiest and most powerful lay leaders of Muscovite Russia. Their careers serve as illustrations of the sources and nature of power in their society: the more we know about the ways in which they gained power and wealth and how they used and tried to preserve them, the better we will understand the workings of the Muscovite administrative system and the social and economic conditions and the values that shaped the lives of the dominant groups in society and thus, in broader terms, of society as a whole. Moreover, knowing Muscovite Russia a little better will give us a clearer

impression of its place on the spectrum of seventeenth-century polities
and societies.

Given these goals, this collective portrait of the boyar elite begins by
describing the entire group statistically and tracing the changes in its
composition over the course of the seventeenth century. Throughout
that age of turmoil and rapid change, as we shall see, a group of distinguished old families successfully maintained its traditional claim on the
ranks of boyar and okol'nichii. These aristocrats dominated the Duma
under Tsar Mikhail and, although their fortunes waned in Aleksei's reign,
they staged a significant recovery under the latter's weak successors. At
the same time, the personal composition of the Duma changed dramatically over the course of the century. First of all, from mid-century, far
more talented or well-connected social upstarts rose to power and Duma
rank than in Mikhail's time. Secondly, in an attempt to rally political
support, the weak regimes of the late 1670s and 1680s conferred Duma
rank on unprecedented numbers of men, many of them undistinguished
or obscure. This inflation served only to discredit the honors awarded so
promiscuously. As a consequence, after 1676, Duma rank no longer meant
very much, and the government sought new ways of organizing its inner
circle of councillors and new, more valuable rewards for its leading servitors. The first such attempts failed to take root; it remained for Peter
I to build viable new institutions at the core of government and to create
a new hierarchy of ranks.

Next, in the second chapter, we will examine the careers of the individual members of the boyar elite and their relationship to the royal
government as a whole. In the seventeenth century, the members of the
Duma remained active servitors of the crown. Until the relaxation of
traditional standards in the 1670s and 1680s, most future members performed useful assignments for the government for twenty or thirty years
before reaching the Duma, and continued to do so once they had joined
the council's ranks. At the same time, most of them found the conditions
of service considerably more secure, comfortable, and rewarding than
had their predecessors at the end of the previous century.

In our period, as before, the members of the boyar elite can be divided into two identifiable categories—representatives of the traditional
military nobility and full-time bureaucrats. Most of the former continued
to serve the royal government in the same capacities as their ancestors:
they led the armies of Muscovy and, on occasion, acted as military governors in the provinces. Oddly enough, the "military revolution" that
spread from western Europe in the early seventeenth century failed to
dislodge the most distinguished representatives of the military nobility
from their traditional position at the head of Russia's army. Changes in

military technology and organization, however, allowed a very small number of talented upstarts to rise to Duma rank, thanks to their mastery of the new techniques.

Dramatic change in another sphere had a much greater impact on the boyar elite. In the seventeenth century, the bureaucracy grew greatly in size and in its claims on the time and treasure of all of the tsars' subjects. It goes without saying, then, that the leading representatives of the second group within the Duma—the career bureaucrats—were men of great power and influence.

Over the course of the century, however, they faced increasing competition within their own realm: members of the military nobility became directors of many chanceries and bore the responsibilities and reaped the rewards that went with leadership in the bureaucracy. These noble officials constituted a new type of servitor, the man who served both on the battlefield and in his office. Moreover, the appearance of many such men presaged the melding of the military nobles and bureaucrats into a single group of servitors—a process which Peter I furthered when he established the Table of Ranks.

The third chapter examines the Duma members' ties with their own clans and intimate families. As we shall see, the men of the boyar elite lived in a tight circle of family relationships. A number of them, particularly the aristocrats who reached the ranks of boyar and okol'nichii, were the sons or grandsons of men who had earlier enjoyed the same distinction. Such men were well aware of their genealogical standing within their own clans. At the same time, for much of the seventeenth century the Muscovite government did not take genealogical seniority into account consistently when promoting men to Duma rank. Other family ties also helped to hold the boyar elite together: nearly half of all new Duma members had close relatives—often by marriage—who had preceded them into its exalted ranks.

A web of marriages bound many Duma families together. In seventeenth-century Russia, prominent nobles arranged their children's marriages for political and social, not economic, reasons. The most desirable brides and grooms were those whose families had close ties to the ruling dynasty and its relatives. As a consequence, the aristocratic clans at the center of the boyar elite repeatedly made matrimonial alliances with one another. Their members also married the children of powerful social upstarts, particularly new royal in-laws and outstanding chancery officials. Finally, the matrimonial strategy of some aristocratic clans seems to have been defensive in nature: as a form of insurance, they married their offspring to as wide a variety of partners as possible.

In the fourth chapter, we will investigate informal personal ties within

the boyar elite—in particular, court parties and factions and patronage
networks. Political alignments within the Muscovite court and administration were apparently in a state of continuous flux. Detailed investigation of the political crises of 1648 and 1682 suggests that court parties
in the seventeenth century were small and short-lived. Personal ties to
a prominent statesman or family held them together; as far as we can
tell, their members did not share any special economic interest or political program. Indeed, men with exceptional energy and clearly defined
ideas posed a threat to the other members of the inner circle at court.
Before long, such individuals had far more enemies than partisans.

Patronage relationships were ubiquitous in seventeenth-century Muscovy. Men of all ranks sought one another's protection and support. Of
course, the most powerful statesmen made the best patrons. Men like
B. I. Morozov and Prince V. V. Golitsyn had a large number of clients
and suppliants. Indeed, it is well-nigh impossible to reconstruct seventeenth-century patronage networks precisely because contemporaries took
them so much for granted.

The following chapter will study the Duma members as "economic
men"—as landlords and entrepreneurs. In Muscovy, most high nobles
derived their income from only one source—ownership of land and control of the peasants on it. They acquired their estates by inheritance, by
purchase, or through grants of crown land as a reward for service or a
mark of royal favor. By and large, the boyar elite prospered in the seventeenth century. The fund of available land grew steadily, thanks, in
part, to the opening of the southern frontier to settlement. This change
made it possible for Duma members to acquire steadily increasing amounts
of land in many parts of the country. The great aristocratic clans did
particularly well in guarding and expanding their holdings. They owed
their good fortune primarily to their political influence: although the
available evidence is ambiguous, more often than not, it would seem,
power came before wealth in land for aristocrat and parvenu alike. As
landowners, most high nobles treated their estates as resources to be
exploited, not economic opportunities to be pursued. With very few
exceptions, they showed little initiative or imagination in managing their
properties.

As we shall see in the sixth chapter, the members of the boyar elite
showed a deep concern for their personal security and their honor. They
fought jealously to defend their social standing, particularly as reflected
in their positions (*mesta*) on the hierarchy of precedence at court and in
service. On the positive side, they took pleasure in a wide variety of
formal expressions and symbols of the tsars' favor. Moreover, they did

their best to present an image of prosperity, respectability, and magnanimity to the rest of the population.

Duma members normally spent much of their lives at court and knew that Moscow was the nerve-center of the royal administration. They lived in the capital in solid houses and, if possible, owned a small estate near the city to supply their households with the necessities of life.

As members of the Eastern Orthodox Church, moreover, Duma members followed the conventional requirements of their faith. Many of them made generous bequests to monasteries and maintained churches for their dependents. Few, however, followed their convictions to the point of abandoning their conventional style of life or risking their careers. Equally few showed much serious interest in the new schools of learning or cultural styles penetrating seventeenth-century Russia from central Europe.

In the concluding section, we will briefly compare the boyar elite with similar groups in other societies in the sixteenth and seventeenth centuries. Like the administrative elite of the Ottoman Empire, Duma members were the ruler's servitors. Like the high nobles of western Europe, the boyars enjoyed a traditional monopoly of the highest ranks in the army and the provincial administration, occupied prominent social positions at the royal court, and owned large estates which provided them with a comfortable and, at times, lavish style of life. Moreover, boyars and western aristocrats shared close family ties and a keen sense of their distinguished ancestry and tradition of leadership in society. Yet the similarities to Turkey and western Europe were limited and superficial. The boyar elite was distinct from comparable groups elsewhere precisely because its members' lives combined obligatory service to the crown, with the traditions and rewards of aristocrats.

CHAPTER I

The Boyar Elite

The rank of boyar has an ancient history in Russia. Beginning with the late tenth century, chronicles used the word along with several others when referring to the leading counselors of the ruling princes.[1] What the word "boyar" originally meant, however, is not entirely clear. Philologically, it may mean a warrior or one who takes responsibility for something.[2] The ambiguity is fortuitous, for, in later times, the boyars were a warrior elite who assisted the prince in governing his realm.

By the seventeenth century, the boyars stood at the top of a complex hierarchy of ranks and institutions. The council of royal advisers, known to historians as the Boyar Duma, consisted of the holders of four ranks— boiarin, okol'nichii, dumnyi dvorianin, and dumnyi d'iak.[3] The rank and function of okol'nichii existed from the thirteenth century. At first the okol'nichie were servitors who accompanied the prince on his travels and saw to his needs. By the sixteenth century, however, the term simply designated members of the Boyar Duma slightly less distinguished than the boyars proper.[4] In the course of that century, the government created two new ranks as a way of bringing social upstarts into the inner circles of the administration and giving them appropriate recognition. Early sixteenth-century sources describe the dumnye dvoriane precisely as "lesser nobles (*deti boiarskie*) who serve in the Duma." The dumnye d'iaki were the most important officials in the rudimentary but remarkably efficient Muscovite bureaucracy. In reality, they played leading roles in the governing of the realm from the late fifteenth century if not earlier. The rank of dumnyi d'iak which formalized their status emerged, however, only in the latter half of the sixteenth century.[5]

The boyars of the seventeenth century had a social as well as a juridical history. The families whose members tended to dominate the ranks of boyar and okol'nichii in our period gradually came together at the court of the rulers of Moscow over the course of three centuries. As a social group, the boyars and okol'nichie consisted of two elements. First came the princes, the descendants of the numerous branches of the Rus-

sian ruling house, the Riurikovichi, and the Lithuanian dynasty of Ge-
dimin. All bore the title of prince which all sons inherited from their
father, and all had once ruled their own small principalities somewhere
in the plains and forests of northeastern Europe. The second element in
the boyar group was made up of the so-called non-titled families who
had achieved power and social prominence by serving the princes of
Moscow for several generations. Their masters rewarded their efforts
with positions of authority and, in many cases, rank. The rulers of Muscovy, however, did not grant patents of nobility or hereditary titles in
the western European sense. Either a man was born a prince or he was
not. The non-titled became nobles through ownership of land and informal social concensus.

In strictly chronological terms, the group of non-titled servitors coa-
lesced first. A number of leading families of the sixteenth and seventeenth centuries occupied prominent positions at the court of the princes
of Moscow in the fourteenth century.[6] In the next two centuries, the
ranks of non-titled boyars continued to grow; new men whose talent and
loyalty made them invaluable to the ruler joined the evolving core of
distinguished families at court. By contrast, the princes came to Moscow
relatively late. Many of the leading princely houses of later centuries
jumped on the Muscovite bandwagon in the latter half of the fifteenth
and first decades of the sixteenth centuries when the princes of Moscow
clearly won the struggle for hegemony in northeastern Europe. Ivan III
and his successors welcomed the princes into their service with honors
appropriate to their distinguished ancestry. At the same time, their new
masters watched them carefully and kept them from positions of real
power until they had proved their trustworthiness.[7] Like the non-titled
boyars, the princes as a group continued to evolve, adding new recruits
to their number, including a small number of immigrants from the north
Caucasus as well as native Russians.

At the beginning of the sixteenth century, the distinctions between
the princes and non-titled boyars were clear and important.[8] A hundred
years later, I am convinced, most of the differences between them, apart
from the title of prince itself, had disappeared. As we shall see, the
careers of princes and non-titled boyars followed the same patterns: they
owned and managed land in the same way, and, if marriage alliances are
any indication, they regarded one another as social equals. For these
reasons, this study will make no systematic distinction between the princely
and non-titled families among the boyars of the seventeenth century.

Before proceeding, we must deal with certain problems of terminology. First, by the phrase "boyar elite" I mean all of the individuals who
served in the Boyar Duma in any of its four ranks. Secondly, I will use

the word "boyar" in two meanings, both current in the seventeenth century itself.[9] In the narrow sense, a boyar was a man who held the highest rank in the Duma. In passages in which precise distinctions must be made, I will use the word in this technical meaning. In popular usage, however, the word "boyar" could denote any high noble or person in power. On occasion, when the context permits, I will use "boyar" in this broader sense for reasons of style.

To the consternation of some of my colleagues, I will also use the terms "aristocracy" or "aristocratic element" when discussing the families which dominated the top two ranks of the Duma. The terms come, of course, from western European historical vocabulary and do not fit Russian reality precisely.[10] When I use them to describe the Muscovite high nobility, I am not suggesting that the "Russian aristocracy" enjoyed great political and economic power in their regions of origin and thus remained largely independent of the authority of the ruler, as was the case with their western and central European counterparts in earlier times. As we shall see, quite the contrary was true.

By the Russian aristocracy, I mean those families which served in high office and enjoyed material comfort and an exalted social standing over the course of several generations. In that sense, many of the boyars of the seventeenth century were aristocrats, for, throughout that period, a central core of distinguished old families within the boyar elite was remarkably successful in maintaining its claim on high rank and office, its wealth, and its standing at the pinnacle of the social hierarchy.

Seventeenth-century boyars lived in tumultous times. Nothing that they experienced between 1613 and 1689, however, compared with the chaos and bloodshed of the preceding decades. To begin with, after a period of military triumph abroad and gradual reform at home, Ivan IV launched the *oprichnina* in 1565.[11] Dividing Muscovy in two and creating his own private security force and administration, the tsar lashed out at his enemies, real and imagined. Between 1565 and 1572, several waves of terror claimed thousands of victims from all walks of life. Many members of Duma families died at the hands of Ivan's executioners. Whether the oprichnina was a systematic attack on all or on parts of the aristocracy or represented Ivan's revenge on individuals whom he distrusted, it cost Muscovite society dearly.[12] So far no historian has successfully added up the exact price that the boyars paid for Ivan's experiment. Clearly, some lost friends and relatives, others their careers or their estates, and all of them their self-confidence. The plight of the peasants is not in dispute. The government's exactions in order to win the war for Livonia and the excesses of the oprichnina made life unbearable for many of them. By

the thousands, they fled from their homes to the frontiers of Muscovy
and beyond, thereby setting off an economic depression and social crisis
of enormous proportions.

For three decades after his death in 1584, Ivan's legacy haunted Russia. The government of his son, Fedor, under the leadership of Boris
Godunov, made limited but sensible attempts to cope with the social,
economic, and diplomatic problems that Ivan left behind and succeeded
at least in giving the country a few years' respite. When Fedor, the last
of the Riurikovich dynasty, died in 1598, Muscovy slid slowly but inex-
orably into chaos.

With good reason, Russians remember the years between 1598 and
1613 as the Time of Troubles.[13] A myriad of problems undercut the
effectiveness of the government and destroyed the social fabric of the
country. First came the problem of political legitimacy. After Fedor,
Boris Godunov, his chief minister and brother-in-law, ascended the throne
but was unable to convince his restless subjects of his right to rule.
Moreover, his government faced problems that would probably have
overwhelmed any seventeenth-century administration. Two consecutive
years of crop failure in 1601 and 1602 produced widespread famine and
social unrest. Once again peasants fled from their homes in a desperate
bid for survival. In this emergency, doubts about Godunov's right to rule
proved fatal to his regime. An adventurer claiming to be Dmitrii, the
youngest son of Ivan IV, appeared in Poland and quickly won support
among the discontented elements in Muscovy—nobles, Cossacks, and
peasants alike. With Polish backing, he invaded Russia, gathered his
forces, and, after initial setbacks, overthrew Godunov's regime and took
power in 1605.

With his accession, Russia's plight grew worse. The False Dmitrii did
nothing to fill the vacuum on the throne. As was well known, the real
Dmitrii had died as a child in 1592. Before long, a group of boyars,
playing on doubts about the pretender's legitimacy and the Polish flavor
of his court, overthrew him and installed their leader, Vasilii Shuiskii,
as tsar. Shuiskii sat on the throne for four years, from 1606 to 1610, but,
for much of his reign, ruled little more than the city of Moscow. Indeed,
for many months, his government faced the direct challenge of another
false Dmitrii, who set up a competing regime in Tushino, just outside
the capital. Meanwhile social discontent burst forth in a series of massive
rebellions. In desperation, Shuiskii added the final ingredient to the
crisis: to shore up his tottering throne, he invited the Swedish government to send troops to support him. Once on Russian soil, the Swedish
forces settled in and stayed long after Shuiskii had disappeared from the
scene. Moreover, their presence prompted King Sigismund III of Po-

land, who was already fishing in Muscovy's troubled waters, to launch a campaign of open intervention. At one and the same time, Polish troops invaded the country, and their king began negotiations with some of the boyars in hopes of securing the throne of Russia for his son, Wladyslaw.

In this moment of chaos and national humiliation, leaders appeared to rally the remaining forces of Russia. With the encouragement of Patriarch Germogen, the nobles of eastern and southeastern Muscovy formed a coalition with the townsmen of east and north for the purpose of expelling the foreigner and restoring the fortunes of Orthodox Russia. The national coalition brought together a strange conglomeration of elements, including large numbers of Cossacks who had thrived on the chaotic conditions of recent years. From the beginning, the movement for national revival suffered from acute internal divisions, and its first attempt to capture Moscow from a Polish garrison failed. At the end of 1612, however, Prince D. M. Pozharskii and Kuz'ma Minin led a second attempt that ended successfully.

As the leaders of the national revival realized, their first task was to elect a tsar whose administration could establish its right to govern. With this in mind, they called a meeting of the *zemskii sobor* (national estates) which, in 1613, chose Mikhail Romanov, a young member of a distinguished non-titled family related by marriage to the old dynasty. Mikhail's coronation gave Russia a new ruling house. It also served as a first step in the campaign to rid the country of the disastrous consequences of the Troubles, a campaign that, in a broad sense, lasted most of the seventeenth century.

In the years between Mikhail's accession and 1689, the Russian government faced many problems. As elsewhere in Europe, the most urgent issue was mobilizing the country for war. For most of the century, Russia faced two principal enemies—Poland to the west and the Ottoman Empire and the Crimea to the south. At first Poland was the primary target. Although the Truce of Deulino in 1618 finally put an end to Poland's part in the Time of Troubles, the agreement only gave the parties time to rest until the next round of fighting. That took place in 1632-1634, when Russia, taking advantage of the disruption of the Thirty Years' War in central Europe, tried unsuccessfully to recapture Smolensk, lost during the Troubles.[14] In the reign of Mikhail's successor, Aleksei Mikhailovich (1645-1676), the two powers clashed again, this time over control of the Ukraine, which, under Khmel'nitskii's leadership, revolted against Polish control and accepted Russian protection. In the first three years of the war, 1654-1657, the Russian army marched relentlessly westward, aided by the fact that, at the same time, the Swedish army invaded and devastated the heartland of Poland. After Sweden left the war, however, the Poles staged a remarkable recovery and re-captured a good deal of lost territory before the Truce of Andrusovo ended the conflict in 1667. [15]

In the seventeenth century, the security of the southern frontier re-mained a major concern of the Russian government. For centuries, war-lords from the neighboring Turkic societies had raided the southern bor-derlands of Muscovy and occasionally penetrated the heart of the country, looting and carrying off prisoners for sale as slaves. Beginning in the fifteenth century, the Muscovite government took systematic measures to meet the danger of invasion. These included maintaining an army on the southern frontier throughout the year, constructing a series of forti-fied defense lines, and developing an elaborate system of reconnaissance and warning signals. After the Time of Troubles, the new government of the Romanovs faced the same Tatar threat and responded in the same way. Particularly in the late 1630s and 1640s, when the western frontier was quiet, the government made a major effort to repair the existing defense perimeter and to construct the new Belgorod line farther south in the steppe. In the long run, the campaign paid off handsomely: in the middle and later decades of the century, Crimean raids no longer threat-ened the heartland of European Russia, and the rich "black soil" belt to the south of the capital was secure for settlement as never before. [16]

The successes of Russian arms brought enormous gains of territory. The wars with Poland extended Moscow's rule to the eastern or "left bank" Ukraine, with its distinct local political and cultural traditions. During the seventeenth century, moreover, Russia extended her bor-ders eastward across Siberia to the shores of the Pacific and established a common border with China.

Expansion brought new entanglements. The southward extension of Russia's borders led to a bloody but inconclusive war with the Ottoman Empire between 1676 and 1681. Then the regency of Princess Sophia and Prince V. V. Golitsyn, which ruled from 1682 to 1689, joined the general European coalition against the Turks and, as its contribution, made two disastrous attempts to conquer the Crimea and to put an end to border raids once and for all. [17]

Like other governments in seventeenth-century Europe, the new re-gime in Russia had to pay dearly in order to wage war almost continu-ously. [18] First, even before the debacle at Smolensk, its leaders realized that they had to rebuild the Russian army along modern European lines. First, as elsewhere in Europe, the total size of the army grew rapidly, particularly in the 1650s and 1660s. [19] Second and more importantly, the government created new units of infantry and cavalry trained to use the latest firearms and maneuvers in the field. After initial failures, these new-style units took hold and, by the height of the war with Poland in the mid-1660s, made up the great majority of the whole army.[20] Military reform had momentous consequences. At the same time, we should not forget that the traditional units of noble cavalry which the boyars often commanded continued to exist until the end of the century.

As elsewhere, the new style of warfare strained the government's financial resources. In addition to the costs of the old-fashioned units, the Russian administration had to buy weapons for the new cavalry and infantry and find the cash for the salaries on which they lived. According to one estimate, the cost of the army rose two-and-a-half times over the course of the century.[21] As a result, the Russian government struggled desperately throughout the period to increase its income from taxes and other sources.[22]

Financial necessity in turn spurred the growth of the central bureaucracy. The same development took place in other European countries in response to the same needs. In Russia, however, the bureaucracy had a greater weight than elsewhere on the continent because the royal administration faced no other centers of political authority and power except the Eastern Orthodox Church. During the seventeenth century, the central bureaucracy grew larger and more complex. By the 1680s, about 2,000 men worked in chancery offices in Moscow alone.[23] Moreover, the number of chanceries burgeoned: more than 75 existed at some time or another during the century.[24] To be sure, the very growth of the system posed serious problems, in particular excessive division of responsibility and the tendency of several chanceries to perform essentially the same function. Yet, in spite of its problems, the Muscovite bureaucracy performed its basic functions—collecting taxes and drafting men into the army—remarkably well.[25]

As the seventeenth century passed, moreover, the pretensions of the central administration grew steadily. With increasing success, the bureaucracy spread its tentacles into the provinces, even reaching to the peasant communities of the far north and the Cossack hosts of the southern borderlands, where the tradition of local autonomy had deep roots. Rising governmental demands set off a rising tide of local opposition. Nevertheless, the bureaucracy prevailed, as it seems inevitably to do. By the end of the century, opponents of official policy could find no corner of Russia remote enough to hide in.[26]

Popular resistance to the government welled up from many sources. Throughout seventeenth-century Europe, peasant revolts and urban uprisings were common occurrences. Russia was certainly no exception. Once unleashed during the Time of Troubles, popular discontent was never still for long. The legal and social status of the manorial peasants declined steadily in the first decades of the century as the government slowly but surely gave in to the demands of the nobility, particularly its lower strata. Finally, the Law Code of 1649 gave the lesser nobles precisely what they wanted—the full enserfment of the peasantry.[27] "Second serfdom" took a particularly virulent form in Russia and created an explosive situation. When set in motion by Cossacks, manorial peasants and indentured laborers quickly rose in revolt. In the most spectacular case, the revolt led by Sten'ka Razin spread over many thousand square miles of southern and eastern Russia in 1670 and 1671 and forced the government to mount a major military campaign to put it down.[28] The urban population also chafed under the burden of high taxes. A wave of riots swept through a number of cities and towns between 1648 and 1650.[29] After that, most urban areas were quiet, but Moscow remained a tinderbox, thanks, in part, to the presence of a large and restless garrison.

In the midst of institutional change and social unrest the Russian economy remained relatively stable.[30] During the seventeenth century, most Russians continued to live in economic isolation, supporting themselves by growing their own food with traditional techniques and implements. The outside world impinged on them only when agents of their landlord or the government came to collect rent or taxes.[31] As we shall see later, these outside pressures began to force many peasants to sell on the market part of their crop or some items that they had made. Changes of this type took place very slowly, however.

Urban life in Russia differed greatly from that of the most highly developed regions of western Europe. Except for Moscow, a large city by any contemporary standard, urban centers were quite small, and many of them, especially in the south, served primarily as administrative centers and military garrisons. Russian cities, moreover, looked different from their counterparts in western Europe: many covered very large areas since their populations often combined extensive gardening with the usual urban pursuits. Nevertheless, we should not exaggerate the primitive quality of urban life in Russia, particularly when compared with the less developed regions of central Europe.[32] Russian towns produced a wide variety of goods in small workshops and were known for their lively markets. At the same time, there were no intense concentrations of workshop production like the textile industry in some other parts of the continent. Indeed, the largest concentrations of industrial production, if we may call it that, were located in the countryside, where a few wealthy nobles and other entrepreneurs, native and foreign, exploited local natural resources and labor to produce salt, potash, and iron.

By comparison with their western European counterparts, the merchants of Russia occupied a weak and unstable position. They were relatively few in number and often suffered from the government's demands on their time and treasure, to say nothing of its direct and unfair competition with some of their enterprises. At the same time, as recent studies stress, the merchants sometimes made goodly fortunes from their trading ventures, and a very few even reached high office in the administration.[33] Moreover, as a group, they enjoyed limited political influence: in response to their petitions, for example, the government set limits to the rights and privileges of their foreign competitors operating inside Russia.[34]

Seventeenth-century Russia carried on a lively foreign trade. In international commerce, she served primarily as a source of raw materials and imported manufactured and luxury goods. Like other parts of eastern Europe, Russia hewed wood and grew grain for the more highly developed parts of the continent, particularly the Netherlands.

No survey of Russian life in the seventeenth century, however brief, would be complete without mentioning the Eastern Orthodox Church. Since Russia's official conversion to Christianity many centuries earlier, the church ministered to men's spiritual needs and shaped high culture. As time passed, moreover, it gained great wealth and considerable political influence. Despite the church's abundant resources, however, the seventeenth century was a time of crisis. Three issues proved particularly vexing. First, was Russian Orthodoxy a uniquely authentic form of Christianity, the only coin in the economy of salvation, in Michael Cherniavsky's memorable phrase?[35] Secondly, who ultimately held authority within Russian Orthodoxy, the patriarch or the whole church as represented by all of its leaders in council? Finally, how much power over it did its lay protector, the tsar, and his government rightfully enjoy?

In his brief but momentous term in office from 1652 to 1659, Patriarch Nikon brought all of these issues to a head. As his first concern, he tried to restore the church's moral, spiritual, and legal authority and to free it from excessive dependence on the secular power. As he was well aware, to do so meant to reverse the direction which the relations between church and state had taken in the preceding century and a half. As one part of his program, he attempted to make the Russian church an integral part of universal Eastern Orthodoxy. Unfortunately for him, his decision to implement this policy by bringing the liturgical practices of his flock into conformity with contemporary Greek usage led to conflict with many of the faithful, who believed passionately that Russia alone was authentically Christian. Before long, Nikon was a man besieged. His attempts to increase his own authority as representative of the church angered Tsar Aleksei, devout though he was. Within the church, Nikon's autocratic style of administration made him many enemies, and, in the country as a whole, large numbers of parish clergy, monastics, and concerned laypeople rebelled against his liturgical reforms and all that they implied.

In the end, Nikon brought disaster to the church for which he cared so much. By the end of the century, the government exercised, if anything, even more authority over the church than before. Moreover, many thousands, and eventually millions, of Russians left the official church altogether and set up their own religious communities, where they hoped to preserve the one true faith, authentic Russian Orthodoxy, from the corruption of Nikon's liturgy and the dangers of a changing world.[36]

In this century of change and strife, the boyar elite occupied the top position on the administrative and social hierarchies of Russia. In the seventeenth century as before, the Duma served as a group of royal advisers who met regularly, usually in one of the large chambers of the great Kremlin palace, to discuss important matters of state. At any given time, to be sure, a number of its members might be absent from Moscow. Those in the capital, however, made frequent regular appearances at court. The rhetoric of official decrees underlined the Duma's participation in the process of making decisions: phrases such as the "boyars' decree (*boiarskii prigovor*)" or "the Sovereign ordered and the boyars decreed (*Gosudar' ukazal i boiare prigovorili*)" appear frequently in seventeenth-century legislation.[37] Moreover, the Duma stood over the administrative chanceries (prikazy). Its members heard the reports of their directors and, by law, also decided difficult or ambiguous judicial cases which the chanceries referred to them.[38] The Duma's ties to the bureaucracy were personal as well as legal. At a time when the chanceries were growing rapidly in number, size, and claims to jurisdiction and when their administrative routine was becoming more precise, more and more Duma members served as their directors.

The boyar elite also constituted the topmost rung on the ladder of service ranks. All Muscovite nobles had a formal rank which brought with it certain duties and privileges and conveyed a particular standing in society. At the bottom were the provincial nobles who made up the core of the traditional cavalry army of the Muscovite state. Between them and all of the servitors based in Moscow was a clear line of demarcation that could be crossed only with difficulty. Many nobles formally served in the capital. The official service lists for 1629 include the names of about 1,000 men, those for 1692 more than 3,500.[39] Those who were not members of the Boyar Duma held one of several court ranks (*spal'nik*,

stol'nik, striapchii, or *zhilets*) which entitled them to perform certain
ritual functions. The lowest echelon of servitors in the capital was known
simply as the Moscow nobles (*moskovskie dvoriane*). From their vantage
point, the boyars occupied an awesomely exalted position and rank.[40]

What ultimately interests us about the members of the Duma, however, is not their high formal position, but the fact that almost all of the
most powerful laymen of seventeenth-century Russia reached its ranks
at some time in their careers. Our goal is to investigate the sources of
their political influence, social standing, and economic prosperity. By so
doing, we can look behind the hierarchical facade of Muscovite life and
see more clearly the ways in which men gained, maintained, and lost
power.

This objective forces us to make a number of tactical decisions. For
one thing, we must establish the chronological limits of our enterprise.
The choice of 1613 as a starting-point hardly needs justifying. After the
Time of Troubles, the new government of Mikhail Romanov had to rebuild the boyar administration from scratch and restore order to society.
Finding a suitable finishing date is more difficult. The Boyar Duma continued to exist until Peter I replaced it with the Senate in 1711. Peter's
government, however, virtually ceased to appoint new members by 1693.
Moreover, in the 1690s, the Duma was swollen with undistinguished
men while the ambitious and power-hungry clustered around the young
ruler.[41] For these reasons, we will end our study in 1689, when Peter
overthrew the regency government of Sophia and Prince V. V. Golitsyn
that had ruled Russia since 1682 in the names of the young tsar and his
elder half-brother, Ivan.[42] The dates we have chosen, of course, have no
absolute significance and, when appropriate, the discussion of particular
themes will range beyond the frontiers we have rather arbitrarily established.

Let us turn now to a general profile of the boyar elite in the seventeenth century. The first thing that strikes us is a remarkable inflation of
honors. To begin with, the size of the Boyar Duma increased fivefold
over the course of the century, as Appendix A shows.[43] In one sense,
there is nothing surprising in this development; throughout its history,
the number of its members changed continually. Moreover, by the
standards of previous reigns, the Duma under the first Romanov was not
exceptionally large; with between 28 and 39 members, it was considerably smaller than Ivan IV's council in the 1550s and early 1560s, but
larger than at most other times in the sixteenth century.[44] In addition,
we should note that, in the course of the seventeenth century, the number of the tsar's courtiers of all ranks also grew rapidly; the proportion

of Moscow nobles who reached Duma rank remained about the same throughout our period.

After all is said and done, however, the Boyar Duma grew to absolutely unprecedented size after 1645. Its ranks swelled primarily in three short periods—between 1645 and 1652, in the late 1670s, and in the first years after the regency came to power in 1682. In the last two decades of Aleksei's reign, the number of its members levelled off at between 65 and 75, but, after his death in 1676, the size of the group expanded steadily until, by the beginning of 1690, the Boyar Duma nominally had 151 members. In view of its traditional role as an inner council of royal advisers, it had become swollen beyond recognition. No wonder that the regimes of the late seventeenth century experimented with new and smaller conciliar bodies to perform the Duma's executive and judicial functions![45]

Moreover, the relative size of the four ranks within the Duma changed equally dramatically. At the top, the number of boyars increased as the whole Duma grew; it ranged between 14 and 28 under Mikhail, rose quickly into the high 20s and low 30s in the early years of Aleksei's reign, then levelled off until the late 1670s, when it shot up to a high of 61 in 1683. The size of the second aristocratic rank in the council, that of okol'nichii, evolved in much the same way. Under Mikhail, the number of okol'nichie remained well within sixteenth-century norms. Thereafter it grew from 8 in 1645, the year of Aleksei's accession, to 54 in 1690.

The most startling novelty of the late seventeenth century was the large number of dumnye dvoriane and dumnye d'iaki. In the sixteenth century, a very small number of non-aristocratic courtiers and officials of outstanding merit held these ranks. The situation remained the same until about 1650; in the first half of the seventeenth century, there were one, two or three dumnye dvoriane and between two and five dumnye d'iaki. After that, once again, unprecedentedly large numbers of men rose to these ranks. To be sure, the patterns of development were somewhat different. As before, the dumnye d'iaki were career chancery officials, in other words, professional bureaucrats, who had demonstrated their particular skills for many years before receiving Duma rank as their reward. Since the qualifications for the rank were rigorous and the requisite skills rare in Muscovite Russia, the number of dumnye d'iaki remained relatively small. At most, 11 men held the rank. Becoming a dumnyi dvorianin required far less. The rank served as a catch-basin for courtiers and favorites of undistinguished social origin and no special training. As might be expected, then, the number of men who achieved this rank grew as the Duma as a whole expanded, from 1 in 1645 to a high of 41 in 1689. At the same time, the size of the group did not change at precisely the same time as the other ranks or the council as a whole. The number of dumnye dvoriane rose sharply in the mid- and late 1660s, when the other ranks remained relatively stable and actually fell somewhat in the late 1670s while the other ranks grew. The reasons for this eccentric pattern will soon become clear.

To an unprecedented degree, members of the Duma in the seventeenth century treated its four ranks like a staircase, rising from one to the next. Indeed, to introduce an anachronism, the Muscovite hierarchy of ranks resembled an escalator much more than a flight of stairs. Normally a man could move steadily upward, but not downward. Demotions took place rarely in the seventeenth century and were usually a temporary sign of royal disfavor.[46] On the other hand, a promotion entitled the fortunate servitor to occupy his new rank for life if he could not rise still higher.

In short, seventeenth-century Duma members played a game whose formal rules made it difficult to lose. At the same time, as a small minority of Duma members discovered to their chagrin, powerful and prominent men could fall from power and suddenly lose not just their high rank, but also their property, freedom, and even life itself. Behind the secure hierarchy of rank lurked the very real danger of disgrace and its consequences.

As the century passed, the system of promotions became more flexible. Advancement within the Duma's ranks became a common occurrence. A number of its members held two or three ranks in turn, and S. I. Zaborovskii set a record by rising from dumnyi d'iak all the way to boyar during a long and rather undistinguished career.[47] In some ways, this new pattern stretched, but did not radically change the significance of Duma rank. Men who entered the council as boyars came from slightly more distinguished families than those who first became okol'nichie, but otherwise there was little to choose between them.[48] Both usually represented the highest strata of the traditional warrior nobility. In other respects, however, the practices of the regimes of the second half of the century introduced radical change. In the sixteenth century and, indeed, through most of Mikhail's reign, a wall of custom separated the two lowest Duma ranks from the two highest. Dumnye dvoriane, for example, rarely rose to the rank of okol'nichii. In the last decades of the seventeenth century, however, such promotions became common; twelve men made the jump in the reign of Fedor Alekseevich, and twenty-two did so under the regency. These figures suggest that the social exclusiveness of the Duma's upper ranks was beginning to break down.

To test the validity of this observation, we should examine the social origin of the men who held Duma rank. Historians of the period agree that the composition of the group changed dramatically over the course of the seventeenth century. Without question, some distinguished families disappeared from the scene and a number of "new men" rose to power. There is considerable debate, however, on the time at which these changes took place and on their significance. At one end of the historiographical spectrum, S. F. Platonov claimed that, at the end of the Time of Troubles, ". . . the Moscow boyars disappeared forever from the historical arena. . . ."[49] In their place, the "middle classes" of Muscovite society came to power. To be sure, in some of his other writings, Platonov moderated his position, arguing that a number of old boyar families continued to thrive under the Romanovs, but did so only by serving the new regime under the same conditions as the newcomers with whom they had to share power.[50] A number of his contemporaries disagreed with his views. In his book on the reign of Mikhail Romanov, E. V. Stashevskii rejected Platonov's thesis that the "middle classes" emerged victorious from the Time of Troubles. As he sensibly pointed out, it is a strange victory that brings the victor no spoils! Indeed, the provincial nobility, the core of the "middle class" coalition, had to fight for nearly half a century more in order to achieve its primary objective, the complete enserfment of the peasantry. Instead, Stashevskii suggested, the composition of the boyar group and the political relationships within it changed slowly and subtly in Mikhail's reign.[51] The greatest historian of the boyars, V. O. Kliuchevskii, placed even heavier emphasis on the gradual pace of the change. Slowly but surely over the course of the seventeenth century, he argued, increasing numbers of social outsiders entered the inner circles of government to take their place beside the survivors from the traditional service aristocracy. Their rise to power reflected broad changes taking place in the administration and in society, in particular the increasing importance of the bureaucracy and the greater political weight of the lower nobility. In Kliuchevskii's opinion, these changes took place primarily in the second half of the century, beginning with the crises of the late 1640s.[52]

A close examination of the changing composition of the Duma reveals that, if anything, Kliuchevskii understated the case. To test the prevailing theories, let us divide its members into representatives of old and new families. We will define as a member of an old family any man who had a relative within three kinship links in the rank of boyar or okol'-nichii at least thirty years before his own appointment. The relative importance of such old clans—what I call the aristocratic element—and of previously unrepresented families will tell us much, not only about the boyar group itself, but also about the policies of the government which its members dominated.[53]

Measured in this way, the composition of the boyar elite in the reign of Mikhail Romanov accurately reflects the profound conservatism of the new regime.[54] First, the new government did its best to heal the wounds that the ruling group had suffered during the Time of Troubles. By 1613, all prominent courtiers and officials had served several governments in succession and, in struggling to survive, many had flitted back and forth between contending factions, particularly in the years when Vasilii Shuiskii and the Pretender of Tushino had vied for recognition as Russia's ruler. The new regime overlooked these compromises and betrayals. Within the ranks of the Duma after 1613, we find former supporters of any and all factions in the Troubles.[55]

In its appointments, moreover, the new regime showed a strong preference for the clans whose members had dominated the political life of the court before the years of crisis. Between 1613 and 1645, slightly more than half of all members of the Duma came from old aristocratic families. Moreover, more than one-third were direct descendants of men who were boyars or okol'nichie at least thirty years earlier. Finally, under Mikhail, two-thirds of the new appointees to the aristocratic upper ranks of the Duma were the eldest members of the senior branch of their clan in their own generation. Taken together, these figures suggest that Tsar Mikhail and his advisers regarded the surviving representatives of the sixteenth-century aristocracy as the natural leaders of society.

Other facts confirm this hypothesis. When we examine the "new men" in the boyar elite in the first three decades of the new regime, we discover that they were often scions of branches of the great princely clan groupings whose members had not achieved Duma rank in earlier times. Prince D. M. Pozharskii, the national hero in 1613, is a good example. He was a descendant of the eldest branch of the Starodub princes. Before long, other princes of distinguished lineage but a modest tradition of official service—the Khovanskiis, Mezetskiis, Volkonskiis, Litvinov-Mosal'skiis, L'vovs and Prozorovskiis—joined him. These families replaced some of the casualties of the crises of the previous generation and, in several cases, quickly adjusted to their exalted new rank. In contrast, genuine social upstarts rarely appeared in Mikhail's council and, when they did, they usually occupied the two lowest ranks, traditionally reserved for men of their ilk. The only real parvenu to become a boyar under Mikhail was the tsar's father-in-law, L. S. Streshnev. There was nothing radically new about his promotion, however; royal in-laws received equally favorable treatment in the sixteenth century.

Surely, the reader is entitled to suggest, these facts represent only one side of the story. What of the once-great families which declined into obscurity in the seventeenth century? Such there were, to be sure, but there were remarkably few of them. Eleven families which placed at least one member in the Duma in the period 1462-1584 survived the Time of Troubles but failed to retain their former eminence.

If, as Lawrence Stone has suggested, social groups are like busses whose passengers change continually, the fact of these families' fall should not surprise us.[56] Understanding the reasons why they fell from power, however, would throw much light on the sources of the boyars' power. The question is extremely difficult to answer, in part because the families that failed left virtually no records behind them. Some probably suffered biological failure; three or four of the eleven families had few male heirs, all of whom seem to have died young. At least one clan lost the battle against poverty. In 1630 one of the Tatevs won his release from a service assignment by arguing that he was too poor to support himself while carrying it out. He must have made a very good case since the Muscovite government accepted such petitions only with the greatest reluctance. In several other instances, however, all we can do is guess. None of the numerous Saburovs of the seventeenth century amounted to anything. Perhaps none of them showed much ambition or talent for service. Perhaps their family relationship with the fallen Godunovs weighted them down like a millstone. We simply do not know.

With these significant exceptions, then, the surviving aristocratic families of Russia retained and, in a number of cases, even improved their position in the first decades after 1613. Indeed the extent to which Tsar Mikhail's council was aristocratic in composition, and the care with which genealogical seniority was recognized, suggest that the new regime was consciously trying to rebuild the shattered sixteenth-century elite. It is probably no accident that the years in which the archconservative Patriarch Filaret dominated the government were the time when the regime took genealogical considerations most seriously when appointing new members of the Duma.

In this as in many other ways, Mikhail's reign was a period of restoration.[57] The government's central concern was to bring back the good old ways and to encourage the good old families. In reality, as restoration governments are apt to discover, the old order, like Humpty Dumpty, was irretrievably smashed. When all the king's horses and all the king's men failed to recapture Smolensk from the Poles, Mikhail's government launched a campaign of reform that continued in fits and starts for the rest of the century.

The reign of Aleksei Mikhailovich was a time of dramatic change in many areas of national life. At the same time, the "most gentle tsar" was no revolutionary; traditional institutions and social customs continued to shape national life. The changing composition of the Duma reflected the situation well. Representatives of the well-established aristocratic families continued to become boyars as before: they made up about 45 percent of the new members of the Duma in Aleksei's reign as a whole. When we subdivide the reign into smaller units, however, we notice a remarkable change. In the years 1645-1658, nearly 60 percent of the Duma's new members were aristocrats while for the period 1667-1675 they made up less than 20 percent of the recruits to the boyar elite. Clearly Aleksei's government opened up its ranks to far more new men than had Mikhail's.

Who were these new men? As in Mikhail's day, some were members of previously unrepresented princely clans—Boriatinskiis, Urusovs, Velikogo-Gagins and Kozlovskiis, among others. Others, as before, were prominent chancery officials like Almaz Ivanov. Still others came from a third well-established category, the royal in-laws. A number of Streshnevs, Aleksei's maternal relatives, and Miloslavskiis, his wife's kin, enjoyed high rank at his court. Many new members of Aleksei's council, however, do not fit into any of these traditional categories. Often the sources at our disposal make it extremely difficult to guess what qualities or which personal connections helped a man rise to Duma rank from comparative obscurity. We can, however, offer two general observations. First, as we shall see in greater detail, a number of the new men in Aleksei's inner councils were favorites in the usual sense of the word. The tsar enjoyed their company. How did he get to know these particular individuals from among the hundreds of lesser court servitors or thousands of provincial nobles? As we shall see, the sources hint at one possible answer—a powerful patron at court.[58]

Secondly, and even more significantly, Aleksei's government promoted a number of experts in military or diplomatic matters in recognition of their services. Most of these men rose from the Moscow or provincial nobility and entered the swelling ranks of dumnye dvoriane. The most dramatic example is the celebrated diplomat and statesman A. L. Ordin-Nashchokin. He was not alone, however. Distinguished military careers apparently won promotions for Z. V. Kondyrev, O. I. Sukin, Z. F. Leont'ev, I. I. Rzhevskii, and V. N. Panin, among others. Diplomacy was the forte of A. O. Pronchishchev, I. I. Chaadaev, and A. I. Nesterov.[59]

Their promotion to the Duma suggests that Aleksei and his advisers deliberately opened up its ranks to outstanding servitors, regardless of their social origin. To be sure, since the fifteenth century, most Duma members could legitimately take pride in their distinguished record of service. They received their rank on two grounds—aristocratic birth and personal achievement. Under Aleksei, however, the latter alone brought an increasing number of men into the once-exclusive boyars' club.

In this, as in so many areas of official life, Aleksei anticipated the far more radical changes of his son Peter. His policy on appointments to the Duma prefigures the Table of Ranks. Moreover, some of the families whose members reached high rank in his reign—the Boriatinskiis and Tolstois, for example—remained prominent in later centuries. At the same time, we should not exaggerate the degree of novelty of Aleksei's policies. As usual, his government poured its new wine into old institutional bottles. Moreover, as Peter later discovered, allowing talented new men to rise to the top did not seriously undermine the power of the great aristocratic families of the realm. However the government changed the rules of the political game, the aristocrats kept on winning.[60]

After Aleksei's death, the government of Russia entered a prolonged period of crisis. The central problem was the succession to the imperial throne. Aleksei's sons by his first marriage, Fedor and Ivan, were sickly and, in Ivan's case, retarded as well. Neither could be expected to reign for long. On the other hand, Peter, Aleksei's only son by his second marriage, showed real promise. When his father died, however, he was only three years old. For the next thirteen years, a succession of statesmen tried to build stable regimes and to establish coherent policies in domestic and foreign affairs.

In these circumstances, governments struggling for stability set off an inflation of honors. Not only did the number of Duma members rise spectacularly, but the new appointees' claims to exalted rank also appear far weaker than under Mikhail and Aleksei. At first glance, the composition of the Duma under Fedor and the regency which followed him appears more conventional than in Aleksei's last years. For example, over 40 percent of its new members came from aristocratic families as we have defined them. Below the surface, however, the situation had changed radically. In earlier times, men won Duma rank, in part, by the quality of their service to the ruler. In the last years of the seventeenth century, however, many new members were men of no discernible distinction. More than 20 percent of them performed no service at all before receiving Duma rank other than participation in court ceremonies.[61] In the past, moreover, men had usually reached the Duma only after a number of years in service. In the last decades of the century, however, disproportionately large numbers of very young men became members; two-thirds of all those who did so during the century achieved this dubious feat after 1676.[62] Significantly, a goodly number of these young men came from distinguished aristocratic families—the Golitsyns,

Odoevskiis, Romodanovskiis, Saltykovs, Cherkasskiis, and Sheremetevs—and those most rapacious of in-laws, the Naryshkins.

As the facts we have presented imply, virtually all male members of
some of the most powerful court families received Duma rank whether
or not they deserved it by conventional standards. In this area—as in so
many others—the practices of the weak regimes of the late seventeenth
century represent a distortion of well-established norms.

Throughout the century, a number of aristocratic clans had an exceptionally strong claim on Duma rank. In his work, written in Sweden in
1666 or 1667, Kotoshikhin, the former Muscovite chancery clerk gave
one obvious measure of these families' special standing; when entering
the Duma, they immediately became boyars, while members of less favored clans initially held the lower rank of okol'nichii.[63]

Another test gives an even better sense of the relative standing of
prominent Muscovite families. Over the course of the century, seventeen aristocratic families placed all of their men who reached the usual
age of appointment—their early forties—in the Duma.[64] These families—princes like the Kurakins and Trubetskois and non-titled servitors
such as the Saltykovs and Troekurovs—usually had relatively few members in each generation.[65] Below them on the ladder were nine well-
established families with significant numbers of mature and apparently
competent men who never attained Duma rank. Among them, two types
predominated—non-titled servitors who had been prominent in the sixteenth century, like the Golovins, Kolychevs, and Pleshcheevs, and newly
promoted princes, like the Dolgorukiis and Volkonskiis. In their cases as
well, the size of the family played an important role. Several of these
nine had numerous members in our period. They thus ran afoul of the
apparent assumption that only a limited number of any one family could
hold Duma rank at any one time.[66] All the same, the size was not necessarily decisive; some small families had mature members with records
of significant service who nevertheless never reached the Duma.[67] Moreover, we might assume that, within the largest clans, all appropriate
members of one particular branch might become Duma members. Generally speaking, this was not the case, however; M. L. Pleshcheev, the
one member of his family to reach the Duma in our period, had several
close relatives of roughly equal distinction who did not win that honor.
All things considered, then, it would seem that, in the eyes of the Muscovite government and high society, the Golitsyns were, quite simply,
more distinguished than the Pleshcheevs.

Before proceeding further, we need to remind ourselves that many of
the realities of seventeenth-century life remain closed to us. The outlines
of men's careers, for example, tell us far less than we would like to know.

In the final analysis, we simply do not understand why one man received Duma rank and another from the same family did not, in spite of the fact that, outwardly, their records of service seem almost identical. Does, for example, the failure of several apparently qualified Khilkovs to reach the Duma prove that the family stood lower on the social ladder than, say, the Sheins or Pronskiis? We cannot be sure.

No such mystery shrouds the rapid growth in the size of the Duma in the last decades of the century. For one thing, some newly represented clans succeeded in placing all of their male members in its ranks. Once the first of them had joined the inner circle at court, the other Miloslavskiis, Khovanskiis, and Khitrovos all followed, whether or not they displayed any exceptional personal qualities. When they took their places alongside the members of the distinguished old families and the individual newcomers of sundry origin, they helped to swell the Duma to unprecedented size.

The inflation of honors in the late seventeenth century had political roots. As far as I know, the government of Muscovite Russia never sold offices or rank. Instead, the unstable and short-lived regimes of the late seventeenth century gave away such honors in a desperate attempt to reward their supporters appropriately and to win new adherents to their cause. The most spectacular example of such promiscuity was the promotion of eighteen men to Duma rank within four days at the end of June 1682. Sophia's new government rewarded an improbable group ranging from members of aristocratic clans to three Khitrovos, relatives of one of Aleksei's favorites, to men like M. I. Sunbulov, I. I. Sukhotin, V. F. Izvol'skii, and V. D. Miasnoi, of whom no one had ever heard before.

What were the consequences of this inflation of honors? Lawrence Stone has argued that, in England under the early Stuarts, the inflation of honors contributed to a mood of resentment and contempt toward the aristocracy and the government which rewarded it so lavishly.[68] The same attitudes probably pervaded much of Russian society in the late seventeenth and early eighteenth centuries. Certainly articulate Russians shared with their English counterparts a hierarchical vision of society. In both countries, a man who rose above his station offended the sensibilities of his fellows, especially when he behaved arrogantly or adopted a flamboyant style of life.[69]

The vastly different political traditions and institutional structures of the two countries meant that dissatisfaction with the inflation of honors took very different forms. In Russia in the late 1670s and 1680s the provincial nobility had no regular forum in which to express its resentment at the pretensions of the ruling elite. When an opportunity arose, however, its representatives made their feelings perfectly clear. When, in the fall of 1681, Prince V. V. Golitsyn and other leaders of Fedor's government appointed a commission to study the state of the army, the lower nobles' "selected representatives" recommended the abolition of *mestnichestvo*, the traditional system of precedence ranking, arguing that such a reform would put an end to the arrogant behavior of commanders from the aristocratic families of the court.[70] Moreover, at several times in the eighteenth century, notably in 1730 and in Catherine II's Legislative Commission, the representatives of the provincial nobles adamantly opposed any proposal for reform that smacked to them of aristocratic privilege, and displayed a profound attachment to Peter's Table of Ranks, which theoretically conferred high rank only as a reward for a man's individual merit. Clearly the inflation of honors reinforced a strong current of bitterness among rank-and-file nobles.

Aristocratic pretensions also stirred up resentment among chancery officials, if Kotoshikhin's testimony can be trusted. In his celebrated description of the Muscovite government written in exile, he included the rather nasty comment that some boyars were too ignorant or incompetent to play any real part in governing the realm.[71] What he would have said about the swollen ranks of the Duma in the 1680s we can only guess! Whatever the accuracy of Kotoshikhin's well-known remark, it expresses a very real grievance. The size and importance of the bureaucracy grew steadily throughout the seventeenth century. The traditional hierarchy of ranks, however, gave chancery officials fewer rewards than they deserved. At the same time, the system did give outstanding bureaucrats a little room at the top, and the inflation of honors made that space wider. In the course of the century, some chancery officials succeeded in winning Duma rank, a moderate fortune, and a measure of social acceptance among the first families of the court. If Kotoshikhin's career had turned out differently, he would undoubtedly have been delighted to take his seat in the council and to marry his daughter to the grandson of one of the boyars whom he caricatured.

The inflation of honors changed the Boyar Duma as a body. With seventy-five or a hundred members, it could hardly function any longer as a council of royal advisers. The Muscovite government dealt in several ways with this problem of its own making. First, on certain occasions, the tsar apparently met with only some of the Duma members who were at court or nearby.[72] Secondly, the royal administration created new and more effective institutions to take over some of the council's functions. The Raspravnaia Palata, for example, gradually emerged to hear judicial appeals. On May 9, 1681, it consisted of twenty-two men, including several chancery officials who did not hold Duma rank at all.[73] Finally, the council's unwieldy size guaranteed that a small number of royal advisers and favorites within it actually made governmental policy, while the other members only gave their passive consent.

In addition, the change posed vexing problems for the boyars as individuals. Governmental leaders like Prince V. V. Golitsyn had to bid for men's loyalties by distributing Duma rank generously. At the same time, Golitsyn was well aware that "when everyone is somebody, then no one's anybody." As a result, he and other statesmen of aristocratic lineage experimented with new titles that would set them above the common herd of Duma members. As head of the regency government, for example, Golitsyn adopted a splendid series of honorifics, especially "guardian" (oberegatel') of the realm.[74] In the latter half of the century, moreover, official records sometimes used the title blizhnii boiarin (privy boyar) to designate particularly distinguished courtiers. The practice dated from the sixteenth century and, in the seventeenth at least, apparently did not have any precise political or institutional significance.[75]

The dissatisfaction of leading officials took most dramatic form in a proposal for reform debated within the administration in 1681. This project recommended dividing Russia into a number of large provinces over each of which a courtier of particularly distinguished lineage would be appointed governor for life. Interestingly enough, the proposal emphasized that the governors would have the right to use the grand title of "boyar, governor, and prince of Kazan'" or of Novgorod or Siberia. Apart from changing the system of administering the realm, then, the reform would have left no doubt as to who were the most distinguished and powerful statesmen of Russia. In the end the reform ran aground on the opposition of Patriarch Ioakim, a man who came from the lowest nobility.[76] As was to be the case in the eighteenth century, a reform that appeared to further the ambitions of the aristocratic families of the court was doomed to failure.

The only reform to emerge from the discussions of 1681 was the abolition of mestnichestvo in the following year. This change, as I have argued elsewhere, was long overdue and altered very little. This traditional system of rank order had given the boyars certain psychological rewards but, in practical terms, had long been more of a headache than a blessing.[77]

The most serious resistance to the inflation of honors came from the mature Peter I. After a long period of neglect of domestic affairs, he turned on the moribund Boyar Duma and its swollen ranks and, with characteristic ruthlessness, simply abolished them. With the creation of the Senate and the formulation of the Table of Ranks, the boyars ceased to exist in name, but not as families or as a social group. That, however, is a story for others to tell.

CHAPTER II

Servitors

Historically,, service to the crown made the boyars who they were. The great non-titled aristocratic families of Muscovy rose to prominence in the fourteenth and fifteenth centuries by serving in the army and administration of the princes of Moscow. Occupying high positions from generation to generation gave them the influence, social standing, and style of life that made them aristocrats. Princes, by contrast, had a title that no ruler could confer or take away. Nevertheless, serving in the court in Moscow became, in the fifteenth and sixteenth centuries, their way of life. Moreover, these two groups within the aristocracy stood at the top of a hierarchy of royal servitors. Ivan III and his successors developed the *pomest'e* system of conditional land tenure precisely to create a large group of noble cavalrymen who could be trusted to appear for muster under all circumstances.[1] Then, in the mid-sixteenth century, Ivan IV extended to all noble landowners the obligation to serve in the army.[2] All nobles were, by definition, soldiers. By the beginning of the seventeenth century, then, the Russian nobility wore the harness of service like a well-trained horse.

To be sure, the fact that the high nobility regularly served in the royal army and administration was not uniquely Russian. In England in the late sixteenth and early seventeenth century, for example, the aristocracy eagerly sought offices in the king's government as a source of influence and income.[3] Nevertheless, the tradition of service ran unusually deep in Russia. As far as I know, no Russian noble of the seventeenth century, great or small, questioned the tsar's right to call him into the army. A significant number of minor nobles objected to the government's decision to call them up at the particular moment, and hid in order to avoid the muster.[4] I suspect, however, that their grounds for objection were exceedingly mundane; the tsar had the perfect right to summon anyone he chose—except them. Principled objections to official policy often stressed that the abuses in question hindered the nobles in the performance of their service obligations. This strain runs, for example, through the gentry petitions of the late 1630s and 1640s which attacked the inefficiency and corruption of the central bureaucracy and demanded the complete enserfment of the peasantry.[5] The obligation to serve itself did not come into question.

Many forces besides governmental policy impelled Russian nobles to serve. First of all, a highly successful career brought a man to the locus of political power. His efforts attracted the favorable attention of the tsar and his advisers, brought him to the court in Moscow, and perhaps won him one of the Duma ranks as his reward. Muscovy offered an ambitious man no other options. In Russia, by the sixteenth century, there were no local magnates or marcher lords whose power in their own region of the country surpassed that of the monarch. On the contrary, a Russian noble who stayed at home on his estate—assuming that the government allowed him to—simply faded into oblivion. Moreover, he ran the risk of falling into poverty. As we shall see in greater detail in a later chapter, Russian nobles practiced partible inheritance; they divided their lands roughly equally among all their sons. Over the course of several generations, then, a family's estates would be subdivided several times until each individual heir received only a tiny fragment of the original holding. Official service provided the only counterweight to this custom.[6] The Muscovite government frequently rewarded its noble servitors with grants of land. Moreover, service in the administration gave one the opportunity to collect fees and bribes which might well be invested in real estate. Those who did not serve with distinction lingered, like the poverty-stricken princes whom Giles Fletcher described, on the fringes of official society, dependent on the patronage of their more powerful neighbors.[7] Finally, service to the state provided the nobles, including the most aristocratic, with their *raison d'être*, their source of self-esteem. We should remember, for example, that a man's ranking under the mestnichestvo system depended on his previous assignments in service and those of his close relatives, as well as on his family genealogy.[8] Indeed, service was sometimes the more important criterion. To mention only one, rather extreme, example, in 1623 members of two branches of the sprawling Buturlin clan quarreled over their respective roles in a wedding at court. The okol'nichii Fedor Leont'evich Buturlin successfully warded off the challenge of his cousins by pointing out that, while their branch of the clan might be senior to his in a technical genealogical sense, its members had lost their high standing by serving as provincial nobles in Novgorod rather than in the capital.[9]

In the seventeenth century, the members of the boyar elite continued the tradition of working in the army and administration of Muscovy. In this chapter, we will examine the ways in which they served the crown and the impact of their official duties on their lives. The patterns of service naturally evolved over the course of time in response to changing political and economic conditions and the policies of particular rulers.[10] One of our tasks, then, is to see how these patterns changed during the seventeenth century and, more broadly, how the practices of our period differed from those of earlier and later times.

Before we begin the discussion, we should remember that two very different types of servitors made up the boyar elite. The vast majority belonged to the high nobility whose primary obligations were military. By and large, the men of the aristocratic families of the court served as army officers from generation to generation. At the same time, the most talented or favored of them also received postings as provincial governors or high office in the court itself. As far as we know, young aristocrats received no formal training for their future careers and had no special expertise. Indeed, illiteracy, while probably rare among the men of the aristocracy in the seventeenth century, did not necessarily bar a noble from a career in service.[11] What the aristocrats offered the tsars was a family tradition of leading armies and attending the ruler. Young men had the experience of growing up among fathers, uncles, and older brothers who carried it on and of serving alongside them, beginning in their mid-teens. As Brenda Meehan-Waters puts it, their specialty was leadership.[12]

The other type of Duma member was the chancery official. The men in this category entered the council with the rank of dumnyi d'iak. They were the outstanding representatives of the growing army of specialists in bureaucratic techniques. Recruits to the ranks of chancery clerks came from many groups in society, particularly the lesser nobility and the urban population. By the seventeenth century, however, chancery officials were tending to become a hereditary elite like the aristocracy. The boys who entered the prikazy in their earlier teens were expected to be literate and often had family connections within the world of the chanceries. Once hired, they went through a rigorous program of training in the copying and drafting of official documents. As mature men, their specialty was their mastery of the exacting routine of paperwork through which the Muscovite bureaucracy functioned. If they had exceptional knowledge of a particular subject—finance, for example, or a geographical region—that was an additional feather in their caps.[13]

The relationship between these two groups within the ruling elite was complex. The line that separated them became less and less distinct as the seventeenth century passed. Moreover, the relative importance and power of the members of the two groups is very hard to determine. Without doubt, leading chancery officials played an enormously important role in the administration of Russia. At the same time, the outstanding representatives of the traditional nobility also adopted policies and made decisions that affected the fate of the country. Moreover, if we can judge by the rewards that the system brought them, the outstanding boyars did considerably better than the great chancery officials. Ultimately, at the present stage in the discussion, we cannot decide definitively which group had greater power. Indeed, the question is ultimately unanswerable, for, in any society, men achieve and exercise power in an incomparable variety of ways.

In the seventeenth century, just as earlier, the members of the boyar elite served a lengthy apprenticeship. By making a rough statistical comparison of the careers of all Duma members during the period we can establish a rough *cursus honorum,* a pattern of advancement up the ladder of ranks and offices.[14] First of all, most men achieved Duma rank in the prime of life. Over the course of the century, the majority of new recruits to the boyar elite was in early middle age, that is between thirty-five and forty-nine. If we assume that they had begun to serve in official capacities at the normal age of fifteen, they had taken twenty or thirty years to reach the top of the Muscovite hierarchy. As we might expect, men of well-established aristocratic families entered the Duma at a slightly earlier age than those who had to work their way up the ladder of service without the aura of a great name or the support of a powerful clan. A clear indication of this is the fact that newly appointed dumnye dvoriane, usually men of comparatively undistinguished social origin, were, on the average, significantly older than men who were first appointed to the Duma as boyars. There were relatively few spectacular exceptions to these general norms. Over the course of the century, not many men reached Duma rank in their old age. At the other end of the spectrum, very young men rarely joined the boyar elite before 1676. After that date, however, as traditional patterns of advancement were breaking down, about one new Duma member in five was under thirty.[15]

The future members of the boyar elite worked while they waited for their reward. In the seventeenth century, they served chiefly in the army as their ancestors had done. Over half of them functioned exclusively as officers or military administrators in the provinces. Another one-fifth combined army duties with service in the civil bureaucracy during their apprenticeship.

Interestingly enough, in spite of the government's determined attempts to carry out radical military reforms, almost all of the future Duma members served in the old-fashioned cavalry units. In some respects, this pattern is understandable. Apparently members of aristocratic fam-

ilies were reluctant to serve in new-style military units for fear of compromising their precedence ranking.[16] At the same time, contrary to
what we might expect, few of the numerous "new men" of the century
rose to the boyar elite on the technological wave of the future. Only five
spent their early careers in the new-style regiments. The most notable
of them, A. A. Shepelev, by origin a provincial noble, fought with distinction in the wars with Poland and Turkey in the latter half of the
century and served as a consultant on reform of the army before receiving the new rank of *dumnyi general*, the equivalent of okol'nichii, in
1687.[17] Why did service in the new-style regiments help so few men to
reach the boyar elite? In order to answer the question, we must have
the results of detailed research on the command structure of the Russian
army in the second half of the seventeenth century. At present, however, we can hazard an observation or two. To begin with, many of the
commanders of the new units were unassimilated foreigners—men whom
custom excluded from the ranks of the Duma and the social elite of the
Muscovite court. The five Russians who rose to the boyar elite were
among the most prominent commanders of the 1670s and 1680s. Other
native officers of roughly equal stature, however, remained on a lower
plateau, commanding modern regiments and holding lower court rank
until the end of the century.

Oddly enough, the strel'tsy units, the supposedly obsolete infantry
founded in the sixteenth century, actually proved a better springboard
to high rank. Eight future members of the Duma, including the celebrated A. S. Matveev, served for years as commanders of strel'tsy.[18] In
evaluating their careers, we should bear in mind that, in the last decades
of the seventeenth century, these old-fashioned musketeers acted as garrison troops in the restless towns of Russia. Their primary function was
to keep order. They also carried significant political weight. In 1682, for
example, they made and unmade governments in the best tradition of
the Praetorian Guard.[19] No wonder the tsar and his advisers tried to
control the strel'tsy either by wooing the units' commanders or by placing their own partisans at their head.

In short, most future Duma members served in the army. The types
of units in which they fought, however, suggest that it was their lineage,
personal connections, and political weight, rather than their importance
in strictly military terms, that distinguished them from thousands of other
soldiers.

In striking contrast to the traditions of their caste, a significant minority of Duma members in the seventeenth century had done little or
nothing to justify its high rank. Over the whole period, more than one
man in ten performed only ceremonial functions at court in the early

years of his career.[20] From the young noble's point of view, hanging around the court had its advantages; it was a good deal safer and more comfortable than life at the front, and it provided opportunities for personal contact with the ruler and his ministers and favorites. At the same time, it had its drawbacks, as Prince V. V. Golitsyn was to discover. Once a boyar, the courtier in question might well have to lead an army or administer a province as a prominent member of his caste was expected to do. And he had to serve in these capacities without the benefit of experience![21] Despite his brilliance in other fields, Golitsyn was a disastrously inept general. If he had served on campaign at the beginning of his career, he might have learned how to lead an army or else, failing that, to leave military matters to men of competence.

The unstable conditions of the late seventeenth century magnified this flaw in the system of promotion. Up until 1676, the number of Duma members with no experience outside the court remained small. Moreover, the group included men of the caliber of B. I. Morozov, who used his position as tutor to the future Tsar Aleksei to make himself first minister when his protégé came to power.[22] After 1676, however, more than one man in five reached Duma rank without ever working outside the court; many of them, moreover, had little to recommend them except membership in one of the powerful court clans. In the 1670s and 1680s, then, the boyars showed signs of becoming courtiers in the pejorative sense.

As we might expect, chancery officials rose to the boyar elite by distinguished service in their area of expertise. Within the world of the chanceries, men's careers followed a rigid pattern of promotions and, with few exceptions, only those who had already reached the top could hope to become dumnye d'iaki. In the seventeenth century, the directors of only two particularly important chanceries—the Foreign Office (*Posol'skii Prikaz*) and Military Records Office (*Razriadnyi Prikaz*)—automatically held that rank. A number of the heads of the Land Grant Office (*Pomestnyi Prikaz*) also joined the Duma's ranks.[23]

These men were specialists in every sense of the word. They not only served exclusively in the bureaucracy, but often spent their early careers in a single important chancery. G. V. L'vov, Almaz Ivanov, and E. I. Ukraintsev, for example, worked almost without interruption in the Foreign Office. I. A. Gavrenev and V. G. Semenov stayed in the Military Records Office, while F. K. Elizarov and G. S. Karaulov spent many years in the Land Grant Office. Officials' lives were not always so simple, however. Some men, like M. F. Danilov, switched from one of the main chanceries to another in mid-career. Others worked in a wide variety of offices; F. F. Likhachev and G. S. Dokhturov, for example, both served their apprenticeship in several chanceries, most of which collected taxes or managed the government's finances. D. M. Bashmakov's numerous early positions included several which brought him into close personal contact with the tsar and his family. A few, like A. S. Durov, rose through the bureaucracy in steps that, on the surface, have no obvious inner logic, and a very small number had no experience at all in the bureaucracy before reaching Duma rank.[24] The most celebrated of the latter was A. S. Kirillov, a merchant who, after working for the government as a tax farmer, stepped directly into the royal council as head of several financial chanceries. His Moscow palace still stands and reflects his wealth and solid good sense.[25]

In the latter half of the century, these relatively simple patterns of advancement through chancery service began to change. Under Tsar Aleksei, the Office of Secret Affairs acted as a stepping stone to high rank. This new chancery functioned as the ruler's personal secretariat and, under his direction, dealt with a remarkable range of problems. In spite of its sinister name, its most important responsibility was to manage the royal family's estates, including the tsar's prized collection of falcons.[26] Given Aleksei's intense interest in its operations, it is no surprise that three of its officials whom he surely knew well—D. M. Bashmakov, F. Mikhailov, and D. L. Polianskii—eventually became dumnye d'iaki.[27]

Moreover, the careers of outstanding officials reflect the increasing political importance of the strel'tsy in the second half of the seventeenth century. Several members of the boyar elite worked in the Musketeers' Office (*Streletskii Prikaz*) early in their careers. Moreover, four dumnye d'iaki—Durov, Polianskii, Larion Ivanov and F. L. Shaklovityi—were in charge of this chancery at one time or another.[28] Shaklovityi, who began his career as a clerk in the Office of Secret Affairs, achieved great power in the 1680s and cut a fine figure, thanks to his control over the strel'tsy. Princess Sophia and Prince V. V. Golitsyn regarded him as a particularly staunch ally and, in the course of consolidating their power in the summer of 1682, promoted him to the Duma and made him head of the Musketeers' Office. In that capacity, he restored order in the Moscow garrison and acted, in effect, as the head of internal security for the regency government. When it fell in 1689, vengeance swiftly followed. He was executed on October 12 of that year for plotting to kill Tsar Peter I.[29] Whatever the truth of the accusation, Shaklovityi's position as commander of the strel'tsy forced Peter to destroy him.

Bureaucratic specialists were not the only men who worked in chanceries on their way to the Duma. In the course of the seventeenth century, many representatives of the warrior nobility served alongside them for a time in the course of their careers. As we shall see in greater detail later, these noble officials represented a new and important stage in the evolution of the governing elite in Russia.

In the early stages of their careers, one future Duma member in five served in the chanceries as well as in the army. These men came more often from the lower echelons of the nobility than from the great aristocratic families of the court. Since they rose from a social group with a tradition of military service, they usually began their careers in the army and punctuated their stint with an occasional job in a chancery. Understandably, they were most likely to do so in a period of peace immediately after one of the major wars with Poland.[30]

Usually these budding noble officials held only one or two chancery positions in their early careers, and these were usually in offices of secondary importance. A number of them, for example, served briefly in one of the judicial chanceries or those closely connected with the court and the royal family like the *Bol'shoi Dvorets* (Great Court) and Equerry Office (*Koniushennyi Prikaz*). There were, to be sure, some exceptions. A few men directed chanceries of major importance before receiving Duma rank; in the early 1630s, for example, F. V. Volynskii served as head of the Land Grant Office.[31] An equally small number stayed in one post for many years—twenty-seven, for example, in the case of I. P. Matiushkin's stint as second in command of the Great Treasury (*Bol'shaia Kazna*).[32] Finally, in the last decades of the century, a significant number of future Duma members served briefly in as many as four or five bureaucratic posts, mostly in relatively unimportant chanceries.

Admittedly what we have discussed so far seems to have little significance either for the functioning of the Muscovite bureaucracy or for the education of these noble officials as leaders. Certainly these budding boyars had no special training in the exacting routines of chancery work. The bureaucracy would probably have functioned just as well without them. Moreover, it is difficult to imagine what they learned in very brief assignments to minor chanceries. What they did acquire was a taste for chancery service and the advantages it brought. As we shall see shortly, once members of the military nobility reached the Duma's ranks, they began to perform chancery service much more often than before and in much more vital offices.

Bureaucratic specialists and members of the traditional nobility shared one other governmental activity—diplomacy. The Foreign Office was the nerve center of the Muscovite diplomatic service.[33] Its officials and translators handled the daily routine of contacts with other countries and their representatives in Moscow and prepared very detailed instructions for Russian diplomats going abroad. At the same time, the government often chose its ambassadors from the military nobility. In his work on the

Muscovite administration, Kotoshikhin indicates that ambassadors were chosen primarily for their social standing, with the most distinguished aristocrats representing Russia in negotiations with her most important neighbors to the west.[34] We will examine his contention in greater detail later. Noble diplomats, however, contributed more than aristocratic glamor to the conduct of Muscovite diplomacy. Clearly the tsars' government valued the services of a number of them and saw to it that they received appropriate rewards.

Serving as an ambassador, for example, might be the crucial moment in the early career of a young noble. A small number of them received Duma rank for a single important diplomatic mission—A. I. Ziuzin for his role in the conclusion of the Treaty of Stolbovo in 1617 and S. M. Proestev for his success in winning Polish confirmation of the Treaty of Polianovka in 1634.[35] The pattern continued throughout the century. Prince I. P. Boriatinskii and I. A. Pronchishchev seem to have won promotion for the Treaty of Kardis in 1661, B. I. Nashchokin for the Truce of Andrusovo in 1667, and V. I. Tiapkin for the Treaty of Bakhchisarai in 1681.[36]

Under Aleksei, moreover, noble diplomats began to play entirely new roles. First, his government belatedly responded to the quiet revolution in European diplomacy by appointing Tiapkin as Russia's first resident ambassador.[37] In 1673 it assigned him to Warsaw, where he served for several years before negotiating the peace with Turkey.[38] Secondly, in the latter half of the century, several men rose to great power primarily through their skill as diplomats. A. L. Ordin-Nashchokin was, of course, the outstanding example. A provincial noble from Pskov on Russia's western frontier, Nashchokin spent his first adult years in the army. When he was in his thirties, his intelligence, ambition, and skill with words attracted the attention of the royal treasurer, B. M. Dubrovskii. He began to receive diplomatic assignments. His performance so pleased successive governments that he rose rapidly in the service hierarchy and, in 1658, reached Duma rank. After he concluded his masterpiece, the Truce of Andrusovo, Aleksei made him head of the Foreign Office and, in effect, first minister of the realm.[39] His rival and immediate successor, A. S. Matveev, followed his example. Although more a military man and less a diplomat than Nashchokin, he carried out a number of delicate negotiations with leaders in the Ukraine. Once he reached the top, he too acted as prime minister, using his position as director of the Foreign Office as the main buttress of his administration.[40] These men's careers serve as a tribute to the tsar's openness to new ideas and techniques of governing and his willingness to work closely with men from outside the court aristocracy. Nashchokin, in particular, must have tried Aleksei sorely. He was notoriously difficult to work with, but the tsar continued to support him until his retirement from service.

Our lengthy reflections on the Duma members' early careers allow us to draw several conclusions. First of all, theoretically and in practice, men did not advance in the Muscovite service hierarchy by merit alone. Many members of the military nobility owed their high rank, in part, to their family heritage and connections. As I have argued elsewhere, men of aristocratic birth did particularly well under Tsar Mikhail, whose regime deliberately encouraged the revival of the great court families of previous centuries.[41]

At the same time, through most of the seventeenth century, most Duma members earned their rank with twenty years or more of useful service. To judge by externals—offices held and formal appointments in service—in the absence of more revealing testimony, some of them showed considerably more talent and promise than others. Almost all, however modest their gifts, made some contribution to the defense or governing of the realm in their early careers. The boyar elite was a working group.

The ways in which men qualified for membership in the Duma changed dramatically in the latter half of the century. In making promotions, Aleksei's government gave less weight to a man's family background than Mikhail's and placed greater emphasis on his gifts and record of service. As we have seen, a high proportion of new Duma members in the 1660s and 1670s were specialists in several fields of expertise.

After Aleksei's death, the regimes that followed turned the boyar elite into a caricature of its former self. Not only did they inflate the number of Duma members, but they also destroyed its image as a group of servitors. To be sure, some members still preserved the aristocratic tradition of service in the army and at court, and others worked hard to rise from obscurity to high rank. Far too many, however, had done nothing to merit their reward; they were indeed parasites—cousins of cousins, friends of friends, or partisans of factions. Their presence discredited the boyars as a group in the eyes of Peter and of many of his subjects.

Once they had reached the top of the Muscovite ladder of ranks, what did the Duma's members do to justify their exalted position? To begin with, they must have spent many hours in council sessions, listening to reports from the chanceries, ruling on difficult legal cases, and deliberating questions of foreign and domestic policy. To be sure, we do not know who attended particular sessions of the Duma. Moreover, most members probably did relatively little to set the course of government policy; it stands to reason that only the tsars and their closest advisers from the court and the bureaucracy actually steered the ship of state.

Nevertheless, the Duma as a body was an integral part of the Muscovite administration and, in addition, individual boyars routinely served on the commissions that took charge of the city of Moscow and the royal administration when the tsar was away from the capital. Prince M. P. Pronskii, for example, served in this capacity on a number of occasions. When Tsar Aleksei left for the Polish front early in 1654, Pronskii stayed behind in the capital and died there at his post in the epidemic that struck in the fall of the same year.[42]

Seventeenth-century Duma members, like their predecessors, performed many other functions as well. As we might expect, many members of the traditional military nobility continued to serve in the army. Over the course of the seventeenth century, one Duma member in five performed only military functions. Despite alternating periods of peace and war, the figures remained quite stable throughout the period. In addition, roughly two more men in five combined military and civilian duties.

Chancery service was even more popular. Over the course of the century nearly 60 percent of all Duma members held at least one post in the bureaucracy. Of these, one in ten was a full-time administrative specialist who rarely, if ever, served outside the central chanceries. The remainder—all 209 of them—were the noble officials, men from the traditional military elite who nevertheless held bureaucratic office.[43] As often as not, these men alternated between their traditional vocation, the military, and their newly acquired one. Oddly enough, although the central administrative apparatus grew steadily through the century, there were relatively more noble officials in the boyar group under Mikhail and Aleksei than in the regency period.

The most obvious reason for this anomaly was the remarkably high number of Duma members who, in the last decades of the century, did nothing except attend court ceremonies. After 1676, nearly one of them in three performed no other function.[44]

Let us now look at these general patterns in much greater detail in order to see in what specific ways the boyar elite served the crown and to evaluate its contribution to the common weal insofar as we can at so great a distance from their time. By tradition, the boyar's primary responsibility was to provide leadership, particularly in the army. As we have seen, they continued to do so throughout the seventeenth century. The ways in which they did, however, underwent considerable change.

Before proceeding, we should note that the line between military and civilian functions was not always clear in our period. In particular, by the early seventeenth century, the same term, voevoda, could mean either a general in the usual sense or a provincial governor. The ambiguity was not merely semantic. The same nobleman often acted as garrison commander and civil governor of the town to which he was assigned.[45] In the discussion that follows, we will try to distinguish between these two functions, bearing in mind that such precision is not always possible.

In the last decades of the sixteenth century, the boyars led the armies of Muscovy. In time of war, one of them was invariably the commander of the main corps of the army. On other occasions, the situation was a little more complicated. In the late sixteenth century, the Muscovite government maintained an army along the southern frontier at all times. Its commanders were usually not yet boyars, but came from a small circle of aristocratic clans of the court. Many of their families had a long tradition of boyar rank, and a number of the individual commanders later received that distinction themselves.

The aristocrats' virtual monopoly of military command did not come cheap. Most of the main generals of the late sixteenth century qualified for their positions with long years of service in the wars of Ivan IV's reign. Moreover, even the most distinguished of them worked very hard, remaining in the field for years at a time and often moving quickly from one distant frontier to another.[46]

To what extent do these patterns hold true for the seventeenth century? The rapid changes in military organization and technology in that period make comparison difficult. In Mikhail Romanov's reign, the noble cavalry continued to provide the core of the army, and the mobilization and deployment of manpower took place in much the same ways as earlier. From the beginning of Aleksei's reign in 1645, the pace of change was rapid. New-style regiments played an increasingly important role in the field, and the traditional cavalry lost much of its significance. Moreover, the improvement in the southern defenses against Crimean raids allowed the government to place less emphasis than before on keeping regular army units mobilized along the frontier. Finally, in the second half of the century, the rigid centralization of military matters gave way to a system of local military districts whose commanders exercised some initiative in supplying and deploying their troops. The Belgorod military district (*razriad*), the most important of these, gradually took shape in the late 1640s and 1650s.[47]

By the end of the Polish wars in 1667, then, the Muscovite army bore little resemblance to its sixteenth-century predecessor. To be sure, reform was far from complete, and the army remained in a state of flux. Nevertheless, old patterns of service had largely disappeared, and old methods of keeping records had changed, to the despair of the historian who wishes to make clear comparisons or to reach neat conclusions about the impact of the changes.

Throughout the seventeenth century, the tsars and their closest advisers proceeded on the assumption that the best commanders were to be found in the traditional military elite, the aristocratic families of the court. In time of war, boyars and okol'nichie commanded the army. In the first and last major wars of our period, the situation was the same; in 1632, M. B. Shein, A. V. Izmailov, and Prince S. V. Prozorovskii led the armies that set out to recapture Smolensk, and Prince V. V. Golitsyn and Shein's great-grandson took the lead in the futile attempts to conquer the Crimea in 1687 and 1689. To be sure, our choice of examples is hardly flattering. As far as we know, these generals received their commands for political rather than for military reasons. Among the leaders in the Smolensk War, only Prozorovskii had a lot of military experience. Shein and Izmailov had spent years away from the army; indeed, the former's last military action was to surrender Smolensk to the Poles in 1611. The government's decision to appoint such apparently unqualified men puzzles historians; it is quite possible that they got the jobs only after more promising candidates such as Prince B. M. Lykov and Prince D. M. Pozharskii had turned them down.[48] Golitsyn's decision to make himself commander of the invasions of the Crimea is equally mysterious. As an astute politician, he knew full well that his regency for the young Peter stood on shaky ground and that, as the tsar grew up, time was his enemy. Golitsyn's government desperately needed the glamor of brilliant military success to give it an aura of legitimacy and a chance to survive. Yet contemporary rumors claimed that Golitsyn did not want to take command himself but was forced to do so by his enemies at court.[49] In any case, both wars turned out disastrously for Russia and for the ill-chosen commanders-in-chief. Shein and Izmailov were executed in 1634 for failing in their mission, and Peter overthrew Golitsyn and sent him into remote exile for the rest of his life soon after the second Crimean expedition.

In these instances, the government's mistake was not in choosing aristocratic boyars, but in picking the wrong ones. In the Thirteen Years' War with Poland, in which, with some spectacular exceptions, the Russian army gave a good account of itself, the list of commanders looks like a set of military orders from the reign of Ivan IV or the list of guests at a great celebration at Aleksei Mikhailovich's court. Many of the great aristocratic names are there—Prince Ia. K. Cherkasskii, Prince N. I. Odoevskii, Prince M. M. Temkin-Rostovskii, V. P. and V. B. Sheremetev, Prince A. N. Trubetskoi, A. V. Buturlin, Prince Iu. A. Dolgorukii, Prince G. G. Romodanovskii, and Prince I. A. Khovanskii.[50] Indeed, in a sense, the wars of the 1650s and 1660s were a grand finale for the traditional military organization of Muscovy. When Tsar Aleksei declared war on his enemy, the King of Poland, he marched off to the front in May of 1654 with most of his court.[51] Two years later, on the outbreak of war with Sweden, the tsar once again went to the front, where, from a safe distance, he watched the efforts of several of the same generals.[52]

The boyars also led the armies in another kind of war—social war against the tsar's rebellious subjects. In 1650, Prince I. N. Khovanskii directed operations against the rebellion in Novgorod, and the government sent Prince F. F. Volkonskii to pacify Pskov.[53] The most serious threat of all, the peasant revolt led by Sten'ka Razin in 1670 and 1671, prompted Tsar Aleksei to use the full weight of the army.[54] The most celebrated commanders of the day, Prince G. G. Romodanovskii and Prince Iu. A. Dolgorukii, led the government's forces, assisted by a number of secondary commanders from leading court families. When faced with revolts that threatened the power, property, and very lives of the boyars, the government had no doubt that it could count on their support.

In the first half of the seventeenth century, while the army still consisted largely of old-fashioned cavalry, Duma members rarely took routine command posts on the southern frontier. For example, only three times did a member of the boyar elite serve as commander in Tula or Riazan' and, on two of those occasions, war with the Crimea seemed imminent.[55] At the same time, just as in the previous century, the government drew its southern commanders from the court aristocracy. All but a very few came from Duma families, and a number reached the council's ranks later in their careers.[56] Indeed, in the early years of Aleksei's reign, the command in Belgorod, the new center of the southern defenses, acted as a stepping-stone to the Duma; all three men who served in that capacity received promotions within a matter of months.[57]

After about 1650, the command structure of the Russian army began to feel the impact of reform. In Belgorod, for example, the main commander was the commander-in-chief of the entire southern front. Very prominent generals from the court aristocracy usually received the assignment; Prince G. G. Romodanovskii served in this capacity several times, as did V. B. Sheremetev and Prince B. A. Repnin. At the same time, the court aristocracy lost its grip on the lower echelons of the command structure. After mid-century, the men who served under these generals came from much more obscure noble backgrounds than their predecessors.[58]

In one sense, indeed, a new group of specialists, leading new-style regiments, took over the most important secondary commands. By the time of the war with the Ottoman Empire in the years 1676-1681, the new trend was already clear. On the battlefield, Romodanovskii remained commander-in-chief, but the real heroes were all warriors of the new type—I. I. Rzhevskii, who died defending Chigirin, A. A. Shepelev, and G. Kosogov.[59] Moreover, in the army units not involved in the fighting, the administration often assigned such men as subordinates to aristocratic commanders.[60] In return for their services, the government rewarded these talented newcomers with Duma rank and other titles. Thus they became part of the governing elite of Russia in theory as well as in reality.

In spite of their efforts, however, aristocrats still held the highest positions of command. How well did such men perform their duties? Making judgments at so great a distance is a hazardous business. Fortunately we have some contemporary opinions about the competence of some of the leading Muscovite generals. To be sure, foreigners' reactions to Muscovite life often reeked of hostility or snobbery. Nevertheless, their comments about seventeenth-century Russian generals sound a remarkably consistent note. As individuals, the commanders were staunch and brave men; Prince G. G. Romodanovskii had extraordinary physical strength and vigor, and Prince I. A. Khovanskii was courageous to the point of insanity.[61] Nevertheless, they were not very effective in the field. Contemporaries and later historians thought that many of them had too little strategic sense and tended to be too cautious. Contemporaries made such remarks about Romodanovskii and Prince Iu. A. Dolgorukii and, it seems in hindsight, V. B. Sheremetev lost an entire army at Chudnovo in 1660 through indecision and paid for his errors with twenty years in the Crimea as a prisoner of war.[62] Moreover, nothing in their training prepared them to take advantage of the new military technology that was sweeping Europe. Theirs was a traditional skill whose time was past.

Why, then, did the governments of the latter half of the seventeenth century keep them on? The answer, I am convinced, is not the mestnichestvo system. While the tradition of precedence ranking interfered with the functioning of the army by justifying quarrels between contentious generals, it did not force the tsar to appoint any particular man to a position of command. As recent scholarship has shown, the rules of mestnichestvo contained many loopholes through which the ruler could advance a man of low estate if he wanted to.[63] The reason why the crown continued to appoint aristocrats as generals is far broader and subtler than any particular system of traditional law. It is the hierarchical view of society through which men viewed the political and social elite as the natural leaders of society. When the tsar needed commanders, the boyars were the most obvious group to which to turn.

By the end of the seventeenth century, the aristocrats, the highest echelon of the traditional military nobility, had outlived their usefulness in some ways, but not in others. Without question, they lacked the education and training to cope with the complexities of life after the "military revolution."[64] At the same time, their collective political power, social standing, and wealth, and their authority over the peasants in their capacity as landlords, made them the natural leaders of society as before. In order for the aristocrats to become effective military leaders once again, they had to be forced to undergo a cultural revolution. That was the goal that Peter I set for himself and for them.[65]

Throughout the seventeenth century, Duma members served as provincial governors. Since the administration of the provinces was an extension of the army, it was natural that the crown recruited its leaders from the traditional military elite. The nature of the assignment made them suitable candidates. Although, in theory, the tsar's government in Moscow administered the whole country on a day-to-day basis, it lacked the instruments to do so in practice. Its agents, the governors, lived in a limited number of provincial towns and attempted to administer the huge areas around them with the help of a small garrison and an even smaller chancery staff. At best, they could hope to collect taxes, submit petitions and other routine business to Moscow, and suppress any serious dissent or social unrest.[66] Yet, while hardly a model of modern bureaucratic efficiency, the system was far from laughable, for it performed its duties reasonably well at very little cost.

From the last decades of the sixteenth century, the network of provincial governors conformed to a single pattern. Throughout our period, it centered on four strongholds—Novgorod, Pskov, Kazan', and Astrakhan'. When they were under Muscovite control, Smolensk and Kiev played an equally important role. To be sure, the system was not static. It could be adapted, not only to the changing fortunes of war, but also to the regime's changing priorities. If we may judge by the rank of the men appointed to these positions, the chief governorship of Siberia, in Tobol'sk, became very important in the first half of the seventeenth century, and Archangel, the administrative center of the European north, increased in significance after mid-century.[67]

The men who occupied these positions came from the same small circle of prominent court families whose members also enjoyed a virtual monopoly of the highest military commands. The vast majority of them had already received Duma rank, and those who had not would, in most cases, soon be so favored.

As the perceptive reader has undoubtedly noticed, we seem to have entered a charmed circle. Novgorod, the argument goes, must have been

a central pivot of the provincial administration because boyars were its
governors. By the same token, boyars must have been important because they served in Novgorod. In all fairness, however, it is the Muscovite sense of hierarchy and propriety that is responsible for the practice of matching the significance of the assignment with the rank and
social standing of the man appointed to it.

The formal rank of a governor tells us little about his fitness for the
position. The main test available to us is his record of previous service.
In the first half of the century, a man became a governor after many
years of service, particularly in the army. At the same time, we should
note that, unlike their sixteenth-century predecessors, many of them had
also served in the central bureaucracy and had carried out diplomatic
assignments. A few, moreover, had served almost exclusively in ceremonial posts at court.[68]

As the century passed, these patterns became even more complicated.
As we would expect, many governors served a long apprenticeship in
the old-fashioned military units. Moreover, a number of the new military
specialists like I. I. Rzhevskii became governors, particularly of strategic
towns of secondary importance.[69] Other men like Prince I. A. Khilkov
became virtual specialists in provincial administration, moving from one
governorship to another.[70]

The most important change of all springs from the ongoing reform of
the Russian army. As the importance of the traditional noble cavalry
declined, fewer and fewer members of the court aristocracy served their
apprenticeship in the army. Although the pattern is not consistent, more
and more governors, particularly after 1676, took up their posts without
the benefit of any military experience. Some, to be sure, had held posts
in the central chanceries or carried out diplomatic missions. In increasing numbers, however, a new governor's prior experience consisted exclusively of taking part in court ceremonies. In Novgorod alone, for example, this was true of Princes M. A. and M. Ia. Cherkasskii and Prince
F. S. Urusov. Such men had somehow to compensate for their lack of
background. In order not to exaggerate the significance of this phenom-
enon, we should remember that among their predecessors and successors in Novgorod were men with very long and varied experience in
administration—Prince I. A. Khilkov, V. S. Volynskii, and P. V. Sheremetev.[71]

From the Duma members' point of view, service as a governor was a
mixed blessing. On the negative side, the job took one away from Moscow. Life in Tobol'sk undoubtedly offered far fewer comforts and pleas-
ures than the capital, to say nothing of the rigors of the long journey
there and back. Far more importantly, service anywhere in the prov-

inces removed the individual boyar from the center of political life, the court in Moscow. While he was absent, a man might lose an opportunity for promotion or suffer from the intrigues of rivals.

Service in the provinces offered the Duma members no political advantages. As Giles Fletcher noted at the time when the seventeenth-century system was taking shape, the tsar and his advisers took care that no provincial governor became too powerful. Terms in office were strictly limited to two or three years.[72] One governor of Tobol'sk set a record for a major post by serving for six.[73] Moreover, the government made sure that no leading courtier put down roots in one particular provincial center. Those who served more than one term as governor—and there were a number—usually received the assignments in widely separated parts of the country. If they served twice in the same place, as sometimes happened, the government removed them for a number of years before sending them back.

Such precautions achieved their main purpose. Moreover, the chanceries of the central bureaucracy tried to keep a close watch on the provincial governors' activities, sent them detailed instructions, and expected those orders to be obeyed.[74] At the same time, some governors misused their office, taking excessive bribes and tyrannizing the people under their authority. In 1645/6, for example, local cavalrymen accused the governor of Novgorod, Prince S. A. Urusov, of mistreating them. Urusov allegedly ordered them to provide excessive quantities of supplies for the army and, when they failed to comply, beat them, and threatened them in filthy language (*"branil ikh materny"*). Predictably, Urusov denied most of their charges.[75] In another case, in 1665, V. Ia. Golokhvastov lost his job as governor of Eniseisk in Siberia for misappropriating funds and mistreating the natives.[76] This setback, however, did not prevent him from reaching Duma rank later in his career. Siberia was the sore spot of the provincial administration. Given the great distance from Moscow, the central bureaucracy could not exercise any measure of effective control over local officials, and scandals were common.[77] Elsewhere, however, cases of spectacular corruption or administrative malpractice were relatively rare.[78]

Being a governor had its good points as well as its drawbacks. Once settled into his new quarters, the governor could act as a little autocrat, at least in the short run. No one in Novgorod or Kazan' could challenge his authority except through the time-consuming and risky procedure of petitioning the tsar for redress. In the meantime, the governor was free to receive routine bribes and favors and to enjoy the practical and psychological compensations of being a very large fish in a small pond.[79]

On balance, the disadvantages of service in the provinces probably outweighed the advantages. What was the impact of service in the army and the provincial administration on the lives of the boyars? In the last years of the sixteenth century, the demands of official service were very onerous. Men like Prince T. R. Trubetskoi and Prince F. I. Khvorostinin received a profusion of assignments, one right after the other.[80] As a result, they remained in motion almost continuously, dashing from one end of the country to the other. They spent many years at a time away from Moscow, with little opportunity to see to their political fortunes, set their personal affairs in order, or simply to rest.

Throughout the seventeenth century, Duma members worked at a much more relaxed pace. In the first half of the century, Prince B. M. Lykov and Prince G. K. Volkonskii, for example, served in a wide variety of capacities in both Moscow and on the periphery.[81] Military obligations alternated with regular periods in Moscow attending at court or holding office in the chanceries. The same patterns held true under Aleksei and his successors. To be sure, a few exceptional men conformed to the earlier pattern, spending long periods of time away from the capital as generals or governors: Prince G. G. Romodanovskii, Prince G. S. Kurakin, and Prince I. A. Khovanskii must have been grateful for their occasional periods of respite in Moscow.[82] In 1674, for example, Romodanovskii complained that his estates had gone to rack and ruin because he had served in the Ukraine virtually without interruption for twenty-two years. His sons, moreover, could offer him no help in managing the family's property since Mikhail was spending his sixth consecutive year in the army and Andrei was a prisoner-of-war in the Crimea.[83] Other boyars whom we think of as generals, however—Prince Iu. A. Dolgorukii and Prince A. N. Trubetskoi, for example—held a wide variety of offices and consequently spent long periods at home as well as on the road.[84] If there is anything new in the last decades of the seventeenth century, it is the number of Duma members who rarely left the shelter of the court. Even men of the stature of A. S. Matveev and B. M. Khitrovo began their careers with a series of limited missions in the provinces, then settled in the capital and built nests for themselves in the chanceries and at court.[85] In this, as in so many other ways, then, the seventeenth century was a good time to be a boyar.

While in Moscow, many Duma members held positions in the bureaucracy. As we have noted, more than two hundred of them who came from the traditional military nobility spent at least a brief period in chancery service. Where and how long they worked there varied greatly from one individual to the next. For a number of these noble officials, assignment to a prikaz was a fleeting episode in a career devoted to other activities. Such men were particularly likely to serve in the judicial chanceries, the Petition Chancery, the offices supplying the court, or in the so-called "Investigative Chanceries." Others founded brilliant careers primarily on chancery office. Before describing some of the ways in which they did so, however, we can draw a few general observations from the bewildering variety of individual examples.

Statistical analysis of the social origin of the noble officials leads to two general conclusions. First, a man from one of the aristocratic families of the court was more likely to serve in a chancery than a social upstart who had just joined the boyar elite. Secondly, the "new man" was more likely to work only in the chanceries than his aristocratic counterpart, who more frequently moved back and forth between his desk and his regiment in the field.[86]

Let us consider the implications of these statements. To begin with, chancery service evidently appealed to many Russian nobles of whatever family background. Administrative office gave the holder income in the form of fees and bribes, command of a body of scribes or soldiers, and opportunities for building networks of clients. For men of the traditional warrior nobility, moreover, serving in an office in Moscow near the court was far more comfortable and safe and offered better prospects for political gain than the obvious alternative, life in the army in the field.

Many nobles felt the lure of office but had no special skills to offer. Members of the great aristocratic clans of the court, however, had advantages that offset their lack of training. In striving for chancery office, they could count on their families' power, political connections, and the tradition of leadership of Muscovite society. As a result, they often received positions as heads of chanceries, especially those that did not require special expertise. The Vladimir Judicial Chancery is a case in point. Over the course of the seventeenth century, the list of its directors contains many of the most distinguished names on the social register. Even the five who were not members of the Duma—Prince I. M. Katyrev-Rostovskii, Prince P. I. Pronskii, N. I. Sheremetev, Prince Iu. M. Odoevskii and M. I. Morozov—came from the same social stratum as the others.[87] It must have been difficult for men of less exalted origin to compete with those who enjoyed such advantages from birth.

Yet compete they did, for they too had special advantages. As we have noted, many of the social upstarts who joined the boyar elite in the seventeenth century had their own areas of specialization. Although they had not served an apprenticeship in the chanceries, a number of them had shown talents or acquired skills that gave them access to bureaucratic office. A. S. Matveev's military and diplomatic experience trained him for the offices that he held at the height of his power. At the same time, his example should warn us that many parvenu noble officials owed their rise to more than talent and energy alone. Like their aristocratic counterparts, they enjoyed the benefits of the right connections—in this case to the tsar himself through marriage or friendship. Matveev was Aleksei Mikhailovich's friend and eventually became his father-in-law in effect if not in fact. The Rtishchevs also had Tsar Aleksei to thank for their offices.

Behind these statistical trends lies a profound change in the relationship between the two elite groups that we are discussing—the highest echelon of the warrior nobility and the specialists who formed the backbone of the chancery system. Over the course of the seventeenth century, the line between the groups became less and less distinct. Men from the traditional military nobility penetrated all but a few corners of the bureaucracy. In the first decades of Romanov rule, the new regime left two of the most important branches of the administration—the Foreign Office and the Military Records Office—in the hands of the specialists. By the end of the century, however, noble officials had served as directors of every chancery on at least some occasions. To be sure, before 1689, only one noble official, Prince M. Iu. Dolgorukii, served as head of the Military Records Office, and his tenure was very brief.[88] Moreover, the three noble officials who directed the Foreign Office— Ordin-Nashchokin, Matveev, and Prince V. V. Golitsyn—were men whose personal qualities made them exceptions to any rule.[89] Finally, Tsar Aleksei's private chancery, the so-called Office of Secret Affairs, enjoyed a special status. No noble official ever directed it. Instead, the tsar himself took a very active part in its operation and worked closely with the specialists on its staff.[90]

These developments in no way negated the importance of the bureaucratic specialists. Without a small army of trained officials and clerks, the growing central administration simply could not have functioned. Moreover, throughout the century, the outstanding chancery officials enjoyed great power and prestige as individuals. We know less about their characters and ideas than about the leading noble officials of the time. The foreigners whose reports are the most important source of personal observations judged them from the perspective of their own self-interest; a Muscovite official was, in their eyes, a good man if he favored their cause and took only modest bribes.[91] Moreover, there may be some truth to the stereotype of the faceless bureaucrat. Long years of training and work in a disciplined and rather rigid hierarchical organization were not likely to make chancery officials colorful characters. Nevertheless, the evidence at our disposal, much of it indirect, suggests that the leading chancery officials were an impressive lot.

First of all, these bureaucratic specialists played a central role in the most important activities of the Muscovite—or any other—state. Throughout the century, they helped in establishing and executing foreign policy, they kept the records of manpower and of the pomest'e estates which together provided the foundation for the organization of the traditional cavalry army, and they oversaw the collection and management of the state's revenue. Under Aleksei and his successors, moreover, some of them, like A. S. Durov and F. L. Shaklovityi, had command of the strel'tsy, the most important internal security force in the land.[92]

In addition, their varied personal destinies provide indirect evidence of their significance. I. A. Gavrenev had a successful career by any standards. Born into the provincial nobility, he rose through the bureaucracy to the rank of okol'nichii. At the height of his influence, he enjoyed a comfortable fortune and the respect of the aristocratic families of the court. He married a Princess Volkonskaia and arranged the marriage of his daughter to V. B. Sheremetev.[93] On a more negative note, rioters in Moscow blamed N. I. Chistyi, A. S. Kirillov, and L. Ivanov for their troubles and singled them out for lynching.[94] F. L. Shaklovityi's fate was no happier. It is a tribute to his power that Peter's government went to such trouble to destroy him in 1689.[95] A timely change of allegiance saved E. I. Ukraintsev from a similar end. The fact that he held prominent positions both under the regency and Peter testifies to his value as an experienced diplomat and official as well as to his political agility.[96]

What I am suggesting, then, is not that the leading chancery officials lost their power in the latter half of the seventeenth century. Quite the contrary! Instead, we see the gradual disappearance of the once-clear line between the upper strata of the military nobility and the bureaucracy. In most cases, it was the warrior nobles who stepped over into chancery service. There are, however, isolated examples of chancery specialists who served briefly in the army.[97]

Whatever the details, the broad pattern of change is clear. Over the course of the seventeenth century, the two elites—the military nobility and the chancery officials—gradually merged. In 1689, the process was still not completed. Peter I finished the job and, in the Table of Ranks, established the formal structure of a single large and varied group of servitors of the crown.[98]

At this point, let us examine the ways in which the noble officials—members of the military nobility—served in the chanceries. As we might expect, the patterns of their careers in service are almost infinitely varied. Some spent many years in a single chancery: N. M. Boborykin, for example, worked only in the Great Income and a subsidiary.[99] Others moved from one office to another. G. M. Anichkov served consecutively in the Great Court, the Court Judicial Chancery, and the *Novaia Chet'*, which collected excise taxes.[100]

In the lives of the most prominent men of the time, we can see at least three general patterns of chancery service. First, at many times in the seventeenth century, contemporaries knew that a single statesman dominated the government of Muscovy. Foreigners often referred to such a man as chancellor. While no such office existed, the dominant political leader founded his power on a whole portfolio of offices in the chanceries. Prince I. B. Cherkasskii began the practice in the early 1620s when he became head of the Land Grant Office, the Great Treasury, the Musketeers' Office, the office that registered and looked after foreign soldiers in Russian service, and the Apothecary Chancery. The combination included control over part of the state's income and over the strel'tsy, the main police force of the realm. Moreover, the directorship of the Apothecary Chancery entailed regular access to the tsar's person.[101] The portfolio must have worked well. B. I. Morozov, who perfected the arts of the seventeenth-century courtier, put together a very similar combination at the very beginning of Aleksei's reign, adding only the *Novaia Chet'* to the package.[102]

The great chancellors of the last decades of the century concentrated on foreign policy. From the incorporation of the eastern Ukraine into Muscovy in 1653 until the "eternal peace" of 1686, the military and diplomatic struggles for control of that rich area took up a large part of the Russian government's resources and attention. Not surprisingly, then, the three great statesmen of these years—A. L. Ordin-Nashchokin, A. S. Matveev, and Prince V. V. Golitsyn—took a keen interest in diplomacy and served, first and foremost, as heads of the Foreign Office. Nashchokin and Matveev also directed the tax-collecting agencies attached to the foreign ministry, the Little Russia Chancery that administered Muscovy's half of the Ukraine, and the chancery that dealt with prisoners of war. To this combination, Matveev added only the Apothecary Chancery. As first minister of a regency of questionable legitimacy, Golitsyn tried to strengthen his power in a number of ways. In addition to the Foreign Office, he took over the directorship of three chanceries that controlled branches of the army, the Artillery Chancery, and those that had jurisdiction over the new-style military units and the foreign personnel in Russian service.[103] In abstract terms, his choice of weapons was excellent. In reality, however, in 1689, when Peter challenged the regency, Golitsyn found out to his consternation that he could not count on the support that his offices should have provided.

Secondly, in the seventeenth-century elite, we can see examples of a

type of official who attracted more attention in the following two hundred
years—the general as bureaucrat. Prince Iu. A. Dolgorukii fit the mold
well. Contemporaries thought of him primarily as a military man, and
indeed he commanded Russian armies in a number of important commands. Between 1658 and 1660, for example, he twice commanded the
forces on the Lithuanian front and served a stint on the southern frontier
as well. A decade later he led the armies sent against the Razin rebels.
In the final analysis, however, he was a jack-of-all-trades like most other
members of the boyar elite. Over the course of his career, he acted as
director of ten different chanceries, the most important of which dealt
with military matters and questions of national security. He spent several terms as head of the Artillery Chancery and twice directed the Kazan' Office that administered the conquered lands of the former khanate.
Moreover, like many of his successors in later centuries, he retired from
the army to spend the last years of his life in the comfort of the court
and the chanceries. After the Razin uprising, his most important office
was the directorship of the Musketeers' Office. The assignment cost him
his life, for, in 1682, members of the Moscow garrison under his command mutinied and lynched him.[104]

Third, friends and favorites built nests for themselves in the court and
in the chanceries that supplied its needs. I. M. Iazykov, Fedor Alekseevich's influential adviser, is an excellent example of the type. At the
height of his power, he held only four formal offices, the directorships
of the Court Judicial Chancery, the Tsar's Workshop, the Gold and Silver Chanceries, and the Armory. All were of minor importance, and all
were closely connected with the court. Together they tell us only that
the tsar held Iazykov in high regard. Similarly, Aleksei's friend F. M.
Rtishchev received formal appointments that gave no real indication of
his influence on the tsar's domestic and foreign policy or of his significance as a patron of scholars. Another of Aleksei's favorites, Rtishchev's
kinsman, B. M. Khitrovo, held a larger portfolio of minor chancery offices of the same type.[105]

What did the noble officials as a group contribute to the functioning
of the administration? Certainly, with the rarest exceptions, they lacked
special training in bureaucratic techniques. While the literature gives us
only the most fleeting glimpses of life inside the prikazy, it is reasonable
to assume that, in many cases, the boyar in charge of a chancery left all
of the routine work and most of the thinking to the specialists who served
under him.[106] Ordin-Nashchokin—a noble official with the skills and determination to establish policy and write innumerable documents defending it—struck contemporaries as a shocking exception to the rule.
At the same time, far less gifted noble officials may well have learned on

the job and made a real contribution to the functioning of the chanceries in their charge. To judge by the formulaic language of chancery documents, contemporaries assumed that the formal head of a prikaz bore ultimate responsibility for its decisions.[107]

The boyars' primary contribution to the chanceries, then, was a tradition of leadership. In the seventeenth century, the Russian administrative system grew very rapidly. The number of chanceries and of their officials increased sharply. In this situation, the tsars' government needed many new administrators. As is well known, Muscovite Russia's urban population, small and poorly developed, could meet only a minute part of the need. The government had no choice but to turn to the warrior nobility. The most valuable recruits, of course, were those who entered the chanceries young, learned the routine of work on the job, and stayed for life. But even the noble officials who lacked such training could make a contribution. They were accustomed to positions of command. Moreover, they gave the chancery milieu a higher social tone and, in their persons, linked it with the Boyar Duma and the ruler's inner circle of advisers and courtiers.[108] In broader terms, the noble officials served as a bridge between the bureaucracy and the military nobility, still the mainstay of the army.

The best proof of the usefulness of the noble officials is the attitude of Peter I, a ruler whose power and strength of character allowed him to treat the nobility as he liked. The reforming emperor counted heavily on the traditional nobility to manage the bureaucracy as well as to lead his armies.[109] In the long run, he and his successors demanded, not that the nobles leave administration to specialists, but rather that they educate themselves to perform their duties, both military and bureaucratic, more effectively.[110]

The boyar elite provided many of seventeenth-century Russia's diplomats. The leading officials of the Foreign Office, of course, played the central role. They took part in negotiations with foreign ambassadors in Moscow, sometimes accompanied the most important embassies to other countries, and supervised the day-to-day conduct of foreign affairs. During the course of the century, all but three directors of the Posol'skii Prikaz were bureaucratic specialists. It is precisely the three exceptions—Ordin-Nashchokin, Matveev, and Golitsyn—however, who seem to have exercised the greatest influence on the general outlines of Russian policy. In the minds of contemporaries, each of them stood for a definite diplomatic program. Nashchokin wanted an alliance with Poland against Sweden, and Golitsyn aimed at a general anti-Turkish coalition. Matveev took the opposite tack; as his first priority, he insisted that

Muscovy keep control of Kiev and the eastern Ukraine, a policy that inevitably meant conflict with Poland.[111]

These three were the outstanding representatives of a large number of military nobles who performed diplomatic functions. Leaving aside the bureaucratic specialists, nearly eighty or one-fifth of all members of the boyar elite served as diplomats at some time in careers mainly in the army and the chanceries. A few like the Pronchishchevs and I. I. Chaadaev devoted a large part of their careers to diplomacy.[112] They were specialists in the same sense as their three more famous colleagues.

What did the noble diplomats as a group have to contribute to the conduct of Russian foreign policy? Kotoshikhin, the former employee of the Foreign Office, suggested that the Muscovite government used a man's ancestry as the main criterion for making him ambassador to another country. The tsar sent to Poland boyars of the most distinguished ancestry, to Sweden Duma members of good, but less exalted family, and to the Hapsburgs men of slightly less distinction still. Normally men of the boyar elite did not serve as ambassadors to the other countries of Europe or the Near East.[113]

A survey of the literature on Russian diplomacy confirms the accuracy of Kotoshikhin's testimony. In practice, the most important delegations that conducted negotiations with Poland—those that took part in meetings on the frontier between the two countries—normally consisted of a boyar and other Duma members of lower rank, and usually included the dumnyi d'iak who headed the Foreign Office. A boyar, an okol'nichii, or, less commonly, a dumnyi dvorianin led the Muscovite delegations to the Polish court. When dealing with Sweden, the Russian government usually appointed okol'nichie to lead missions to Stockholm, but, on occasion, boyars took part in negotiations on the frontier. Once again, less prominent courtiers and officials of the Foreign Office made up the rest of the negotiating team.[114]

The tsars' government had good reasons for this pattern of appointments. The social standing of the ambassador left little doubt of the relative importance to Russia of the country to which he was sent. Moreover, in the seventeenth century, European rulers took an intense interest in the symbols and rituals of diplomacy. They were determined that rivals whom they considered their equals or inferiors accord them their full titles and receive their representatives with full ceremonial honors. Any change in these symbolic patterns they perceived as an attempt to change the nature of the relationship between the two powers. The Muscovite government understandably took pains to see that aristocratic Polish and Swedish diplomats negotiated with men who could unquestionably be considered their social equals. To help its noble diplomats make a suitably grand impression, it conferred on them the honorary title of governor (*namestnik*) of a town whose importance suited their standing in Muscovite society.[115] This concern with social and ceremonial equality may help to explain an anomaly in Kotoshikhin's testimony. No seventeenth-century European, least of all a Russian, could doubt that the Ottoman Empire was a formidable power; yet the Muscovite ambassadors to the Porte were men of low rank. The reason probably lies in the Turkish practice of appointing as ambassadors men of comparably low rank and standing.[116]

Did the noble diplomats contribute anything to Russian diplomacy besides their distinguished names? The evidence on this point is ambiguous. Kotoshikhin suggests that the professionals in the Foreign Office did the ambassadors' thinking for them. At one point, he remarks nastily that, out of arrogance and ignorance, some aristocratic envoys dared to improvise on their written instructions. More recent commentators, however, take the ambassadors as a group more seriously. Since we know very little about the inner workings of Russian missions abroad, we cannot answer the question definitively.

Indirect evidence, however, allows us to make some tentative judgments about the qualifications of Russia's noble diplomats. First, we must bear in mind that the government did not choose aristocrats at random as ambassadors. Many boyars of impeccable lineage never served in that capacity. Moreover, the careers of those who did suggests at least a limited degree of specialization. Twelve noble diplomats repeatedly represented Russia in negotiations with the same foreign country—eight with Poland and four with Sweden. Prince N. I. Odoevskii, G. G. Pushkin, and I. I. Chaadaev often met Polish representatives on the border between the two countries, and I. A. Pronchishchev made missions to Stockholm a specialty.[117] Likewise, foreign representatives in Moscow dealt over and over again with the same courtiers. They saw a great deal of the four we have just mentioned and a number of others—Prince Iu. A. Dolgorukii, Prince F. F. Volkonskii, and V. S. Volynskii, for instance.[118] The government did not show complete consistency in appointing these men as negotiators.[119] Nevertheless, on a number of occasions, the same Muscovite team dealt with representatives of the same power on separate occasions. In 1658 and 1659, Volkonskii and two chancery officials did business with the Danish envoy, Oldeland, on consecutive visits to Moscow.[120] Representatives of the Hapsburgs dealt with the same men—Prince A. N. Trubetskoi, Prince G. S. Kurakin, Dolgorukii, B. M. Khitrovo, and A. Ivanov—during missions six years apart.[121]

These fragments of evidence suggest that Kotoshikhin's observations are correct, but one-sided. Undoubtedly their exalted births helped make

Odoevskii and Dolgorukii appropriate spokesmen for the Muscovite state. At the same time, the nobles who served repeatedly as diplomats surely displayed some aptitude for negotiation and considerable familiarity with the rituals, if not the issues, of diplomacy. There were plenty of substitutes at court for aristocrats who played the game of diplomacy with disastrous ineptness. On a more positive note, a few men besides the three famous chancellors apparently became specialists in diplomacy. By all accounts, for example, Pronchishchev was an expert on Sweden, with detailed knowledge of the issues, men, and customs that dominated relations between the two countries.[122]

In broader terms, the pattern of developments is the same as we have observed in our discussion of the chanceries. At the beginning of the seventeenth century, we can see two distinct groups, the specialists of the Foreign Office and the amateur noble diplomats who served in many capacities. By the latter half of the century, however, the two groups were merging, thanks, in large measure, to the emergence of expert diplomats from the military nobility, of whom Ordin-Nashchokin was the prototype and most brilliant example.

Over the course of the century, nearly one-fifth of the Duma's members did nothing except attend court ceremonies. After 1676, the proportion rose to nearly one in three. Some men who fall into that category had received Duma rank as a retirement gift at the very end of a long and useful career. Many, however, particularly toward the end of the century, did little or nothing of note at any time in their lives. These men were courtiers in the strict sense.

Courts served a number of useful functions in seventeenth-century Europe. All over the continent, rulers spoke to their own people and to foreign rivals through ceremonial and entertainments. In such symbolic language, kings and queens advertised their power, piety, or good taste— even when they did not have them. Beginning in the early sixteenth century, European rulers and artists collaborated in developing new forms and techniques to delight and awe men. In Versailles, Louis XIV worked the new magic to perfection.[123] At the other end of Europe, the Muscovite court usually spoke a different, much older symbolic language. Even so, its appeal to the loyalties of men was essentially the same.[124]

In this sense, courtiers had their uses. A man who put on a gold brocade robe, probably borrowed from the royal treasury, and stood with a throng of others at the reception of an ambassador contributed to the impression that Russia was a wealthy and powerful country, not to be trifled with. When he took part in an ecclesiastical ceremony, he helped to spread the message that the tsar was a devout Christian whom all faithful sons and daughters of Eastern Orthodoxy should revere and obey.

Moreover, as many historians have observed, Louis XIV imprisoned the French aristocracy in a golden cage when he built Versailles.[125] There he held them under his watchful eye and kept them busy waiting on him and attending ceremonies from morning until night. In many ways, the court of Aleksei Mikhailovich superficially resembled its French counterpart. There too the ruler and his leading subjects spent their days and nights in an exhausting round of liturgies, sacred and secular.[126]

In Russia, however, there was no need to take the nobility prisoner. Since the fourteenth century, its leading representatives had responded to the lure of power or the pressure of political or economic adversity by moving to the capital on their own initiative. Indeed, in the seventeenth century provincial nobles would have been only too glad to join the thousands who had already reached the court.

In Russia, then, the appearance of a large number of courtiers who served only decorative functions signified the decay of the Muscovite tradition of a working nobility. As we have suggested, the political instability of the late seventeenth century produced a striking inflation of honors. Many new members of the boyar elite were nonentities who received the honor only because they belonged to one of the parvenu families that dominated court politics or one of the factions that they led. Their promotion reflected their clans' desperate need for prestige or their obligation to reward allies, not their merit. For this reason, they brought Duma rank and those who bore it into disrepute.

A student of the history of western Europe may be surprised that, in a discussion of the careers of Russian nobles, we have not mentioned the church. The omission is deliberate. As far as I know, Muscovite nobles rarely sought a career in the church.[127] Certainly the extensive genealogical and service records of the seventeenth century reveal no younger sons of great noble families who became bishops. On the contrary, the little we know about the social origins of members of the ecclesiastical hierarchy suggests that men of all backgrounds could rise to positions of influence. In modern terms, the church was the most "democratic" institution in Russia.

Accordingly, family relationships very rarely linked the high nobility of the court and the high dignitaries of the church. The Savelovs provide the only exception. Three of them rose from obscurity to join the boyar group, thanks to the support of their energetic kinsman, Patriarch Ioakim.[128] In this exceptional case, power in the church brought recognition in the secular world, not the other way around.

Why did the church fail to attract members of the high nobility into its service? There are, I think, two reasons. First, in the seventeenth century, Russian nobles set their hopes for advancement and prosperity on service to the state and the rewards that it conferred. Moreover, in a period when all arms of the government swelled rapidly, the administration needed all the soldiers and officials it could find. Thus, if a man had ten sons, it suited him and the government to enroll them all in its service.

Secondly, the traditional rules of the Eastern Orthodox Church made it an unattractive alternative to state service, particularly for the wealthiest and most powerful nobles. In order to become a bishop, a man had to spend a long apprenticeship in a monastery. Moreover, even after a period of rigorous preparation, there was probably no guarantee of a bishop's throne. Certainly the Russian church had no teen-age hierarchs and no bishoprics controlled by a single family. In short, a genuine religious calling was the only reason why a seventeenth-century noble would take monastic vows. Moreover, the pressures to serve the government kept even the most devout high nobles from answering the call until very late in life.

As the reader is surely aware by now, most boyars of the seventeenth century worked for their keep. At the same time, the conditions in which they served were, by and large, considerably more favorable than those faced by their predecessors in the late sixteenth century and by their successors under Peter. Their official obligations frequently gave them opportunities for political gain and economic profit, and many of them enjoyed periods of respite from active duty and the prospect of a comfortable retirement at the end of it.

In some respects, however, the patterns of their service careers, particularly in the second half of the century, resemble those of the eighteenth. Historians have often noted that, in many ways, the practices of Aleksei Mikhailovich's government anticipated the reforms of Peter I.[129] In our previous discussion, we observed the gradual emergence of a single group of royal servitors woven from several social and institutional strands. As in later periods, most men of high rank were generalists, serving interchangeably in military and civilian capacities. At the same time, the system left room for specialists in both the narrow and the broad sense; the outstanding chancery officials of the time won advancement through their mastery of the skills of the bureaucrat and, in addition, some prominent representatives of the military nobility who served in many capacities gained recognition primarily for their efforts in one particular area of governmental activity. Finally, seventeenth-century practice admirably combined social continuity and openness. Members of the well-established aristocratic families of Muscovy continued to prosper and to play important roles in the political life and administration of the realm. At the same time, talented newcomers could rise to high rank and great power and did, especially in the reign of Aleksei. Most of the main components of the eighteenth-century system of promotion were already evident.

We should be very careful, however, not to exaggerate the degree of resemblance.[130] Peter the Great attacked real problems, and his reforms made important changes in the institutions and administrative practices that he inherited. In establishing conditions of service for the administrative elite, Peter made two major changes in seventeenth-century patterns. First, he treated the high nobility as a drill sergeant. He forced its members to serve him continuously under very rigorous conditions. Many of those who felt his fists—figuratively or literally—must have yearned for the good old days of his father, to say nothing of the genial chaos of the early 1690s. Secondly, he insisted that all of his leading servitors act as bearers of a new cultural style. In the latter decades of the seventeenth century, a few statesmen developed new artistic and cultural tastes on their own initiative. Peter, however, required all nobles to educate their sons for service and to shape their social lives according to his notions of civilized European styles. Contemporaries thought that Peter's policies represented a radical departure from those of his predecessors, and they were right.

In addition, we must bear in mind that the second half of the seventeenth century was a time of experiment and of flux. By the time of Aleksei, the leaders of the government realized the inadequacy of existing practices and began to make important changes in a number of areas of national life. In most, however, they did not succeed in creating a new system to replace the old. Over the course of the century, we have seen the slow and ultimately incomplete fusion of two elite groups, the warrior nobles and the chancery specialists, into a single cadre of leaders. It remained, however, for Peter to give structure and coherence to these tendencies by instituting the Table of Ranks.

CHAPTER III

Family and Marriage

Many boyars were aristocrats as well as servitors. By that, I mean that, for several generations, members of their families had held the rank of boyar or okol'nichii, served in important posts, and enjoyed exceptional wealth and prestige. At the same time, unlike their western European counterparts, they owed their standing largely to a tradition of service to the crown rather than to their entrenched power in the region of their origin.

As he was acutely aware, each boyar belonged to a family and, beyond that, was one small part of a complex mosaic of relationships of blood and marriage. Moreover, within the boyar elite, we can see an inner core of powerful clans, often related to one another. Some of them were those small but distinguished families which stood out by placing virtually all of their mature male members in the Duma during the seventeenth century. Many of these same clans enjoyed exceptional wealth and made particularly good marriages for their children. They constituted the social elite of Muscovite Russia. As we shall see, traditions of genealogical seniority played a significant role in their lives, and they expressed their convictions about their social standing, above all, in the choice of marriage partners for their children.

In seventeenth-century Russia, these aristocratic traditions seem to clash with the equally traditional demand that all men serve the crown in order to win high rank. The rulers of Muscovy found ways to reconcile these apparently contradictory principles. In examining the service careers of the members of the Duma, we noted that, for centuries, the Russian government looked to a slowly evolving group of aristocratic clans for leaders for the army and the administration. In more specific terms, moreover, we cannot understand the careers of many seventeenth-century statesmen unless we take into account the families into which they were born and married.

Strictly speaking, Russian nobles belonged to lineages, not clans, since they could trace their descent from a known ancestor.[1] In what follows, however, we will use the more familiar words "clan" and "family," which, although less precise, will not distort our discussion. As elsewhere in Europe, Russian clans transmitted names, titles, and property through the male line. At the same time, as we shall see, women could play significant roles in the life of their clans and of society at large, and ties of marriage might have a more important influence on an individual's fate than those of birth.

To study Russian noble clans means to enter a world of slow but steady change. In earlier times, as noble families grew in size, younger sons sometimes founded new clans designated by new surnames or hyphenated versions of the old. In the seventeenth century, this type of proliferation did not take place, as far as I know. The Great Velvet Book, the official genealogical compilation begun in 1682, records families whose names remained stable throughout the century.[2]

The clans themselves continued to evolve, of course. Some went on growing in size; the Buturlins, for example, were very numerous in our period.[3] At the other extreme, some clans, once very large, had dwindled down to a single line, as was the case with the royal family, the Romanovs.[4] Still others, like the Odoevskiis and Sheremetevs, fell into the middle ground, passing their power and wealth from a small group of fathers to an equally small number of sons over several generations.[5] The structure of these families undoubtedly helped them to maintain a preeminent position among the Russian nobility throughout the seventeenth century and later.

Finally, the make-up of the web of clans that dominated the court and administration of Russia changed as well. Distinguished old families like the Mstislavskiis and the Sitskiis died out.[6] Other clans rose from the lower echelons of the nobility to replace them, thanks to distinguished service, an advantageous marriage, or the favor of the tsar or his closest advisers. Families like the Pushkins, Tolstois, and Chaadaevs of later literary renown, for example, reached the boyar group in the seventeenth century.[7]

The obvious but mysterious natural processes of birth and death decided the fate of noble families. Sudden catastrophes, whether man-made or natural, took individual lives, but seem to have had comparatively little impact on entire clans. Ivan IV's reign of terror, the oprichnina, for example, affected different families in different ways. His purge of the high nobility in the years 1565-1571 hit some prominent families particularly hard. Of the clans that were still represented in the Duma in the seventeenth century, the Kolychevs and Pleshcheevs felt the tsar's rage especially keenly, losing nine and eight men respectively. In the seventeenth century, both families enjoyed less influence and prestige than before the catastrophe, if we can judge from the offices they held and the marriages they made. At the same time, in purely biological terms, they continued to thrive.[8] Theirs were extreme cases; most prominent seventeenth-century families had suffered less at Ivan's hands. The related clans, the Morozovs and Saltykovs, lost a total of five members in his purges. Before they died, however, all but one of the victims had heirs who carried on the family line. Moreover, in the seventeenth century, they suffered opposite fates: the Morozovs died out and the Saltykovs continued to multiply.[9] The execution of its senior member contributed to the extinction of the elder branch of the Repnins and increased the chances that the whole clan would die out. The younger branch, however, beat the odds and produced prominent statesmen in the seventeenth century and beyond.[10] Finally, the Shuiskiis, who, to the surprise of historians, went through the crisis unscathed, became extinct when Prince Ivan Ivanovich died in 1638.[11]

Sudden death stalked the population of Russia in the seventeenth century as well. In its first years, the Time of Troubles brought warfare, material hardship, and chaos to all strata of society and to all parts of the country. Later decades were more tranquil, but the great wars and uprisings of the century claimed thousands of lives, and the epidemic of 1656 took many more. Nevertheless, as far as we know, these tragic events do not explain why one noble family waxed and another waned.[12]

All we know for certain is that many high nobles died young. The genealogies of Duma families contain the names of many male members which appear rarely in official records of service or not at all. Yet the completeness of the court registers for most of the seventeenth century makes it likely that any adult man of a Duma family would be recorded as a participant in ceremonies and religious observances even if he showed no aptitude for more demanding forms of service.[13] A man who disappeared from the records altogether had probably died.

Moreover, nearly one Duma member in five for whom we have information had children, none of whom married, if we can believe the extant records.[14] To be sure, our information on seventeenth-century noble marriages is spotty and unreliable. Nevertheless, the number of such families with children who never married seems to me too high to blame on inadequate sources alone. Concern for the survival of the clan and the lure of political and social connections impelled high nobles to marry off all their eligible children, probably at a comparatively early age. When a Duma member did not marry off any of his children, it is probably an indication that they died before reaching maturity.

Study of family genealogies confirms the impression that some clans lost a disproportionately high number of males at an early age. We can find examples among all types of Duma families—the princes Pozharskii, the Izmailovs, a well-established non-titled clan, and social upstarts like the Likhachevs and Narbekovs.[15]

Even worse, a surprisingly large number of Duma members had no children at all. Popular wisdom holds that "it's not hard to become a father." Russian nobles had every reason to question this axiom. In an age of high mortality rates among all groups in society, men and women wanted large numbers of children to guarantee that the family did not die out. Large families, of course, had their disadvantages. As I have suggested, the most favored clans were those which had roughly the same number of active men from one generation to another. Yet, I suspect, this pattern of family development was a fortunate accident. I know of no direct evidence that Duma families practiced birth control. Moreover, in seventeenth-century conditions, the reasons for having many children outweighed those for having few: prominent noble families could expect to provide extra sons with service positions in the growing army and bureaucracy and to replenish their estates from the steadily expanding fund of land. Nevertheless, in spite of the pressures to reproduce, more than one-fifth of the Duma members had no children who lived long enough to be recorded in the family genealogy. One can easily imagine their sorrow and frustration.

Armed with these general observations, let us examine the ways in which the structure and connections of their clans affected the lives of seventeenth-century Duma members. At the outset, we must bear in mind that family membership has both objective and subjective dimensions. On one level, a man or woman belongs to a family because he or she shares a common ancestor with the other members. On another, people are relatives if they recognize that they are and if the connection means something to them. Scholars of Muscovite Russian history have proceeded, probably quite correctly, on the assumption that there was no distinction between the two meanings of membership in a family; men who shared the same surname and appeared in the same genealogy recognized their kinship.[16]

Whether this assumption actually held true in the seventeenth century is a moot point. By that time, some clans—the Saltykovs and Buturlins, for example—had grown very large without subdividing definitively. But did all of the Buturlins still think of all the others as their relatives? The testimony of the main body of evidence on this question, the records of precedence disputes, is ambiguous. When it suited him, a litigious noble claimed that everyone who bore his name ranked higher than all kinsmen of his rival. All Buturlins, the argument ran, automatically stood above all Volynskiis or Sheremetevs above Pleshcheevs.[17] On other occasions, the shoe was on the other foot. Ambitious courtiers petitioned to dissociate themselves from men of the same name whose standing and record of service were undistinguished. Two branches of the Buturlins fought one such battle and the Iazykovs another.[18] Given such an ambivalent contemporary attitude to the meaning of membership in a clan, we cannot proceed on the assumption that all men with the same name were related in a meaningful way. We can, however, make tactical choices to distinguish between close and very distant relatives.

Family ties held the boyar elite together in several ways. First of all, a group of families which transmitted high rank from father to son or from grandfather to grandson dominated the upper ranks of the Duma. Over the entire seventeenth century, 36 percent of all boyars and okol'-nichie were direct descendants of men who had held the same ranks at least thirty years earlier. Their families' tradition of leadership and their ties to the court and to each other undoubtedly helped the sons and grandsons to retain the gains of their forefathers.

Secondly, the patterns of descent within the Duma illustrate once again the government's changing policy toward its leading servitors. As we have noted, Mikhail and his advisers showed a marked preference for members of the well-established aristocratic clans of the court. In his reign, 45 percent of all newly appointed boyars and okol'nichie were direct descendants of earlier ones. Aleksei's regime, however, opened the Duma to unprecedented numbers of social upstarts, particularly in the last decades of his reign. Between 1659 and 1676, only 16 percent of the new appointees to the Duma's top ranks had direct ancestors who had served in the same capacity.[19]

In addition, we must take into account that boyars, like all married men, enjoyed the benefits and headaches of membership in two families. Ties of marriage as well as of blood linked Duma members to one another. To illustrate this point, let us see how many men had a relative within three kinship links in the Duma at the time of their own promotion to its ranks. The following diagram illustrates what I mean by three kinship links.[20]

By this measure, close to one-half (43 percent) of all Duma members in the seventeenth century had a close relative who was already in the council when they entered it. Interestingly enough, this figure remained almost constant throughout the entire century.[21]

This numerical fact has two important implications. First, it suggests that, in the course of his career, ties to blood relatives or in-laws in the boyar elite helped a man to reach the pinnacle of the Muscovite system.

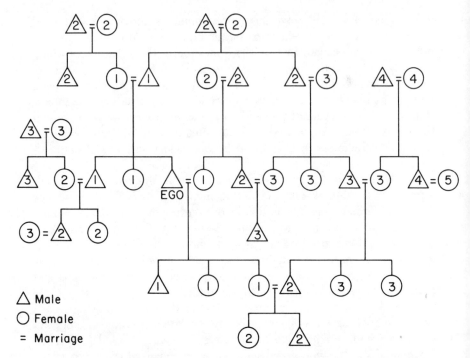

DIAGRAM I.   Kinship Links between Individual (Ego) and Selected
Relatives.

Secondly, the consistent importance of these connections throughout the
century indicates that men of all social origins profited from such links
of kinship. Further investigation substantiates the latter hypothesis. A
little less than half of the men with such connections (42 percent) came
from families that did not have a long history of Duma rank.[22] A relative
in the council helped aristocrat and parvenu alike.

    A brief look at individual clans gives a better sense of the meaning of
these figures. As we would expect, the distinguished old families that
thrived throughout the century—the Golitsyns, Odoevskiis, and Sheremetevs, for example—scored very high on our test.

    So, not surprisingly, did those which profited from the policy—unan-
nounced but apparently conscious—of marrying the heir to the throne
to the daughter of an obscure local noble. Such marriages had their
advantages. They kept the heir from marrying outside the Orthodox faith
or from bringing a convert of doubtful sincerity into the Russian court.
Moreover, marriage to a woman of obscure origin kept the royal family
from becoming the ally of one particular aristocratic clan at the cost of

bitter animosity from the other great families of the realm. The custom also had its price. Such marriages saddled the tsars with greedy parvenu in-laws who strove to take advantage of their good fortune. In our period, the Miloslavskiis, Naryshkins, and Lopukhins entered the boyar elite in droves. In other cases, the connections that brought parvenus into the council were more complicated. I. P. Matiushkin seems to have reached Duma rank because he married F. L. Streshneva, the sister of Tsar Mikhail's wife.[23] Later, three of his kinsmen rose to the same dignity on his or one another's coattails. Clearly marriage alliances with the royal family and with one another changed the fate of many noble families. We will return to this theme later.

Finally, let us look at the genealogical position of Duma members within their own clans. In one sense, this is the least rigorous test of all since it treats all members of very large families as relatives. In another, the criterion is a demanding one. Genealogical seniority means something quite specific. In Kievan and Mongol times, for example, in the ruling clan of East Russia, the Riurikovichi, seniority passed from the head of the family to his younger brothers in the first instance. According to one application of this general principle, the two oldest of the younger brothers were considered senior to the oldest son of the family head, and the third younger brother was regarded as his equal. After this, the fourth member of the older generation, the succession passed without question to the sons.[24] In her recent dissertation, Nancy Shields Kollmann argues that boyar clans of the fourteenth and fifteenth century followed precisely the same pattern.[25]

To what extent did the Russian high nobility follow such a pattern of succession in the seventeenth century? By implication, this question contains another. What role did genealogical seniority play in the careers of Duma members in our period? Put more crudely, did many of them owe their high rank to the fact that they were the senior representatives of distinguished old families?

Before answering these questions, we should make certain qualifications. It would be unreasonable to expect social upstarts who reached high rank because of their talent or the tsar's favor to conform to principles of genealogical seniority. For this reason, we will consider only the aristocratic members of the boyar elite, that is, the princely and non-titled clans which had a representative in the Duma at least thirty years before the promotion of the individual whose genealogical standing we are considering. To this group we will add the one other set of clans which we might expect to take genealogical considerations seriously— the princes who were newcomers to the Duma.

Over the course of the seventeenth century, slightly more than one-half (56 percent) of the members from these families entered the ranks of the Duma according to genealogical seniority within their clan.[26] At first sight, our conclusion seems impressive. On further reflection, however, this figure means both more and less than it appears to.

First, our test tends to exaggerate the extent to which boyar clans consciously observed the rules of genealogical seniority. To give one important example, when a member's son reached Duma rank earlier than his younger brother, we count the uncle as the senior representative, for he was precisely that when he entered the boyar group. In a more rigorous sense, however, both the nephew and the uncle broke the rules that we have outlined by accepting promotion to the Duma in reverse order.

Secondly, examination of family genealogies tests much more than the observance of traditional principles of seniority. For one thing, there is a close relationship between the size of a clan and the extent to which its members followed one another to Duma rank in the appropriate order. For example, none of the Buturlins to reach the council in our period was the senior representative of the family. On the other hand, small aristocratic clans like the Odoevskiis followed the rules quite closely. To put it bluntly, the fact that a clan received a high score on our test may prove only that it was small and that it had very few adult men from among whom the government could choose boyars. In addition, in the seventeenth century, most men reached the Duma in early middle age after many years of service. The order in which members of a clan won promotion to the boyar elite may simply reflect their age rather than a conscious determination to respect their genealogical standing. Finally, the fact that a new council member occupied the senior position in his clan may simply be a coincidence. Even among the parvenus who rose to Duma rank, a goodly number were the senior members of their clans.[27] Two families of royal favorites, for example—the Rtishchevs and the Matiushkins—consistently followed the rules of genealogical succession.[28] Moreover, in families like the Romodanovskiis or the Naryshkins, whose members reached Duma rank in no observable order, some new council members nevertheless happened to be the eldest men available, in genealogical terms.[29]

In the light of these reservations, we must take our statistic with the proverbial grain of salt. At the same time, the investigation of family genealogies permits certain limited conclusions.

To begin with, our model of promotion by genealogical seniority does not fit the facts of seventeenth-century life with any consistency. The boyar elite and a number of the clans from which its members came had both grown too large to conform to any simple set of rules or principles.

By implication, then, no single key opens to us the careers of seventeenth-century Duma members. Whatever its importance in earlier times, genealogical seniority alone does not explain why one man became a member and another did not. Of course, that does not mean that contemporaries did not take genealogical considerations seriously. They did indeed, as the records of precedence disputes eloquently testify. We can also see their awareness of seniority at work at particular times and within individual clans.

First, as I have argued elsewhere, the government of Tsar Mikhail consciously sponsored a revival of the great aristocratic families of the realm. To a remarkable degree, the boyar elite in his reign consisted of the eldest living descendants of the same clan, both princely and nontitled, that had dominated the Muscovite administration in previous centuries. To be sure, not all great sixteenth-century families survived and thrived in the seventeenth. Many died out, and a limited number— eleven, by my count—lived on, but faded into obscurity. Most of the old elite families, however, retained their prominence and their hold on high office under the new dynasty.[30]

Perhaps the clearest proof of the newly crowned Romanovs' predilection for the traditional aristocracy can be seen in the number of new boyars and okol'nichie who entered the Duma as the senior representative of their clan. In the first years of Mikhail's reign, the new regime virtually ignored genealogical considerations in appointing new boyars. The young tsar's advisers showed a marked preference for the Romanov family's cronies and in-laws like the Cherkasskiis and for experienced military men like Prince D. M. Pozharskii. Once the head of the clan, Patriarch Filaret returned from prison in Poland and assumed control of the government, however, the revival of the aristocracy began in earnest. In the years of his preeminence, 1619-1633, all but one of the new boyars and okol'nichie came from the aristocracy, and well over half of them were the senior members of their clans.[31] In Mikhail's last years, when a succession of favorites from the aristocracy dominated his government, the revival reached its zenith. With two exceptions, all new boyars and okol'nichie were aristocrats and, of their number, more than 80 percent occupied the senior position in their families when they entered the Duma.[32] This remarkable figure strongly suggests that Mikhail's government took genealogical considerations very seriously indeed when making appointments.

Negative evidence, if we can call it that, also supports our position. In only one instance in Mikhail's time did the government promote a junior member of one branch of an aristocratic clan earlier than its senior member. Prince I. I. Odoevskii became a boyar in 1622, eighteen years before Prince Nikita Ivanovich, his first cousin who was genealogically his senior, but probably some years younger.

As we have already seen, after 1645, Tsar Aleksei's government followed new policies in several areas of national life. For one thing, the aristocracy lost its near monopoly on high rank. Nevertheless, throughout the rest of the century, we can hear echoes of the aristocratic revival of earlier decades. When we examine the composition of the boyar elite in the second half of the century, we come across men with only one evident claim to high rank—their positions as the senior members of distinguished old clans. In particular, F. B. Dolmatov-Karpov, Prince M. M. Temkin-Rostovskii, Princes V. A. and M. V. Obolenskii, A. D. Kolychev, Prince I. A. Vorotynskii, and Prince S. Iu. Zvenigorodskii seem to have owed their eminence to their family standing. Their careers reveal no other reasons why they became boyars or okol'nichie.[33]

Secondly, some of the most distinguished families of Muscovy preserved the tradition of genealogical seniority throughout our period. One after another, Sheremetevs, Kurakins, Pronskiis, Repnins, Sitskiis, and Troekurovs entered the Duma in precisely the correct order.[34] As we have noted, the small size of these clans made it relatively easy for them to observe such niceties. Other equally distinguished families broke the rules only occasionally under special circumstances. The relative ages of the men in the clan might dictate a breach in tradition, as the example of the Odoevskiis illustrates. Political circumstances might also deflect a family from the usual practice; all of the numerous Khovanskiis entered the boyar elite in precise order of seniority except two of the sons of Prince Ivan Andreevich the Younger, who received Duma rank at an early age during their father's ill-fated bid for power in 1682.[35]

To conclude, respect for genealogical seniority was an important element in the family tradition and world view of the Romanovs and the other aristocratic clans of seventeenth-century Russia. The attitude contributed to the conservative approach of Tsar Mikhail's government and the resulting aristocratic revival of his reign. After 1645, however, we can see the impact of genealogical considerations primarily in some aristocratic clans. If there was ever a time when genealogical seniority determined who became a boyar, that time had certainly passed by the middle of the seventeenth century.

Over the course of history, marriage has taken many different forms and met many different social needs. Among the boyars of seventeenth-century Russia, parents married off their sons and daughters with two objectives in mind. First, they hoped to guarantee that the paternal clan would survive. As our scattered evidence makes clear, noblemen and women married for the first time when they were very young, often while in their late teens.[36] Then, if all went well, children came soon and often. Tsar Aleksei and his first wife, Mariia Miloslavskaia, set their subjects an impressive example: in twenty-one years of marriage, they produced thirteen children, often at intervals of twelve to fifteen months. When Mariia died, the tsar remarried as soon as discretion allowed, and had three more offspring in the last five years of his life.[37] Subsequent events bore out Aleksei's concern about the succession to the throne. Only three male heirs survived him, and Peter, the youngest, alone proved to be a competent ruler. Many prominent noblemen followed the same pattern. If a man's wife died young, as many did in childbirth, he usually remarried soon. Often, although by no means always, the second or third wife was a young woman who had never been married before.[38] To such unequal matches, the bride brought the prospect of many years of child-bearing.

Secondly, marriages formed the cement that held the Russian high nobility together. Making statistical statements about the marriage customs of boyar families is a risky undertaking; much of our information comes from nineteenth-century genealogical compilations of doubtful accuracy and, even there, there are serious gaps in the data. In particular, we know the dates of only a few seventeenth-century marriages, and educated guesses are of little help in determining when a particular union took place.

Even so, the frequency with which Duma families made marriage alliances with one another is remarkable. Leaving aside the cases for which we have no information, roughly three-quarters of the members of the boyar elite in our period married at least one son or daughter to someone from another Duma clan. As a result, over the course of time, well-established aristocratic families built matrimonial bridges to most other prominent clans. In other words, if we look hard enough, we will discover most boyars were one another's in-laws. If that is so, can such ties of marriage have meant anything at all?

On the face of it, not all matrimonial connections had equal significance. Recent marriages likely meant far more to a clan's members than ties established many years earlier. At the same time, some distinguished families remained closely linked with one another over several generations of mutually reinforcing marriages. Moreover, at any given time, a large boyar clan undoubtedly had fresh links with a wide variety of other families. What sense can we make of such a tangled skein of family relationships?

Before addressing this issue, let us examine the economic dimension of marriage. In a stimulating essay on the family in early modern England, Lawrence Stone stated that ". . . the key to the system of controlled marriage was the exchange of property. . . ."[39] I strongly suspect that this was not the case in Russia. To be sure, Russian noble brides brought their husbands estates as part of their dowries. The young man and his parents undoubtedly appreciated the addition to the family holdings. At the same time, acquiring land was probably not their primary motive in making the match. For one thing, the high nobles of Russia lived much of the time in Moscow and owned lands scattered in many parts of the country. Under these circumstances, it was most unlikely that a boyar would marry his son to the daughter of a neighboring proprietor in order to round out one of his estates. The fragmentary evidence supports this hypothesis; dowry lands were separate properties located at a distance from the rest of the husband's family holdings. Moreover, within the family portfolio, the dowry estate occupied a special place and passed to the wife's heirs or to a monastery in return for prayers for her soul.[40] These considerations suggest that economic gain, while probably important, was not the primary concern of Duma members when they married off their children.

Above all, it was the power and social standing of their clans that made young people valuable marriage partners. However, the reasons behind some seventeenth-century matrimonial alliances remain a mystery. It is impossible even to guess, for example, why Sheremetevs married members of obscure families like the Shliakov-Chezhskiis, Shishkins, and Svin'ins.[41] Such cases were relatively rare, however. Leafing through the genealogical records for information on marriages, one repeatedly sees the same aristocratic surnames in pairs. Moreover, some of the infrequent exceptions underline the political and social implications of marriage in the Muscovite elite. When a young aristocrat married the daughter of a prominent social upstart, the union brought together, not so much an old name and new money, as in many other societies, as an old name and new power. In the most striking cases, the great chancery officials of the late sixteenth and early seventeenth centuries, Elizar Vyluzgin and I. A. Gavrenev, capped their careers by marrying their daughters to Sheremetevs.[42] These alliances rewarded both families. Through them, the officials won entry into the social elite of the court. In return, the Sheremetevs linked themselves to men who had important parts in governing the realm and enjoyed the influence and wealth that flowed from high office.

In the kaleidoscope of elite marriages, several patterns stand out. Most dramatic are the concentric circles of noble clans spreading out from the throne. Successive royal in-laws made up the inner circle. Indeed, in the seventeenth century, their position differed very little from that of the new Romanov dynasty itself. While royal propaganda stressed the Romanov's distinguished ancestry, their real claim to the throne, as they knew full well, rested on the marriage of their kinswoman to Ivan IV.[43] They were the epitome of the successful royal in-laws. Moreover, the new dynasty needed time to distance itself from the boyar elite from which it had come. As tsars, the first Romanovs enjoyed the aura of their imperial office and the sacerdotal role of shepherds of the Orthodox flock, to say nothing of the coercive weight of the state. At the same time, the first rulers of the line were, by and large, relatively weak or ineffectual men who reigned but could not really rule. Only Aleksei showed much strength and determination, and he did so erratically. Otherwise, small groups of courtiers and favorites from the court nobility ruled in the tsar's name. Some of these men came from clans like the Cherkasskiis and Sheremetevs, who, like the Romanovs, had married into the old dynasty.[44]

Since the new dynasty preferred to marry its young men to Russian noblewomen, each royal nuptial brought a new clan of in-laws to court. After Tsar Mikhail's tragically brief marriage to a Princess Dolgorukaia, all the royal consorts came from obscure provincial families. No one doubted that the Streshnevs, Miloslavskiis, Naryshkins, Apraksins, Grushevskiis, and Lopukhins were upstarts. The government, for example, carefully kept them away from situations that might lead to precedence disputes, for fear of embarrassing all concerned.[45] At the same time, the aristocrats who might laugh at them behind their backs sometimes found them indispensable.

In Muscovite Russia, power flowed primarily through personal channels. Even in the seventeenth century, when the bureaucracy grew in size and efficiency, the most powerful men were often those who stood closest to the throne and who came into regular personal contact with the tsar. F. M. Rtishchev provides a particularly good example. If we judge him by his formal offices and titles, he was a relatively insignificant figure. In reality, however, his contemporaries and later historians give him credit or blame for decisively influencing official policy in several spheres.[46] Even such imperious figures as A. L. Ordin-Nashchokin and Patriarch Nikon owed much of their power and the offices that embodied it to the favor of Aleksei Mikhailovich.[47]

This is where the in-laws came in handy. Whatever their merits—and most seem to have been very undistinguished—they unquestionably lived close to the tsar, and one of their kin shared his bed and board. As a result, court clans, great and undistinguished, eagerly allied themselves with the newcomers, in spite of their disdain. If our guesses about the timing of the marriages are correct, the Streshnevs managed, between

Mikhail's marriage to Evdokiia and the end of the century, to forge ties
with the Golitsyns, Lykovs, Vorotynskiis, Troekurovs, and Saltykovs,
among others.[48] Their successors, the Miloslavskiis, cashed in quickly on
their good fortune. B. I. Morozov, Aleksei's mentor and first minister,
arranged his protégé's wedding to Mariia, then married her sister almost
immediately afterward. Before long, the family was enmeshed in a web
of alliances with other court clans.[49] In much the same way, suitors appeared as soon as Aleksei Mikhailovich took Nataliia Naryshkina as his
second wife.[50] Only the royal in-laws of the last years of the century—
the Grushevskiis, Apraksins, and Lopukhins—failed to win social recognition quickly. In the case of the first two clans, their ties with the
royal family lasted a very short time. As for the Lopukhins, contemporaries quickly figured out that no one won Peter's favor by observing
traditional social niceties, let alone by paying court to his abandoned
wife and her kinsmen.

Men and women made somewhat different moves in the game of matrimonial chess. Although the evidence is far from unanimous, social
upstarts like the great chancery officials or the new royal in-laws tended
to marry their daughters to aristocratic young men.[51] In a world of pat-
rilineal clans, the groom's name and social standing were more important
than the bride's.

Moving our kaleidoscope a little, we can see rectangles and more complex geometric figures emerge. Over the course of the seventeenth century, a group of four interrelated families occupied the central position
in the network of marriage that bound together almost all families of the
court. The Romanovs, the Cherkasskiis, the Sheremetevs, and the
Odoevskiis had complex ties with one another dating back to the sixteenth century.[52] In the seventeenth, the latter three clans renewed
their ties with four more marriages with one another and with the complex transfers of property that these connections produced.[53] Moreover,
as the Romanovs gradually changed from a noble clan into a ruling dynasty, the Golitsyns replaced them in the central configuration thanks,
once again, to well-made marriages.[54] Around this central core gathered
many other clans. In Mikhail's reign, the group had ties to the Sitskiis,
the Lykovs, the Litvinov-Mosal'skiis, the Golovins, and the Pronskiis.[55]
Thereafter, the net spread wider and wider.

In the early years of Aleksei's reign we can see another configuration
emerging. Three closely related provincial families—the Khitrovos,
Rtishchevs, and Sokovnins—appeared at court at about the same time.
Moreover, since they reached the inner circle shortly before the young
tsar married a woman from another provincial clan, the Miloslavskiis,
historians have speculated that the latter already had matrimonial ties

with one of the three, probably the Sokovnins. However accurate this guess, the four families of newcomers soon had clear connections with one another through a fifth clan, the Morozovs. Although he was the scion of a distinguished aristocratic family, Boris Morozov, the tsar's chief adviser, had no qualms about marrying the sister of his master's new bride. Incidentally, it is quite likely that, at the time, the first minister was a widower in late middle age and his new wife a woman in her early twenties. To complete the figure, in the following year, 1649, Morozov's brother, Gleb, married a Sokovnin.[56] Many years later, that young woman, now a widow, openly rejected Patriarch Nikon's reforms and, with her sister, Princess Urusova by marriage, died a martyr in defense of native Russian tradition. Once these upstart families had solidified their position around Aleksei's throne and established ties with his powerful in-laws, they had no trouble marrying into distinguished families.

Let us complete our observations with a glance at the marriage patterns of several different types of clans. Distinguished old princely families like the Odoevskiis and Golitsyns usually married their offspring to the children of other aristocrats. The Odoevskiis, a comparatively small clan, were particularly discriminating, showing a marked preference for other princes and accepting ties with parvenus like the Rtishchevs only after the latter had established their position at court and in high society.[57] The more numerous Golitsyns cast their nets wider; while most of them married fellow aristocrats, both princely and non-titled, they also made matches with the new royal in-laws, the Streshnevs, and the Khitrovos and two or three families of no great distinction in any sphere.[58] Their most distinguished non-titled colleagues, the Sheremetevs, displayed even more catholic tastes. In the middle of the seventeenth century, for example, they had connections with four princely families of distinction, one fine old non-titled family like themselves and several of humbler origin. Indeed, as we have noted, the Sheremetevs stand out for their willingness to marry their children to talented and powerful upstarts.[59]

What do these patterns suggest? First, the distinguished old families of the Muscovite court formed a self-conscious social elite. As the records of precedence disputes make clear, they were acutely aware that they occupied the top rung of the social ladder, and they guarded that position jealously. Marriages to their social equals emphasized their distance from the less distinguished members of society.

Secondly, in a world of rapid change, the boyars used marriage as a defensive weapon. The Golitsyns and, in particular, the Sheremetevs made alliances with a wide variety of families. When they married below their station, the reasons may have been personal. It may well have been difficult, for example, to find a suitable mate for an ugly or sickly child. All the same, the general pattern suggests that the more prudent aristocratic clans tried to build ties to as many other families as possible. The practice served, I suspect, as a form of insurance. In a political crisis at court, relatives by marriage might not prove reliable allies—they might well be related to one's enemies too—but would perhaps at least remain uncommitted in the struggle for power.

The princely clans that entered the boyar elite in the seventeenth century occupied a middle position. Their title and lineage distinguished them from the rest of the nobility, but they had just climbed into Muscovy's political elite and joined the inner circle of the court. Understandably, they adopted a flexible approach to marriage. In our period, the Lykovs, a branch of the distinguished Obolenskii lineage, were a small clan. On the whole, they married very well, mixing matches with newly elevated princes like themselves, royal in-laws, and old boyar families, including the Romanovs and Odoevskiis, who held central positions in the matrimonial network.[60] At the opposite pole, we find the Volkonskiis. They were a large clan, and their numbers increased rapidly in the seventeenth century. Their numerous marriages linked them to a very wide variety of other clans, many of them relatively obscure. Oddly enough, the Volkonskiis who reached Duma rank married women of particularly undistinguished origin. They very rarely made ties with the most powerful families of the realm; I know of only one example, the marriage of I. P. Sheremetev to Princess M. V. Volkonskaia in 1634. When they arranged matches with other families in the boyar elite, they often chose newcomers like themselves—royal in-laws, new princes, or recruits from the provincial nobility or from the chanceries.[61]

The fate of these two princely clans shows us the two faces of the Muscovite social elite. As measured by marriages, the Lykovs were simply more distinguished than the Volkonskiis. Their lineage and history gave them an aura that the Volkonskiis, solid though they were, simply could not match. At the same time, the rank of boyar or okol'nichii reinforced a family's social distinction and, in the long run, could make aristocrats out of parvenus. In this sense, the Lykovs and Volkonskiis were both outsiders who sought marriage alliances in many quarters as they moved toward the inner circle. By the end of the century, the Lykovs had reached the goal; the Volkonskiis were still on the road.

Non-titled newcomers to the boyar elite faced the same problems without the protection of a great name. Royal in-laws understandably found the going easiest. The Naryshkins married into many different families. They accomplished their first matrimonial coup, a match with the Lykovs, in 1673, very soon after Nataliia became Aleksei Mikhailovich's second wife. By about the end of the century, they had ties with the Golitsyns and Cherkasskiis, as well as with many other clans, distinguished and obscure.[62] Others, even the families of royal favorites, found it hard to gain recognition. The numerous Khitrovos made a few good matches; members of the clan married a Golitsyn, a Prozorovskii, and a Troekurov.[63] The Rtishchevs did not fare quite so well. They made matches within the lesser nobility from which they had risen, with one brilliant exception, a tie with the Odoevskiis.[64] In the case of both families, these exceptionally fine marriages were the result of their rapid advancement, not its cause.

When we examine the family structure and marriage patterns of the boyar elite, we can see the rough outlines of an aristocracy. Many members of the group in our period could not be called aristocrats by any stretch of the imagination. Yet, within its ranks, we find a number of clans like the Golitsyns and Sheremetevs, whose members held high office and occupied prominent positions at court through several generations. Families like these remained cognizant of the tradition of genealogical seniority and took care to make appropriate matches for their children.

At the same time, the word "aristocratic" has a somewhat special meaning when applied to seventeenth-century Russia. There a family could not belong to the highest echelon of society without a long record of distinguished service and high rank. A fine genealogy alone guaranteed nothing. Marriage patterns serve as the best test of a family's acceptance into the aristocracy. Despite their princely lineage, the Gorchakovs had only one representative in the boyar elite in our period. Largely for this reason, I would suggest, they rarely made marriages with Duma clans. By way of contrast, the Dolgorukiis, a Duma family of no greater genealogical distinction, made more than half of its recorded matches in our period with other clans within the boyar elite.[65]

The Muscovite aristocracy gradually changed over the course of time, like other historical elites. Although the lack of precision of our data prevent us from tracing clear patterns, we can nevertheless see hints of the process by which new families slowly won acceptance into the highest echelon of society. The royal in-laws provide our best examples. Once they occupied their positions around the throne, the high and mighty began to accept the reality of their presence by arranging marriages with their children. If upstart families succeeded in holding onto high office and the resulting social and economic advantages for long enough, they could congratulate themselves on becoming full members of the elusive Russian aristocracy.

CHAPTER IV

Politics, Parties, and Patronage

Within the boyar elite, informal personal relationships supplemented ties of blood and marriage as sources of social cohesion and order. This chapter examines two ways in which Russian high nobles reached beyond the family circle for support—political factions or groupings and networks of patronage.

Informal groupings of powerful courtiers have played an important role in the political life of many centralized monarchies.[1] Small, informal alliances of noble courtiers and bureaucrats took shape in the shadow of the throne and fought with rival groups for power or simply for survival. Such cliques could function in two directions—as alliances of roughly equal partners and as vertical patronage hierarchies in which powerful figures gave protection and help to less fortunate clients in return for their support.

In Russia such groupings were long an important feature of the political landscape. In the eighteenth century, for example, knowledgeable Russians and foreigners recognized their significance and left us records of their composition and policies.[2] In the seventeenth century, foreign observers likewise assumed that such groupings existed at the court in Moscow. Their reports and the other sources of the period, however, give us little help in identifying such groupings, outlining their contours, and finding the common family link, vested interest, or policy that united them. Even when describing the great political crises of the seventeenth century at first hand, contemporaries tried mainly to identify the leaders of contending factions and their policies and showed little interest in their less prominent allies and followers.

The family genealogies and patterns of marriage which we have just examined also shed very little light on the political life of the Russian court. Family relationships provided the underlying structure of the social and economic life of the Russian aristocracy. They did not necessarily determine an individual's political affiliation, however. The reason lies in the large number and the complexity of each man's family ties. If we look hard enough, we will discover that most prominent figures of seventeenth-century Russia were related to each other at least remotely.[3] As a result, the fact that two men had common family connections does not tell us whether they were allies or enemies or remained indifferent to one another's fates.

In order to understand elite politics in seventeenth-century Russia, then, we must take into consideration everything that might determine a man's political allegiance and affect his behavior in moments of crisis—his career in service and the personal connections that he made while on official duty, his economic interests, his family connections, and his ideological predilections and cultural tastes. Examining all of these features of men's lives will help us to weigh the significance of contemporaries' brief remarks on court groupings and perhaps to fill in the sketchy outline that they have given us.

This chapter is an attempt to study the structure of court politics in particular times and places. It is not a political history of seventeenth-century Muscovy. In particular, we will examine the two most important political crises within our period—those of 1648 and 1682—in detail in order to understand better the composition and workings of court parties and factions. Moreover, we will study the political position and role of a few prominent and relatively well-documented figures of the middle and late decades of the century.

In 1648, Russia experienced its own version of the "general crisis of the seventeenth century."[4] Some elements in Russia's crisis will be familiar to a student of western European history; others reflected particular local traditions and problems. As elsewhere on the continent, royal taxation ignited popular opposition. In 1645, Aleksei Mikhailovich ascended the throne, and B. I. Morozov, his former tutor, became the leader of his government. Morozov had a clear sense of Russia's needs; in a world of continuous warfare, the country had to have a better, more modern army and that, in turn, would cost money. As a result, the new regime took serious steps to increase royal revenues, tightening the enforcement of tax collection and introducing a heavy new levy on salt. Understandably, the salt tax aroused bitter opposition, and Morozov's administration repealed the measure at the end of 1647, less than two years after its introduction. At the same time, in compensation, the government tripled the levy of other direct taxes. Moreover, as though higher taxes were not provocation enough, Morozov and his closest associates in the government earned a reputation for their personal greed and corruption.

The predictable explosion took place at the beginning of June 1648.

Attempts of citizens of Moscow to petition the tsar for redress of their grievances quickly flared into a full revolt. Angry crowds took control of the streets of the capital, looted the homes of a number of prominent courtiers, officials, and merchants, and lynched three unpopular members of Morozov's government—N. I. Chistyi, P. T. Trakhaniotov, and L. S. Pleshcheev. For several days, Tsar Aleksei and his court were at the mercy of the rebels. Even the young ruler's remarkable presence of mind won only one concession for the royal government; he saved Morozov's life by agreeing to exile him to the St. Cyril-Beloozero Monastery far to the north of Moscow. The fallen favorite's departure from the city completed the collapse of his administration and the repudiation of his policies. Into the resulting political vacuum stepped a new regime led by Prince Ia. K. Cherkasskii and N. I. Romanov, men with close personal ties to the throne and with reputations as Morozov's enemies.

Although tempers quickly cooled in Moscow, the June uprising had momentous consequences. First of all, it proved to be only the tip of the iceberg of popular resentment toward the government's policies and the officials who enforced them. Over the course of the next two years, violent protests broke out in many of Russia's urban centers. While social conditions and particular local grievances varied considerably from one town to the next, the government heard the same general themes over and over again. Men and women from many walks of life bitterly resented high taxes, the arbitrary behavior of local governors and other officials, and the inequities and endless delays endemic in the courts of law. Moreover, on a number of occasions, rioters also directed their anger at the more privileged members of local society.

Secondly, as successive administrations in Moscow knew all too well, those leading members of provincial society on whose support the government depended also had long-standing grievances. During the crisis of 1648, representatives of the local nobility once again demanded that the manorial peasants be deprived of all right to leave their lords' estates and that those who left illegally be liable to extradition for all time. In the same year, spokesmen for the urban population renewed their demand that all property in the towns and all people living on it have the same legal status and be subject to the same taxes. In view of its obvious vulnerability, the royal government had no choice but to take these demands with the utmost seriousness.

In order to restore political and social stability, the new regime of Cherkasskii and Romanov proposed to meet the long-standing need for a full and up-to-date code of laws. With this in mind, on July 16, 1648, its leaders appointed a commission, under the direction of Prince N. I. Odoevskii, to draft a new code. Moreover, they realized the political necessity of winning the cooperation of the leading groups in society. Consequently, on the same day, they issued instructions for the convocation of a zemskii sobor or national estates, which began on September 1. Soon it became clear that a compromise was in the offing. In return for their support, the government gave in to the demands of the provincial nobles and the urban elite and included the provisions that they desired in the code that was formally adopted early in 1649.

While the work of codification went on, the political alignments at court changed once again. Aleksei Mikhailovich had never lost confidence in Morozov and, once relative stability returned to the capital, he began to work for the restoration of his former favorite. By mid-September, Morozov had moved to the Holy Trinity Monastery not far from Moscow. A little over a month later, he came back to the capital. Cherkasskii apparently saw the handwriting on the wall, for he abruptly left the city without the tsar's permission, thus, in effect, giving up his leading role in government. Morozov was back in power, but this time he behaved more circumspectly. The tsar's father-in-law, I. D. Miloslavskii, took over the bureaucratic offices abandoned by Cherkasskii and, although Morozov remained close to the tsar in the 1650s, he never fully regained the overwhelming power that he had exercised before the crisis of 1648. Moreover, whatever his own preferences may have been, he had no choice but to accept the provisions of the new law code as formulated by his defeated rivals.[5]

What does the crisis of 1648 tell us about the nature of political factions at the tsar's court?[6] First, let us examine the direct testimony of the sources at our disposal. In describing the events of 1648, contemporary observers, both foreign and Russian, left no doubt that two factions or groupings struggled for power. The most important foreign commentators—Pommerening, the resident ambassador from Sweden, and Adam Olearius, the former ambassador from Holstein, who kept himself informed about events in Russia—give particularly clear evidence on this point. On one side, they saw Morozov and his close associates, Pleshcheev and Trakhaniotov. On the other, they clearly identified two of Morozov's enemies, Cherkasskii and Romanov. Beyond these few names, contemporary observers were not sure who belonged in which group; some considered Chistyi a member of Morozov's faction, while others saw him as an independent figure who happened to pay the price for his own unpopularity during the uprising against Morozov's regime. Other less notorious figures such as Prince A. M. L'vov and Prince A. N. Trubetskoi sometimes appear on lists of possible allies of Morozov.[7] To sum up, contemporaries believed that rival court groupings existed, but could identify only a few of their adherents with any degree of certainty.

Up to this point, our inquiry may reflect only the bias of sources on seventeenth-century Russia. We have very few eyewitness accounts of events and interpretations of their meaning. At the same time, we know a great deal about the formal careers of prominent noblemen of the time. What do the boyars' records of service tell us about their political affiliation? Before answering the question, we must establish rules for using the mountain of evidence at our disposal. The fact that two men occasionally served together tells us very little. Each Duma member probably shared assignments in the army, the administration, or in court ceremonies with virtually every other one of his colleagues at some point in his career. To show that two men probably belonged to the same political grouping, we must demonstrate that their careers ran parallel for much of their length. In particular, for example, we would rightly expect one of Morozov's partisans to rise to high office in 1645 or soon afterwards, to fall into oblivion in the middle of 1648, and then to return to power when the faction's leader made his come-back.

As we might expect, a comparison of career patterns adds relatively little to the direct testimony of contemporaries. We can identify a few men—G. G. Pushkin, Prince V. G. Romodanovskii and Princes F. F. and P. F. Volkonskii—who may well have belonged to Morozov's faction and one of his probable opponents, Prince I. A. Khilkov.[8]

Clearly, then, the court factions that fought for power in 1648 were small. When we combine all of our evidence, we can tentatively identify, at most, thirteen members of the Morozov grouping. On the other side, we find only three active enemies of his—Cherkasskii, Romanov, and Khilkov. In the years between 1645 and the beginning of 1650, however, a total of 70 individuals enjoyed Duma rank, and 118 men in all served Tsar Aleksei in at least one important military, administrative, or diplomatic capacity.[9]

By either measure, then, most powerful courtiers or active servitors remained uncommitted in the factional struggles at court.[10] Only in the most exceptional circumstances was the majority of the boyar elite forced to commit itself to one particular faction. In 1689, for example, when the young Peter I issued a direct challenge to Sophia's regency, he left the leading nobles no room to maneuver. Either a man was for Sophia or he was for Peter. Within hours of the beginning of the crisis, virtually the entire court joined the stampede to Peter's side. Most of the time, however, Duma members could and did avoid such radical choices.

Moreover, the court factions of 1648 were very unstable. It took Morozov nearly two years to build up his grouping. In particular, Pleshcheev achieved prominence only in August 1647.[11] Then the holocaust of 1648 virtually destroyed the group. Within a few days, Trakhaniotov,

Pleshcheev, and Chistyi were dead and Morozov in exile. After his return to power, the composition of his party continued to change. I. D. Miloslavskii, who may well have been Morozov's ally all along, began to play a more prominent role.[12] Moreover, three of the less prominent adherents of the faction went their own way in 1649, and B. F. Narbekov, a client and kinsman of Miloslavskii, joined in their place.[13]

In addition, the court groupings of 1648 did not represent any clear economic or social vested interest. P. P. Smirnov, the author of the most interesting Soviet accounts of the crisis, has suggested that precisely such ties held together both Morozov's allies and his enemies. In his interpretation, Cherkasskii, Romanov, and their adherents shared a bitter opposition to any change in the legal status of the urban population. Moreover, he suggested, Morozov's enemies were aristocrats, while his supporters were social upstarts. As I have argued elsewhere, however, neither of these suggestions provides much help in understanding the crisis of 1648. The first simply does not hold water; among the boyars, only Romanov owned large quantities of urban property and therefore had a vested interest in preventing reform. The second of Smirnov's arguments has more merit; Romanov and Cherkasskii were indeed aristocrats, and Morozov, himself a man of equally distinguished lineage, commanded a motley crew. Still, the social distinctions between the two groups were not so dramatic as to explain why men joined one grouping rather than the other. After all, most Duma members, whether aristocrats or upstarts, belonged to neither.[14]

Ideology likewise does not explain how court groupings formed. Although possible, it is not likely that men allied themselves with Morozov primarily because they shared his determination to modernize the Russian army and to improve the state's finances. Indeed, as we shall see, those rare individuals who put forward a distinct personal philosophy or political program—Patriarch Nikon and A. L. Ordin-Nashchokin, for example—found themselves in isolation from most members of the boyar elite.

Marriage ties and family connections, however, seem to have helped to hold court groupings together. If we can believe the testimony of contemporaries, by 1648 Morozov, Miloslavskii, Pleshcheev, and Trakhaniotov were all one another's in-laws.[15] Without doubt, Morozov cemented his ties to the throne when he presided over Tsar Aleksei's marriage to Miloslavskii's daughter and then married her sister. In effect, his faction constituted a new group of royal in-laws. His chief rivals likewise could boast close family connections with the ruling house. Romanov, of course, was the leading member of its cadet branch, and the

Cherkasskiis' connections with the Romanovs dated from the previous century.

Marriage alliances did not necessarily lead to political commitments, however. On occasion, indeed, the relationship of marriage and factional allegiance was precisely the opposite; Morozov's marriage, for example, strengthened personal and political ties that were already well-established. Moreover, since marriages linked many Duma clans to one another, only the most immediate and direct matrimonial ties could have any political meaning. At roughly the mid-point in the century, for example, both the Sheremetevs and the Prozorovskiis were related by marriage both to the Cherkasskiis, the clan of Morozov's chief rival, and the families of some of his allies. As far as can be determined, however, these three-cornered family connections ended just before 1648 or came into being soon after the crisis.[16]

The political system of which the crisis of 1648 gives us a glimpse revolved around individual favorites or relatives of the ruler. Ultimately a man like Morozov enjoyed great power because Aleksei Mikhailovich trusted him and therefore named him to high office and threw the weight of the throne behind his favorite's policies. Once such a man had achieved preeminence, he attracted a number of allies and, as we shall see, probably set up a network of clients as well. The personal composition of such alliances seems to have changed continually as old allies deserted or left the scene and new ones took their place.

In a political world in such rapid flux, most Duma members seem to have stayed neutral, keeping in touch with all such factions, but committing themselves to none. Membership in a victorious court grouping had its rewards, but close associations with an unpopular ruling clique could exact a terrible price, as the events of 1648 demonstrated. A cautious, defensive stategy of avoiding factional entanglements was the better bet in the long run.

The crisis of 1682 confirms a number of these conclusions. In some ways, the events of that year resemble those of the earlier crisis. Once again, rebels took control of Moscow and lynched a number of unpopular officials. Behind the superficial similarities, however, the two crises differed in many respects. In 1682, the strel'tsy of the Moscow garrison led the opposition to the government. These privileged units of old-fashioned infantry had long-standing grievances against some of their officers, whom they accused of disciplining them harshly and withholding their pay. Early in the year, while Tsar Fedor Alekseevich was still alive, the strel'tsy twice petitioned the government for redress. In the first case, officials ordered the petitioners whipped, but, when the second complaint threatened the government with mutiny, its leaders agreed to discipline the most unpopular of the garrison's officers.

Moreover, a complex succession crisis added fuel to the flames. When Fedor died on April 27, 1682, it was not clear who would succeed him on the throne. Among Aleksei Mikhailovich's numerous children, there remained only two sons—Ivan, son of Mariia Miloslavskaia, his first wife, and Peter, only son of his second marriage to Nataliia Naryshkina. Logically, Ivan should have ascended the throne, but contemporaries agreed that he was unfit to rule since he was physically handicapped and retarded as well. The ten-year-old Peter, however, showed considerable promise. The two boys' personal qualities were far less important than the political needs of their maternal relatives. The Miloslavskiis and Naryshkins both owed their prominence entirely to their proximity to the throne. Ever since Aleksei's death, the two clans had vied for power, and, once the succession crisis began, neither could afford to see the other's candidate become tsar.

Within a matter of days, the restlessness of the strel'tsy and the ambition of contending court factions came together. Very soon after Fedor's death, a coalition of courtiers, including the Naryshkins, the Iazykovs, and Likhachevs, favorites of the late ruler, and Patriarch Ioakim arranged to have Peter declared tsar. Within three days, the strel'tsy renewed their campaign against their commanders and quickly brought the shaky new government to its knees. The new regime agreed to arrest a number of commanders and, in a long-standing Muscovite custom, to have them beaten publicly at regular intervals until they paid back large sums of money that they had allegedly embezzled.

These sweeping concessions bought the government only a short respite. The garrison remained in ferment. Moreover, as a number of contemporaries suspected, the court grouping around the Miloslavskiis, losers in the first stage of the struggle over the succession, made contact with the rebellious troops. Precisely who served as intermediary was—and is—a matter of debate. Without question, however, the new regime's chief enemies, the strel'tsy and the opposition at court, pursuing their own separate goals, cooperated in overthrowing it.

Responding to rumors that the life of Prince Ivan was in danger, the strel'tsy revolted on May 15 and, in effect, took control of Moscow. For three days, they stormed through the city looking for their enemies, probably following a list of targets which they and their advisers had drawn up in advance. They lynched the most visible of the Naryshkins—Ivan Kirillovich—and A. S. Matveev, the most energetic and talented of their allies. The victims of the uprising also included well-known generals, prominent chancery officials, two unpopular officers, two foreign

court physicians, and a number of less prominent individuals who happened to be in the wrong place at the wrong time. At one stroke, the
strel'tsy had destroyed the Naryshkin regime and left the way open to
their rivals at court. The Miloslavskiis and their allies took control of the
government and, on May 26, had Ivan proclaimed co-ruler alongside
Peter. Three days later, the new regime declared Princess Sophia, Ivan's
older sister, regent for the two boys.

The revolt of the strel'tsy unleashed other forces of opposition to the
Muscovite government. During the chaotic days of mid-May, bondslaves
raided the office of the Slavery Chancery and destroyed the documents
that they found there. Moreover, the conservative religious opposition,
the Old Believers, whose ire at Patriarch Nikon's liturgical reforms served
to bring together many strains of resistance to the prevailing conditions
of Russia's church, state, and society, won many adherents among the
troops of the garrison. Both the strel'tsy and the Old Believers found a
champion among the boyars in the person of Prince I. A. Khovanskii, a
general who apparently enjoyed widespread popularity in spite of a very
undistinguished record in the field. Whether Khovanskii sincerely sym-
pathized with the Old Believers' opposition to the Nikonian reforms is
impossible to determine. Apart from his conduct in 1682, nothing in his
biography suggests principled opposition to the ecclesiastical policies of
the government and the hierarchy. Moreover, his reputation—derived,
to be sure, from hostile sources—suggests that his primary motives were
ambition and egotism, not moral scruple. At the same time, it is possible
that he had strong convictions and kept them to himself; open adherence
to the Old Believer camp would certainly, at the very least, have destroyed his career. Under the circumstances, we cannot be sure what, if
anything, he really believed.

In any case, with Khovanskii's help and the backing of the strel'tsy,
leaders of the Old Believers forced the regent, her courtiers, and members of the ecclesiastical hierarchy to take part in a public disputation in
the Kremlin on July 5. In the final analysis, however, the strel'tsy pursued their own interests as an elite military formation, if necessary at
the expense of their temporary allies. Immediately after the May uprising, the mutineers received many favors from the government, including
payments of money and the circulation of an official proclamation justifying their actions during the revolt. Thereafter, the new regime found
that it could count on the strel'tsy to do its bidding. Late in May, when
bondslaves petitioned the government for their freedom, the troops put
them down savagely. Later, immediately after the government's confrontation with the Old Believers, the strel'tsy obeyed orders to arrest
and execute the chief spokesman of the religious opposition.

By early summer, then, the strel'tsy were satisfied, and the court became the center of the political conflict. No sooner had the Miloslavskiis and their allies displaced the Naryshkin group than they began to quarrel among themselves. From the time of Khovanskii's emergence as the hero of the strel'tsy, the other leading figures at court looked on him with deep suspicion. Before long, their wariness and his own arrogance left him in isolation. During the summer of 1682, the balance of power within the government shifted toward Sophia and Prince V. V. Golitsyn, her reputed lover and chief adviser. In retrospect, their rise to preeminence is hardly surprising. Although, as a woman of the imperial family, Sophia had lived a sheltered life until her sudden emergence in 1682, the regent quickly proved to be a very intelligent and, when necessary, ruthless politician. Moreover, in Golitsyn, she had a highly educated and astute counsellor. In the long run, Khovanskii was no match for them. After her frightening encounter with the Old Believers, Sophia, aware of her vulnerability, withdrew from Moscow with the court. Khovanskii, however, failed to take advantage of her absence. The bureaucracy continued to follow her directives, and, as time passed, she and Golitsyn established their position more and more firmly. Finally, from the safety of the Holy Trinity Monastery, the government summoned Khovanskii from Moscow, arrested him and his son, and summarily executed them on September 17.

With their deaths, the crisis abruptly ended. Within a few days, the strel'tsy submitted to the new regime, and, from that time on, the regency ruled Russia without serious challenge until Peter I abruptly overthrew it in 1689.[17]

The court groupings that struggled for power in 1682 bear a number of general resemblances to those of 1648. Once again, the factions were relatively small, and most members of the boyar elite belonged to none of them. At first glance, the Naryshkin and Miloslavskii groupings appear much larger than their precursors of 1648. In his memoir many years after the events, A. A. Matveev, son of the Naryshkin group's leader, listed twenty-two supporters of the faction apart from the Naryshkins themselves. The names he mentioned included those of the most distinguished aristocratic clans—Odoevskiis, Cherkasskiis, Dolgorukiis, Sheremetevs, and others of their ilk. Indeed, in case his reader should miss the point, he summarized: ". . . in general, powerful personages of honorable and distinguished families (*iz chestnykh i znatnykh rodov palatnyia osoby*), and the entire nobility and all the people except one opposing party or gang and the Moscow strel'tsy then stood unwaveringly and faithfully on the Tsar's side as mentioned above."[18]

Almost everyone—certainly all the best people—supported the Naryshkins. Although highly partisan, Matveev knew a great deal about the dramatic events of his youth, and his remarks on the attitude of particular boyars may well be true. At the same time, these men may have owed their allegiance, not to the Naryshkin faction as such, but to its policy of crowning Peter as tsar. As subsequent events were to prove, Peter was the only male of the royal line who showed any promise as a ruler. Leading figures such as Patriarch Ioakim probably thought that arranging his accession to the throne as quickly as possible was the best way of avoiding a crisis over the succession. Many boyars probably supported Peter's candidacy for the same reason, whether or not they liked his maternal relatives.[19]

As the crisis unfolded, the mutinous strel'tsy killed sixteen prominent men, in addition to Matveev and Naryshkin—nine of them members of the Duma. In addition, they forced the government to exile a number of other individuals.[20] In all but a few cases, the rebels evidently knew what they were doing. Before the mutiny, the strel'tsy drew up a list of their intended victims, probably with the help of their friends at court. Matveev charged—and most recent historians agree—that the Miloslavskiis and their allies put ideas into the mutineers' heads.[21] But were the victims of the May uprising necessarily allies of the Naryshkins and thus enemies of the Miloslavskiis?[22] The answer varies from one victim to the next. A. S. Matveev and I. K. Naryshkin undoubtedly led the group that bore the latter's name. Moreover, I. M. Iazykov may have been their ally, at least for the moment; Tsar Fedor's favorite had apparently broken with the Miloslavskiis in about 1680 and, in the interregnum following his patron's death, agreed to let Matveev return to Moscow, perhaps in order to strengthen his own endangered position. Often, however, the strel'tsy had their own reasons for resenting the men in power. In the proclamation issued at the moment of their victory, for example, the troops accused Iazykov of treating them oppressively while head of the government. Once again, as in 1648, moreover, prominent administrators like A. S. Kirillov and Larion Ivanov died for the sins of the entire bureaucratic system as well as for their own; the mutineers accused them of corruption and, in Ivanov's case, added the imaginative charge that he kept a collection of poisonous fish, presumably proof that he had conspired with foreign court physicians to poison the late Tsar Fedor. In 1682, moreover, the rebels killed two of the most prominent Russian generals of the period, Prince G. G. Romodanovskii and Prince Iu. A. Dolgorukii. In Romodanovskii's case, the strel'tsy may actually have believed that he had shown disastrous cowardice in battle against the Turks. By way of contrast, the sources suggest several possible reasons for Dolgorukii's death. There may indeed be truth in the mutineers' claim that he died because he had oppressed them while their commander-in-chief.[23] At the same time, contemporary accounts suggest that he may have fallen victim to bad luck and a sharp tongue, killed by strel'tsy whom he insulted while they were bringing him the body of his murdered son.[24] In any case, neither general seems to have died primarily for his allegiance to the Naryshkins. Indeed, Dolgorukii had served as head of the Office of Strel'tsy in an administration dominated by the Miloslavskiis and had remained in that office when the Iazykovs and Likhachevs had eased them out of power.[25]

The Naryshkin grouping, then, while large by the standards of 1648, was probably considerably smaller than either Matveev's testimony or a list of the mutineers' victims would suggest. At its core stood Matveev, the Naryshkins, and their momentary allies, the Iazykovs and Likhachevs. Moreover, the younger Matveev's testimony that Prince F. S. Urusov informed his father of the impending revolt and that Prince M. A. Cherkasskii risked his own life to save him from lynching suggests that these two men may have belonged to the faction.[26] Whether the other prominent courtiers, bureaucrats, and generals mentioned in the sources were allies of the Naryshkins or merely happened to take the same political position or to suffer the same fate is impossible to determine with any degree of certainty.

Contemporary accounts preserve considerably less information about the Miloslavskii faction. Matveev consigns only the Miloslavskiis themselves, certain officers of the strel'tsy, and M. I. Sunbulov to the camp of his enemies. The latter suddenly emerged from obscurity by opposing Peter's accession with shouts in support of the candidacy of his older half-brother, Ivan.[27] Once the Miloslavskiis had won the struggle for power, he received the rank of dumnyi dvorianin for his pains.[28]

As contemporaries were well aware, the Miloslavskii grouping changed its composition quickly, once in power. Sophia emerged as its leader and found a skillful collaborator in Golitsyn. Before long the Khovanskiis broke away and formed their own grouping. In the process, they cast the faction's previous leader, I. M. Miloslavskii, into temporary eclipse.[29]

While these changes were taking place, the divided governing faction worked hard to attract a reliable group of supporters at court and in the bureaucracy. In the four months between the Moscow uprising and the final clash between Sophia's government and Khovanskii, the new regime appointed twenty-six men to Duma rank, a remarkably high number for so short a time. Moreover, its leaders appointed new heads of a number of chanceries.[30] Which of these new Duma members and administrators could be considered members of the Miloslavskii faction is difficult to say. Some were the kind of people who would probably have

held high rank and office under any government. Among the new boyars, for example, were two Sheremetevs and a Saltykov and, in the
ranks of the new prikaz directors, we find men like Prince I. B. Repnin
and Prince I. B. Troekurov, who had held similar positions on several
previous occasions.[31] Others clearly owed their rank to their connections
with the ruling faction. The list of the new boyars included three Khovanskiis, a Miloslavskii, and a Golitsyn. Moreover, three members of the
Khitrovo clan may well have received Duma rank because of their family's ties with the Miloslavskiis; certainly their biographies reveal no other
reason for the honor.[32] Some of the newcomers to high office, however,
defy neat categories. A. I. Rzhevskii and Prince F. F. Volkonskii, among
others, received their first important bureaucratic posts just after the
Moscow uprising; they may well have been partisans of the Miloslavskiis.[33] Similarly, several new Duma members of undistinguished family
with very ordinary records of service—V. L. Pushechnikov, B. F. Polibin, and the celebrated Sunbulov, for example—may have been clients
of the victorious court party.[34] Finally, the official records of the time
suggest strongly that Golitsyn and E. I. Ukraintsev worked closely together, not just as colleagues in government, but as political allies in a
bond that lasted until they went their separate ways in 1689.[35] Given
these uncertainties, we can only suggest that the core of the Miloslavskii
grouping—like the Naryshkin faction—consisted of roughly ten or twenty
individuals at most.[36]

Moreover, we must remember that these two factions, like the Morozov grouping before them, dominated the government for a significant
period of time. In 1682, each of them in turn took the reins of state at a
time of uncertainty and confusion. In such circumstances, men with no
stake in any court party rallied to the focal point of political authority.
In particular, once the Khovanskiis and their allies, the strel'tsy had
posed a threat to the established political order, most courtiers turned
away from them in panic and rallied around the only rival force, the
emerging regime of Sophia and Golitsyn.[37]

Despite his apparent strength in the summer of 1682, Prince I. A.
Khovanskii never succeeded in creating a political grouping among Russia's governing elite. The most imaginative historians can point to only
two allies in the boyar elite outside Khovanskii's own family—I. I. Chaadaev and K. O. Khlopov.[38] Moreover, once Khovanskii's fortunes waned,
Sophia and Golitsyn had no trouble winning the two over and rewarded
them with money and important service assignments.[39] When the show-
down came in mid-September, Khovanskii and his son went to their
deaths in complete isolation.

We can see several reasons for his political failure at a glance. First,

Khovanskii paid the price for long absence from court. Between 1669 and 1681, he spent almost all of his time as a commander in the field and thus had no opportunity to build personal connections in Moscow.[40] Secondly, contemporary sources strongly suggest that Khovanskii's arrogance and naked ambition frightened and repelled his fellow boyars. Finally, his allies stepped directly out of the nightmares of Muscovite courtiers. After the May uprising, no one had to tell the boyars to fear the strel'tsy. The Old Believers were even worse; with the rhetoric of fire and brimstone, they drove Sophia and most of the court out of Moscow and into an alliance to destroy Khovanskii.

To return to our comparison: the discussion of the composition of the court groupings in 1682 indicates that they were almost as unstable and short-lived as their predecessors at mid-century. As we have seen, the lynchings of May effectively destroyed the core of the Naryshkin faction. Almost immediately after that, the victorious Miloslavskii grouping split. After the destruction of the Khovanskiis, the surface of court politics became tranquil once again, and, just as in earlier periods of domestic peace, the outlines of court groupings faded out. All was quiet until 1689. Then, the regency, which appeared in command of the political stage, collapsed before the challenge of Peter and his supporters, a number of whom were survivors of the earlier Naryshkin grouping.[41] In the confrontation, Sophia and Golitsyn saw their base of support quickly shrink to a group of fifteen or twenty diehards who could not abandon ship in time.[42] For these loyalists, all that remained was to throw themselves on Peter's mercy.

Once again, as in 1648, men joined court groupings for reasons of political ambition or personal loyalty. As far as we can see, no common vested economic interest united the members of the Miloslavskii and Naryshkin factions. Moreover, except for Khovanskii's flirtation with the Old Believers, ideology likewise played no evident part in determining men's loyalties. The leaders of the Miloslavskiis and the Naryshkins had distinctly different cultural standards and tastes; Sophia and Golitsyn supported learning and the arts and showed great interest in foreign cultural achievements, particularly in Poland and the Ukraine, while the Naryshkins seem to have been nativist know-nothings until the young Peter broke away and discovered the delights of Moscow's German Quarter.[43] It is most unlikely, however, that these cultural differences affected men's political choices.

Family connections did more to hold the two groupings together. As contemporaries knew perfectly well, the succession struggle of 1682 pitted two clans of royal in-laws against each other. Apart from the Miloslavskiis' and Naryshkins' ties to the Romanovs, however, marriages rarely brought men into one grouping or the other. Only one clear example comes to mind; I. M. Miloslavskii's marriage to Princess E. P. Prozorovskaia probably brought her father and brother into her husband's faction.[44] At the same time, some marriages clearly ran across political lines; A. P. Saltykov and V. S. Zmeev both received Duma rank from a government dominated by the Miloslavskiis, even though they apparently had matrimonial ties to their defeated rivals, the Naryshkins.[45] Moreover, the most notorious match of 1682 had very little to do with politics; at the height of his power, Khovanskii, a widower with grown children, married the widow of the murdered official, Larion Ivanov, in order to gain control of his considerable fortune.[46]

Finally, as before, most prominent courtiers apparently stayed clear of all contending factions. Of the 110 Duma members in May of 1682, only about 40 at most can be identified as adherents of one grouping or the other. Moreover, the uncommitted majority included the most distinguished aristocratic clans, with some notable exceptions. As we observed, A. A. Matveev listed Odoevskiis, Cherkasskiis, and Sheremetevs among the courtiers who supported the Naryshkins in advancing the candidacy of Peter. At the end of the summer, the same names appear, along with the Golitsyns, among those whom Khovanskii allegedly intended to kill when he overthrew Sophia's regency and took power.[47] The anonymous document revealing Khovanskii's supposed plans was almost certainly a falsification used by Sophia and Golitsyn to discredit and isolate their rival.[48] In spite of its obvious unreliability, however, the document shows the new government's eagerness to claim the finest families of the realm as its supporters. In reality, the Odoevskiis, Cherkasskiis, Sheremetevs, and many other less glamorous courtiers probably stayed out of the struggle of contending factions, throwing their weight behind any regime that offered the promise of political stability and domestic tranquillity.

To sum up, the complex, fragmented, and shifting world of court politics took the following shapes during the crisis of 1682. When Fedor died, leaving a confused succession, the favorites of his last years, the Iazykovs and Likhachevs, made an alliance of convenience with the Naryshkins, relatives of the more promising of the surviving heirs. Together the allies won the first round of the struggle and appeared to have shut the Miloslavskii grouping out of power. The latter had its revenge when the strel'tsy revolted in May. After the riots and lynchings of May 15-17, the Miloslavskiis seemed to be in complete charge of the situation. Certainly their chief rivals had, for the moment, ceased to exist as a political force. In the moment of victory, however, the anti-Naryshkin coalition split, and Prince I. A. Khovanskii pursued his own designs.

Over the course of the summer, he fought and lost a struggle for power. The unaligned courtiers who, before the May uprising, had rallied to the Naryshkin government, now turned in increasing numbers to Sophia and Golitsyn. By September, Khovanskii was alone and an easy target. The new regency had no rivals. At the same time, the memory of old battles remained strong, and, in 1689, the young Peter rallied a number of Naryshkin partisans to his banner when he rose to challenge Sophia's regime.

The dramatic events of 1648 and 1682 give us an unusually good opportunity to look through the orderly surface of court life to the political alignments beneath. By their very nature, however, these crises were nightmarish exceptions to the usual flow of court life. For a different perspective on seventeenth-century court politics, let us examine the positions of three particularly well-documented individuals—Patriarch Nikon, A. L. Ordin-Nashchokin, and A. S. Matveev in the years before 1682. Once again we are dealing with the exceptional; all three men were social and political outsiders.

As such, they had a great deal in common. All rose from comparatively obscure social origins. Nikon, the most dramatic success story of the seventeenth century, began his life as a peasant. All performed a variety of important official functions on their way to the top of the civil or ecclesiastical ladder. In the final analysis, however, they owed their power to the friendship or support of their royal patron—Tsar Aleksei. Moreover, in part because of their dependence on the ruler's changing policies and moods, they occupied preeminent positions for a relatively short time. Nikon performed the functions of patriarch for six years, Matveev acted as Aleksei's chief adviser for five, and Nashchokin served as head of the Foreign Office for only four. In each case, moreover, they left office under a cloud; Nikon and Nashchokin resigned when the tsar failed to support them against their enemies, while Matveev's foes drove him from court soon after Aleksei's death. All three wound up in exile far from Moscow, Nikon and Nashchokin by their own choice.

In some ways, the latter figures stand apart from Matveev and the rest of their contemporaries. Both put forth clear and unconventional ideas which they tried to carry out in practice. Nikon threw the whole weight of his office into a struggle to revivify the Russian church and to restore its corporate autonomy and integrity. As a diplomat, Nashchokin looked past the recent history of enmity between Russia and Poland to a vision of harmony between the two great Slavic nations. Moreover, Nikon and Nashchokin struck their contemporaries as difficult men—self-assured, arrogant, and uncompromising. Certainly, as we shall see, both had an unfortunate knack for antagonizing their subordinates and ultimately tired their patron with their fractiousness and nagging.[49]

Their combativeness, the bane of their contemporaries, has served historians well, however. All three left extensive complaints about their mistreatment at the hands of their enemies. Their letters and petitions give us a clear, although perhaps distorted, look at the political life of the court.

If we can believe their own statements and other contemporary records, all of these energetic parvenus had more enemies than friends. The two ideologues—Nikon and Nashchokin—are particularly obvious cases.

The celebrated patriarch's role in secular politics is not easy to trace. Scandinavian observers regarded him as a protégé of B. I. Morozov. They suggested that he used his authority to convince N. I. Romanov, Morozov's enemy, to support the government dominated by his patron.[50] Moreover, contemporary observers and later historians assumed, quite plausibly, that, while in office, Nikon exercised considerable influence on the policies of Tsar Aleksei's regime.[51] At the same time, there are few clear indications of his position in the political firmament of the court. If Nikon indeed acted as head of the government while the tsar visited the battlefront in 1654 and 1655, he must have worked closely with the Duma members left behind to manage the affairs of state. Nevertheless, we have no record of Nikon's relations with Prince M. P. Pronskii, Prince G. S. Kurakin, or their subordinates; they played no role in his subsequent career and had no hand in his fate.[52] In a nutshell, most of the hard evidence about the patriarch's entanglements with the tsar's courtiers comes from the years after he left office and tells us little about his years in power.[53]

Once he withdrew from office, the former patriarch retained only one loyal supporter among the boyars—N. A. Ziuzin. He had worked in the patriarchal chancery in the early years of Nikon's term and, in 1664, wrote to his former mentor, urging him to return to Moscow unannounced. By all accounts, Ziuzin aimed at reconciling Nikon and the tsar. His good intentions brought only disaster, however. The patriarch's sudden reappearance in the capital shocked and frightened the government and further worsened his relations with the tsar. Moreover, for his pains, Ziuzin was exiled from court and suffered the confiscation of his property.[54]

When questioned about the episode, Ziuzin claimed that two other members of the Duma, Ordin-Nashchokin and Matveev, had urged him to write to Nikon. When confronted with his testimony, the two denied their involvement in the intrigue and were exonerated.[55] In a broader

sense, however, Nashchokin and F. M. Rtishchev may have been sym-
pathetic to Nikon.[56] Rtishchev's biographer identifies him repeatedly as
the patriarch's friend and ally.[57] He does not make clear, however, the
time in Nikon's complicated career to which he is referring. In the late
1640s and early 1650s, Rtishchev and the future patriarch stood together
in the front ranks of a force of clergy and laymen, working to reform and
purify the Russian church. Once Nikon assumed the patriarchal dignity,
however, the reforming coalition began to break apart. We do not know
how Rtishchev reacted to Nikon's liturgical reforms or to his monarchical
style of administering the church. As a sponsor of Ukrainian scholars in
Moscow, he probably had little sympathy for the nativist element in the
bitter protests of Avvakum and his colleagues against Nikon's reforms.
At the same time, as a devout layman, he was undoubtedly troubled by
the signs of impending schism among the faithful. Nikon's open conflict
with the tsar must have exacerbated his concern for the fate of the church.
All the same, he took no clear action to support Nikon and indeed carefully dissociated himself from the former patriarch. After 1658, then,
Rtishchev appears to have been the anguished man in the middle, eager
to reconcile all of the contending factions that were destroying the peace
and unity of the church. By his action, or rather inaction, he sided, in
effect, with his friend, Tsar Aleksei, both against Nikon's pretensions
and against the Old Believer movement.

In the world of the laity, the patriarch had no lack of enemies. His
clash with B. M. Khitrovo in 1658 brought their bitter antagonism to the
surface and opened a festering enmity.[58] Moreover, in his statements in
his own defense, Nikon repeatedly attacked Prince N. I. Odoevskii, whom
he blamed for the secularizing provisions of the Code of 1649, and S. L.
Streshnev, who took a leading part in the campaign to disqualify him
from the patriarchal office, once he had ceased to exercise it.[59] In addition, he was not amused when Streshnev named one of his hounds Nikon
and taught it to imitate the patriarchal blessing with its paw.[60] Nikon
also quarrelled publicly with the Boborykin brothers over land and re-
portedly clashed with Prince Iu. A. Dolgorukii, who objected when he
ordered the tsar's chaplain to withhold his blessing from his royal charge.[61]
Finally, in a letter to the tsar, Nikon referred to an earlier clash with
B. I. Morozov, with whom he desired to be reconciled.[62]

In the period of uncertainty between 1658 and the church council of
1666-1667, a number of Duma members and other officials carried on
negotiations with Nikon or brought him messages from the tsar. Were
these men active opponents of the patriarch or officials who were only
carrying out their official duties?[63] In most cases, we cannot be sure.
Some, however, may well have disliked Nikon and accepted their as-

signments in order to help drive him from power. For example, Prince A. N. Trubetskoi's frequent participation in the government's campaign against Nikon may well stem in part from the patriarch's earlier criticism of his conduct of the war against Sweden.[64] Whether or not they had old scores to settle, most members of the boyar elite went along with the government's campaign to remove him from office and to defeat the cause he championed.

In the final analysis, Nikon fought against ideas and attitudes, not against men. He was a man of intense loves and hates and tended to equate his own dignity with the integrity of the church as a whole. The man against whom he railed most bitterly—Odoevskii, usually a trimmer, and Streshnev, otherwise a nonentity—symbolize the pretensions of the state to legal and practical hegemony over the church. For their part, most courtiers returned the compliment. Like Aleksei Mikhailovich himself, they seem to have rejected Nikon's claim that the church stood over the state as its judge. Certainly, only one of them risked martyrdom in support of the deposed patriarch. Moreover, as a group, they closed ranks against a man who was an outsider in every sense—a social upstart and a clergyman to boot. The boyars saw priests and bishops almost every day of their lives but were apparently at ease with them only as long as they kept to their traditional role and refrained from challenging the established order of the secular world. Against a crusader like Nikon, they built a wall of hostility.

The boyar elite reacted to Nashchokin in a very similar way. Like Nikon, he had very few friends at court. In the early years of his career, he enjoyed the protection of B. M. Dubrovskii and F. I. Sheremetev, under whom he served.[65] In later years, when under pressure from enemies, real and imagined, Nashchokin pointed to Rtishchev as a true friend; the latter, he claimed, felt such antagonism from other courtiers because of their relationship that he was afraid to continue their correspondence.[66]

Throughout his career, the master diplomat remained isolated and depended entirely on the continued favor of his chief sponsor, Tsar Aleksei. Evidently the monarch had a deep regard for Nashchokin's talent, energy, and integrity. Certainly he put up with endless complaints, particularly in Nashchokin's embattled last years as head of the Foreign Office. In an extreme instance, the latter lashed out: "You have destroyed me . . . how shameful it is for you not to support me, not to do things my way, to give joy to my enemies who, in working against me, also work against you."[67] Such desperate attempts to retain the support of his royal master probably served only to alienate the tsar further.

In Nashchokin's mind, he was surrounded by enemies. First and foremost among them he named other diplomats. From the very beginning of his career, his mission to Moldavia, he attacked the officials of the Foreign Office as incompetent and corrupt.[68] After that, in the late 1650s, he clashed with I. A. Pronchishchev and in the 1660s openly fought with the other leading officials of the Foreign Office, Almaz Ivanov, G. S. Dokhturov, L. Golosov, and E. Iur'ev.[69] These conflicts had several roots. Nashchokin was an abrasive character who tended to impute sinister motives to anyone who opposed him. For their part, his colleagues resented his superior attitude toward them and his notion that, as an outsider to the world of the chanceries, he did not have to conform to the usual bureaucratic routines in which they had been trained.[70] Finally, as Nashchokin knew all too well, his policy of peace with Poland enjoyed very little support at court.

At several points in his career, Nashchokin also feuded with prominent aristocrats, largely, he believed, because he came from humbler social origins than they. Once again, there is more than a grain of truth in his charges. His feud with Prince I. A. Khovanskii in the late 1650s arose from their differing origins as well as from the latter's refusal to send troops to cover the Russian ambassadors entering negotiations with the Swedes.[71] Likewise, Prince N. I. Odoevskii probably had Nashchokin in mind when he made derisive comments about low-born diplomats in Russian service.[72] Earlier biographers have also identified Prince Iu. A. Dolgorukii, B. M. Khitrovo, and I. D. Miloslavskii as his enemies, and Scandinavian observers added Prince I. S. Prozorovskii to the list.[73] A. S. Matveev's position is harder to categorize. As Nashchokin's successor in the Foreign Office, he adopted very different and more popular policies—Russian expansion into the Ukraine and hostility toward Poland. At the same time, there is no record of direct clashes between them before Nashchokin left office and entered a monastery.

In short, then, Nashchokin did not get along with a number of prominent aristocratic courtiers and royal favorites. His enemies could hardly be considered a court faction or party, however; at other points in their careers, they fought one another for power. Nashchokin, the articulate outsider, encountered two powerful barriers—the entrenched routines of the chanceries and the network of families that dominated the court. In each case, his assaults caused the walls to bend but not to break. In the end, moreover, each group of opponents stiffened its resistance to him, and together they drove him from office.

Matveev occupied a more conventional place in court life.[74] Long a friend of the tsar, he became the nearest thing to a royal in-law when Aleksei married his ward, Nataliia Naryshkina. That, in turn, made him leader of the nascent Naryshkin grouping and chief opponent of the Miloslavskiis, the kin of the tsar's first wife. Once again, we know far more about Matveev's enemies than about his friends. Apart from the Miloslavskiis themselves, Matveev or his contemporaries counted B. M. Khitrovo, V. S. Volynskii, Prince B. I. Troekurov, Prince S. P. L'vov's heirs, and I. S. Gorokhov, a prominent chancery official, as his foes.[75]

Khitrovo stands out in this group. As we have indicated, he alone actively opposed all three of our heroes. At the same time, Khitrovo himself remains something of a mystery. We have conflicting testimony about his character and attitudes; some contemporaries regarded him as a statesman of talent and distinction, while others saw him as a scheming courtier with a weakness for wine and women.[76] One thing is certain: he could not afford to be a snob since he too came from obscure social origins. Moreover, we have no indications that he had distinct political ideas, cultural tastes, or was exceptionally pious. The outline of his career reveals him as a courtier and favorite from first to last, entrenched in offices close to the tsar's person.[77] He jealously maintained that position, beating back any challenges to his power or threats to his dignity.

The strengths and weaknesses in Matveev's political position came from his ties of marriage to the tsar and the new royal in-laws. Ideas played very little role in his political fate. Moreover, Matveev seems to have fitted into the social life of the court far better than Nashchokin, to say nothing of Nikon. Perhaps, then, it is no accident that he retained the tsar's favor until the latter's death.

The examination of the political positions of these three individuals allows us to make several observations. First, as we have seen in another context, the boyar elite was extremely fragmented. Even such exceptional men as these elicited the open support or naked hostility of very few other members of the Duma. In such cases, too, most Duma members remained uncommitted. At the same time, the reaction of a minority among them suggests that, as a group, they tended to close ranks against ambitious outsiders. Khitrovo's example suggests, moreover, that parvenus who had already penetrated the inner circle of the court were particularly hostile toward other social upstarts who might supplant them. The Sheremetevs and their like had far less reason to worry.

To achieve prominence and power, even the most talented newcomer needed the support and evident favor of the tsar. Bright ideas helped a man very little; indeed unconventional theories could make enemies but had little power to attract support. Appropriate marriage and family ties helped a man far more, for they brought some possible allies along with the inevitable rivals. Finally, without the help of a powerful patron at the beginning of his career, even the most talented of new men stood little chance of attracting the tsar's favorable attention and thus receiving high rank and important offices.

In the complex and fluctuating world of court politics, patronage provided a modicum of coherence and order. As in later times, the life of a Russian noble revolved around direct personal relationships. We have already noted the importance of a man's ties to his relatives by blood or marriage and to his political allies. These two types of relationship, however, may well pale in significance before those of patron and client.

Patronage relationships among seventeenth-century courtiers are very difficult to study. Contemporary commentators—Russian and foreign alike—rarely mentioned them, probably because they simply took them for granted.

In the eighteenth century, patronage hierarchies appear in plain sight of the historian because of the fashion for writing personal letters. Moreover, as David Ransel has convincingly argued, Russian nobles of that time felt a tension between the ideal of Petrine legislation that society functioned according to legal norms and the everyday reality of a world in which patronage, bribery, and nepotism still shaped men's lives and careers.[78] As far as we can tell, seventeenth-century nobles felt no such ambivalence. Patronage was simply a fact of life.

Their attitudes make it virtually impossible to reconstruct seventeenth-century patronage hierarchies in any detail. For one thing, they rarely wrote private letters—the primary source on informal personal relationships—except to the stewards of their estates. The rare exchanges of correspondence at our disposal, however, do allow us a few glimpses into the world of patronage, show us the variety of different forms that it took, and give us a rough sense of the relative importance of such relationships as a source of social cohesion within the Russian nobility.

The correspondence of the Golitsyn and Khovanskii families abounds in requests for support, pleas for help, and personal recommendations.[79] In a typical case, Prince V. V. Golitsyn's mother wrote to him at the front in the Turkish war of the late 1670s, asking for news and urging him to pardon one of his subordinates, an artillery officer who was late reporting for duty.[80]

Such requests and recommendations came from many sources and covered a wide variety of situations. Prominent courtiers sometimes wrote short, formula-strewn letters to Golitsyn or to one of the Khovanskiis, reminding them simply that they existed and might one day need support.[81] In other instances, members of the Duma recommended their kinsmen or subordinates to the tsar or to one another. For example, a parody of an official petition of Tsar Aleksei written for the amusement of the court in 1645 or 1646 mentions that six different Duma members had asked him for promotions, transfers in service, or other favors for more obscure individuals.[82] In such cases, it is hard to explain why a particular man wrote to Golitsyn, a Khovanskii, or one of their colleagues. To be sure, sometimes the writer and the recipient of the request were relatives by marriage.[83] A few were political allies.[84] Far more often, however, no family ties or common experience of service bound the two people together. Most likely, men as diverse as the powerful chancery official, Larion Ivanov, the boyar, Prince Iu. I. Romodanovskii, and an obscure figure like I. Divov all appealed to Golitsyn because his wealth, power, and family connections would allow him to give them what they wanted if he were so inclined.[85]

As we might expect, close relatives, particularly women, played a vital role in establishing networks of informal personal relationships. Winning the support of Golitsyn's mother—a woman of formidable determination, to judge by the tone of her letters—was a very effective way of gaining his attention. His father-in-law, his uncles, and even his young son also recommended someone to him on occasion.[86] Among the relatives with whom he corresponded, only his wife, daughter, and mother-in-law refrained from such suggestions.

The men who appealed for support came from many backgrounds and faced a variety of problems. The suppliants included members of the Duma, courtiers of lower rank, and officers of special military units, both native and foreign. In their ranks we also find chancery officials and clerks and merchants. A number of the lower-ranking members of the court carried letters of introduction to Golitsyn when they reported to his command in the field.[87] Some of the requests for support arose from service in the military administration of the provinces; two of Prince P. I. Khovanskii's former subordinates in Archangel asked him to recommend them to the new governor, and two well-born governors of remote regions asked Golitsyn's help in escaping from their God-forsaken posts.[88] The most desperate of all was undoubtedly M. O. Kravkov. Long a close associate of the Khovanskiis, he fell victim to the rage of the soldiers under him in the succession crisis of 1682. At their demand, the shaky new regime that ruled in the name of the young Peter arrested him and subjected him to public humiliation until he paid the enormous sum that he had allegedly embezzled from the pay of his men. In their desperation, he and his wife wrote frantic letters, begging the Khovanskiis to help pay off the debt in return for part of Kravkov's property.[89]

What is striking, then, is the number and variety of people who felt the need for informal personal ties designed to provide them with support and protection. In spite of their power, wealth, and social prominence, the boyars needed patronage relationships no less than their more obscure contemporaries.

For one thing, ambitious social upstarts sometimes reached Duma rank with the help of a powerful patron. In mid-century, B. I. Morozov evidently played such a role. A number of historians, for example, have suggested that N. S. Sobakin, B. M. Khitrovo, and his relatives, the Rtishchevs, owed their rapid advancement to his patronage. Moreover, a number of other powerful figures of later decades received their first important service assignments in the first years of Tsar Aleksei's reign, when Morozov was at the height of his power.[90] In their turn, moreover, Morozov's clients later sponsored protégés of their own; Khitrovo, for example, furthered the career of Larion Ivanov.[91]

Anyone who had close personal contact with the tsar or exercised moral authority over him might make an effective patron. The royal in-laws seem to have advanced the careers of clients; the Matiushkins, for example, probably enjoyed the sponsorship of the Streshnevs. At mid-century, B. F. Narbekov began his rapid advancement, in all probability thanks to the patronage of his kinsman by marriage, I. D. Miloslavskii, the tsar's father-in-law.[92] Even the patriarch might act as a patron of laymen. Nikon clearly advanced—and subsequently destroyed—the career of N. A. Ziuzin, and, later in the century, Ioakim pushed forward his own relatives, the Savelovs.

Among Russian diplomats of the seventeenth century, we see similar patterns. As we have noted, A. L. Ordin-Nashchokin received his first diplomatic assignments with the help of B. M. Dubrovskii and F. I. Sheremetev. Then, in later life, Nashchokin returned the favor, promoting the careers of his younger colleagues, V. M. Tiapkin and P. I. Potemkin.[93] These well-known examples probably provide only a small sample of the workings of patronage in the careers of Duma members; it is entirely possible that most of the many successful parvenus of the century began their careers as clients of prominent courtiers and officials. The reticence of contemporaries, however, prevents us from testing this hypothesis.

The limited evidence at our disposal suggests that patronage networks were very flexible. None of the fragments we have examined indicates that a patron's clients and suppliants belonged to a rigidly exclusive group. At the same time, a client apparently owed his patron the decency not to oppose him openly or to join a rival network. None of the people who asked for Golitsyn's support or favor, for example, also turned to the Khovanskiis for protection.

If a man were desperate enough, however, he might well turn to anyone who could possibly help him in his need. In his eagerness to escape from an assignment on the Don, Prince P. I. Khovanskii asked his connections in Moscow to appeal to the patriarch, Prince Iu. A. Dolgorukii, and A. S. Matveev to arrange for his transfer to a more pleasant post.[94] Even more remarkable—and equally understandable—was the conduct of Matveev himself. After his fall and exile to the far north, the former first minister wrote to the patriarch, the Tsar's former confessor and an imposing array of prominent laymen, including his enemies, I. M. Miloslavskii and B. M. Khitrovo, protesting his innocence of the charges against him and begging for an improvement in his treatment.[95] Any friend—or even enemy—at court might stand a man in good stead.

Like marriage alliances, then, patronage ties often had a primarily defensive purpose. In the confusion of seventeenth-century court politics, individuals and families strove to avoid isolation and to maintain working relationships with as many of their fellows as possible.

Informal personal relations of the kind we have described were certainly not unique to Russia or the seventeenth century; they have played a significant role in the social and political life of many societies at many times in history. For the boyars, they probably loomed especially large, however, even though we can see only small fragments of their workings.

In seventeenth-century Russia, personal contacts with the ruler and his leading courtiers allowed a man to survive and helped him to climb to high office and social distinction. At the same time, belonging to a powerful aristocratic clan by birth or marriage, while still of enormous importance, probably provided fewer guarantees than in previous centuries. Moreover, the century was a time of rapid change; Russia's government and ruling elite had to meet the challenges of new technologies and cultural standards, and the boyar elite took in many new members, particularly in the latter half of the century. Under the circumstances, the boyars badly needed the security of informal networks of personal ties.

CHAPTER V

Landlords

Ownership of populated land was the boyars' primary source of economic survival and prosperity. All Duma members owned land and controlled the peasants who lived on it. To say so naturally raises many questions. In what ways did men acquire landed property in seventeenth-century Russia? In particular, what was the relationship of wealth in land to political power? Or, put more crudely, did the rich gain power, or did high office bring with it wealth? Moreover, once the boyars had acquired land, how did they administer it and exploit its resources? What role did other members of their families play in the ownership of their estates? In particular, to whom did they bequeath their property?

Answers to these questions will, of necessity, be fragmentary and speculative. Despite the intense interest of prerevolutionary and Soviet historians in the legal and economic aspects of the ownership and management of landed estates, no one has undertaken a systematic study of landholding patterns in all of seventeenth-century Russia. To do so would require many years of arduous work with unpublished land cadasters. Short of that, however, we are left with a tantalizing, but limited and distorted, body of sources. We have summary lists of the boyars' landholdings for particular years. Those for 1613, 1638, 1647, 1653, 1678, and 1696 have been published, and I have discovered an incomplete unpublished list for 1670.[1] In addition, we have at our disposal a number of individuals' wills, a few marriage contracts, and a significant body of documents and secondary literature on the management of particular estates. In all cases, however, such documents shed light on the economic lives of only a few members of the Muscovite high nobility and may give a very distorted picture of that social stratum as a whole.

Several preliminary observations are in order. First, as many scholars have noted, some Russian nobles of the seventeenth century were very much richer than others. The members of the Duma included the richest and most powerful laymen in the realm, but, even within their company, the wealthiest individual owned roughly one hundred times as much land or labor as the poorest. The economic divisions within the boyar group remained very deep throughout the century. In the list of prominent landowners in 1613, the Duma members' estates ranged in size from Prince F. I. Mstislavskii's 32,606 *chetverti*, or roughly 134,000 acres, down to M. M. Godunov's 208 chetverti, or about 850 acres.[2] Toward the end of the century, Prince I. A. Vorotynskii headed the list for 1678 with a total of 4,609 peasant households, while fellow Duma member, N. K. Streshnev, had only 14.[3] All of the other summary lists reflect the same disparity. Any generalization about the economic life of the boyar elite as a group must be tempered by the realization that their individual fortunes were extremely diverse.

Secondly, Russian nobles of the period owned two different types of estates. The first type, the *votchina*, they held on allodial tenure and could dispose of as they wished within broad legal limits. The second, the pomest'e, appeared in Russia in significant numbers only in the late fifteenth century, when Ivan III confiscated much land in conquered Novgorod and gave it to his followers on condition that they serve him loyally. As is well known, pomest'e estates remained theoretically the property of the crown. Through most of the sixteenth century, their occupants could not sell them or bequeath them to their heirs. Only if the son showed his capacity for service would the government grant him his father's estate. By the mid-seventeenth century, however, the pomest'e system had lost much of its rigor. In practice, the owner of the pomest'e could pass it on to his sons or trade it to another noble for land that he found more desirable.[4] In other words, the legal distinctions between votchina and pomest'e estates were becoming fainter and played a less and less significant role in calculating the landed wealth of the nobles. At the same time, the boyars by no means forgot these differences. Whenever possible, they gladly paid the government for the right to change the form of ownership of their lands from pomest'e into votchina. There were apparently two main reasons for this preference. Ownership of a votchina probably carried with it greater prestige than possession of a pomest'e. On a more practical plane, moreover, the owner of a votchina could move his peasants to any of his other estates, whereas the population of a pomest'e was bound, in theory, to that particular tract of land and could not be resettled elsewhere.[5] Be that as it may, the following discussion of boyar landholding will take no further note of these distinctions except in the treatment of individual cases in which they seem particularly important.

Finally, we should bear in mind that ownership of land was not the only source of income of the boyar elite. As Kotoshikhin pointed out, all Duma members and many lesser servitors of the crown had the right to claim an annual salary in money and in pomest'e estates of a particular size. Each individual received an amount of these two forms of salary (*oklad*) in accord with his position on the Muscovite service hierarchy. All Duma members theoretically received at least 200 rubles a year. Moreover, the government regularly gave its leading servants raises for outstanding service, particularly in military campaigns. Thanks to the generosity of Aleksei, Fedor, and, above all, the shaky regency of the 1680s, money salaries rose rapidly. In the last decades of the century, thirteen boyars reached a level of 1,000 rubles a year by the end of their careers.[6]

What do these figures mean? We must approach the question on two levels. To begin with, we need a rough idea of the value of Russian currency in the seventeenth century. Except for a brief experiment in the 1650s, the ruble remained a unit of reckoning only. The chief coins in circulation were the *kopek* and the *den'ga*, worth one one-hundredth and one two-hundredth of a ruble respectively. Over the course of the century, the royal treasury reduced the amount of silver in these coins slowly but steadily. Between 1610-1611 and 1698, successive devaluations reduced the weight of the kopek by about 19 percent. Although these changes were indeed significant, their impact was small enough to allow us, in our very rough calculations, to proceed as though the value of Muscovite currency did not change over the course of the century.[7]

The purchasing power of the coinage likewise changed comparatively little during our period. The price structure of seventeenth-century Russia is a complex and controversial subject. The sources of the period record innumerable prices of individual items in various places and times, but make it difficult to construct a series of genuinely comparable figures over time. The best recent attempt to solve the problem concentrates on two major agricultural commodities, rye and oats. Leaving aside extreme local variations and the impact of the disastrous experiment with copper coinage in the early 1660s, the price of oats remained roughly stable during the century, and the price of rye declined sharply in both nominal and real terms in the 1640s and the 1670s. For purposes of this study, then, we can consider prices roughly stable in the period with which we are concerned.[8]

A few examples provide illustrations of the practical value and purchasing power of money in the seventeenth century. According to Iu. A. Tikhonov's calculations, for example, peasant households in central Russia paid their lords an annual rent in money ranging from 5 kopeks to 2½ rubles a year.[9] Nobles paid their servants between 2 and 10 rubles a year and might have to expend 20 rubles a year to hire a skilled craftsman. In some cases, it cost between 200 and 300 rubles to hire a contractor for a building project.[10] On a more mundane level, a *chetvert'*, normally about 289 pounds, of rye cost anywhere from 40 kopeks to 1.33 rubles.[11] Depending on type, age, and condition, a horse cost from 1 to 5 rubles.[12] Icons, treasured heirlooms, and devotional objects cost anywhere from 2 to 100 rubles, the latter when enclosed in a lavishly jewelled cover.[13] The Moscow house in which the icons might hang could cost from one to many thousands of rubles.[14]

In the light of these figures, then, the boyars' annual salaries seem significant, but far from lavish. More than that we are not in a position to say. First of all, we cannot be sure that the government actually paid the Duma members their salary on an annual basis. Kotoshikhin, that well-informed contemporary, claims that it did, and, in the absence of any confirming evidence, we would be wise to take him at his word since independent evidence supports the rest of his discussion of the subject.[15] Secondly, when they wrote petitions requesting a raise in salary, Muscovite nobles seemed more concerned with their prestige among their compatriots than with the state of their pocketbooks. Even more than extra income, the petitioners wanted the government's formal recognition of their rank and the value of their services.[16] In seventeenth-century Russia, then, salaries did not make men rich. They did, however, provide a useful source of cash in a largely natural economy.

Ownership of land, however, was the primary economic resource of the seventeenth-century nobility. To understand the boyars, then, we must investigate how they acquired and maintained their landholdings and how they administered them, beginning with the thorny issue of the relation of landholding to political power.

Let us turn first to the summary lists of the holdings of Duma members. Several general observations can be made at once. First, as one would expect, the members of the Duma and holders of high court office had, on the average, considerably larger estates than the lesser courtiers, the stol'niki, and Moscow gentry. In 1613, for example, the mean holding of the Duma members and court officers was 4,274 chetverti, or about 17,500 acres, while that for all members of the lower ranks on the list of that year was 1,170 chetverti or 4,800 acres.[17]

Secondly, within the membership of the Duma, the higher the rank the richer the man. Throughout the century, those who held the rank of boyar owned roughly four times as much land, on the average, as the okol'nichie. In 1638, for example, the boyars owned a mean of 883 peasant households and the okol'nichie 221.[18] The figures for 1678 are 862 and 226 households, respectively. Moreover, the okol'nichie in turn usually owned twice as much land as the holders of the two lowest Duma ranks.[19]

So far our findings are ambiguous. These very rough averages could serve as proof either that boyars became rich or that the rich became boyars. They show unequivocally, however, that power and wealth went together and that almost all Duma members owned more than the roughly 20 households necessary to support a noble in service.[20]

Further study of the list of 1613 leads us in two opposing directions at the same time. On the one hand, the data on the list suggest that those individuals among the lower ranks of courtiers who would later rise to membership in the Duma were, on the average, wealthier than their fellows whose later careers would not be so distinguished.[21] A large estate, it would seem, was helpful in climbing the political ladder, but was by no means a decisive advantage. Comparative poverty could be overcome and often was.

On the other hand, many of the richest landowners in 1613 owed much of their wealth to the generosity of the recent rulers of Russia. As one regime succeeded another in the chaotic Time of Troubles, its leaders tried to win support by granting prominent nobles large tracts of crown or confiscated private land.[22] Prince F. I. Mstislavskii's estates, for example, consisted largely of lands granted him by the regime of Vasilii Shuiskii, and Prince I. B. Cherkasskii's were made up of grants from Shuiskii and the boyar administration of the last period of the Smuta. The military leader of the national revival, Prince D. M. Pozharskii, likewise received large grants from both Shuiskii and the boyar regime. Other wealthy boyars received grants from less savory sources, the first False Dmitrii and King Sigismund of Poland.[23] In such cases, men received grants of land because they were competent servitors, influential courtiers, or personal favorites of successive rulers. Insecure governments tried to buy their allegiance.

The policies of the governments of the Time of Troubles were by no means unique. At various times after 1613, the new regime of the Romanovs gave away extensive tracts of crown land. In the first years of the restoration, Tsar Mikhail's government made grants mainly to groups of the provincial nobles who made up the core of Muscovy's cavalry army. Then, in 1627, the government forbade further alienation of crown land. Within a few years, the tsar began to break his own rules by giving extensive tracts of land to particular favorites. Such generosity was also the order of the day in the 1670s and 1680s.[24]

Although only one of many ways of acquiring land, such royal grants laid the foundations of some of the largest fortunes of seventeenth-century Russia. Let us look at one celebrated example to which we shall return later. B. I. Morozov, the great statesman and favorite of the late 1640s, inherited a fine name and a distinctly modest fortune. In the

second decade of the century, he and his brother owned family lands
with a total population of 233 peasant households. In 1617 he received
his first royal grant, the core of his future holdings in the district of
Nizhnii-Novgorod. Thereafter his royal masters, Mikhail and Aleksei,
continued to reward him generously, particularly in the 1630s and 1640s,
when he became the second richest layman of the realm. Most of his
acquisitions in this period, including his small empire in the Arzamas
district, were carved from crown lands. After his fall from power in 1648,
Tsar Aleksei's government treated him with greater reserve; he bought
most of the land that he added to his portfolio in the last decade before
his death in 1661.[25] A man like Morozov owed his great wealth to the
favor of successive tsars and the power that flowed from their regard for
him.

Morozov's estates, although exceptionally large, were typical in another respect. At the height of his power in 1647, he owned tracts of
land in eleven different districts of Russia, to the north, west, and east
of Moscow.[26] In the same year, six other Duma members owned estates
in at least ten districts. Such portfolios of widely scattered estates were
even more common in 1678; on the summary list of that year, 18 of the
88 individuals owned land in 10 or more of the 72 districts mentioned.
In the most remarkable case, Rodion Matveevich Streshnev had small
estates in 18 districts in all four corners of the realm.[27] At the other end
of the scale, only 5 of the men on the list held land in only one district,
presumably a single estate.[28] Among the boyars, then, scattered landholdings were the order of the day. We will examine the practical consequences of this pattern later.

These lists provide evidence of another well-known feature of boyar
landholding in the seventeenth century—the drive to acquire fertile land
on the eastern and southern frontiers of Muscovy. In the first half of the
seventeenth century, a systematic campaign to improve the southern
defenses of the realm bore fruit.[29] As the danger of Crimean raids declined, settlers of all types moved southward into the rich lands of the
"black soil" belt. The boyars used their influence to profit from the
southern land boom. A number of individuals on the lists of 1647 and
1678 owned lands in southern districts, and others held extensive tracts
east and southeast in the direction of the former Khanate of Kazan'. The
most notorious southern colonists were, of course, the Romanovs, particularly Ivan Nikitich, the uncle of Tsar Mikhail, who acquired large
holdings in several frontier districts and who conducted a ruthless campaign to populate them with peasants. His efforts made him rich, but,
in the process, he became the terror of his poorer noble neighbors and,
one assumes, of his unfortunate peasants as well.[30]

Other features of the boyars' landholdings become clear when we examine lists of the ten wealthiest individuals and families at several points
in the seventeenth century (Tables 1 and 2).[31] The continuity from one
list to the next is remarkable. Families like the Sheremetevs, Cherkasskiis, Kurakins, Odoevskiis, and Saltykovs remained in the top ten
throughout the century and provided many of the wealthiest individuals.
Others, like the Mstislavskiis, Morozovs, Sitskiis, Vorotynskiis, and the
cadet branch of the Romanovs remained wealthy until the male line died
out. Without question, wealth provided some of the advantages that helped
members of these families to remain rich and powerful for generation
after generation.

At the same time, as Morozov's example illustrates, political power
and favor could bring wealth. The classic success stories of the period
provide particularly striking examples. At various times in the century,
I. T. Gramotin, L. S. Streshnev, I. D. Miloslavskii, and L. K. Naryshkin
rose from obscurity to prominence and wealth through talent, energy,
ambition, or good luck. At the time of his death, for example, the chancery official L. Ivanov owned more than 3,500 chetverti of land in eight
districts.[32] The Streshnevs, Miloslavskiis, Naryshkins, and Lopukhins all
got rich by marrying into the royal family. Political influence brought
economic rewards, at least in their cases. Roughly the same is true of
families like the Pozharskiis, Dolgorukiis, and Khovanskiis. All three enjoyed a distinguished lineage and a distinctly modest fortune until one
of their family members became a celebrated military leader and reaped
the appropriate rewards.[33]

Summary lists of landholding admittedly give only a superficial
impression of the changing political and economic fortunes of individuals
and families in Muscovy. For a closer viewpoint, we should turn to a
detailed study of particular families over several generations. Unfortunately, this task is well-nigh impossible, given the present state of the
literature. As a rough beginning, we can look at some features in the
political and economic lives of three interrelated families, the Sheremetevs, the Odoevskiis, and the Cherkasskiis. These three clans stand
out for their stability in a period of rapid change; they were prominent
and prosperous at the end of the sixteenth century and remained so into
the eighteenth. As such, they stand at the opposite pole from Morozov,
a man who made a great fortune in his own lifetime but left no male heir
to enjoy its fruits.

As we examine the changing fortunes of these families, we must bear
in mind the most important rule of the game that they played. From the
beginning of its history, the Russian nobility followed the custom of partible inheritance of land. Before he died, each man divided his property

TABLE 1 Ten Wealthiest Individual Lay Landowners in Russia

	1613	1638	1647
1	F. I. Mstislavskii	I. N. Romanov	N. I. Romanov
2	D. T. Trubetskoi	F. I. Sheremetev	B. I. Morozov
3	F. I. Sheremetev	I. B. Cherkasskii	Ia. K. Cherkasskii
4	I. M. Vorotynskii	D. M. Pozharskii	F. I. Sheremetev
5	I. B. Cherkasskii	L. S. Streshnev	I. V. Morozov
6	V. P. Morozov	Iu. E. Suleshev	M. M. Saltykov
7	I. N. Romanov	D. M. Cherkasskii	N. I. Odoevskii
8	A. Iu. Sitskii	B. M. Lykov	G. I. Morozov
9	I. m. N. Odoevskii	I. T. Gramotin	L. S. Streshnev
10	D. M. Pozharskii	A. M. L'vov	V. I. Streshnev

	1653	1670
1	N. I. Romanov	M. Ia. Cherkasskii
2	B. I. Morozov	P. M. Saltykov
3	Ia. K. Cherkasskii	Iu. A. Dolgorukii
4	I. D. Miloslavskii	Ia. N. Odoevskii
5	I. V. Morozov	A. S. Shein
6	G. I. Morozov	R. M. Streshnev
7	N. I. Odoevskii	Iu. P. Trubetskoi
8	M. M. Saltykov	I. B. Miloslavskii
9	L. S. Streshnev	M. S. Pushkin
10	V. I. Streshnev	M. I. Morozov

	1678	1696
1	I. A. Vorotynskii	M. Ia. Cherkasskii
2	P. M. Saltykov	L. K. Naryshkin
3	Ia. N. Odoevskii	Ia. N. Odoevskii
4	G. S. Kurakin	A. S. Shein
5	P. V. Sheremetev	M. A. Cherkasskii
6	I. B. Troekurov	F. P. Saltykov
7	I. A. Golitsyn II	M. G. Romodanovskii
8	N. I. Odoevskii	I. B. Troekurov
9	I. B. Repnin	S. I. Saltykov
10	F. F. Kurakin	A. I. Golitsyn

TABLE 2 Ten Wealthiest Families in Russia

	1613[a]		1638		1647	
1	Mstislavskii	32,606	Romanov	3,473	Morozov	10,213
2	Trubetskoi	19,172	Cherkasskii	3,031	Romanov	7,012
3	Sheremetev	15,586	Sheremetev	2,417	Cherkasskii	5,173
4	Cherkasskii	9,975	Pozharskii	1,449	Streshnev	3,895
5	Vorotynskii	7,265	Streshnev	1,430	Sheremetev	3,446
6	Sitskii	6,800	Saltykov	1,013	Saltykov	2,736
7	Kurakin	6,410	Morozov	999	Odoevskii	1,728
8	Morozov	6,051	Lykov	829	Kurakin	1,297
9	Romanov	5,074	Golitsyn	819	Trubetskoi	1,104
10	Odoevskii	4,842	L'vov	738	Golitsyn	880

	1653		1670	
1	Morozov	11,636	Cherkasskii	6,730
2	Romanov	7,689	Saltykov	2,606
3	Cherkasskii	6,790	Odoevskii	2,501
4	L'vov	3,172	Dolgorukii	2,259
5	Streshnev	3,116	Shein	1,100
6	Saltykov	3,066	Khovanskii	934
7	Odoevskii	1,934	Miloslavskii	877
8	Kurakin	1,802	Streshnev	855
9	Trubetskoi	1,490	Buturlin	808
10	Repnin	1,234	Trubetskoi	755

	1678		1696	
1	Odoevskii	4,248	Cherkasskii	9,083
2	Golitsyn	3,541	Naryshkin	8,049
3	Saltykov	3,019	Saltykov	5,103
4	Kurakin	2,828	Prozorovskii	3,833
5	Dolgorukii	2,733	Sheremetev	2,312
6	Sheremetev	2,106	Odoevskii	2,185
7	Troekurov	1,551	Shein	1,889
8	Romodanovskii	1,411	Lopukhin	1,835
9	Repnin	1,336	Golitsyn	1,518
10	Streshnev	1,074	Miloslavskii	1,513

NOTE: For the sake of consistency, the figures include only the lands of family members who served in the Duma.

[a] 1613 figures in chetverti, all others in peasant households.

among all of his sons and made provision for his widow and daughters
as well. Over the course of several generations, this custom could well
lead to economic ruin. If the number of family members grew steadily,
each individual's share in the common inheritance became smaller and
smaller.[34] Before long, the entire clan could sink into poverty and obscurity. Despite the obvious dangers of the system, the nobles of Russia
could not envision a viable alternative, as Peter the Great was to discover. His attempt to force the nobles to bequeath their entire landed
estate to a single heir encountered strong opposition and was soon abandoned. The nobles' stubborn attachment to this ruinous custom sprang,
not from suicidal tendencies, but from a lack of economic and institutional alternatives. Like any concerned parents, the nobles wanted to
provide for all their children, but could find only one way of doing so.
Owning and managing land was the main source of income for the vast
majority of well-to-do Russians in the seventeenth century and certainly
the one that was most appropriate for a noble. Official salaries were too
small to live on, even if paid regularly, and trade was out of the question.
Moreover, unlike their western European counterparts, Russian nobles
did not arrange ecclesiastical careers for their younger sons. The custom
of partible inheritance, then, seems to have been the best of a bad bar-
gain.

Noble families could escape its consequences in several ways. First,
they could limit the number of heirs in each generation. As we shall see,
some of the richest families of seventeenth-century Russia had relatively
few children who lived to inherit a share of the family patrimony. There
is no evidence, however, to indicate the use of any form of birth control.
Second, nobles could acquire more land so that each heir would have
enough. By and large, they counted on government grants to improve
their fortunes. The wealthiest and best-connected families could also increase their holdings through purchases or marriage settlements.

The three families under consideration provide illustrations of the successful use of all of these techniques. They were, of course, not typical
of the entire boyar elite, let alone of the nobility as a whole. All three
are exceptional for their wealth and for the relatively full surviving documentation on their lands. Even so, there are serious gaps in the available sources that make our discussion fragmentary and our conclusions
tentative.

During our discussion of these families and their landholdings, we
should keep in mind the prevailing laws governing inheritance in seventeenth-century Russia. According to the Code of 1649 and other decrees, a man's sons normally inherited his votchina lands. If he had no
sons, then his daughters divided his estate. A man's widow inherited

one quarter of his movable property and could receive some or all of his
purchased estates. His inherited land was, under all circumstances, to
remain in the male line of his family. By law, a widow also retained
control of her dowry and any purchased estates that she had inherited
from her own family. In the case of pomest'e land, sons usually retained
possession of their deceased father's land if they fulfilled the service
obligations that accompanied it. The law guaranteed their widowed mother
a fixed proportion of their father's pomest'e land as a form of pension.[35]
As we shall see, these guidelines gave the boyars considerable flexibility
in disposing of their property.

Even among the boyars, the Sheremetev family stands out. The Sheremetevs were non-titled aristocrats who entered the service of the princes
of Moscow in the middle of the fourteenth century. There they thrived
and, by the end of the sixteenth century, were already wealthy and
powerful.[36] In the seventeenth, they formed a relatively small and co-
hesive, if not always harmonious, family group. Throughout the century,
they remained one of the very wealthiest families of Russia, occupying a
place between third and sixth on the summary lists of boyar landholdings. Most remarkable of all, however, was their longevity; the Sheremetevs remained among the richest and most prominent noble clans
until the end of the last century.

Our picture of the Sheremetev estates begins to take shape in the last
decades of the sixteenth century. By that time, the family had evidently
gathered the resources needed to survive the upheavals of Ivan IV's later
years and the Time of Troubles. Among the first signs of their rising
fortunes was the acquisition of the village of Kuskovo, near Moscow.
Vasilii Andreevich Sheremetev (fl. 1500-1537), the progenitor of all of
the famous Sheremetevs of later generations, got it from the Pushkins
in exchange for another property. From that time on, Kuskovo remained
a treasured possession of the family.[37]

In the sixteenth and seventeenth centuries, ownership of land near
Moscow was a particularly valuable asset. Since the capital was the central mustering point for the army, both the government and the nobles
themselves recognized that it was crucial to own an estate within a short
ride of the city. Ivan IV's plan to give lands near Moscow to about 1,000
servitors attempted to meet that need, whether or not it could actually
be implemented in practice.[38] Moreover, the court and the central offices of the royal administration were located in Moscow. As a result,
courtiers and officials maintained residences in the city itself. As we shall
see in greater detail, these leading citizens brought many of their provisions into the city from their country estates. Land within easy reach
of Moscow made the provisioning of city residences particularly conven-

ient and economical. Finally, the great nobles of the capital used their
estates around the city as places of recreation. Particularly in the seventeenth century, some of the most prominent officials of the realm began to build large houses on these estates in order to live comfortably
and to entertain on a grand scale.[39] Kuskovo became just such a property, treasured not because of its intrinsic economic value but because
of its location. Several generations of Sheremetevs transformed it into
one of the most imposing of the Russian nobility's country seats near
Moscow.

Our first full picture of an individual Sheremetev's estates is impressive. Ivan Vasil'evich the Younger, the fifth of Vasilii Andreevich's six
sons, inherited seven estates from his father and his brother, Ivan the
Elder, each in a different district of Russia. To these he added several
tracts of land which he bought or acquired on exchange. He concentrated particularly on gathering land around Moscow and in rounding
out his holdings at Kuskovo and at Pesochnia in the Riazan' area. Ivan
the Younger undoubtedly owed part of his good fortune to the chaotic
times in which he lived. Landed property seems to have changed hands
very rapidly during the oprichnina, when Ivan IV purged many members of the nobility. Even though two of his own brothers were among
Ivan's victims, Ivan the Younger thrived. He evidently enjoyed the tsar's
confidence, for Ivan granted him two new estates, one of which had
belonged to the fallen favorite, Aleksei Adashev, and a palace in the
Moscow Kremlin. The core of Ivan the Younger's holdings consisted,
then, of lands gathered by the Sheremetevs over previous generations.
Royal favor accounted for a minority of his holdings, albeit a significant
one.[40]

Building on his father's foundation, Ivan the Younger's only son, Fedor, became one of the richest men in Russia in the first decades of the
seventeenth century. It was a struggle to preserve his inheritance in the
storms of the Time of Troubles. The Sheremetevs fell into Boris Godunov's disfavor, along with the Romanovs. The new tsar confiscated the
family's palace in the Moscow Kremlin and in 1600 took away the Riazan'
property, Pesochnia, and gave it to one of the Cherkasskiis. During the
next few years, Fedor Ivanovich Sheremetev pestered several governments for the return of these properties. In the end, his efforts paid off;
in 1610, the Polish occupation regime of King Sigismund granted him
title to the Riazan' property, and in November 1612 the leaders of the
Russian national revival allotted him space in the Kremlin on which to
build a new palace to replace the one he had lost. Thus, in 1613, he had
reassembled his father's portfolio of lands and was well on the way to
making substantial additions of his own.[41]

Fedor Ivanovich was not the only resourceful Sheremetev. Although the data on their estates are less extensive, it is clear that his cousin, Petr Nikitich, and the latter's sons, Ivan, Vasilii, and Boris were comfortably well off. At some point, Petr Nikitich seems to have regained the Kolomna estate, Chirkino, from the St. Cyril-Beloozero Monastery, to which a pious ancestor had granted it. This property passed to his youngest son, Boris, and became one of the core estates of the family.[42] In all probability, he willed his sons a number of other properties as well. In the summary list of 1647, all three had significant, but modest, holdings in various parts of Russia, ranging from Ivan's 331 peasant households to Boris' 112.[43] Before long, moreover, the three brothers were to inherit the sixteenth-century core of the Sheremetev lands.

For the moment, however, Fedor Ivanovich enjoyed undisputed preeminence in the clan. In 1647, he owned lands with a population of almost 3,000 peasant households.[44] When he made his will, two years earlier, he listed a total of 29 estates outside the cities of Russia, four properties in Moscow, and one in Nizhnii-Novgorod. The foundation of his wealth was still the ancestral (*rodovye*) estates that he had received from his father.[45] These were to remain the property of the Sheremetev clan. Since he had no children, he willed them to his nephews, the three sons of Petr Nikitich, and to their heirs.[46]

By the 1640s, however, ancestral estates made up only about one-third of Fedor Ivanovich's fortune. The rest consisted largely of royal grants, particularly Ivan IV's gifts to his father, and of lands that he and his father had purchased. Evidently, Fedor Ivanovich had not been idle. Over the first decades of the seventeenth century, he bought tracts of land from the crown and from a variety of individual proprietors, most obscure but including the prominent official Fedor Likhachev and one of the Pleshcheevs. Moreover, he took legal steps to see that he could will as many of his holdings as possible to the heir of his choice. For example, in 1639 he petitioned the tsar to let him treat estates granted for service as though he had bought them. In reply, Tsar Mikhail's government allowed him to change the legal classification of three properties granted for service during the Time of Troubles.[47]

Having freed his hand, he designated as his primary heirs his son-in-law, Prince Nikita Ivanovich Odoevskii, and his favorite grandson, Prince Iakov. In addition, he carefully set aside smaller portions of his estate for Nikita's other sons and his daughter. His decision altered the economic fortunes of both families. Thanks to his generosity, the Odoevskiis' fortunes increased until, on the summary list of 1678, they were the wealthiest single family in Russia. The Sheremetevs continued to thrive, but their wealth was divided among a number of family members so that no individual of Fedor Ivanovich's stature as a landowner emerged in the rest of the seventeenth century.

Even before the marriage alliance with the Sheremetevs, the Odoevskiis were no mean family. They were descendants of the Chernigov branch of the Riurikovich princes and owned their family principality, Odoev, on the southwestern frontier of Muscovy, until well into the sixteenth century. The first Odoevskiis entered the service of Moscow's rulers late in the fifteenth century.[48] From that time on, each generation of Odoevskiis produced distinguished servitors over the course of the sixteenth and seventeenth centuries.

No available sources throw light on the economic position of the Odoevskiis before 1613. In the summary list of landholding of that year, they appear as the tenth wealthiest family of the realm, largely thanks to the holdings of Prince Ivan Nikitich the Younger. He apparently inherited some of his lands from his father and received the rest as a grant from the boyar government in 1612 or 1613.[49] Our next solid evidence dates from 1647, when Prince Nikita Ivanovich, Prince Ivan the Younger's nephew, owned at least fourteen properties in eight separate areas of the country, with a total population of 1,728 peasant households. His two older sons, Prince Mikhail and Prince Fedor, also owned property in their own right.[50]

Where Prince Nikita Ivanovich got his land is not clear. Fragmentary evidence suggests that he purchased some of it from the government.[51] His will makes clear that he bought land to round off a number of his properties and that he bought several houses and lots in the city of Moscow from private individuals and from the government.[52]

The location of his estates is considerably more revealing. The three Odoevskiis listed in the survey of 1678—Prince Nikita Ivanovich, his son, Prince Iakov, and his great-nephew, Prince Iurii Mikhailovich—together owned 4,248 peasant households in 15 different districts of Russia.[53] None of their many estates, indeed none owned by any Odoevskii in the seventeenth century, was located in or near Odoev, their ancestral home. At some time in the sixteenth century, the Odoevskiis had lost their roots in their ancestral territory, begun to center their lives around Moscow, and acquired lands wherever they could, just like other successful servitors.

Prince Nikita Ivanovich bequeathed his extensive lands to his direct descendants, as was usually the custom. When he made his will in 1689, he had already outlived all but one of his sons and all of his grandsons. As a result, he devoted much of the document to adjusting previous inheritance arrangements, including the will of Fedor Ivanovich Sheremetev. As stipulated long before, Prince Iakov Nikitich Odoevskii re-

mained in possession of his Sheremetev inheritance and acquired some
of his father's estates as well. The rest of the estate went to Prince Nikita
Ivanovich's great-grandsons and remained in the Odoevskii family.[54] Prince
Iakov's inheritance, however, had a complex history. Since he had no
sons, the bulk of his estate passed on to two daughters and their husbands, Prince Dmitrii Mikhailovich Golitsyn and Prince Mikhail Iakovlevich Cherkasskii. Then, later in the eighteenth century, further matrimonial alliances brought some of the Sheremetevs' ancestral lands back
into their hands.[55]

In the Cherkasskiis, the Odoevskiis allied themselves with one of the
most remarkable clans of seventeenth-century Russia. As their surname
suggests, the Cherkasskiis came as immigrants from Kabarda in the
northern Caucasus. A number of princes from the area entered Muscovite service in the 1550s and 1560s and immediately occupied prominent
positions in the army and at court. Before long, the Cherkasskiis made
matrimonial alliances with the throne through Ivan IV's marriage to Mariia Temriukovna and with the Romanovs, kinsmen of Ivan's first wife,
who were later to rule Russia in their own right.[56] Thereafter those
members of the clan who accepted conversion to Eastern Orthodoxy won
recognition as regular members of the Muscovite aristocracy and collected the appropriate rewards.

Unlike the Sheremetevs and the Odoevskiis, the Cherkasskiis were a
large sprawling clan, a loose coalition of comparatively distant relatives.[57]
Two advantages made up for their lack of cohesion. First, the evidence
suggests that the Cherkasskiis stood at the center of a group of immigrants from several neighboring Near Eastern societies. Secondly, the
clan's close association with the Romanovs paid off spectacularly, once
the latter became the ruling dynasty in 1613.

As immigrants, the Cherkasskiis received their lands as grants from
the rulers whom they served. In the late sixteenth century, several
members of the clan acquired estates that had been confiscated from
other nobles.[58] After the Time of Troubles, the trend continued. The
boyar administration that restored the monarchy gave large tracts of land
to both Prince Ivan Borisovich and Prince Dmitrii Mamstriukovich
Cherkasskii, making them two of the wealthiest men of their time.[59]
Indeed, one member of the clan or another stood near the top of the
summary lists of landholding throughout the century. As Prince Dmitrii
Mamstriukovich's will and other sources make clear, a continuing stream
of royal grants and the clan's purchases, often from crown land, provided
their wealth.[60]

The inheritance patterns of the Cherkasskiis differ somewhat from
those of the other families we have discussed. Members of a large clan,

they had no qualms about leaving their property to comparatively distant relatives as long as it remained in the possession of the family group.[61] For example, lacking a direct heir, Prince Dmitrii Mamstriukovich left most of his land to a second cousin, Prince Iakov Kudenetovich Cherkasskii, and the rest to another second cousin, Prince Grigorii Suncheleevich, who also shared briefly in the inheritance of his father-in-law, Prince Nikita Ivanovich Odoevskii.[62] Prince Grigorii, it would seem, contested the will on the grounds that his branch of the clan was genealogically closer to the deceased than Prince Iakov Kudenetovich's.[63] The government, however, disallowed his protest.

Prince Grigorii's resentment is understandable, for Prince Iakov Kudenetovich was already very wealthy. In 1647 he owned 5,173 peasant households on at least 21 estates in thirteen different districts.[64] He received his lands from several different sources. Apart from probable royal grants, he inherited land from both Prince Ivan Borisovich Cherkasskii, his first cousin, and Prince Iu. E. Suleshev, a prominent immigrant from the Crimea to whom he was related not by blood but by common status and background as immigrants from Near Eastern societies.[65]

More fortunate than earlier kinsmen, Prince Iakov Kudenetovich had a son to whom he apparently willed his fortune intact. Certainly Prince Mikhail Iakovlevich was the wealthiest private individual in Russia in the last years of the seventeenth century.[66]

What does the fate of the three families' lands suggest? Given the very small number of examples we have discussed, our conclusions will serve as hypotheses to be confirmed or amended by future studies. First, as we have noted, boyar families took pains to keep their fortunes intact. Whenever possible, men and women bequeathed their lands to their own sons, daughters, and grandchildren. Lacking direct heirs, they handed on their estates to more distant relatives or even, on occasion, godchildren or friends. By and large, however, they went to considerable pains to guarantee that their fortune stayed within the family (rod), however they defined that elusive concept. As our examples illustrate, a number of prominent seventeenth-century families succeeded brilliantly in holding on to and, indeed, increasing their wealth in land.

Secondly, royal favor contributed to their economic success. Clearly wealth accompanied high office and rank. Poverty and political obscurity likewise went hand in hand. In our period, however, the relationship between wealth and power seems to vary from one family to the next. Most of the Sheremetevs' estates were, by the seventeenth century, hereditary family possessions, while, at the opposite end of the scale, the Cherkasskiis' estates were all recent gifts of the crown.[67] Like them, the numerous "new men" of the seventeenth century owed their wealth primarily to high office or royal favor.

In the longer view, service in high office probably helped to make all three families wealthy. By 1613 the Sheremetevs could look back on a century and a half of service in Moscow and the resulting rewards. How many of their seventeenth-century estates they had earned through that service, however, is unclear and will probably remain so. The case of the Odoevskiis is a good deal simpler. By the seventeenth century they had lost touch with their ancestral homeland. Everything that they owned, then, was in some sense the product of their service in Moscow.

Finally, in this as in other respects, the seventeenth century was a very good time for the high nobility of Russia. In contrast with the confusion of the period of the oprichnina and the Time of Troubles, individual and family fortunes remained relatively stable and their fate predictable. The government of the early Romanovs provided the conditions in which many Duma families thrived. The tsars of the new dynasty gave generous grants to their favorites and supporters. At the same time, the new regime rarely interfered with the orderly transfer of family lands from one generation to the next. To be sure, there were spectacular confiscations; particularly in the last decades of the century, fallen favorites paid for their sins with exile and the loss of all of their property. Such cases, however, were highly exceptional. By and large, seventeenth-century governments helped Duma members to increase their fortunes and to pass them on intact to their descendants. By comparison with the recent past the seventeenth century was, in this respect, a golden age for the high nobility of Russia.

The economic prosperity of the nobles of Russia depended on their ability to get the most benefit from the natural resources and the labor under their control. The peasants were particularly important, for without them the land itself was essentially worthless. In judicial terms, then, the lord owed his well-being to the legislation that bound the peasants to his land. The political and legal process of enserfing the peasants reached its culmination only in the middle of the seventeenth century, in the Law Code of 1649. Nevertheless, the Ulozhenie seems to have made little change in the fabric of life on the noble estates. Clearly, even though most of our evidence comes from the latter half of the century, landlords' attitudes and practices appear to have remained essentially the same throughout the period.

How did Russian high nobles manage their estates? Thanks to the efforts of pre-revolutionary and Soviet historians, we can answer this question with some degree of confidence. There are several studies of

the estates of B. I. Morozov, an excellent book on those of A. I. Bezobrazov, and shorter works on N. I. Romanov, Prince N. I. Odoevskii,
and Prince I. A. Vorotynskii's widow as landowners.[68] The nature of the
published and archival sources sets definite limits to the value of these
works, excellent though they are. First, the surviving seventeenth-century documents on estate management do not preserve enough statistical
data to permit a systematic analysis of even one estate or the use of
economic models. What we have instead is a large number of impressions of the ways in which a high noble managed his lands. Secondly,
we have sources on these particular estates precisely because they were
exceptional; excluding Odoevskii's holdings, all soon ceased to exist as
economic units and escheated to the crown when Morozov, Romanov,
and Vorotynskaia died without heirs and when Bezobrazov fell into disgrace and was executed. Having recognized these problems, however,
we can still look at a remarkably detailed picture of seventeenth-century
estates, large and small.

Given the high quality of the existing studies, there is no need to
describe a typical estate. Instead, we will concentrate our attention on
the economic attitudes of seventeenth-century estate owners and the
concrete practices in which they implemented their ideas. What, in their
minds, were the principal resources that ownership of land gave them?
How, then, did they exploit those resources? To what extent was their
thinking traditional? Were they aware of new opportunities, and, if so,
how did they meet the challenge?

Before long, indeed, we will have to deal with questions that are not
strictly economic in the modern sense. By the definitions of their own
society, all of the landlords whom we are discussing were relatively
wealthy; in the eyes of contemporaries, Morozov was fabulously rich,
and even Bezobrazov was comfortably well off.[69] Yet, as we shall see,
the concept "wealth" had a somewhat different meaning for them than
it does for us. In addition, we must bear in mind that the dictates of
social custom influenced many of the high nobles' economic decisions
just as they do our own.

In the seventeenth century, managing extensive holdings was a complicated business. As we have observed, most prominent noble servitors
owned estates in several different parts of Russia. Moreover, a man like
Morozov or Bezobrazov was, first and foremost, a servitor of the crown.
As officers in the civil administration or the army, they had to remain in
Moscow or in the region to which they had been assigned. Indeed, as
far as we know, most Duma members remained in Moscow and its en-
virons as much as possible. Men like Bezobrazov who tried to retire from
service did not receive permission to do so; at the age of about 60, he

tried to retire to his favorite estate, but the government recalled him to service and kept him there in spite of his protests and his attempts to win his freedom through the intervention of influential friends.[70] Whether by choice or not, then, Russian high nobles managed their estates from afar.

The wealthiest landowners ran their estates from their residences in Moscow. Their administration was intensely personal. Morozov, Bezobrazov, Odoevskii, and Romanov—all took a deep interest in the detailed management of each of their properties. In the rhetoric of their business correspondence, peasants and local officials addressed petitions directly to them, and they often couched their replies in equally personal terms. At the same time, the enormity of the task of administering many properties forced them to hire staffs of subordinates. All of them except Bezobrazov employed a chief steward for the central Moscow office and presumably a small secretarial staff to assist him. On each of the main estates, the lord employed a local steward to report on the condition of the property and to carry out orders from the center. The stewards, usually bondslaves of Russian or foreign origin, owed their position to the lord's favor and had no choice but to put up with his whims. At the same time, as his representatives, they enjoyed arbitrary power over the peasants, tempered only by the threat that the latter might successfully appeal to the lord if they carried out their duties with excessive corruption or brutality. At the bottom of the chain of command were the peasant officials who collected some of the lord's revenues and the commune itself.[71]

In many respects, then, the administration of a large estate resembled the government of the Muscovite state. Like the tsar, Morozov or Bezobrazov theoretically exercised personal authority over his peasants. In reality, however, they worked in isolation in Moscow, dependent on local agents for their knowledge of conditions in the far corners of the realm. Moreover, it was only through the efforts of those local agents that their orders would have any effect. The problem of distance alone made the lord's personal authority, to a degree, an illusion. A conscientious or frightened local steward might well ask the lord for instructions on dealing with a problem which would be resolved for better or worse before there was time to receive an answer. Morozov saw the problem clearly. In 1651 he chastised the steward of an estate near Nizhnii-Novgorod for reporting a problem directly to the central office in Moscow rather than to his immediate superior, the steward in Murashkino, one of his large Arzamas properties; in an emergency, the steward in question could ride to Murashkino in two days, while it would take four or five weeks to receive an answer from Moscow.[72] Moreover, even when time and space did not make efficient administration of the lord's lands an impossibility, it was difficult to run the business entirely by correspondence. Romanov, for example, was uncomfortable with written documents and preferred to give his stewards a completely free hand.[73] Even a diligent lord, however, found that misunderstandings between himself and his stewards played havoc with the smooth operation of the estate. In one instance, Bezobrazov dressed down a semi-literate steward whose written reports he simply could not understand.[74]

In the light of these difficulties, the administration of the estates of the high nobles was understandably rudimentary. When a new steward took office, the lord issued him a list of instructions that must have seemed utopian; his duties, for example, included keeping the peasants from drinking excessively, smoking, and gambling.[75] When he fell short of these high expectations, the lord's only means of keeping him in line was a steady stream of recommendations, criticism, threats, and occasionally a public beating administered by other local officials.

In broad terms, all large landlords of the seventeenth century administered their estates in essentially the same way. At the same time, as the local stewards and peasants were well aware, the impact of the lord's administration varied subtly but significantly from one estate to another. As many scholars have observed, owners of very large estates could afford to be more flexible in their dealings with the peasants than their counterparts with more limited resources. Morozov was no saint; he was capable of vindictiveness and had a well-established reputation for greed.[76] Nevertheless, he showed a great deal of flexibility and restraint in managing his huge holdings; peasants in difficult circumstances often received temporary relief from their obligations to him.[77] Prince N. I. Odoevskii's attitude alternated between relative flexibility and unrelenting severity, depending on the condition of his financial affairs.[78] The lord's personality, of course, also colored his administration. An irascible disposition as well as comparatively limited resources made Bezobrazov a most unpleasant landlord. He demanded a great deal from his underlings and, when thwarted, unleashed on them torrents of obscenity remarkable even in seventeenth-century Muscovy.[79] Even in the best of circumstances, however, local officials and peasants remained ultimately powerless in the face of the lord's demands and whims.

With few exceptions, high noble landlords had a rudimentary understanding of the purpose and economic potential of their estates. Their attitude was frankly exploitative. Ownership of land gave them the right to use its natural resources and population as they saw fit. For the most part, moreover, they saw only the short-term advantages that their lands provided. Even the most ambitious lords like Morozov concentrated on exploiting these resources for their own immediate gain.[80]

In the lord's eyes, the peasants' first responsibility was to feed him and his household. He counted on his estates to meet all of his basic material needs. In all of the recorded cases, the lord's peasants provided his household with a wide variety of products—grain and flour of various types, meat, fish and poultry, eggs and dairy products. The peasants also provided simple manufactured products such as cloth and alcohol.[81]

Boyar landlords demanded both large quantities of such "table supplies" and high quality as well. From her largest estate, a unit with 770 peasant households in the fertile Lebedian' district of the black soil belt, Vorotynskaia received roughly 9 tons of pork, 500 sheep, 500 hens, 200 each of geese, ducks, and piglets, and more than 10,000 small carp, some alive and some already cleaned. The quantities of grain she received are also staggering—between 22 and 44 tons of rye, between 7 and 14 tons of rye malt, half that amount of oat groats, and smaller, but still considerable, amounts of wheat, and buckwheat and millet groats. Her peasants also presented her with lard, hemp oil, and alcohol. Unfortunately, we do not know the period of time during which Vorotynskaia collected these supplies.[82]

If the lord felt that the quality of his supplies was not high enough, his local stewards felt his wrath. In spite of the size and diversity of his estates, to say nothing of his duties in other spheres of life, Morozov devoted a considerable part of his surviving correspondence to the proper provisioning of his household. When mice nibbled into a shipment of ham, for example, he wrote a scathing rebuke to the steward whom he held responsible.[83] On another occasion, his Riazan' peasants complained that they could not catch their full norm of fish because of low water. Noting sarcastically that those peasants had earlier sold fish on the market, Morozov asked angrily, "How come there are no fish? The Oka is flowing as usual."[84]

Within each large landlord's portfolio of holdings, some estates played special roles. Morozov's Zvenigorod estate specialized in the raising of livestock and in growing fruits and vegetables for his table. Bezobrazov used his Vologda lands in the infertile north primarily as a source of hay; indeed, he instructed the peasants there to distill any surplus grain they had rather than trying to ship it to Moscow. This sensible recommendation must have been small comfort to peasants who still faced the formidable job of hauling hay roughly 280 miles from the Vologda area to the capital.

For his material well-being, the lord depended on the labor of his peasants. Many of the lord's supplies came from the peasants' own fields and livestock and were paid to the steward as dues in kind. Moreover, it was the peasants who had to transport the provisions to Moscow or to the country residence where the lord needed them.

Carting made heavy demands on the resources and time of the peasants. The lord expected them to provide their own horses and carts according to certain established norms and, if they would or could not do so, to make a payment of money as a substitute. Bezobrazov, a notorious cheapskate, took particular pains to see that the peasants used their own horses rather than his.[85] Peasants who brought their lord his provisions lost valuable time from their own activities; the trip from Bezobrazov's Belev estates to Moscow took between ten days and three weeks and the lord was not above employing the peasants for several days on projects in the city before letting them return home.[86]

Carting was only one of many forms of labor service (barshchina). All the lords whom we are discussing demanded that their peasants work for them in their fields, in making hay and cutting wood on the common lands of the estate, on construction projects, and in any industrial enterprise in which the lord might be engaged.[87] The amount of barshchina required varied from lord to lord and from region to region. On Bezobrazov's lands, for example, the peasants worked for him between two and four days a week on the average.[88]

Barshchina allowed the lords to set aside part of their land as their own demesne. Morozov designated about 33 percent of the arable land on his estates for his own purposes.[89] Understandably, the proportion of a given property that the lord exploited directly varied from one region to another; by and large, the lord's demesne was larger in the fertile regions to the south and east of Moscow. On some northern estates, there might be no demesne at all.[90]

Like their eighteenth-century successors, seventeenth-century lords were prisoners of traditional attitudes and routine. The peasants who worked the land usually grew the same crops with the same techniques they used on their own plots. As far as we know, they usually planted the staple grain crops. As a result, some lords, notably Morozov and Bezobrazov, produced a surplus of grain which they sold on the market.[91] Indeed, if a recent study is correct, Morozov's operations may represent a conscious attempt to expand grain production in his demesne in order to respond to the demands of the market.[92] Even if this hypothesis is correct, however, Morozov departed from the traditional practices of his fellow lords to only a very limited extent.

In addition to produce and labor, the peasants provided their lords with cash. All the lords for whom we have detailed studies collected money rent (obrok) from some of their peasants. Bezobrazov, whose operations were comparatively small and primitive, collected money rent from only two of the eleven separate estates in his holdings.[93] On the other hand, Morozov collected money obrok from all his many estates. While precise figures are not available, it would seem that Morozov and Bezobrazov collected one ruble per year from each peasant household.[94] Romanov apparently demanded considerably less from most of his peasants.[95] To judge by these figures, then, Morozov stood to collect up to 9,000 rubles a year in cash at the height of his fortunes. We know for certain that, in 1650, Odoevskii collected a little over 325 rubles from his Galich peasants who, three years earlier, numbered 517 households.[96] Even at the more modest rate suggested by these figures, then, the richest landowners of Russia collected large amounts of cash from their peasants.

These obrok payments loomed large in the lives of lords and peasants alike. They were the lord's only regular source of cash, except for official salaries and other perquisites of high office which, in any case, they may not have collected regularly. Yet the boyars could not live without a considerable cash income. Even Vorotynskaia, who ran an austere and old-fashioned household, regularly bought items like vinegar, lemons, and caviar on the market and, at times, had to buy staples in order to supplement the inadequate supplies from her estates in order to feed her city household.[97] Moreover, as we shall see, to live like a boyar required cash to support oneself while on a service assignment, to buy luxury goods, to pay the salaries of hired craftsmen and household dependents, and to perform conspicuous acts of charity. The more ambitious the boyar, the more money he needed.

The lord's needs put heavy pressure on the peasants. They lived in an essentially natural economy and yet had somehow to make enough money to pay obrok to their lords and taxes to the state as well. Since the lord's demands for labor service prevented most peasants from leaving the estate on which they lived, their main hope of raising money was to sell their surplus grain or other produce on the market.[98] Often the lord's demands for cash seemed overwhelming. The extant estate documents resound with the complaints and pleas of peasants who insisted that their assessment of obrok was excessive and could not possibly be paid.[99] From their side, the lords doggedly struggled to extract the money owed them. When the lord needed money urgently, he hounded his peasants with particular ferocity, as Odoevskii's correspondence makes clear.[100]

As the high nobles were well aware, the peasants on their lands were their main economic resource. The land itself, however, also provided benefits besides tillable soil—in particular forests, lakes and rivers, and minerals. These natural resources the lords exploited in the same direct

manner in which they treated the peasants. The forests provided fuel
and timber for lord and peasant alike. Fish from the estate occupied a
prominent place on the lord's table. It was a vital source of animal pro-
tein for the entire population, particularly in seasons when the Eastern
Orthodox Church's regulations on fasting prohibited meat. The boyars
regarded the finest fish as great delicacies; when preparing to entertain
Tsar Aleksei Mikhailovich, Morozov gave his stewards particularly detailed instructions to ensure that his larder was well supplied.[101]

High noble landlords made some attempts to improve upon nature.
In order to raise and preserve fish, Morozov and Bezobrazov both built
artificial ponds on their main estates. Both also took care to develop
orchards, particularly around their favorite country residences. Morozov
frequently instructed his stewards as to when and how to graft new limbs
onto his fruit trees.[102] In these cases, the lord did his best to improve
the quality and regularity of the supply of food for his own consumption.
The market played no role in his planning.

Many of the processed goods from the estate likewise served the lord's
household. When the peasants distilled vodka from surplus grain or wove
cloth, they worked within the limits of a natural economy.

Seventeenth-century noble estates produced only one commodity primarily for the market—potash. One of the earliest industrial chemicals,
potash had many uses in the seventeenth century. It was especially important in the manufacture of soap and glass. Russia had ideal conditions
for its production—a limitless supply of wood and a labor force that could
be made to work in very unpleasant conditions. In the latter half of the
century, a number of boyars took advantage of their opportunities. I. D.
Miloslavskii, Prince Iu. P. Trubetskoi, Prince N. I. Odoevskii, the Cherkasskiis, and the Rtishchevs all produced potash.[103] The Rtishchevs' venture, however, quickly collapsed because of the disruption caused by the
war with Poland and by peasant unrest.[104]

All of these lords' efforts paled before Morozov's. He took energetic
steps to develop production in his Arzamas and Nizhnii-Novgorod estates, especially the village of Sergach. His stewards received very detailed instructions from their lord, backed up by the usual stream of
threats. Morozov scolded one of them severely, for example, for waiting
until June to begin preparing oak ash, the raw material from which potash was made.[105] His peasants also paid the price of his ambition. Most
of the workers at the potash sites were serfs performing barshchina. They
bitterly resented this assignment and plagued the stewards by complain-
ing or by simply fleeing. As their resistance mounted, Morozov had to
turn increasingly to the practice of hiring workers on salary. In particular, in 1660, he recruited 346 workers from his Galich estates and sent

them to the potash works. Apparently they performed their duties well, unlike local peasants performing labor service, but their presence did not change the basic nature of the enterprise.[106]

Morozov's operation rested on the foundation of serfdom. His estates symbolized the position of the boyar elite as a whole. The entire group's prosperity rested, in part, on its members' control over the serfs on their lands. As Morozov discovered, the peasants bitterly resented their lords' demands and resisted as best they could. Most of the time, they took small and undramatic steps to defend themselves. On occasion, however, the peasants' resentment poured forth in massive revolts that momentarily swept away the power of the landlords and the government which supported them. In 1670-1671, the peasants of Morozov's former properties near the Volga enthusiastically joined the jacquerie led by Sten'ka Razin.[107] As he probably realized, a man like Morozov lived on a powder keg.

For the moment, however, Morozov was surely pleased with the results of his industrial efforts. At the high point in their development, his potash works produced roughly 1,400 to 1,600 tons annually.[108] The profits from the venture were equally impressive. First of all, potash was in great demand; Morozov apparently had no trouble selling his product to the Muscovite government and to foreign merchants. Secondly, the costs of production remained relatively low. Morozov had to pay for the simple equipment used in the manufacture, the salaries of the hired workers, and the costs of transporting the finished product to Moscow or the northern ports. At the same time, he had free access to the basic raw material—wood—and to the forced labor of most of his workers. Finally, the government supported him by granting him exemption from internal tariffs on his shipments of potash. With all of these advantages, a recent study concludes, Morozov regularly made a profit of at least 50 percent on his investment in the potash industry.[109]

Morozov's one other venture in manufacturing ended in failure. In the mid-1640s he invested briefly in the company founded by the Dutchman Vinnius to exploit the deposits of iron ore in the Tula area. A few years later, Morozov tried to establish his own iron factory on his estate, Pavlovskoe, in the Zvenigorod district near Moscow. The venture, however, did not bring him success. Apparently the local ore was of low grade, and the estate's production remained irregular and small. Indeed, Morozov had to buy iron products on the market.[110]

Although limited, Morozov's entrepreneurial efforts made him an exception among the boyars. For the most part, high noble landlords managed their estates in a very traditional way. As we have seen, they stayed within the confines of a natural economy, relying on their land and the labor of their peasants for most of the necessities of life.

Like their eighteenth-century descendants, the boyars shared the attitudes of their peasants toward farming.[111] By and large, they were content to let the peasants grow the traditional crops, especially rye and oats, in the traditional way. As a consequence, the productivity of their lands remained low. On Morozov's estates, for example, the rye crop ranged between 2.5 and 5.2 times the amount of seed sown; the yield of oats fluctuated between 2.1 and 5.4 to one.[112] Attempts to improve the situation usually followed traditional peasant practice; most commonly, the lord and his staff expanded the area of land cultivated when they sought to increase the amount of food and feed at their disposal.[113] A few lords made very limited attempts to introduce new crops or forms of animal husbandry. In these respects, however, private landlords launched fewer new ventures than the managers of Tsar Aleksei's estates.[114] On the whole, then, the boyars let peasant tradition govern their estate management. As landlords they had two main concerns. First, they saw to it that their peasants continued to farm; in a bad year, even the most rapacious of them loaned the peasants seed grain for the following season.[115] Secondly, they made sure that their stewards extracted from the estate the supplies, money, and labor needed to support them and their households. However limited their vision, the boyars knew full well that their primary resource was not, strictly speaking, economic at all. It was their legal and administrative control over their peasants.

This power of coercion supported a wasteful style of life. Although the boyars' extravagance paled before the prodigality of their eighteenth-century descendants, many features of their public and private lives played havoc with their household economy. As we shall see in greater detail, being a boyar demanded a certain style of life. Whenever possible, high noble families owned one or several houses in Moscow, and a number of prominent individuals began to develop their suburban properties into country residences fit for a tsar. Wherever they lived, their social standing demanded that they be surrounded by large numbers of servants who had little to do.[116] Swollen household staffs devoured the lord's resources, for, in addition to paying their miserable salaries, he had to feed and clothe them from the production of his estates. Moreover, the boyars' life style included entertaining and taking part in public ceremonies, both of which required fine clothes as well as suitable provisions for the table. All these expenses, of course, were part of the price of being a noble anywhere in Europe.

Secondly, being socially prominent members of the Russian Orthodox Church had its cost. Whether personally pious or not, all Duma members apparently gave considerable sums to their favorite monasteries in return for prayers for their souls and for those of their departed relatives. A number of them built and maintained parish churches and monasteries. Moreover, some, like Vorotynskaia, supported groups of poor dependents in their homes as an act of Christian charity.[117] All these activities, however laudable, cost money.

Finally—and perhaps strangest from our point of view—boyar households accumulated remarkable quantities of "dead capital." Wills and lists of confiscated property mention large numbers of rich brocade robes, icons with lavish jewelled covers, gold and silver ceremonial vessels, and richly decorated swords and guns suitable only for show. Heirlooms provide aesthetic pleasure and stimulate family pride in many societies. In comparison to the other economic resources of a seventeenth-century boyar household, however, their number and value seem wastefully high. Moreover, like the man of one talent in the parable, some boyars simply hid their treasures away. N. I. Romanov, for example, kept thousands of rubles in cash in chests in his cellar.[118] Vorotynskaia went even further; at one point, after selling off some of the linen woven by her peasants, she still kept more than four miles of the cloth in her storehouse![119] These examples illustrate particularly well the essentially passive attitude of the boyars toward their economic resources and opportunities.

Such behavior points up the difficulty that we face in explaining how rich the boyars really were. On the surface, people like Morozov, Prince N. I. Odoevskii, and Vorotynskaia had great wealth in land. They were undoubtedly the envy of almost all their contemporaries. At the same time, as we have seen, much of their wealth took unproductive forms, and their values and style of life regularly ate away at the roots of their prosperity. Many fell into debt; at the same time, they were models of financial responsibility and solvency as compared to their descendants in the following century. Moreover, many of them, including Odoevskii and Vorotynskaia, often suffered from an embarrassing shortage of ready cash. On several occasions, Odoevskii admitted that he desperately needed money, and Vorotynskaia was reduced to borrowing from her chief steward.[120] Indeed, of all the landowners whose estates are the subject of special studies, only Morozov seems to have made frequent use of large sums of cash; we know, for example, that he occasionally loaned large sums of money to the wealthiest of his peasants.[121]

Most boyars, then, had great wealth, but not in easily negotiable form. What their large estates gave them was material comfort and security. They knew that, as long as they had control over an adequate number of peasants, they and their dependents would have enough to eat and a solid roof over their heads. That very knowledge reduced most boyars to exploiting the natural resources and inhabitants of their estates simply and directly. Only exceptional men like Morozov tried to take advantage of even the very limited opportunities for initiative offered by the economy of seventeenth-century Russia. Even in cases like his, moreover, new ventures constituted only a small part of a simple and traditional economic system.

In the final analysis, the boyars' wealth sprang from their political and social eminence. The prevailing system of state service, the nature of social relationships, and the policies of the government of the early Romanovs all helped the most prominent men and families of Russia to maintain or even to increase their wealth in land. As the fund of available land steadily grew, old aristocratic families like the Sheremetevs kept their fortunes, and parvenus used their influence to get rich. In the economic sphere the seventeenth century was a good time for the boyars.

Juan Carreño de Miranda. Portrait of the Russian ambassador to Spain,
Peter Ivanovich Potemkin.

The Palm Sunday celebration of Christ's entry into Jerusalem.

The tsar and his courtiers receiving a foreign embassy.

Prince V. V. Golitsyn's palace.

The Church of the Holy
Trinity, Ostankino. Photo by
Dr. Jack E. Kollmann.

The Church of the Savior, Ubory.

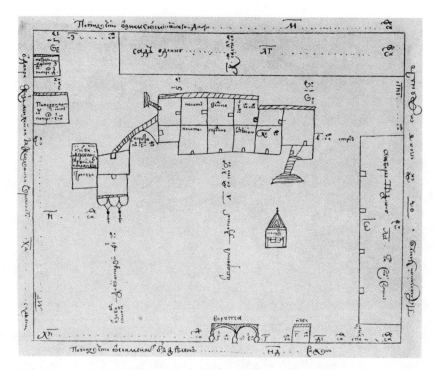

The house and yard of V. I. Streshnev in Moscow.

A boyar's estate, Nikol'skoe, near Moscow.

Semen Uskakov's icon, "Christ, the Great Hierarch."

CHAPTER VI

Courtiers and Christians

Any study of the boyars must come to grips with a paradox. We cannot understand how and why they acted without taking into account their beliefs and values. At the same time, given the nature of our sources, their assumptions and attitudes often appear most clearly in their deeds. We must therefore look at their style of life and their relations to one another, to the court and to the church, in order to learn how they saw themselves in their roles as the tsars' leading subjects and as members of the Eastern Orthodox fold.

This chapter will consist of a series of brief sketches of several important features of the boyars' public and private lives. When seen together, they will, I hope, form an impressionistic picture of the mental and spiritual world in which the boyars lived.

People of our day enter the boyars' world like visitors from another universe. As we read the records of their time, we are struck by attitudes and customs which they frequently took for granted. Yet it is precisely these most obvious features of their lives and view of the world that best explain their behavior.

To an outsider, the boyars seem insecure and obsessed with the defense of their honor and social standing. Their history as a group and the conditions of their life in the seventeenth century go a long way toward explaining their attitudes. As we have seen, even the most aristocratic clans of Russia had long served the ruler and depended on his favor for rank, offices, and much of their landed wealth. In the seventeenth century, royal favor played an even larger and less predictable role than before. The new dynasty, former aristocrats themselves, honored and rewarded their relatives and favorites, and the most powerful of their ministers did the same. A considerable number of the most prominent courtiers in the latter half of the century were men who owed everything to the tsar's personal friendship or respect. On the negative side, the disfavor of Ivan IV had brought distinguished and powerful men to a horrible and humiliating death. Under the early Romanovs very few boyars suffered such a fate, but the memory of sixteenth-century atrocities must have remained fresh. Moreover, even in the seventeenth—the best of times—individual Duma members might suffer disgrace, or even execution, and whole clans could sink into oblivion.

Court literature of the late seventeenth century underlined the lessons of life itself. The poems and plays composed at the court of Aleksei praise the tsar as the source of harmony in the world. Yet the royal power provides only a measure of coherence in a dark and threatening universe. Disaster stalks the individual, and chaos looms before the people as a whole. Happiness is fleeting; the smallest change in a man's condition can bring complete disaster. Indeed, the benevolent tsar might himself be the source of calamity; for, if royal favor made a man powerful, its loss would bring his destruction, as Aman, the villain of the Play of Artaxerxes, discovered to his rue.[1]

In short, despite the boyars' prominence and power over society, they had very limited control over their own fate. No wonder their conduct shows many signs of insecurity and defensiveness!

The scene is a familiar one. The tsar and his courtiers gather in a banquet hall in the Kremlin palace. One of the nobles present loudly objects to his assigned place at the table, on the grounds that it demeans him and his family. At the tsar's command, attendants force him, kicking and screaming, to take his place. When kicks and screams prove useless, he goes limp and slides to the floor.[2]

We have seen one of the more colorful manifestations of mestnichestvo or precedence ranking. Historians have written volumes about its workings and its impact on the functioning of the royal administration.[3] In theory, the tsars' leading courtiers and servitors occupied rungs on an unwritten but clearly understood ladder of precedence. Ancestry, genealogical position within his own family, and his family's record of service, particularly in recent times, combined to determine each man's position in the social and service hierarchy.

As I have argued elsewhere, in the seventeenth century the system's impact was essentially negative and its importance primarily psychological. Most of all, men feared to accept a military assignment or sit at a place at the dinner table that would set a precedent lowering their families' social standing and prospects in service. Rather than tolerate such dishonor, they fought back fiercely with angry words and formal lawsuits. The court registers of the century, particularly those for the reign of Tsar Mikhail, record large numbers of such obscure legal quarrels.

That the boyars engaged in them is an indication of the seriousness with which they guarded their honor, for, in practical terms, litigation carried great risks and brought very limited rewards. At best, a man might receive the judgment that he stood higher on the ladder of precedence than his rival. On balance, however, the scales of justice tilted heavily to the negative side. At the very least, a litigant lost time and effort and probably money for fees or bribes as well. Moreover, he ran the risk of embarrassment when judges examined his family's genealogical claims and past record of service. The case might also lead to a public exchange of insults with his rivals in the presence of the court.[4] A man who lost a case suffered much more than mere embarrassment. Most often a litigant who insulted a superior by raising false claims of precedence suffered the humiliation of being ceremonially surrendered (*vydan golovoiu*) to his opponent, or of going to jail for two or three days, or the physical pain of a beating. Occasionally an unsuccessful litigant spent several years under a cloud waiting for his next assignment in service, and, in the most extreme case, that of Prince I. V. Golitsyn, lost his estates and was exiled from the capital for the rest of his life.[5] Yet litigate they did, stubbornly and vehemently!

With the exception of a few combative individuals, Duma members ran these risks as part of a strategy of self-defense. They preferred to avoid litigation if they could do so without compromising their standing. Sometimes, when they received postings in service, they asked the government to state officially that their assignments would not serve as precedents in future disputes.[6] Moreover, entire areas of official life and whole categories of people lay outside the precedence hierarchy. Disputes usually arose from military service and court ceremonies; postings in the chanceries, the most sought-after assignments, had no bearing on a man's standing. As a result, chancery officials had no place on the precedence hierarchy, although, on occasion, they refused to recognize that fact. The same is true of the vast majority of the traditional military nobility whose family origins or recent record of service held them below the bottom rung of the ladder. At the opposite extreme, royal in-laws and favorites remained safe from challenges to their standing, in practice if not in theory. Since the tsar was the final judge of precedence disputes, courtiers quickly learned the futility of challenging those who enjoyed his personal protection.[7]

Most boyars would, I suspect, have been glad to escape the mestnichestvo system altogether. When Tsar Aleksei's government took a stern attitude toward precedence disputes, the number of such clashes fell dramatically.[8] Even more remarkably, the proposal to abolish the system of rankings aroused no opposition of which I am aware.[9] The leading families of the court had apparently discovered that mestnichestvo was a poor weapon in the struggle to defend their honor. The government's commitment to maintain official genealogies of the finest families of the realm gave promise of accomplishing the same end at far less risk to the boyars and far less cost to all concerned.

In many respects, precedence disputes were duels, only without bloodshed. At the same time, they lacked the glamor of swordplay. While no less concerned with defending their honor than their counterparts elsewhere in Europe, the high nobles of Russia had no love for brilliant chivalric gestures. The taste for dueling captured the Russian aristocracy at a later date. In the seventeenth century, the boyars preferred to defend themselves in ways that were less dramatic, but far more reliable.

Mestnichestvo served as a channel for the boyars' feelings of anger, jealousy, and wounded pride; it did not cause them. We meet expressions of the same feelings in their private letters. Both the forms of address and the contents of their correspondence reveal their sense of their own vulnerability.

Their concern for their honor appears in many contexts. Servitors frequently petitioned for raises in their salaries and allotments of service lands, on the grounds that they were being dishonored by receiving less than colleagues of similar background with the same records of service.[10] Private letters reveal the same anxiety. In her correspondence with her son, Prince V. V. Golitsyn's mother expressed concern not only about his health and safety, but also about his standing in service. With her usual delicacy, she scolded him for accepting the celebrated general, Prince G. G. Romodanovskii, as a colleague without protest.[11]

As they were well aware, the members of the boyar elite occupied an intermediate position between the state which they served and the lower orders of society over whom they enjoyed virtually unlimited power. When addressing the throne, they customarily adopted a self-effacing tone, referring to themselves as the tsar's slaves and using a lower-class form of their names—a nickname and surname without the patronymic, the sign of social distinction.[12]

They vented their anger and frustration on their social inferiors. Toward such people—their stewards, for example—they behaved arrogantly, pouring forth threats and demands and sometimes lapsing into language that would make a peasant blush. Landlords punished insubordinate peasants severely, and, in a particularly dramatic instance, Prince Iu. A. Dolgorukii and his fellow commanders treated captured survivors of the Razin revolt with savage cruelty.[13] The boyars knew their place in the cosmic scheme of things and made sure that their inferiors did not forget theirs.

The position and attitudes of the chancery officials within the Duma are harder to determine. The fact that they owed their rank and power to their expertise probably gave them a secure sense of their position in society. At the same time, that place was distinctly inferior to that of the tsar's aristocratic courtiers. As such, their social standing did not accurately reflect their importance to the government or their power to shape other men's lives. To judge by their actions, their solution to this anomaly had two prongs. First, they took care to distinguish themselves from the other non-aristocratic groups in society. For example, L. D. Lopukhin petitioned the government to guarantee that he, as a chancery official, would not be dishonored if prominent merchants signed the Code of 1649 above him and his colleagues.[14] Secondly, the most prominent officials took steps to duplicate the aristocrats' style of life and to win, through the marriages of their children, recognition that they had reached the pinnacle of Muscovite society.

For its part, the government of Muscovy appealed to the Duma members' need for recognition with an elaborate system of symbolic, as well as practical, rewards. Often it combined the two. Many times during the century, the tsar received successful generals or diplomats, home from the field, congratulated them, and gave them gifts, including luxurious fur coats or robes, furs, gold coins and goblets, or drinking cups, as well as a raise in their salaries and allotments of service land.[15] In purely material terms, the gifts were not to be sneezed at. The items of clothing and the pelts were very valuable, and, at their best, the vessels not only contained a considerable quantity of silver, but reached very high standards of craftsmanship.[16] If the surviving inventories of the boyars' personal effects are any indication, the recipients treasured these royal gifts and added them to their families' collections of heirlooms.[17]

On some occasions, men being promoted or rewarded in other ways for their achievements received formal documents outlining their careers or describing their personal qualities in the most flattering light. They must have been deeply moved by these generous expressions of royal favor.[18] In moments of tragedy, Aleksei Mikhailovich sometimes wrote his courtiers far more personal letters of consolation. He informed Prince N. I. Odoevskii of the sudden death of his eldest son, Mikhail, and urged him to ". . . hope in God, His Most Pure Mother and all the saints and rely on us, the Great Sovereign. If God wills, we will not abandon you. . . ."[19]

Purely ceremonial gestures spoke almost as eloquently. The very fact of an individual or group audience with the tsar told the returning warriors or diplomats that the ruler appreciated their performance. When the government wanted to encourage commanders in the field, it chose a young courtier to travel to the front to bring the tsar's congratulations on recent victories or simply to "ask about the health" of the generals.[20]

Such gestures undoubtedly gave the recipients a sense of their importance and worth and the conviction that the tsar and his ministers recognized and valued their efforts. Moreover, they provided an excellent opportunity for the monarch to remind his subjects of the divine origin of his prerogatives. In language very similar to the rhetoric of absolute monarchs to the west, these ceremonial statements stressed that, as God's agent, the tsar presided over an orderly and just universe in which virtue had its reward. As Tsar Aleksei remarked in scolding V. B. Sheremetev for his arrogant attitude, even the rank of boyar itself "is awarded through the will of the great and eternal Tsar and heavenly Lord and not mortal appointment."[21] To the government, the cost of maintaining such comforting and encouraging impressions was very small if it helped to keep the boyars content with their lot in service. One measure of the degree to which Tsar Aleksei's servitors believed these messages is the profound bitterness of men like Ordin-Nashchokin and A. S. Matveev when they came to believe that the tsar no longer gave adequate recognition to their efforts on his behalf.

On April 10, 1636, a foreign visitor standing on Red Square in Moscow saw the following scene:
". . . the Grand Prince . . . emerged from the Kremlin, with the Patriarch, in a solemn procession. In front on a very large, wide, low-slung wagon was carried a tree to which were fastened many apples, figs, and raisins. By the tree sat four boys in white shirts, singing Hosannahs. Behind them came many priests in white choir robes and costly ecclesiastical vestments, carrying banners, crosses, and ikons, on long staffs, and singing in unison. Some of them held censers, which they swung toward the people. Following them were the foremost merchants or gosti, the d'iaki, the scribes, the secretaries, and, last of all, the princes and boyars, some of them carrying palm branches."[22]

After attending a service in one of the sanctuaries that made up St. Basil's, the tsar and his retinue stopped to pray at the Lobnoe Mesto on the square, then reenacted the drama of Christ's triumphant entry into Jerusalem. The tsar, as leader of the secular arm, played the subordinate role. In the part of Jesus, the patriarch sat sidesaddle on a horse, blessing the onlookers, while the tsar walked in front, leading the animal by the reins. With the accompanying host of ecclesiastical and lay dignitaries, the central figures in the pageant reentered the Kremlin, where they concluded the celebration of Palm Sunday.[23]

The members of the Duma played an important supporting role in many dramas like this one. When they were in the capital, they lived by the rhythm of the tsar's court and spent many hours in his entourage in the churches and palaces of the Kremlin or on tour of charitable institutions and monasteries in the vicinity of Moscow.

The ceremonial life of the Russian court revolved around the person of the ruler and presented him as the epitome of the benevolent and pious ruler. His daily routine conformed to a rigid schedule of religious and secular activities. Like his contemporary, Louis XIV, Aleksei Mikhailovich was almost always on stage and so were his courtiers. The tsar arose early in the morning and, after private prayers, attended matins with his wife in their private chapel. Meanwhile, the members of the Duma gathered in the palace. When the tsar appeared, they bowed low before him, then accompanied him to a nearby church for a celebration of the liturgy. Only after they had finished their public devotions did the ruler and his counsellors get down to the affairs of state. After a break for dinner and a siesta at home, the members of the Duma often returned to the palace for an evening session.[24] Whether or not most of them had much to contribute to the governing of Russia, they certainly kept busy attending the ruler and listening to reports on the condition of the realm.

The tsar's courtiers lived by a second recurring pattern of ceremonies as well—that of the liturgical calendar of Eastern Orthodoxy. The Palm Sunday procession was only one of many dramatic highlights of the Christian year. Easter, Epiphany, Christmas, and other holy days had special observances in which Duma members were expected to participate.[25] Indeed, to be absent without good cause was a punishable offense.[26] Finally, the life of the court turned on the great events in the life of the imperial family—coronations, marriages, and funerals. Elaborate public rituals marked each of these occasions.

The continuous round of liturgical ceremonies spoke to the tsar's subjects, great and obscure alike, in the language of Eastern Orthodox piety. The tsar appeared as the pious servant of God and the defender of His flock on earth. As such, he had the right to demand the loyalty and obedience of the faithful whom God had entrusted to him.

The Duma members' presence at official ceremonies served to reinforce these impressions. If the ruler's most mighty subjects bowed before him and followed in his train, how much more should lesser mortals obey him?

On one type of occasion, I would argue, the public posture of the ruler and his courtiers articulated a distinctly different message. In the surviving pictures of the tsars' formal audiences for foreign ambassadors, the monarch sat on his throne only a little higher than the Duma members who were present.[27] Without doubt, the tsar was head of state. At the same time, the spatial arrangements suggested, he did not negotiate in isolation but with the support of his people, whose leading representatives appeared as his junior colleagues. This image corresponded particularly closely to the political and personal realities of the seventeenth-century court.

For most of the century, social life at court revolved around official banquets. As the court registers testify, the tsar and the patriarch both regularly wined and dined large numbers of guests. As hosts, the emperors tried to create an impression of magnificence and lend an aura of dignity to the proceedings. In Aleksei Mikhailovich's time, in particular, the ruler's piety and sense of decorum made these dinners dignified affairs, a far cry from the notorious parties of Ivan IV.[28] In the banquet hall, displays of the royal plate dazzled the guests.[29] Servants brought them staggering quantities of food and drink.[30] At the same time, the dinners followed precise norms of etiquette and ritual.[31] The courtiers who received invitations to dine with the tsar must have been flattered, especially if they were guests of honor on the occasion in question. After they had attended scores of these functions, however, they may well have greeted the ruler's summons with as much resignation as joy.

For Duma members, participation in court ceremonies was a privilege that brought practical advantages and psychological rewards. To begin with, it underlined their superiority to other strata of society. Only the most powerful or favored individuals had the right to enter the imperial palace and, even more remarkably, the tsar's private apartments. Lesser courtiers could advance to the palace porch but no farther.[32]

Moreover, as in other societies, the clothes that they wore on formal occasions marked the aristocracy off from the poorer sort.[33] Boyar families treasured their lavish fur-trimmed brocade robes and, if they had none, turned to the government rather than appear in court in attire that was unsuitably modest. For its part, the royal administration loaned the needy costumes from its treasury so that they would make a suitably dignified impression on their fellow citizens and on foreign dignitaries.[34]

In a far broader sense, taking part in the ritual observances of the court gave the boyars a heightened sense of their own worth and the reassurance that the tsar and his closest advisers recognized their distinguished qualities. As in other courts, some ceremonial functions carried more weight than others. The courtiers who walked beside the tsar and helped him hold the reins during the Palm Sunday ceremony must have felt particularly honored. Likewise, the men and women who took prominent parts in royal coronations and weddings probably felt a particularly deep sense of satisfaction. On a more mundane level, at dinner, receiving a choice morsel directly from the tsar's hand was understood as a clear sign of favor.[35]

Life at court brought practical advantages as well as symbolic rewards. The courtiers lived at the nerve center of political and social life. The core of the royal administration, the most important chanceries, had its offices right in the Kremlin. Moreover, for many ambitious nobles, winning the favor of the tsar or of his chief adviser provided the key to advancement. Seventeenth-century courtiers had to endure interminable services in icy churches and to sit through endless ceremonies and meetings.[36] The exertions were the price they paid for a crucial advantage—physical proximity to those who could "make the lesser great."

Even the best-connected aristocrat felt isolated and vulnerable when on assignment far from Moscow. Prince V. V. Golitsyn's letters from the southern front reveal a thirst for news of court life and anxiety about being cut off from the central source of power in society.[37] As Golitsyn was well aware, a man could do little to defend himself from his enemies at court if he stayed away too long.

Finally, we will turn for a moment to a group to which we have devoted very little attention—the women of the Russian high nobility. By and large, social convention limited their activity to their own households and families. There they could wield considerable influence, particularly over the disposition of property which they had inherited or brought into their marriage as a dowry. Outside the home, the court and the church provided the main avenues to power. A number of noble ladies served in the household of the empress, where they came into daily contact with the person closest to the tsar himself. How well they used their opportunities is, of course, impossible to determine. The influence of a woman like Anna Petrovna Khitrovo, housekeeper to several successive tsaritsas and nanny to their sons, must have been considerable.[38]

In order to keep in daily contact with the court, Duma members lived in Moscow.[39] A few of the most privileged had palaces inside the hallowed walls of the Kremlin. Throughout the seventeenth century, the Trubetskois owned a large property in the center of the complex. Other buildings changed hands more rapidly, passing between some of the most distinguished of the boyars—F. I. Sheremetev, Prince N. I. Odoevskii, B. I. Morozov, Prince B. M. Lykov, and two of the Cherkasskiis.[40] Two fathers-in-law of tsars flaunted their newly exalted status by living in the same distinguished neighborhood.[41] Despite the distinction of their owners, however, boyar properties in the Kremlin tended to fall into the hands of the royal administration or neighboring monasteries over the course of time.

The vast majority of the boyar elite lived in other parts of the city. The fragmentary evidence available indicates that present and future Duma members lived in many different districts. Indeed, the wealthiest and most powerful men owned more than one property in Moscow. In addition to his palace in the Kremlin, Prince Ia. K. Cherkasskii bought a house in St. Nicholas parish and owned garden plots on either side of the outer defense perimeter on the northern outskirts of the city.[42] At the time of his fall from power, Prince V. V. Golitsyn owned a large palace just across from the northwest corner of the Kremlin, a more modest house farther west on Arbat Street, a property on the Smolensk road, and gardens southwest and east of town.[43]

Outside the Kremlin, the Duma members' neighborhoods were anything but exclusive. In 1629, in the section west of the Kremlin where they tended to congregate, their properties were scattered among those of chancery officials and clerks, lesser nobles, and commanders of strel'tsy. For the good of its residents' souls, this one relatively small area had thirty-three churches and three monasteries. Within the district some residents lived better than others; several boyars or boyars-to-be—Prince I. I. Shuiskii, Princes A. V. Khilkov and I. A. Khovanskii, V. I. Streshnev, B. I. Morozov, and I. N. Romanov—owned exceptionally large properties in particularly good locations.[44] The east side of town was apparently less densely settled and had an even more motley population. The likes of F. I. Sheremetev lived near lesser nobles, employees of the bureaucracy, priests, ordinary townsmen, artisans like jewellers, furriers, and silversmiths, and foreigners, particularly military officers. Once again there were churches and monasteries in all corners of the district.[45]

The size of their houses distinguished Duma members from their less fortunate neighbors.[46] In most cases, their arrangement and architectural style were essentially the same as the houses of other prosperous citizens.

When Duma members built their city homes, they aimed at solidity and practicality rather than magnificence. For most of the seventeenth century, the typical house stood in the center of a large lot, surrounded by a fence or wall. The visitor entered the complex through a large gate leading from the street and passed stables, sheds, workshops, and servants' quarters before reaching the house itself. Orchards and gardens took up much of the yard. Evidently prominent Muscovites aimed at making each large house as nearly self-sufficient as possible.[47]

The finest homes consisted of two stories of living quarters above a ground floor used primarily for storage. Over the course of the sixteenth and seventeenth centuries, the wealthiest Russians gradually replaced wooden dwellings with brick structures and incorporated some of the decorative elements that the new medium made possible. In a number of instances, boyars maintained their own house chapels, and these, located very near the family dwelling, shared many of the same stylistic features.[48]

Despite their lack of striking originality or elegance of design, the best of the Duma members' houses created an impression of power and grandeur. The lavish decoration and appointments of Prince V. V. Golitsyn's mansion, just across from the Kremlin, testified to its owner's ambition and exalted taste.[49] Indeed, as a recently published study shows, Golitsyn's fall interrupted extensive remodelling of the house, aimed at making it grander.[50] The house of the Kirillovs, financiers and chancery officials, eloquently reflected their wealth and solid practicality.[51] In rebuilt form, it stands as one of the sights of old Moscow. Toward the end of the century, moreover, the boyars' architects began to build houses along new lines. The Troekurov house, near Golitsyn's, had its facade right on the street and followed a more unified architectural plan than more traditional residences.[52] It served to advertise its owner's standing in the world simply and effectively.

The Duma members' houses in Moscow stood as eloquent testimony to their privileges, power, and wealth. They continually reminded less fortunate Muscovites of the realities of social and political life. As such, they could become easy targets of popular resentment. In times of unrest—in 1648 and 1682, for example—rioters attacked and sacked the houses of unpopular aristocrats and chancery officials as symbols of their arbitrary power and ill-gotten wealth. In spite of their solidity, the Duma members' Moscow homes provided no guarantee of peace and security in a troubled world.

Within their residences, the boyars cultivated a style of life that emphasized their distinctiveness from the rest the population. Like the nobles elsewhere in Europe, they did their best, in their own fashion, to create an aura of magnificence and liberality.

For one thing, they maintained "luxurious and extensive households" of servants and retainers.[53] When investigating the loss of life in the great plague of 1654, census takers discovered that, after the catastrophe, the household of Prince Ia. K. Cherkasskii still contained 533 people, N. I. Romanov's 486, and B. I. Morozov's 362.[54] Prince I. A. Vorotynskii's widow retained more than 100 servants, including several scribes, tailors, cooks, and bakers and a considerable number of stable hands. Some retainers had special functions; a number of the Vorotynskiis' servants had been part of the old prince's military retinue.[55] It was appar-

ently a custom for the most prominent nobles to maintain small units of
troops at their Moscow residences.[56] Moreover, on some ceremonial occasions, Duma members were expected to appear with a retinue of followers in suitable costumes.[57] Other retainers helped their patron to
fulfill his obligations as a Christian. Vorotynskaia supported a small number of pious poor women in her home as an act of charity. Finally, some
of her dependents lived with her simply to keep her company.[58]

From a modern point of view, the wealthiest boyars' staffs of servants
were absurdly large. Still, practices that are indefensible in one social
context may make sense in another.[59] Their wealth and power and their
legal status as owners of serfs allowed Duma members to support large
households at little cost. Moreover, this apparently wasteful practice
provided work, shelter, and food for some members of society who might
otherwise have gone without. Ultimately, however, the swollen household had symbolic meaning. The bigger the retinue, the greater the lord!

Like their counterparts elsewhere, the boyars celebrated their exalted
status with a "consumer style of life."[60] They practiced conspicuous hospitality. As at court, social life revolved around elaborate banquets. At
these functions, the host provided a large quantity and variety of simple
food and prodigious quantities of alcohol. Women normally took no part
in these celebrations, but, as a special sign of favor to the guests, the
hostess might appear briefly and greet them before disappearing into
her own quarters once again.[61]

Despite elaborate etiquette, banquets often became rowdy, drunken
affairs. Foreigners frequently noted the tendency of Russians of all classes
to drink to excess and, as guests, suffered their share of hangovers for
their part in the merriment.[62] Indeed they occasionally registered their
surprise when a prominent Russian entertained them with urbanity and
restraint.[63]

This image of generosity and open-heartedness is only one part of the
boyars' social and emotional profile. Like hosts everywhere, they were
capable of using hospitality as a weapon. Olearius remarked, for example, that high nobles sometimes invited wealthy guests to dinner in order to get the gifts that custom required them to bring.[64] Moreover, the
hosts whose liberality knew no bounds were the same men who kept
trunk after trunk full of valuables locked in their storerooms and fought
like wildcats to defend their honor from the challenge of rivals. Generosity and insecurity went hand in hand.

Since Moscow was the center of their political and social lives, Duma
members valued country estates on the outskirts of the capital highly. A
manor in the Moscow district could provide provisions—food, fodder,

and firewood—within easy reach of their city houses and might serve as a welcome refuge from the pressures of the court and the dangers of urban life.

Through most of the seventeenth century, practical considerations came first.[65] For example, V. B. Sheremetev, a prisoner of war in the Crimea, wrote home expressing his fear that, now that his only son was dead, his second wife and daughter would lose their land near Moscow to the Gavrenevs, his first wife's family; the estate had been part of the first wife's dowry and her kinsmen apparently wanted to reclaim it. In his mind, the loss would be a serious blow since the women depended on the estate for wood to heat their house in the city. Whatever the legal issues, he felt, they desperately needed the property, and the Gavrenevs did not since they already owned other estates near the capital.[66]

Estates near Moscow played a special role in the domestic economy of the wealthiest nobles. In most cases, properties in the Moscow district were far smaller than the Duma members' most important holdings elsewhere. Those exceptional figures like B. I. Morozov who developed specialized economic enterprises usually did so on larger estates in other more suitable parts of the country. Indeed, in some instances, high nobles deliberately neglected their Moscow lands in order to develop properties more remote from the capital. Perverse as always, A. I. Bezobrazov tried to get rid of his small Moscow holdings while making his Belev estate the center of his operations and his country seat.[67]

Most Duma members were glad to have a foothold near the capital. For its part, the government did its best to oblige them, distributing crown land and setting limits on the size of service estates that men of particular ranks could hold within the Moscow district. According to the Law Code of 1649, boyars could own up to 200 chetverti, or about 800 acres, around the capital, okol'nichie and dumnye d'iaki 150 chetverti, or 600 acres each.[68]

Thanks, in part, to such support, Duma members usually got what they wanted; over two-thirds of the members of the boyar elite owned some land in the Moscow *uezd*.[69] The district of Zvenigorod, immediately to the west of the capital, served essentially the same function, but, if the inventory of landholdings for 1678 gives a fair impression, Duma members owned considerably less land there.[70]

Ownership of land near Moscow reflected a man's rank and power. The summary inventory for 1678 gives a good indication of this relationship. Of the 41 boyars listed, 37 owned land in the Moscow district. Among okol'nichie, 19 had holdings near the capital, and 1 had an estate in Zvenigorod district, while 7 did not hold property in either. Men in the lower Duma ranks were not so fortunate; 10 of the 19 dumnye dvo-

riane and 4 of the 9 dumnye d'iaki owned no land near Moscow. Moreover, the size of a man's Moscow estates varied with his rank. On the
average, the boyars in 1678 owned far bigger holdings than men in the
other three Duma ranks.[71] To be sure, such figures provide only the
roughest of measures, for, within each category, the size of individual
estates varied enormously. Among the boyars, Prince Ia. N. Odoevskii
owned lands with 261 peasant households, while Prince V. V. Golitsyn's
estate had only 1 household.[72] A man's fortune could change rapidly with
time, however. As he approached the zenith of his career, Golitsyn rapidly acquired new estates so that, by the time of his fall, only eleven
years later, he owned 9 different properties around Moscow with at least
180 peasant households.[73]

Other evidence supports the view that an estate near Moscow was one
of the fruits of political power or of good connections at court. Over the
course of the seventeenth century, land in the district around the capital
tended to fall into the hands of the most powerful individuals and families of the realm. By a variety of means, they acquired crown lands,
abandoned properties, and the estates of lesser nobles whom they displaced.

In particular, as we might expect, the aristocratic clans closest to the
throne and the royal in-laws and favorites did particularly well in the
scramble for land.[74] The tsars' in-laws, the Streshnevs and Naryshkins,
made particularly remarkable gains. The former bought, sold, and bequeathed Moscow properties in a bewildering pattern, but, thanks largely
to the efforts of two of their number, Rodion Matveevich and Tikhon
Nikitich, came out considerably the richer.[75] The Naryshkins made even
more effective use of their position at court. From the time they became
Tsar Aleksei's in-laws in 1671 until the end of the century, they acquired
a number of valuable properties with a total population of 882 peasant
households.[76]

The most powerful courtiers usually owned land in the choicest locations. In 1648-1649, the lay landlords who owned property on the very
outskirts of the city included N. I. Romanov, Prince Ia. K. Cherkasskii,
Prince B. A. Repnin, Prince S. V. Prozorovskii, Prince F. S. Kurakin,
V. I. Streshnev, and the widow of Prince D. M. Pozharskii.[77]

As always, royal favor was a two-edged sword. Closeness to the tsar
helped men to acquire land near Moscow. At the same time, Prince
V. V. Golitsyn and F. L. Shaklovityi lost everything when Peter I overthrew them in 1689, and the Naryshkins took over some of the best
properties of their defeated rivals, the Miloslavskiis.[78] At the same time,
those clans which managed to consolidate their hold on power and wealth—

the Cherkasskiis and Sheremetevs, for example—kept their suburban estates or passed them on to other aristocratic clans through marriage.

In the seventeenth century, as we have suggested, most properties near Moscow had an exclusively economic function. As far as we know, landowners usually did not live on their suburban estates. Toward the end of the century, however, some of the boyars began to develop their properties as manors where they could enjoy country life without losing touch with events in the capital.

The first of the great country seats began to take shape in our period. Several signs point in this direction. For one thing, a number of lords began to diversify the production of their estates. They raised a variety of livestock and fowl, built ponds for breeding fish for their table, planted orchards, brewed beer, and produced hemp oil. In addition, some lords took steps to increase the grandeur of their surroundings. When the government confiscated I. G. Morozov's estate, Ziuzino, in 1666, the official inventory of the property mentioned five peacocks in the lord's yard.[79]

Finally, on some properties near Moscow, the owners began to build substantial houses as country residences for themselves and their families. The matter-of-fact descriptions in the land cadasters suggest that the manor houses in Rozhestvennoe, owned successively by A. S. Matveev and Prince M. A. Cherkasskii, and in Prince V. V. Golitsyn's estate, Medvedkovo, were solidly built and comfortable.[80] Like most houses in Moscow, they sat amid outbuildings and sheds and, in all probability, pigs and geese wandered to and fro in the courtyard. Contemporary sketches which have recently come to light support this impression, depicting the country houses of the late seventeenth century as practical log structures made up of several distinct architectural units like a far grander building of the time, the summer palace of the tsars at Kolomenskoe.[81] However practical and comfortable they may have been, these buildings lacked the dignity of the best boyar houses of Moscow, let alone the palaces that appeared on some properties around the old capital in later generations.[82] Compared to their counterparts to the West, the most powerful and privileged Russian nobles of the seventeenth century lived in very simple surroundings while in the country.

In this rustic setting, the boyars occupied themselves with the same kinds of activities as nobles in other societies. Much of their time they spent eating, drinking, and entertaining.[83] The impending arrival of distinguished guests, above all of the tsar himself, set off a flurry of preparations. Like royalty and nobles elsewhere, the boyars and their royal guests greatly enjoyed all forms of hunting, including Tsar Aleksei's par-

ticular favorite, falconry.[84] The cultural style of the Russian aristocrats'
country life differed greatly from that of their western and central European counterparts. A French aristocrat might well have found the boyars
boorish and their country seats unimaginably primitive. Nevertheless,
what the boyars, as country gentlemen, lacked in polish, they made up
for with their earthiness and enthusiasm.

In their own minds, the Duma members owed allegiance to two sov-
ereigns, the tsar and God. All of them belonged to the Eastern Orthodox
Church, and, as part of their duties at court, they took part in many
religious observances. In their private lives, they performed the functions that the church expected of its leading laymen.

Any discussion of Duma members as Christians must, by definition,
have distinct limits. We cannot look into the souls of our own contemporaries, let alone those of men and women of an earlier age. At the
same time, the subject is not completely closed to us, for we can examine what the Duma members said about themselves and each other and
how they expressed their faith or lack of it in action.

As a group, the boyar elite made different impressions on different
observers. Paul of Aleppo, a visitor of Eastern Orthodox faith, praised
them for their diligence in attending the liturgy, their respect for churches
and icons, and their generosity to beggars. At home, their piety showed
in the richly decorated icons and in the household chapels which many
of them maintained.[85] Western European visitors were less favorably
impressed. In the eyes of a Protestant like Olearius, all Russian Orthodox members knew far too little about the Bible and gave too much
attention to the superficial elements of their faith—repeated liturgical
observances and the mechanical performance of acts of devotion and
charity.[86] In essence, the two pictures complement each other, and both
are substantially true. Paul's comments are ultimately the more revealing, however, since, as a fellow member of the Eastern Orthodox community, he shared the boyars' own undertanding of the duties of a Christian. At the very least, his observations reflect the ideals to which they
aspired.

At their best, Duma members as individuals lived up to these ideals.
Tsar Aleksei's charter promoting A. L. Ordin-Nashchokin to the rank of
dumnyi dvorianin praises him as the model of a pious and diligent servitor: ". . . you, remembering God and his holy commands, feed the
hungry, give drink to the thirsty, feed the naked, shelter the homeless,
visit the sick and those in prison, and even wash their feet. You fulfill
your oath to Us, the Great Sovereign, and take care of Our affairs with

fortitude and courage. You treat the soldiers kindly, but do not tolerate criminals. . . ."[87]

The hagiographic biography of F. M. Rtishchev portrays him as a lay saint, a man who, in spite of his official responsibilities, gave his primary loyalty to God. In his private life, he took his faith with the utmost seriousness, fasting rigorously, praying often, remaining chaste, and avoiding frivolity. As a public figure, his biographer states, Rtishchev was modest and concerned about the welfare of all his fellow citizens. He served the tsar diligently, even in the face of malicious opposition, and actively patronized Christian scholarship. Men of all ranks had reason to be thankful for his compassion. When famine struck the Vologda region, he organized relief shipments. In another case, when financial necessity forced him to sell one of his estates, he offered the purchaser a discount on condition that he treat the peasants well. When he realized that the inhabitants of the town of Arzamas needed his near-by property, but could not afford it, he gave it to them free. In short, in his biographer's favorite words, Rtishchev, through all the vicissitudes of his life, remained a man of "meek spirit and humble heart."[88]

Both of these portraits seem flattering. Without doubt, the literary form in which they were cast, and the occasion and purpose for which they were written, led their authors to stress their subjects' positive features and to ignore the darker sides of their characters. Nevertheless, the descriptions of Ordin-Nashchokin and of Rtishchev ultimately ring true. Other evidence confirms their piety. Nashchokin, for example, abruptly left public service in the prime of life and took vows in a small provincial monastery.[89] The portraits are also realistic in what they do not claim. Unlike Rtishchev's biography, the charter issued to Nashchokin does not praise him for humility and long-suffering, qualities that he conspicuously lacked. Indeed, his impatience and irritability with his colleagues may have sprung directly from his virtues as a devout Christian. Knowing that he was himself a righteous man and a conscientious official, he tended to assume that anyone who opposed him did so from base motives or weakness of character.

Undoubtedly most Duma members did not live up to the high standards of Nashchokin and Rtishchev. After all, saints are rare in any community. Nevertheless, many of them took their religion very seriously. Their letters, for example, ring with pious sentiments. Prince V. V. Golitsyn's mother wrote that she prayed to Christ, the Virgin, and St. Sergius for his safety and urged him to remain pure in body and spirit.[90] While preparing for a dangerous mission to the Crimea, Prince P. I. Khovanskii wrote to his wife that, while he hoped to carry out his assignment with unprecedented success, he was resigned to dying if that were God's will.[91]

At the same time, only one form of religious vocation enjoyed any popularity among them. A number of Duma members took monastic vows late in life. Given the size of the boyar elite, the number of such professions is rather small; fewer than one member of the group in ten ended his life as a monk.[92] Moreover, the depth of the postulant's commitment varied considerably from one case to the next. Like Nashchokin, G. G. Pushkin, M. A. Rtishchev, and M. M. Saltykov lived in monasteries for a number of years after they retired from service.[93] In many instances, however, we know only that a man died a monk because his name appears thus in lists of tombstone inscriptions. Often such men continued to work in the government's service almost until they died. In these cases, men apparently followed the old custom of taking monastic vows on their deathbed. Several members of the Dolgorukii family, not otherwise noted for their piety, died as monks. In the most striking instance of all, Prince Iurii Alekseevich must somehow have been tonsured after his death, since he remained in service until the moment he was lynched in 1682.[94] Another old practice—the forcible tonsure of enemies of the ruling faction at court—virtually died out in our period. Only K. P. Naryshkin, another victim of the purges of 1682, entered a monastery as a penance for his political transgressions.[95]

As the pattern of religious professions suggests, Duma members were deeply concerned about the fate of their souls in the next world. Like all men, they wondered about the meaning of death and, as Eastern Orthodox Christians, they had no certainty of eternal bliss. The Orthodox tradition did provide ways of preparing for death and improving their prospects in the hereafter. To these, understandably, they often turned.

The custom of prayers for the souls of the dead occupied a central place in the boyars' devotional life. When they made their wills, they usually opened with an acknowledgment of their sins. The testament of Prince N. I. Odoevskii expressed his anguish with particular eloquence:

"In the name of the Holy and Life-giving Trinity of Father, Son and Holy Spirit, I, the slave of God, the sinful Prince Nikita Odoevskii, write this will in sound mind. I see that old age has overtaken me and frequent and diverse illnesses multiply as a loving punishment from God for my sins. They speak of nothing to me except death and the terrible judgment of the Savior in the world to come. For this reason, my heart is anxious about the departure of my soul. Mortal terror has come upon me and covered me with the darkness of confusion so that I do not know what to do. But I will lay my sorrow on the Lord and He will do what

He wishes, since He wants all men to be saved and to come to true understanding."[96]

In the course of settling his earthly affairs, Odoevskii specified that he be buried in the Holy Trinity Monastery and that the monks and nuns of that and seven other communities be given substantial sums of money or quantities of grain for prayers for his soul. In addition, he noted sorrowfully, his grandfather had instructed him to visit prisons and charitable institutions every Saturday and to distribute one ruble in alms at each. For ten years, he had met these obligations but then stopped because of the pressures of service. To make up for his failings, he ordered his executors to give 52 rubles in alms to the poor and prisoners for every year that he had missed.[97]

Odoevskii's will differs from the testaments of other boyars only in the forcefulness of its language. All whose testaments survive set aside substantial sums of money for memorial prayers.[98] In an exceptionally generous gesture, F. I. Sheremetev allocated more than 6,000 rubles for the purpose.[99]

Boyars gave many kinds of gifts to monasteries in return for prayers for their loved ones as well as for themselves. In the first half of the century, a few of them and their widows donated land. Prince D. M. Pozharskii, for example, gave several properties to the Spasso-Efimevskii Monastery of Suzdal' and to the Holy Trinity Monastery.[100] In 1621, Prince F. I. Mstislavskii gave the Simonov Monastery of Moscow two of his Iaroslavl' properties as memorials for four brothers and six children who had died in infancy.[101] In yet another case, Princess Marfa, wife of P. F. Volkonskii, willed an estate that was part of her dowry to the Koliazin Monastery on the understanding that her husband would have the right to buy it back if necessary.[102] The practice of making bequests of land, which ran counter to longstanding governmental policy, seems to have been relatively uncommon and to have died out altogether by mid-century. One reason for the change was probably the reaffirmation of the prohibition on such bequests in the Law Code of 1649.[103]

Much more common were grants of money and objects for liturgical use. The Khitrovo family gave generously to their favorite foundations over the course of several decades. Their gifts included icons and jewelled icon-covers, liturgical vessels, church bells, vestments or rich fabric from which to make them, and Gospels and other liturgical books, often lavishly decorated. On a less exalted note, they gave the monasteries a number of horses as well.[104] Inventories carefully recorded the value of these gifts, which, over the years, added up to thousands of rubles: in one nine-year period, the Khitrovos gave objects—principally very expensive icon covers—worth over 2,500 rubles to the Holy Trinity

Monastery alone.[105] Although the evidence is less complete, other prominent families—the Cherkasskiis, for instance—seem to have been equally generous.[106]

In a number of cases, families developed close relationships with particular monasteries. As our discussion suggests, the wealthy Holy Trinity Monastery frequently benefited from Duma members' generosity or qualms of conscience. Some clans, however, gave their support to more remote or obscure institutions. The Khovanskiis apparently had a special relationship with the Bogoiavlenskii Monastery of Kostroma, and the Khitrovos gave many of their bequests to the Liutikov Holy Trinity Monastery in the Peremyshl' district, which was abandoned during the Time of Troubles and refounded only in the mid-seventeenth century.[107] At the very end of the century, the Boriatinskii brothers went so far as to found the Polikarpov Monastery in the Briansk area.[108]

The economic impact of the Duma members' bequests is very hard to assess. The individuals and families which gave most generously ranked among the wealthiest of the realm. At the same time, the most openhanded, like the Khitrovos, probably felt the pinch of their generosity. Their giving, however, does not seem to have threatened them with ruin. Like most ordinary believers, the boyars were no fools in Christ.

Their lives intersected with the church at every turn. Many of them founded or rebuilt parish churches on their estates.[109] In seventeenth-century Russia, both the landlords and officials of the church seem to have assumed that it was the responsibility of the owner of an estate to provide a sanctuary and clergy for his serfs and other dependents. The lord also had to set aside arable land and meadow for the priest's support and pay him a salary in cash. By and large, these obligations were not onerous. A common norm for the support of a priest was ten to twenty chetverti of land in each of three fields, ten haystacks worth of meadow, and roughly half a ruble a year.[110] If anyone sacrificed for the faith, it was the peasants themselves, since they had to supply the materials and labor to build the new structure.[111]

There was nothing modest about the finest of these estate churches. The Cherkasskiis' church at Ostankino, the Sheremetevs' at Ubory, the Naryshkins' at Fili, and Prince B. A. Golitsyn's at Dubrovitsy all rank among the most impressive architectural monuments of their time.[112]

Moreover, as foreigners noted, a number of boyars built churches or chapels in or near their Moscow houses. In the 1630s, Prince D. M. Pozharskii, a man of unusual devotion to the church, built the Cathedral of Our Lady of Kazan' on Red Square, as well as the lovely tent-shaped church in the village of Medvedkovo.[113] A few years later, M. M. Saltykov and Prince I. A. Vorotynskii built adjoining churches dedicated to the Holy Trinity and St. Sergius.[114] Such acts of devotion were common. The location of the boyars' household churches varied from case to case. As the drawing of V. I. Streshnev's house indicates, the family church or chapel often stood in the center of the yard near the house to which it was connected by a covered walkway.[115] In other cases, the church opened onto the street. In an ingenious arrangement, for example, the Church of St. Paraskeva, next door to Prince V. V. Golitsyn's palace, had two sanctuaries. Downstairs there was a regular parish church; upstairs the Golitsyn family had a private chapel dedicated to the Resurrection.[116]

By founding churches, Duma members made a public announcement of their piety. Other acts of religious devotion were less obvious. As Olearius grudgingly put it, "One finds among the Russians some who not only contribute large sums to churches and monasteries but also are generous to the poor."[117] Odoevskii's will supports this statement, and so does the practice of Princess Vorotynskaia and Rtishchev of maintaining poor and pious women in their households.[118]

As leaders of society, Duma members regularly intervened in the affairs of the church. Members of the parish clergy and leaders of monastic communities turned to them for support. For example, A. I. Matiushkin and Ia. P. Solovtsov both wrote laudatory letters to the Archbishop of Tobol'sk on behalf of Petr Andreev, a priest in the cathedral in Tiumen' who had fallen out of favor with his superior.[119] Among Prince V. V. Golitsyn's correspondence is a letter from the abbess of the Convent of the Descent of the Holy Spirit, asking him to intercede with Fedor Khrushchev, who was persecuting the sisters by taking wood from their forest to build fortifications.[120] Moreover, as landlords, the boyars took responsibility for the clergy on their estates. They tried to ensure that every church had a priest who performed his functions adequately. B. I. Morozov, for one, took these duties seriously. On one occasion, he intervened to stop a quarrel between two priests which culminated in a fist-fight in church.[121] Such diligence had its rewards; a conscientious priest could help a lord to run his estate since, as a man presumed to be literate, he could serve as a witness to contracts and transmit the lord's orders to the peasants in the absence of a steward.[122]

At the same time, the members of the boyar elite did their best to avoid involvement in the profound crises that shook the Russian church in the seventeenth century. The biographies of individual Duma members show some contacts with Patriarch Nikon, usually as messengers from the tsar, but virtually no sign of the schism over Nikon's liturgical reforms that led to the Old Believer movement. Only N. A. Ziuzin supported the patriarch to the end. Moreover, among the high nobility, only the Sokovnin sisters—better known by their married names as the Boiarinia Morozova and Princess Urusova—followed the path of martyrdom in defense of the native liturgical tradition. All the other members of the boyar elite went along with governmental policy on religious questions.

Yet matters were probably not so simple. All Duma members surely knew Nikon, and many probably came into contact with Neronov, Avvakum, and other leaders of the revolt against the liturgical reform and its implications. The most pious must have agonized over the personal tragedies that the ecclesiastical struggles brought and over the damage the crises wreaked on an institution so central to their lives and aspirations. Undoubtedly, a pious layman like Rtishchev found himself caught in the crossfire. Initially, he worked closely with Nikon, and later, when the struggle over the liturgy threatened to split the church, he tried to mediate between the contending factions.[123] In the end, however, he quietly accepted Nikon's destruction and the enforced reform of the liturgy.

Two general reasons account for Rtishchev's passivity in the face of catastrophe. First, the attitudes and programs of Nikon and the Old Believers did not appeal to him and his fellow courtiers. Nothing in his biography suggests that Rtishchev supported the theory of the superiority of the church to the state, and his openness to cultural influences from other Orthodox countries made him a most unlikely candidate for martyrdom in defense of the minute details of traditional Russian liturgical usage. In addition, the fanatical determination of both Nikon and Avvakum probably repelled him. Secondly, all Duma members inherited a tradition of obedience to the ruler whom they served. They owed everything they had and were to him and, in a crisis, were neither willing nor able to risk jeopardizing their wealth or standing by speaking out. When Peter I introduced reforms that probably shook them far more profoundly than the ecclesiastical struggles of the seventeenth century, they quickly went along once again.

As a group, the members of the boyar elite performed their formal duties as Orthodox laymen diligently.[124] All of them did what the Orthodox tradition required, and none openly challenged the teachings and practices of the official church. To say this, of course, is to describe the surface of upper-class life. In practice, a number of high nobles were undoubtedly impious or dissolute. Moreover, with the exception of men like Rtishchev, the boyars had no desire to purify or to invigorate the life of the church. Early in their campaign to reform parish life, for example, both Neronov and Avvakum clashed with members of the

Sheremetev family who objected to being rebuked by mere parish priests.[125]

In their faith, then, the members of the Duma sought emotional comfort here and the best possible prospects for the world to come. At their best, they tried to live up to Rtishchev's standards of love for God and charity to their fellow men. Few, however, had the intensity of devotion that makes men saints, and none had the martyr's fire.

The boyar elite reacted equally cautiously to the changes taking place in Muscovite culture in the seventeenth century. Throughout the period, Russian society was open to many kinds of influence from outside. As earlier historians have shown, new techniques and attitudes reached Moscow from three general areas. From the Protestant lands of northern Europe, the Russian government borrowed the theories and practical know-how of the "military revolution" and recruited mercenaries and craftsmen to teach their skills to its subjects. Moreover, some of the tsars' courtiers and leading subjects came to admire the appurtenances of a solid and comfortable northern European style of life.[126] In the second half of the century, scholars from the Ukraine dominated Muscovite education and literature, bringing with them the polemical skills, literary forms, and educational techniques of Roman Catholic central Europe in a safely Orthodox guise.[127] Finally, the leaders of the church turned, on several occasions, to the Greek-speaking Eastern Orthodox communities for teachers and scholars to help to strengthen the authority and purify the practices of Russian Orthodoxy.[128] The three currents of foreign influence touched somewhat different areas of national life, although the Ukrainians and the Greeks clashed directly on occasion. All three had a distinctly limited impact on Russian society; they penetrated only Moscow and a few provincial centers and influenced only the leading strata of the church and of lay society.

Most Duma members' biographies show no traces of these cultural innovations and conflicts. Moreover, in those few cases in which we can see the influence of new styles and values, these elements of innovation are usually only a small part of an otherwise conventional pattern of behavior.

Anyone who studies the cultural world of the boyars owes a heavy debt to the giants of the past. Russian scholars of the late nineteenth and early twentieth centuries searched our period diligently for the historical roots of Peter the Great's revolutionary turn to European cultural values and practices as he understood them. Thanks to the efforts of recent translators, the English-speaking reader can now enjoy Platonov's fine treatment of Russia's cultural relations with Europe and Kliuchevskii's brilliant evocation of Muscovite culture in transition and his remarkable portraits of the leading figures of the time. Since they wrote, researchers have uncovered little new material that would change the picture that they have left us. In the shadow of such intimidating predecessors, our discussion will aim at a modest goal: to put the cultural achievements of the few exceptional innovators and dreamers into the context of the whole boyar elite.

Several general observations are in order. First, we should recall Kliuchevskii's useful distinction between the adoption of foreign techniques and the absorption of new values and systems of belief. As he indicated, the Muscovite government and its leading subjects usually tried consciously to limit themselves to learning new languages, mastering new technologies, and enjoying new comforts and entertainments. At the same time, men did not always find it easy to locate the boundary between these individual cultural features and the underlying values from which they sprang. Moreover, the act of learning a new language or of drilling troops or of stating a theological proposition in a new way may have profound symbolic meaning and emotional impact. In one case, in 1650, the future Duma member L. T. Golosov and several of his fellow students protested their assignment to study Latin with Ukrainian monks. Such an undertaking, they argued, would undermine their faith. As Golosov put it, "All who have learned Latin have gone astray."[129]

Secondly, to study the Duma members' collective response to cultural change is not to study the process itself. The leaders in the campaign to diversify and to invigorate Muscovite culture and institutions were most often foreigners—scholars, teachers, and poets from the Ukraine and White Russia, soldiers and craftsmen from western and central Europe, and interpreters from many countries. Moreover, a number of the most interesting cultural figures within the Russian community were not Duma members. Kotoshikhin, who, in exile, attacked many Muscovite traditions, was a minor official of the Foreign Office. Two well-known writers of the early seventeenth century, Prince I. A. Khvorostinin and Prince S. I. Shakhovskoi, came from distinguished families, but never reached Duma rank themselves. Their unconventional ideas and behavior attracted the ire of officials of both church and state. In spite of their great skill as writers, their careers in government service ended in futility and suffering.[130]

Finally, as these men knew all too well, the attitudes of the tsar himself had a decisive impact on the course and limits of cultural change. Under the influence of Patriarch Filaret, Tsar Mikhail's government showed great reluctance to accept any departure from native tradition. Aleksei Mikhailovich played a very different role. As Kliuchevskii's fine portrait shows, he was a complex figure, at once a model of Orthodox piety, a strong-willed and short-tempered ruler, and an enthusiastic patron of foreign novelties.[131] From childhood, fascinating objects from abroad surrounded him. As the years passed, he entrusted the education of some of his children to Simeon Polotskii, the White Russian scholar and poet, who taught them Latin and Polish. Before the end of his life, Aleksei presided over the founding of a court theater. The company under the direction of a German pastor performed original plays in Russian translation, with all the embellishments characteristic of the central European Baroque theater.[132] In their turn, Aleksei's children, Fedor and Sophia, products of a cosmopolitan education, followed similar policies of tolerance and experimentation. Like their father's, their regimes had to contend with the conservative cultural attitudes of the leaders of the church, who tried, with considerable success, to put a stop to innovations that, in their view, might threaten the faith of their flock.

Duma members responded to the changing cultural scene in several ways. A number of them adopted individual features of European life. N. I. Romanov, Tsar Mikhail's cousin, used some of his wealth to buy luxuries from Europe. Among his imported treasures were clocks worth between 50 and 70 rubles and a large armoire that cost 950.[133] Olearius reported that Romanov also loved German music and clothes. On some informal occasions, he dressed in European style until the patriarch tricked him out of his new wardrobe.[134] On the whole, however, he lived well within the confines of the Russian tradition. Other boyars of his generation apparently did likewise. The property of another member of the group, probably I. D. Miloslavskii, included native Russian, Near Eastern, and western European items.[135] Among the latter were firearms and a mirror. Yet a Dutch carbine or a German armoire does not make a man a European, any more than a Damascus sword makes him an Arab.

Russian diplomats of the time learned foreign languages and studied other countries and their cultures as part of their official duties. V. M. Tiapkin, a resident ambassador in Poland, is a good example. In Solov'-ev's words: "Tiapkin was a purely Russian type who died in Poland of homesickness. He could not get along with the Poles and saw them in the worst possible light. All the same, he began to write in Polish, sent his son to a Polish school, and the latter delivered an oration to the king in the fashionable language of the day, half Polish and half Latin."[136]

A. L. Ordin-Nashchokin encountered other cultures with the same ambivalence.[137] The great diplomat came from Pskov on Russia's northwestern frontier. Apparently he knew German and Latin from childhood and later learned Polish as well. During his strenuous career, he kept informed about events in the other countries of Europe. For example, he organized the first postal service between Russia and central Europe and saw to it that the Foreign Office received a regular supply of news digests (*kuranty*) from the West.[138] Moreover, a number of his policies had their inspiration in European theory and practice. In proposing to give the city of Pskov self-government, he consciously tried to follow "the example of other, foreign countries." The New Trade Ordinance of 1667 reflects his mercantilist convictions.[139] Throughout his career, then, Nashchokin fought fire with fire. Foreign ideas and techniques served as weapons in Russia's age-old fight against her enemies. All his life, however, he remained a conspicuously devout son of the Orthodox church. When his own son went abroad without permission, Nashchokin was humiliated and tendered his resignation. Fortunately, Tsar Aleksei understood the young man's state of mind far better than his own father and urged the latter to have patience until the bird flew back to his own nest. Ultimately, however, Nashchokin did resign and made a final declaration of his traditional piety and intense patriotism by entering a monastery in his native region.

A few of the boyars played the useful role of collector and patron of scholarship and art. They gave encouragement to the talented foreigners in Russian service and provided links with the court and the chanceries. B. M. Khitrovo enthusiastically collected manuscripts and, as head of the Armory, proved to be a discerning patron who made the chancery a kind of academy of the applied arts. A number of gifted craftsmen and icon painters—notably Semen Ushakov—worked under his direction, and their best work probably reflects Khitrovo's own taste. To judge from their surviving paintings and the metalwork that he donated to his favorite monasteries, Khitrovo had a refined appreciation of the artists' technical skill and little interest in radical stylistic or thematic innovation. The works that he sponsored are fine examples of the Russian national style of his day.[140]

F. M. Rtishchev's biographers have stressed his love of learning as well as his piety.[141] According to his hagiographic "life," he invited Ukrainian scholars to Moscow and maintained them in the Andreevskii Monastery on the outskirts of the city.[142] More recent and critical scholarship has raised questions about this account, arguing that the invitation came from the tsar himself and that the most celebrated visitors from Kiev worked elsewhere in the city.[143] In spite of these corrections in the details of the traditional account, our picture of Rtishchev remains intact. He undoubtedly promoted Orthodox learning energetically and himself studied Greek and other subjects with erudite monks from abroad.[144] Throughout his career, foreign scholars turned to him for support and encouragement.[145] Moreover, as tutor to Tsar Aleksei's eldest son and namesake, he gathered books for the lad on many subjects, including mathematics, philosophy, history, and geography.[146] Rtishchev was no uncritical lover of novelty for its own sake. In his mind, learning was the handmaid of faith. At the same time, he maintained an open mind and an ecumenical perspective on the world. Any scholar who could help to enlighten or to revitalize Russian Orthodoxy had his fervent support.

A. S. Matveev played the role of patron to foreigners of a very different type.[147] Nothing in his background marked him out as a cultural rebel. The son of a chancery official, Matveev spent many years as a soldier and diplomat before reaching boyar rank, thanks to Aleksei's friendship. At the height of his power, he was, like his master, a complex figure, at once conventional and adventurous. Like Romanov before him, he surrounded himself with the civilized trappings of a good European home—German clocks, mirrors and furniture and portraits and maps from various sources.[148] Through his contacts in Moscow's foreign quarter, he built up a theatrical company to perform for the tsar and his new bride, Nataliia Naryshkina, Matveev's former ward. He recruited foreigners and Russians alike, by hook or by crook. Occasionally, he used rough methods; a White Russian musician complained that, when he refused Matveev's offer of employment, he was kidnapped and held in chains until he agreed to play the organ and violin for theatrical productions.[149]

As head of the Foreign Office, Matveev commissioned the translators and clerks in his employ to write several important works of history and heraldry for the royal court. The *Great Book of Titles* and the *Book about the Election of Mikhail Romanov to the Throne*, to name only two, are magnificent examples of the Romanov court's ideology and artistic tastes. We should have no illusions, however: Matveev gave the orders and encouragement while his subordinates—for example, Nicolae Spafari Milescu, an interpreter of Romanian origin—did the work.[150] Matveev's library gives an even clearer indication of the complexity of his position in the changing cultural world of his day. When he fell into disgrace, the government confiscated a number of books in his possession, most of them in Latin. They dealt with many subjects, especially geography, history, and applied science and technology. At the same time, Matveev could not read them, since, as far as we know, he did not know any foreign language. They apparently belonged, not to him, but to the library of the Foreign Office.[151] Why he borrowed them is not clear. Certainly the fact that he did so illustrates his cultural aspirations rather than his accomplishments.

Only one boyar, Prince V. V. Golitsyn, could claim to be a wholehearted devotee of new cultural standards. Relying on the testimony of

Adrien Baillet, sieur de Neuville, a Frenchman who visited Moscow in 1689 with a Polish mission, Kliuchevskii portrayed him as a man of intelligence and vision who had detailed plans for the radical transformation of Russian life and institutions.[152] Measured by his possessions and his concrete accomplishments, however, Golitsyn appears less radical. Without doubt, he received an excellent education and had good command of several foreign languages, above all, Latin.[153] As an adviser to Tsar Fedor, he led the campaign to abolish mestnichestvo.[154] Once Sophia became regent, Golitsyn took over the direction of foreign policy. In both his public and private behavior, he strove to maintain good relations with many European governments and their subjects. He treated Christians of all denominations with toleration, sheltering the Jesuits and receiving them as guests.[155] His palace, while conventional in design, was decorated more lavishly and furnished more luxuriously even than Matveev's. Moreover, the decorative elements on the facade reflect Golitsyn's interest in the new Moscow or "Naryshkin" Baroque manner, the adaptation of European Baroque styles to Russian needs and tastes. A favorite project of his patroness, Sophia—the Churches of the Transfiguration and the Assumption and the belfry in the Novodevichii Convent—probably reflects even more dramatically his love of the lightness and elegance of the new fashion in architecture.[156]

Like his predecessor as foreign minister, moreover, he entertained in European style. Finally, his library reflected the broad range of his taste. The books confiscated when he fell included works on history, geography, and military affairs, as well as religious works and *belles lettres*. Most interesting of all, the collection contained the manuscript of a work by Iurii Krizhanich, the Yugoslav thinker who savagely criticized much in Russia's present condition but who held out high hopes for her future.[157]

After all is said, Golitsyn remains an impressive but shadowy figure. In many respects, he closely resembled other prominent men of his time.[158] In other areas, particularly his tolerant attitude toward Roman Catholics, he shocked his contemporaries profoundly. Indeed, his blend of new and old, of cosmopolitan spirit and conventional behavior, might have provided a model for enlightening and reforming Russia without the suffering that Peter the Great's policies caused. To make this suggestion, however, may be to indulge in fantasies as farfetched as those that Neuville ascribed to Golitsyn. In reality, he lacked the determination and the firm political base to act on his convictions.

None of the boyars, then, was a consistent cultural revolutionary, a Peter the Great *avant la lettre*. Even the most adventurous of them combined elements of novelty with conventional attitudes and forms of behavior. For many, cultural change meant new furniture and no more.

In another sense, however, the seeds of change were germinating. All upper-class Russians had become accustomed to the new, if only in the area of military organization and technology, and to regular contact with foreigners.

Moreover, the boyars looked to the ruler and his government for leadership in cultural matters. When Peter made radical Europeanization official policy, they went along—reluctantly perhaps, but without protest.

CONCLUSIONS
AND COMPARISONS

Aristocrats and servitors. Strength and insecurity. Such paradoxes shaped the lives of the members of the political and social elite of seventeenth-century Russia.

The members of the Boyar Duma—or the boyar elite, as I have often called them—came from two distinct elements, the traditional military nobility and the chancery officials, who spent their entire careers working within the bureaucracy. In the course of the century, the service careers of some military nobles began to resemble those of the officials, and outstanding bureaucrats gained wealth and adopted a style of life that earned them the respect of aristocrats.

Within the highest echelons of the military nobility, we can see a group of twenty or so families which stood out above their fellows. Almost all the men of these clans achieved the rank of boyar, the highest formal accolade to which a Muscovite noble could aspire. When they served, they often received particularly desirable assignments. As landlords, they succeeded in expanding their holdings and, as leaders of society, they made particularly good marriages for their children and kept out of compromising factional entanglements. In every respect, they formed an elite within an elite and, given their record of high rank and standing over several generations, we have every right to call them aristocrats.

Over the course of the century, the composition of the boyar elite changed considerably. The Duma grew rapidly in size and changed from a remarkably conservative and aristocratic body under Mikhail Romanov to a strikingly motley collection of servitors in the last years of Aleksei's reign; for, after 1645, unprecedented numbers of parvenus—royal favorites and in-laws or men with specialized skills or training—received Duma rank. When they reached the top of the Muscovite hierarchy, they took their places beside the representatives of the great aristocratic clans. In no sense did the newcomers displace the first families of the realm. Indeed, with the partial exception of the royal in-laws, they discovered that equality of formal rank did not necessarily entail equality of wealth or social standing.

Moreover, the meaning of Duma rank—the formal designation that set them above the tsar's lesser servitors—was also changing. In the seventeenth century, the bureaucracy provided the royal government with a reliable and increasingly effective instrument of social control. The administration relied more and more on written documentation and clearly defined procedural norms and made less and less use of older forms of consultation, of which the Duma was one. In this new climate, in the latter half of the century, the zemskii sobor or national estates ceased to meet. At the same time, smaller bodies appeared to take over some of the Duma's functions, and, as always, a handful of courtiers and officials seems to have set the main lines of governmental policy.

Yet, even if the Duma as a body outlived its usefulness, the Russian government continued to need generals and bureaucrats, and rural society rested on the foundation of the nobleman's control over his serfs. Under Peter, the rank of boyar disappeared, but Russia's social and administrative elite survived and continued to evolve.

In other words, Duma members could take comfort from the fact that seventeenth-century governments needed their skills or their tradition of leadership of the army and the administration. Throughout the century, the vast majority of them served and, on the whole, did a reasonably good job.

Moreover, they enjoyed unusually favorable conditions of service. By and large, Duma members did not work as hard as their fathers had in the late sixteenth century nor as their sons were to do under Peter. Most seventeenth-century high nobles spent considerable periods of time in the comparative comfort and security of Moscow between assignments at the front or in the provinces. Indeed, a substantial minority of the boyar elite rarely, if ever, left the court and the capital. In the most extreme case, the weak governments of the late 1670s and 1680s bestowed Duma rank on a number of men who had done nothing but take part in court ceremonies and never would. When he came to maturity, Peter inherited a caricature of the Muscovite system of universal service.

In part, the do-nothing boyars of the late seventeenth century became courtiers in the worst sense of the word because they no longer had a military role to play. By the late 1670s and 1680s, regiments of the modern type had replaced the traditional noble cavalry levies at the core of the Muscovite army. To command new-style infantry and cavalry units required special training and skills which, for the most part, the members of the boyar elite did not have. In the campaigns of Fedor's reign and Sophia's regency, many of the most important commanders of Muscovite troops were foreigners or Russians from outside the high nobility who had mastered the new arts of war. Technological obsolescence threatened to deprive the boyars of their traditional *raison d'être*.

At the same time, the boyar elite met the challenge with flexibility and determination. On one hand, as we have noted, the government brought a few of the most outstanding officers of the new type into the elite by promoting them to Duma rank. On the other, boyars continued to hold the highest positions of command in the major military undertakings of the time. For better or worse, they led the Russian armies in the Turkish wars of the 1670s and the Crimean expeditions of the 1680s. They owed their continued monopoly of the most prestigious commands to their personal ties to the throne and to the tradition that they were the natural leaders of the armies of Muscovy. Indeed, Peter I instinctively accepted the high nobility's claim to leadership, but insisted that the sons and grandsons of the boyars of the seventeenth century undergo rigorous training for modern warfare.

To retain their traditional position as the tsar's leading servitors, moreover, members of the military nobility learned to ride the wave of the future—the bureaucracy. Over the course of the century, more and more traditional nobles became heads of chanceries. Indeed, the most powerful of them built veritable nests of offices within the central administration. There they enjoyed special advantages—executive power, increased income, and close contact with the tsar and the ruling circle around him. At the same time, this new departure allowed the government to make full use of the talents of nobles who had a flair for administration or diplomacy: Ordin-Nashchokin and Golitsyn come to mind. It was in the interest of both the royal government and the military nobility to create conditions in which military and chancery service were interchangeable, and a single corps of noble servitors could perform both. The gradual emerging of this pattern, which took far clearer shape in the eighteenth century, held out advantages to both elements of the boyar elite. To the military nobles, it offered new opportunities; to career chancery officials, greater prestige.

Secure in their position as servitors, Duma members had good cause to worry about the dynamics of seventeenth-century court politics. Political life revolved around personal contacts—above all with the ruler and his most influential advisers. The tsar's favor could make a man powerful and rich; his disfavor could destroy him.

In such a capricious world, Duma members sought security wherever they could. Family ties did much to give coherence to men's lives. Boyar clans, especially the aristocratic inner core of the group, retained a sharp sense of their heritage and standing in society and, within them, each man knew his place. At the same time, neither his ancestry nor his genealogical standing within his family guaranteed a man high office or insured him against a disastrous fall. In addition, numerous marriages connected the core group of families to one another and to the throne. This social elite was exclusive, but open enough to change gradually by receiving new individuals and families which had risen through outstanding service or through royal favor. At the same time, marriage alliances alone could not save Duma members from the hazards of changing political fortune. Rather, marriage ties were a form of insurance; boyar clans pursued a defensive strategy of marriage alliances, forging links with the widest possible variety of potential allies or clients.

Members of the boyar elite also sought safety in informal political groupings. Patronage relationships were ubiquitous in the upper strata of Muscovite society in the seventeenth century. Fragmentary evidence suggests that some men had a particular patron or group of clients. At the same time, men and women, particularly those in trouble, maintained contact with as wide a circle of acquaintances as possible, in hopes of finding among them a powerful protector. Court factions or parties were more visible but affected far fewer men. In the seventeenth century, they tended to be very small and short-lived and took shape around men rather than around ideas or political programs. For the most part, the members of the great aristocratic clans avoided them, for they were a poor risk. If the faction's leader won the struggle for power, his followers would gather the spoils; conversely, however, if he fell, they might well share in the catastrophe. Most men found it wiser to stay uncommitted.

In the economic sphere, the members of the boyar elite had little reason for concern. The leading families of Russia retained a secure grip on their lands and even increased their holdings. To be sure, like later generations of Russian nobles, the boyars took their estates for granted and did little to make them more productive. Moreover, in spite of extensive holdings of land and large collections of family heirlooms and hoarded goods, they often suffered from an embarrassing shortage of ready cash. Nevertheless, by the standards of their time and society, most members of the boyar elite remained wealthy, and, as far as we know, even the least favored among them were comfortably well-off. To my knowledge, no boyar families fell into bankruptcy in our period. Only political disgrace could cause a man to lose his lands.

The boyars enjoyed a material life of solid comfort and security. In their Moscow houses and new country retreats, surrounded by numerous servants and retainers, they lacked nothing. Reassuring rituals governed the social events and ceremonies at court, and the practice of

Eastern Orthodoxy provided emotional stability in life and consolation in the face of death. On the surface, at least, they were content with tried and true patterns of life.

In short, in the seventeenth century, most Duma members thrived. They worked and lived in an apparently orderly world. Beneath the comfortable facade, however, there were signs of insecurity and tension. Like most men, they found death profoundly unsettling and took great pains to ensure the repose of their souls and those of their loved ones. They worried about the attitude of the rulers of this world as well. As servitors of the crown, they owed their power and standing to the favor of the tsar and his advisers. Indeed, as the seventeenth century passed, favoritism came increasingly to dominate political life. Capriciousness and unpredictability became the order the day, although not to the extent that they had dominated nobles' lives in the terrifying time of Ivan IV. In addition, popular revolts regularly reminded them that, as government officials and landlords, they could expect to bear the brunt of the profound bitterness of the enserfed lower orders of society. Popular mythology cast them in the role of the wicked advisers from whom the well-meaning tsar had to be saved. Dependent on the crown for the rank and service assignments that brought power, economic prosperity, and social standing, and threatened from below, they had no choice but to do whatever the ruler required. In spite of their distinguished traditions, exalted rank and accrued wealth, Peter I treated them just as he liked.

Where does the boyar elite of seventeenth-century Russia fit on the spectrum of elite groups of the world in which they lived? With whom should we compare them? Since a central fact of their lives was service to the ruler, we might begin by looking at other societies and political systems in which power and its rewards derived from official service. Perhaps China in the last millenium provides the best example of this type of administration. China, however, does not provide a meaningful point of comparison because its bureaucratic elite chosen by competitive examinations bears little resemblance to the Russian high nobles, whose family origins and traditions loomed larger than talent or education of even the most modest kind.[1]

By contrast, the Ottoman Empire appears remarkably similar to Muscovy in many ways. Both were absolute monarchies whose rulers claimed all land as their own and all citizens as their servants. In each, lavish ceremony surrounded and imprisoned the monarch, whose court became the center of political life. In more concrete respects as well, Ottoman institutions closely resembled Russian. In both, the core of the army consisted of cavalrymen who received lands and their revenues on

conditional tenure in return for service. Then, when lightly armed cavalry alone proved inadequate to meet the demands of the age of gun-
powder, each government created an auxiliary force of musketeers—the
janissaries in Turkey and the strel'tsy in Russia.[2]

These striking parallels between the Ottoman and Muscovite systems,
however, do not extend to the group with which we are concerned. The
sultans applied the principle that all men were their slaves far more
rigorously than did their Russian counterparts. At the core of the Ottoman system were officials who were literally slaves—men taken from
their homes in childhood and raised at court so that no one could doubt
their absolute dependence on the ruler or their loyalty to him. In time,
to be sure, some powerful officials founded their own dynasties within
the administration. The resulting elite derived its power entirely from
service, past and present. Its members, then, bore some resemblance to
the powerful chancery officials of Muscovite and early imperial Russia,
but none at all to the high court nobility.

As far as I am aware, no group in Turkish society combined hereditary
ownership of land with high office and political power. There were apparently groups of hereditary nobles in some of the conquered territories, particularly in the Balkans, but their power was restricted to their
native region and to their own nationality. Unlike the high nobles of
Russia, they played virtually no role in the political life of the empire as
a whole.

One final observation is in order. The Ottoman Empire was truly a
multinational state. At the height of its power, its government recruited
the members of the military and bureaucratic elites almost entirely from
the conquered nationalities. Recruiters took promising boys from their
villages to the court, where they were converted to Islam and taught
Turkish and the other languages of the court. Muscovy was much more
like a nation-state. Despite their fanciful claims to the contrary, most
high nobles, like most of the rest of the population, were of Russian
nationality. In each generation, to be sure, the tsars welcomed into their
service nobles of Turkic origin who agreed to the one condition for join-
ing the Muscovite service elite, conversion to Russian Orthodoxy. Such
men, however, stood out as an exotic element in an overwhelmingly
Slavic group.[3]

At the other end of Europe, the aristocracy or peers of England and
France shared many—utterly different—characteristics with the high nobility of Russia.[4] Before proceeding with our comparison, we should note
that the peerage in these western countries and the boyar elite in Russia
are not precisely equivalent. The members of the Boyar Duma were a
larger and more variegated group than the peers and included some men

whose family background and career made them roughly similar to nobles of the robe or new nobles in France.

The great nobles of Russia and of western Europe were the products of very different historical traditions. In the late fifteenth and early sixteenth centuries, when Russian aristocrats already served the princes of Moscow, their counterparts in England and France enjoyed great wealth and power independent of the crown. In the West, "overmighty subjects" lived in fortified castles on large estates defended by their own private armies. Moreover, when they deigned to serve the king, the great nobles enjoyed a virtual monopoly on seats in the royal council, important military commands, and governorships of the provinces. They regarded the monarch as the first among equals and opposed any significant increase in his power by any means at their disposal, including rebellion.

By the late seventeenth century, the position of the aristocracy in England and France had changed dramatically. Indeed, the historical development of Russia and the West converged, making their position very similar to that of their Muscovite brethren. In the intervening century and beyond, the policies of the Tudors and early Stuarts in England and of Richelieu and Louis XIV in France had slowly but surely reduced the local strongholds of the great. Private armies and fortified castles had disappeared, and aristocratic families kept only enough retainers to maintain the style to which they had become accustomed. Moreover, the rulers of both countries lured the aristocracy to their glittering and expensive courts. There they received financial rewards, social recognition, and direct access to the king's person and favor. In return they gave up their freedom of action and, in the most extreme case, suffered the genteel humiliation of daily life in Versailles.

By that time, the western aristocrats resembled Russian high nobles in many ways. Both groups now served primarily at court. Both, in their choice of marriage partners, showed an acute sense of their special position in society. Courtiers in both East and West defended their honor at the slightest hint of insult, with curses and blows and, in France, in the deadly elegance of the duel.

In all three countries, the high nobles had first claim on positions at court and in the officer corps. In the course of the seventeenth century, the three governments forced them to share their right to high office with more and more men of less distinguished origin. There the similarity ended, however. Aristocrats filled the church hierarchy in France, but not in Russia. In England, where there was virtually no army or central bureaucracy, the crown had few jobs to offer the great nobles.

Despite these superficial similarities, the western European aristocrat faced very different conditions from those of his Russian counterpart. The French or English nobleman did not have to serve; the Russian had no choice. Louis XIV did his best to bring the great nobles of France to Versailles, but, despite his efforts, staying at home on the ancestral estate remained a viable, if less desirable, alternative. The reasons for this state of affairs are evident. First of all, even after the strengthening of the royal administration, the great nobles of England and France still had considerable power in their ancestral homelands. Whether courtiers or not, most still owned one or more substantial homes and estates in the provinces, where they could live far from the king's scrutiny. Moreover, they still retained the loyalty of retainers and clients and filled certain powerful offices in the provinces like that of Lord Lieutenant or commander of militia in England. Secondly, given the tradition of primogeniture, the western European noble could hope, with careful management, to pass his fortune intact to his heir. In Russia, customary law obligated the noble to divide his estate among all his sons and provide for his daughters as well. His family faced gradual impoverishment unless he and his descendants could find a way to replenish their fortune continually. The best hope of escaping the dilemma was to earn grants of crown land through royal service.

The aristocrats of western Europe enjoyed other advantages as well. In practice, their rulers had less effective control over their actions than the tsars had over their Russian counterparts. An English or French grandee might behave disgracefully or flaunt royal ordinances with impunity; an obstreperous Russian faced speedy punishment. On the positive side, western nobles had a better opportunity than Russians to present their views to the king and his ministers. In particular, the House of Lords gave the English aristocracy real power to shape royal legislation. In comparison, representation in the sporadic meetings of the national estates gave the high nobles of France and Russia little opportunity to express corporate grievances or to shape their collective destiny. Last, but not least, many western aristocrats received an incomparably better education than their Russian cousins.

In the early eighteenth century, convergence ended, and the high nobles of western Europe and Russia took diverging paths. Although Peter the Great dressed his courtiers in European fashions, he rigorously reasserted the good old Russian principle that all subjects were bound to serve him in his capacity as first servant of the state. The Emperor practiced what he preached. Under his vigorous leadership, every noble had to serve from adolescence until death. At precisely the same time, the French aristocracy began to free itself from the controls imposed by

Louis XIV and to extend its privileges. Thereafter the Russian high nobles marched out of step with their western brothers.

One other country in eastern Europe took the same path. In the late
seventeenth and early eighteenth centuries, the rulers of Prussia transformed nobles who bore a general resemblance to their counterparts in
England or France into a corps of disciplined servants of the state. Until
the reforms of the Great Elector and Frederick William I, the nobles in
the scattered territories of the kingdom had solid bastions of local power.
The national and local estates gave them a corporate political voice.

To be sure, some local customs and conditions prepared the way for
the garrison state of the eighteenth century. Since it consisted of several
separate provinces scattered across the north European plain, Prussia
was exceptionally vulnerable to attack. Even more than elsewhere on
the continent, warfare was a normal and unavoidable fact of life. Moreover, Prussia had its own tradition that the nobles should serve the king.
In theory at least, until the reform of 1717 nobles held their estates on
condition of service to the crown. Previous kings had not enforced the
obligation to serve. Frederick William's law giving the nobles absolute
ownership of their lands was not an act of royal generosity, but rather
an attempt to give the recipients abstract legal rights in exchange for the
payment of real taxes. Moreover, as in Russia, the nobles of Prussia
clung stubbornly to the custom of partible inheritance. Like their Russian cousins, they sought positions in royal service for themselves and
their sons to compensate for the likelihood that, over time, their fortunes
would decline. In addition, service in the king's army and administration
offered ambitious nobles the only promising path to greater wealth and
power. Indeed fighting as officers in the king's army was the nobles'
raison d'être.

In the light of these points of similarity, it is not surprising that, in
the early eighteenth century, Peter I and Frederick William I were able
to complete the transformation of their respective countries into absolute
monarchies of a peculiarly eastern European type.[5] At the same time,
the position of the high nobles of Prussia and of Russia remained different in very important ways. The Prussian Junkers retained their estates
in the provinces from which they had come. Moreover, they kept their
hold on the local estate institutions, even though the royal administration increasingly turned them to its own ends. Their Russian counterparts, then, were more vulnerable to pressure from the royal government and more dependent on its favor and support.

Elsewhere in eastern Europe, the boyars had very little in common
with the magnates of the Polish commonwealth.[6] The border between
Russia and Poland separated two entirely different societies, polities, and

cultures. Indeed, up to the fifteenth century, Polish magnates more closely resembled the aristocrats of western Europe than the high nobles of Muscovy. By the end of the seventeenth century, however, the stream of historical development had divided into several distinct channels; the Polish-Lithuanian Commonwealth presented a striking contrast both to the monarchies of western Europe and to Muscovite Russia.

In Poland, as the power of the crown waned, overmighty subjects became mightier still. The magnates, especially in Lithuania and the Ukraine, set themselves up as rivals of the king. They could well afford to do so. The richest of them owned enormous latifundias and collected the rents and labor service of thousands of enserfed peasants.[7] On these estates, they lived like independent rulers. Royal officials did not dare to interfere in the internal affairs of these principalities. Their caution is understandable. The magnates used their prestige and wealth to make many minor nobles their dependents. As a consequence, they maintained large private armies, some as large as the royal army itself. The style of life and cultural pretensions of the magnates also made them worthy rivals of the king. The most prominent of them lived in magnificent palaces on their estates, surrounded by legions of servants and retainers lavishing generous hospitality on all comers. The best educated of them, like the celebrated Jan Zamoyski, spread learning and encouraged the arts with a liberality and good taste that were legendary. Their cousins in Russia, one suspects, could only shake their heads in disbelief.

The political role of the Polish magnates reflected their social and economic power. For centuries, members of the great families laid successful claim to the highest offices in the royal administration. At the same time, unlike their Russian counterparts, they worked to weaken the government that they served. The magnates had the leading voice in the *Sejm* or national assembly, but, as time passed, were increasingly content to control the decisions of the *sejmiki* or regional assemblies. In these local meetings, their retainers saw to it that the region accepted royal authority and cooperated with the other parts of the country only insofar as it suited their patron. It has long been a commonplace that the rulers of early modern Europe increased their power, in part, by making an alliance with the lower nobility. Polish society would seem to offer the perfect conditions for such a development. In reality, in spite of their resentment of the magnates, the szlachta shared with their more powerful neighbors a fear of royal absolutism and a deep attachment to the privileges of the noble estate which they shared. We are all familiar with the consequences of the magnates' power—the fatal weakening of the national government and the dismemberment of the Polish state.

By the end of the seventeenth century, the Russian high nobles bore little resemblance to the Polish magnates. Like their counterparts to the West, they derived the core of their income from ownership of land and power over the peasants who lived on it. Like the aristocrats of France and England and the Polish magnates, they had first claim on many high offices, especially in the army and at court. Moreover, they shared with them an acute sense of their collective worth. In other respects, however, the Muscovite high nobility differed greatly from similar groups elsewhere in Europe. Unlike their fellows there, the Russians had little power in the regions from which they had originally come. In this regard, the contrast with England, France, Prussia, and, in particular, Poland, could not be more striking. In addition, the Russian high nobles were imprisoned in a system of universal service to an absolute ruler like the Ottoman. It was precisely this combination of landownership, family solidarity, compulsory state service, and the lack of regional power and corporate rights that made the Muscovite high nobility of the seventeenth century unique.[8]

The Membership of the Boyar Duma*
1613-1690

	Boyar	Okol'nichii	Dumnyi Dvorianin	Dumnyi D'iak	Total
1613	19	8	1	1	29
1614	23	8	2	2	35
1615	23	7	2	2	34
1616	28	7	2	2	39
1617	27	6	1	2	36
1618	27	6	1	3	37
1619	24	6	1	3	34
1620	25	7	1	3	36
1621	26	7	1	2	36
1622	25	7	1	2	35
1623	26	6	1	3	36
1624	27	6	1	3	37
1625	27	6	1	3	37
1626	25	6	1	3	35
1627	25	6	1	4	36
1628	23	7	1	4	35
1629	20	6	1	4	31
1630	17	6	1	4	28
1631	15	8	1	4	28

* The figures for 1613 refer to the time of the coronation of Mikhail Romanov, June 11. Thereafter the figures are for January 1 of each year. Men normally held Duma rank for life. I have therefore considered them Duma members from the time of their first appointment until their death, final exile or disgrace, or until they took monastic vows. In some cases, we know only the year of an individual's appointment or disappearance from the Duma according to the Muscovite calendar, in which the year begins on September 1. For example, the most precise available date of a man's death might be 7196 or, in our terms, 1687/8. In such instances, I have assumed that the individual in question died in 1688.

	Boyar	Okol'nichii	Dumnyi Dvorianin	Dumnyi D'iak	Total
1632	15	8	1	4	28
1633	14	9	1	5	29
1634	14	9	1	5	29
1635	18	7	3	3	31
1636	18	10	3	3	34
1637	19	10	3	3	35
1638	18	11	3	3	35
1639	20	10	0	3	33
1640	19	10	0	3	32
1641	20	9	0	3	32
1642	22	8	1	3	34
1643	20	7	0	3	30
1644	18	7	1	4	30
1645	14	8	1	5	28
1646	22	11	1	5	39
1647	25	13	2	5	45
1648	25	18	2	6	51
1649	27	18	3	4	52
1650	28	21	3	5	57
1651	27	23	5	3	58
1652	28	22	6	4	60
1653	29	23	7	3	62
1654	31	25	6	3	65
1655	27	27	6	3	63
1656	29	29	6	3	67
1657	29	31	6	3	69
1658	31	29	5	3	68
1659	32	30	6	3	71
1660	32	28	8	3	71
1661	29	30	8	3	70
1662	27	31	9	3	70
1663	26	28	10	3	67
1664	25	28	10	3	66
1665	26	26	13	3	68
1666	27	25	12	5	69
1667	25	26	12	5	68
1668	27	20	14	6	67
1669	26	19	16	6	67

	Boyar	Okol'nichii	Dumnyi Dvorianin	Dumnyi D'iak	Total
1670	26	16	17	6	65
1671	22	19	21	7	69
1672	25	16	23	7	71
1673	25	17	24	8	74
1674	25	14	25	8	72
1675	25	15	22	8	70
1676	23	13	22	8	66
1677	37	18	23	9	87
1678	43	25	14	11	93
1679	43	25	16	11	95
1680	41	26	15	10	92
1681	44	26	19	10	99
1682	45	29	22	11	107
1683	61	33	29	8	131
1684	59	38	34	9	140
1685	58	39	36	8	141
1686	57	41	39	8	145
1687	55	42	39	8	144
1688	52	41	37	7	137
1689	55	43	41	6	145
1690	52	54	38	9	153

APPENDIX B

The Members of the Boyar Duma, 1613-1713

The so-called Sheremetev list ("Posluzhnoi spisok starinnykh boiar i dvoretskikh, okol'nichikh i nekotorykh drugikh pridvornykh chinov s 6970 po 7184 (to est' s 1462 po 1676) god . . . ," DRV 20:1-131) gives the names of Duma members up to 1676. The individuals listed below whose names appear in that late seventeenth-century source are indicated by an asterisk (*). I have used data from the Sheremetev list only to fill gaps in other sources or when its testimony differs markedly from theirs. On the whole, the Sheremetev list is quite accurate for the seventeenth century.

Duma members at the time of the accession of Mikhail Romanov, 1613

*Mstislavskii, Prince Fedor Ivanovich—boyar, 1576 (A. A. Zimin, "So-stav Boiarskoi dumy v XV-XVI vekakh," p. 77); last mention, May 13, 1621 (DR 1:473-474); died, Feb. 19, 1622 (Mosk. nekropol' 2:291).
*Vorotynskii, Prince Ivan Mikhailovich—boyar, 1591/2 (DRV 20:64); last mention, Dec. 5, 1626 (Sb. mosk. st. 28, sb. 3:1v); died, Jan. 8, 1627 (G. A. Vlas'ev, Potomstvo Riurika 1, pt. 1, p. 57).
*Shuiskii, Prince Ivan Ivanovich—boyar, 1595/6 (DRV 20:66); tonsured, Nov. 28, 1637 (P. M. Raevskii, Rod tsaria, tsareven i kniazei Shui-skikh, n.p.); died, February, 1638 (BK 2:1r).
*Golitsyn, Prince Ivan Vasil'evich—boyar, 1605 (DRV 20:76); exiled to Perm', Sept. 14, 1624 (DR 1:642); died, May 18, 1626 (Mosk. nekro-pol' 1:297).
*Romanov, Ivan Nikitich—boyar, 1605 (DRV 20:76); died, July 18, 1640 (Sb. mosk. st. 154, sb. 3:2v).
*Trubetskoi, Prince Dmitrii Timofeevich—boyar, 1611/2 (RK 1550 2:264); died, June 24, 1625 (A. V. Barsukov, Spiski gorodovykh voevod i dru-

gikh lits voevodskago upravleniia moskovskago gosudarstva XVII sto-letiia, p. 236, citing *DRV* 3:143).

*Kurakin, Prince Andrei Petrovich—boyar, 1584 (*DRV* 20:61); last mention, May, 1613 ("Utverzhdennaia gramota ob izbranii na moskovskoe gosudarstvo Mikhaila Fedorovicha Romanova," p. 77); died, 1615 (*Mosk. nekropol'* 2:127).

*Morozov, Vasilii Petrovich—okol'nichii, 1600/1 (*DRV* 20:71); boyar, 1606/7 (*RK 1550* 2:240); died, March 9, 1630 (Sb. mosk. st. 51, sb. 3:2v).

*Sheremetev, Fedor Ivanovich—boyar, 1605 (*RK 1550* 1:226); tonsured, after June 22, 1649 (A. V. Barsukov, *Rod Sheremetevykh* 3:402); died, Feb. 17, 1650 (*Ibid.*, p. 404).

*Lykov, Prince Boris Mikhailovich—kravchii, 1605 (*DRV* 20:76); boyar, 1605 (*RK 1550* 1:226); died, June 2 or 8, 1646 (BK 4:2v; *DRV* 19:355).

*Dolgorukii, Prince Vladimir Timofeevich—boyar, 1606 (*DRV* 20:81); last mention, in exile, 1629/30 (Sb. mosk. st. 51, sb. 3:2v); died, 1632/3 (*DRV* 20:96).

*Kurakin, Prince Ivan Semenovich—boyar, 1605 (*DRV* 20:76) or 1607 (*RK 1550* 2:243); last mention, 1618/9 (*DR* 1:427; *KR* 1:663); died, 1632 (*Mosk. nekropol'* 2:129).

*Bakhteiarov-Rostovskii, Prince Vladimir Ivanovich—boyar, Feb. 2, 1608 (P. G. Liubomirov, *Ocherk istorii Nizhegorodskogo opolcheniia*, p. 272); last mention, July 5, 1616 (*AAE* 3:116); died, 1616/7 (*DRV* 20:90)

*Godunov, Matvei Mikhailovich—okol'nichii, 1598 (*RK 1550* 1:166); boyar, Dec. 25, 1603 (*Ibid.*, p. 215; N. P. Likhachev, *Razriadnye d'iaki XVI veka*, pp. 523-524); last mention, June 2, 1638 (*DR* 2:579); died, 1638/9 (BK 2:4v).

*Nagoi, Andrei Aleksandrovich—okol'nichii, 1605 (*DRV* 20:76); boyar, 1605/6 (*Ibid.*, p. 77); died, just before Jan. 4, 1618 (*DR* 1:310).

*Nagoi, Mikhail Aleksandrovich—boyar, 1606 (*DRV* 20:77); last mention, 1615/6 (*AMG* 1:138); died, 1617/8 (*DRV* 20:91).

*Odoevskii, Prince Ivan Nikitich bol'shoi—boyar, 1605/6 (*DRV* 20:77); last mention, April 28, 1615 (*DAI* 2:73); died, March 7, 1616 (Vlas'ev, *Potomstvo* 1, pt. 1, p. 75).

*Trubetskoi, Prince Andrei Vasil'evich—boyar, Sept. 4, 1598 (*RK 1550* 1:164); last mention, Sept. 9, 1618 (*DR* 1:356).

*Shein, Mikhail Borisovich—okol'nichii, 1605 (*RK 1550* 2:221); boyar, 1606 (*Ibid.*, p. 238); executed, April 28, 1634 (*AAE* 3:389).

*Godunov, Nikita Vasil'evich—okol'nichii, Sept. 4, 1598 (*RK 1550* 1:164); last mention, May 1, 1622 (*DR* 1:509); died, 1621/2 (*DRV* 20:92).

*Mezetskii, Prince Daniil Ivanovich—okol'nichii, 1607/8 (*RK 1550* 2:243); · boyar, Oct. 1, 1617 (*DR* 1:299); died, 1628/9 (BK 1:4r); buried, July 17, 1628 (*Mosk. nekropol'* 2:244).

*Khvorostinin, Prince Ivan Dmitrievich—okol'nichii, April 24, 1603 (*RK 1550* 1:211; Likhachev, *Razriadnye d'iaki*, pp. 522-523); died, 1614 (*DR* 1:136-137).

*Golovin, Fedor Vasil'evich—okol'nichii, 1606 (*DRV* 20:82); deprived of rank, 1623 (*DR* 1:565-566n.); died, April 16, 1625 (*Mosk. nekropol'* 1:310).

*Litvinov-Mosal'skii, Prince Vladimir Ivanovich—okol'nichii, 1605/6 (*DRV* 20:78); last mention, 1615/6 (*DR* 1:240).

*Romodanovskii, Prince Grigorii Petrovich—okol'nichii, 1605/6 (*RK 1550* 1:234); boyar, Dec. 25, 1615 (*DR* 1:208) [NB. signed "Ut. gramota" as a boyar, supposedly in May, 1613, p. 78]; last mention, November, 1627 (Sb. mosk. st. 32, sb. 1:3v); died, 1627/8 (*DRV* 20:94).

*Izmailov, Artemii Vasil'evich—dumnyi dvorianin, 1605 (*DRV* 20:77); okol'nichii, 1606 (*Ibid.*, p. 82) or April 8, 1610 (Liubomirov, *Ocherk*, p. 277; *RK 1550* 2:256); executed, April 28, 1634 (*AAE* 3:389).

*Golovin, Semen Vasil'evich—okol'nichii, April 8, 1610 (Liubomirov, *Ocherk*, p. 277); boyar, April 21, 1622 (*DR* 1:507); last mention, Dec. 7, 1633 (*KR* 2:596); died, Jan. 10, 1634 (*Mosk. nekropol'* 1:309).

*Pushkin, Gavriil Grigor'evich—dumnyi dvorianin, 1605 (*DRV* 20:76); died, 1637/8 (BK 3:3r).

Vasil'ev, Sydavnoi—dumnyi d'iak, September, 1610 (*RK 1550* 2:261); last mention, June 1, 1619 (*DR* 1:392); died, Nov. 5, 1619 (S. B. Veselovskii, *D'iaki i pod'iachie XV-XVII vv.*, p. 86).

1613: New Appointments

*Pozharskii, Prince Dmitrii Mikhailovich—boyar, June 11, 1613 (*DR* 1:96) [NB. signed "Ut. gramota" as boyar, p. 77]; died, April 20, 1642 (*Rus. pr. nekropol'* 1:689).

*Cherkasskii, Prince Ivan Borisovich—kravchii, dismissed, 1606 (*DRV* 20:82); boyar, June 11, 1613 (*DR* 1:96) [NB. signed "Ut. gramota" as boyar, p. 78]; last mention, March 1, 1642 (*DR* 2:674); buried, April 3, 1642 (*Mosk. nekropol'* 3:311).

*Minin, Kuz'ma—dumnyi dvorianin, June 12, 1613 (*DR* 1:100); died, before July 5, 1616 (*AAE* 3:116).

Tret'iakov, Petr Alekseevich—dumnyi d'iak, June 13, 1613 (*DR* 1:100); last mention, May 16, 1618 (S. K. Bogoiavlenskii, *Prikaznye sud'i XVII veka*, p. 128).

*Odoevskii, Prince Ivan Nikitich men'shii—boyar, Dec. 6, 1613 (*DR* 1:120); last mention, December, 1628 (*DR* 2:16); died, March 2, 1629 (Vlas'ev, *Potomstvo* 1, pt. 1, p. 76).

*Saltykov, Boris Mikhailovich—okol'nichii and dvoretskii (*DRV* 20:89)

[NB. not confirmed by other sources]; boyar, Dec. 6, 1613 (*DR* 1:120) [NB. signed "Ut. gramota" as boyar, p. 77]; 1625/6, demoted to rank of moskovskii dvorianin (*DR* 1:845-846; Sb. mosk. st. 25, sb. 2:60v); boyar again, by Jan. 12, 1634 (*DR* 2:360); died, July 26, 1646 (BK 4:2r).

1615

*Lobanov-Rostovskii, Prince Afanasii Vasil'evich—boyar, Feb. 2, 1615 (*DR* 1:170); died, 1628/9 (BK 2:4v).

*Suleshev, Prince Iurii Ensheevich—boyar, Feb. 2, 1615 (*DR* 1:170); died, March 8, 1643 (BK 4:2v).

*Khovanskii, Prince Ivan Andreevich—boyar, March 14, 1615 (*DR* 1:170) [NB. listed in "Ut. gramota" as boyar, p. 78]; last mention, 1618/9 (*DR* 1:415); died, May 26, 1622 (*Rus. pr. nekropol'* 1:915).

*Sitskii, Prince Aleksei Iur'evich—boyar, March 25, 1615 (*DR* 1:174); died, July, 1644 (Sb. mosk. st. 216:116v); buried, July 6, 1644 (*Mosk. nekropol'* 3:106).

*Volkonskii, Prince Grigorii Konstantinovich—okol'nichii, Sept. 1, 1615 (*DR* 1:197); died, soon after March 2, 1634 (*DR* 2:367).

*Golovin, Petr Petrovich—boyar, Nov. 27, 1615 (*DR* 1:206); died, Dec. 14, 1627 (*Mosk. nekropol'* 1:309).

1617

*Ziuzin, Aleksei Ivanovich—okol'nichii, Oct. 1, 1617 (*DR* 1:299); last mention, Sept. 9, 1618 (*DR* 1:357; *KR* 1:565); died, 1618/9 (*DRV* 20:91).

Novokshchenov, Nikolai Nikitich—dumnyi d'iak, Oct. 1, 1617 (*DR* 1:299); last mention in service, Oct. 2, 1620 (Bogoiavlenskii, *Sud'i*, p. 120); demoted, 1619/20 (Veselovskii, *D'iaki*, p. 376); tonsured, 1633; died, March, 1637 (Likhachev, *Razriadnye d'iaki*, p. 523, n. 3).

1618

*Gramotin, Ivan Taras'evich—dumnyi d'iak, 1611 (Sb. mosk. st. 1066, sb. 2:2v); first mention as dumnyi d'iak after 1613, April 18, 1618 (*DR* 1:319-320n.); disgraced, Dec. 22, 1626 (*RIB* 9:438); restored to rank of dumnyi d'iak, May 19, 1634 (Veselovskii, *D'iaki*, p. 130); pechatnik, first mention, June 18, 1634 (*DR* 2:380); dumnyi dvorianin, 1634/5 (*DRV* 20:97); died, 1638/9 (*Ibid.*, p. 98); buried, Oct. 4, 1638 (Veselovskii, *D'iaki*, p. 130).

1619

*Cherkasskii, Prince Dmitrii Mamstriukovich—boyar, Jan. 6, 1619 (*DR* 1:385); last mention, Dec. 31, 1645 (*AMG* 2:170); buried, June 2, 1651 (*Mosk. nekropol'* 3:311).

*Buturlin, Fedor Leont'evich—okol'nichii, June 1, 1619 (*DR* 1:392); died, after September, 1639 (Sb. mosk. st. 154, sb. 3, 3v).

*Lugovskii, Tomilo Iudich—dumnyi d'iak, returned from Poland to resume office, June 1, 1619 (*DR* 1:391); dumnyi dvorianin, Dec. 21, 1635 (BK 2:192r); last mention, Sept. 21, 1636 (*DR* 2:521); tonsured, Feb. 25, 1638 (Sb. mosk. st. 1161, sb. 1:3v); died, 1637/8 (*DRV* 20:98).

*Pushkin, Nikita Mikhailovich—okol'nichii, August 15, 1619 (*DR* 1:410); last mention, 1620/1 (*Ibid.*, p. 483); died, 1621/2 (*DRV* 20:92).

1620

*Troekurov, Prince Ivan Fedorovich—boyar, March 12, 1620 (*DR* 1:438); last mention, Jan. 29, 1621 (*Ibid.*, p. 468); died, May 29, 1621 (A. B. Lobanov-Rostovskii, *Russkaia rodoslovnaia kniga* 2:295).

1622

*Sitskii, Prince Andrei Vasil'evich—okol'nichii, Jan. 6, 1622 (*DR* 1:494); boyar, April 26, 1622 (*Ibid.*, p. 507); died, 1628/9 (BK 1:5v); buried, April 29, 1629 (*Mosk. nekropol'* 3:106).

*Odoevskii, Prince Ivan Ivanovich men'shii—boyar, April 14, 1622 (*DR* 1:505); died, August 9, 1628 (Vlas'ev, *Potomstvo* 1, pt. 1, p. 79).

*Lykov, Prince Fedor Ivanovich—okol'nichii, April 28, 1622 (*DR* 1:508); last mention, October, 1626 (Sb. mosk. st. 28, sb. 3:3v); died, 1627/8 (*DRV* 20:94).

*Likhachev, Fedor Fedorovich—dumnyi d'iak, first mention, Sept. 8, 1622 (*DR* 1:525); pechatnik, Oct. 27, 1641 (*Ibid.*, 2:673); dumnyi dvorianin, Oct. 1, 1652 (Sb. mosk. st. 1133:2v); last mention, Oct. 3, 1652 (Bogoiavlenskii, *Sud'i*, p. 115); died, January, 1653 (Sb. mosk. st. 1133:2v).

*Dolgorukii, Prince Daniil Ivanovich—okol'nichii, Dec. 6, 1622 (*DR* 1:529); died, August 9, 1626 (*ChOIDR*, 1909, no. 3, p. 105).

1623

*Khovanskii, Prince Ivan Fedorovich—boyar, Jan. 6, 1623 (*DR* 1:532); last mention, 1623/4 (*AI* 3:265); died, 1624/5 (*DRV* 20:93).

*Saltykov, Mikhail Mikhailovich—kravchii, 1612/3 (*DRV* 20:89); okol'-nichii, Jan. 7, 1623 (*DR* 1:533); demoted to moskovskii dvorianin, 1625/6 (*DR* 1:845-846; Sb. mosk. st. 25, sb. 2:61v); okol'nichii again, by Jan. 6, 1634 (*DR* 2:354); boyar, March 17, 1641 (BK 4:6r-7v); died, Oct. 3, 1671 (*DRV* 20:123).

1624

*Khilkov, Prince Andrei Vasil'evich—boyar, Oct. 17, 1624 (*DR* 1:651); last mention, Jan. 10, 1644 (Bogoiavlenskii, *Sud'i*, p. 184); died, Feb. 18, 1644 (Sb. mosk. st. 216:116v).

1626

*Dolmatov-Karpov, Lev Ivanovich—okol'nichii, Jan. 6, 1626 (*DR* 1:760); died, Dec. 23, 1642 (Sb. mosk. st. 182, sb. 2:2v).

Telepnev, Efim Grigor'evich—dumnyi d'iak, first mention, Dec. 22, 1626 (Likhachev, *Razriadnye d'iaki*, p. 130, n. 1); resigned, July 22, 1630 (BK 2:7v); last mention, July 30, 1630 (Bogoiavlenskii, *Sud'i*, p. 128); buried, Dec. 8, 1636 (*Mosk. nekropol'* 3:195).

1627

*L'vov, Prince Aleksei Mikhailovich—"skazano vo dvorets", 1625/6 (*DRV* 20:93); okol'nichii, Dec. 25, 1627 (BK 1:7v); boyar, July 5, 1634 (*DR* 2:380); last mention, March 17, 1652 (*DR* 3:300); died, 1652/3 (*DRV* 20:109).

1630

*Streshnev, Luk'ian Stepanovich—okol'nichii, Jan. 6, 1630 (*DR* 2:108); boyar, March 1, 1634 (*Ibid.*, p. 365); last mention, March 17, 1647 (*AMG* 2:176); died, 1649/50 (*DRV* 20:106).

*Prozorovskii, Prince Semen Vasil'evich—okol'nichii, March 30, 1630 (*DR* 2:129); boyar, August 15, 1646 (*DR* 3:42); dismissed, March, 1652; reinstated, July, 1652 (Sb. mosk. st. 245, 6v); last mention, Nov. 27, 1657 (*DR Dop. k* 3:112); died, Sept. 14, 1659 (*Rus. pr. nekropol'* 1:712).

*Gavrenev, Ivan Afanas'evich—dumnyi d'iak, first mention, August 15, 1630 (*AMG* 1:311; Bogoiavlenskii, *Sud'i*, p. 145); dumnyi dvorianin, Dec. 21, 1650 (*DR* 3:218); okol'nichii, Dec. 6, 1654 (*DR* 3:455); last mention, Sept. 19, 1661 (Bogoiavlenskii, *Sud'i*, p. 147); died, Jan. 11, 1662 (Sb. mosk. st. 342, sb. 1:5v).

1632

*Korob'in, Vasilii Gavrilovich—okol'nichii, Oct. 1, 1632 (*DR* 2:294); died, Feb. 6, 1635 (Sb. mosk. st. 111, sb. 1:3v); buried, Feb. 17, 1635 (*Mosk. nekropol'* 2:86).

Griazev, Ivan Kirillovich—dumnyi d'iak, Oct. 1, 1632 (*DR* 2:294); last mention, April 17, 1634 (Bogoiavlenskii, *Sud'i*, p. 128); died, May 14, 1634 (*Mosk. nekropol'* 1:339).

1634

*Morozov, Boris Ivanovich—boyar, Jan. 6, 1634 (*DR* 2:354); last mention, Sept. 1, 1659 (*DR* Dop. k 3:197); died, Nov. 1, 1661 (*Mosk. nekropol'* 2:285).

*Streshnev, Vasilii Ivanovich—okol'nichii, Jan. 6, 1634 (*DR* 2:354); boyar, Sept. 28, 1645 (BK 4:12v); last mention, May 24, 1655 (*DR* 3:472); died, 1660/1 (*DRV* 20:115).

*Golitsyn, Prince Ivan Andreevich—boyar, Feb. 2, 1634 (*DR* 2:360); last mention, 1649/50 (*DR* 3:184); died, August 30, 1654 (*Mosk. nekropol'* 1:297).

*Sheremetev, Ivan Petrovich—boyar, Feb. 2, 1634 (*DR* 2:360); died, July 8, 1647 (*Mosk. nekropol'* 3:349).

*Streshnev, Fedor Stepanovich—okol'nichii, Feb. 2, 1634 (*DR* 2:360); boyar, Sept. 30, 1645 (*DR* 3:19; BK 4, 12r); last mention, Sept. 2, 1647 (Bogoiavlenskii, *Sud'i*, p. 210).

*Morozov, Ivan Vasil'evich—boyar, March 1, 1634 (*DR* 2:365); last mention, June 29, 1655 (*DR* 3:483); tonsured, 1654/5 (*DRV* 20:110); died, 1670 (*Mosk. nekropol'* 1:508).

*Proestev, Stepan Matveevich—dumnyi dvorianin, July 5, 1634 (*DR* 2:380); okol'nichii, July 19, 1635 (*Ibid.*, p. 470); last mention, March 25, 1649 (*DR* 3:116); died, 1650/1 (*DRV* 20:107).

*Volkonskii, Prince Fedor Fedorovich—okol'nichii, July 8, 1634 (*DR* 2:382); boyar, Dec. 21, 1650 (*DR* 3:218); last mention, Jan. 27, 1663 (*DR* 3:550); died, February, 1665 (Vlas'ev, *Potomstvo* 1, pt. 3, p. 345).

1635

*Repnin, Prince Petr Aleksandrovich—boyar, May 5, 1635 (*DR* 2:456); died, Jan. 27, 1643 (*DRV* 20:349).

*Volynskii, Fedor Vasil'evich—okol'nichii, June 4, 1635 (*DR* 2:467); died, 1645/6 (BK 4:13v-r); buried, Jan. 17, 1646 (*Mosk. nekropol'* 1:232).

Danilov, Mikhail Fefilat'evich—dumnyi d'iak, July 19, 1635 (*DR* 2:470); last mention, Jan. 1, 1648 (*DR* 3:84; Sb. mosk. st. 1103, sb. 4:30v).

*Litvinov-Mosal'skii, Prince Andrei Fedorovich—okol'nichii, July 25, 1635 (*DR* 2:472); last mention, Sept. 21, 1658 (*DR* Dop. k 3:149); died, 1663/4 (*DRV* 20:117).

*Cherkasskii-Amashukov (or Akhamashukov), Prince Vasilii Petrovich—okol'nichii, August 6, 1635 (*DR* 2:474); last mention, May 7, 1649 (*DR* 3:119); died, October, 1651 (Sb. mosk. st. 245:1v).

1637

*Vel'iaminov, Nikita Dmitrievich—okol'nichii, August 15, 1637 (*DR* 2:544); died, July, 1638 (BK 2:189r).

1638

*Golitsyn, Prince Andrei Andreevich—boyar, Jan. 6, 1638 (*DR* 2:560); died, Sept. 22, 1638 (Sb. mosk. st. 131, sb. 1:2v).

*Sitskii, Prince Iurii Andreevich—boyar, May 15, 1638 (*DR* 2:575); died, August, 1644 (BK 4:5v).

*Morozov, Gleb Ivanovich—boyar, Dec. 25, 1638 (*DR* 2:559); last mention, May 9, 1659 (*DR* Dop. k 3:185); died, 1661/2 (*DRV* 20:115).

1640

*Repnin, Prince Boris Aleksandrovich—boyar, Jan. 6, 1640 (BK 4:5r); died, May 17, 1670 (BS 6:1v; *DRV* 19:349-350) [The date of death, 1642/3, given in *DRV* 20:100 is clearly erroneous.].

*Odoevskii, Prince Nikita Ivanovich—boyar, Jan. 12, 1640 (BK 2:8v); died, Feb. 12, 1689 (BS 28:1v).

1641

*Sheremetev, Vasilii Petrovich—boyar, March 17, 1641 (BK 4:6v); last mention, April 3, 1659 (*DR* Dop. k 3:180); died, 1658/9 (*DRV* 20:113).

*Vel'iaminov, Miron Andreevich—okol'nichii, April 27, 1641 (BK 4:15v-r); died, August 23, 1641 (Sb. mosk. st. 165, sb. 1:3v).

*Birkin, Ivan Vasil'evich—iasel'nichii, 1631/2 (*DRV* 20:95); dumnyi dvorianin, last mention, May 5, 1641 (*DR* 2:656); tonsured, September, 1642 (Sb. mosk. st. 182, sb. 1:3v); died, 1642/3 (*DRV* 20:100).

1643

*Dubrovskii, Bogdan Minich—dumnyi dvorianin and kaznachei, April 4, 1643 (*DR* 2:698); died, 1661/2 (BK 5:19r).

L'vov, Grigorii Vasil'evich—dumnyi d'iak, Sept. 1, 1643 (*DR* 2:711); last mention, Dec. 27, 1646 (Bogoiavlenskii, *Sud'i*, p. 129).

1644

*Pushkin, Grigorii Gavrilovich—dumnyi dvorianin, February, 1644 (*DR* 2:731); okol'nichii, Nov. 27, 1644 (*Ibid.*, p. 743); boyar, August 15, 1646 (*DR* 3:42); last mention, Jan. 6, 1656 (*DR* Dop. k 3:21); died, 1655/6 (*DRV* 20:111).

Volosheninov, Mikhail Dmitrievich—dumnyi d'iak, Nov. 27, 1644 (BK 4:22v); last mention, April, 1653 (Bogoiavlenskii, *Sud'i*, p. 129); died, April 6, 1653 (Sb. mosk. st. 1133, sb. 3:2v).

1645

*Trubetskoi, Prince Aleksei Nikitich—boyar, Sept. 7, 1645 (*DR* 3:13); last mention, Oct. 27, 1662 (Bogoiavlenskii, *Sud'i*, p. 63); died, 1662/3 (*DRV* 20:116).

*Romanov, Nikita Ivanovich—boyar, Sept. 28, 1645 (BK 4:7v); last mention, May, 1654 (*DR* 3:413); died, Dec. 11, 1654 (*Mosk. nekropol'* 3:36).

*L'vov, Prince Dmitrii Petrovich—okol'nichii, Sept. 28, 1645 (*DR* 3:15; BK 4:15r-16v); boyar, Feb. 2, 1655 (*DR* 3:457); last mention, March 28, 1660 (*DAI* 4:193); died, 1659/60 (*DRV* 20:114).

*Cherkasskii, Prince Iakov Kudenetovich—boyar, Sept. 29, 1645 (*DR* 3:18; BK 4:7r, 32v); last mention, June 18, 1664 (S. M. Solov'ev, *Istoriia Rossii s drevneishikh vremen* 6:167-168); died, July 8, 1666 (*Mosk. nekropol'* 3:312) or June 1667 (Barsukov, *Rod Sheremetevykh* 7:8).

*Saltykov, Ivan Ivanovich—boyar, Sept. 29, 1645 (*DR* 3:18); died, Oct. 13, 1670 (*DRV* 20:122); buried, Oct. 14, 1670 (*Mosk. nekropol'* 3:69).

*Volkonskii, Prince Petr Fedorovich—okol'nichii, Sept. 29, 1645 (*DR* 3:18; BK 4:16v); died, December, 1649 or January, 1650 (Vlas'ev, *Potomstvo* 1, pt. 3, p. 346).

*Kurakin, Prince Fedor Semenovich—boyar, Sept. 29 or 30, 1645 (*DR* 3:19; BK 4:33v); last mention, April 1654 (*AMG* 2:376); buried, June 25, 1655 (*Mosk. nekropol'* 2:129).

*Dolmatov-Karpov, Fedor Borisovich—okol'nichii, Sept. 30, 1645 (*DR* 3:19; BK 4:16r); boyar, March 25, 1649 (*DR* 3:116); died, 1659/60 (BK 5:4v).

*Temkin-Rostovskii, Prince Mikhail Mikhailovich—boyar, Oct. 1, 1645 (*DR* 3:20); last mention, May 24, 1655 (*Ibid.*, p. 472); died, 1661 (*Rus. pr. nekropol'* 1:849).
*Sobakin, Nikifor Sergeevich—okol'nichii, Oct. 1, 1645 (*DR* 3:20; BK 4:16r); last mention, June 10, 1655 (*DR* 3:480); died, 1655/6 (*DRV* 20:112).

1646

*Buinosov-Rostovskii, Prince Iurii Petrovich—boyar, March 17, 1646 (*DR* 3:31); died, 1660/1 (BK 5:3v).
*Pushkin, Boris Ivanovich—okol'nichii, March 17, 1646 (*DR* 3:32); last mention, 1656 (A. A. Titov, ed., *Letopis' dvinskaia*, p. 25); died, 1658/9 (*DRV* 20:113).
*Trakhaniotov, Petr Tikhonovich—okol'nichii, March 17, 1646 (BK 4:17v); died, June 5, 1648 (S. V. Bakhrushin, *Nauchnye trudy* 2:50).
*Sheremetev, Boris Petrovich—boyar, March 29, 1646 (*DR* 3:33); last mention, April 4, 1650 (*DR* 3:154-155); died, 1649/50 (*DRV* 20:106).
*Buturlin, Mikhail Matveevich—okol'nichii, March 29, 1646 (*DR* 3:33); died, Oct. 5, 1647 (M. P. Lukichev, "Obzor boiarskikh knig XVII v.," pp. 260-261).
*Romodanovskii, Prince Vasilii Grigor'evich men'shii—okol'nichii, March 29, 1646 (*DR* 3:33); boyar, Feb. 25, 1655 (*DR* 3:459); buried, Oct. 3, 1670 (*Mosk. nekropol'* 3:39).
*Elizarov, Fedor Kuz'mich—dumnyi d'iak, June 13, 1646 (*DR* 3:34); dumnyi dvorianin, by Dec. 25, 1650 (*Ibid.*, p. 218); okol'nichii, March 11, 1655 (*Ibid.*, p. 460); died, between Jan. 11 and July 24, 1664 (*AMG* 3:548, 563-564).
*Anichkov, Ivan Mikhailovich—dumnyi dvorianin, last mention, Sept. 4, 1646 (Sb. mosk. st. 202, sb. 3: 5v); tonsured, October, 1652 (Sb. mosk. st. 1133:1v).
*Saltykov, Lavrentii Dmitrievich—boyar, Oct. 6 or Nov. 8, 1646 (BK 4:9v; *DR* 3:49); last mention, June 4, 1655 (*AMG* 2:415); died, 1659/60 (*DRV* 20:114).
*Pozharskii, Prince Semen Romanovich—okol'nichii, Nov. 8, 1646 (*DR* 3:49); died, June 28, 1659 (Solov'ev, *Istoriia* 6:50-51).

1647

Chistyi, Nazarii Ivanovich—dumnyi d'iak, Jan. 6, 1647 (*DR* 3:55); died, June 2, 1648 (Bakhrushin, *Nauchnye trudy* 2:50).
*Khilkov, Prince Fedor Andreevich—okol'nichii, April 18, 1647 (*DR* 3:56); last mention, September, 1654 (*DAI* 3:458); died, 1656/7 (*DRV* 20:112).

*Pronskii, Prince Petr Ivanovich—boyar, April 22, 1647 (*DR* 3:57); last mention, May 17, 1648 (*Ibid.*, p. 92); died, May 13, 1652 (Lobanov-Rostovskii, *Rus. rod. kniga* 2:136).

*Khilkov, Prince Ivan Vasil'evich—okol'nichii, August 15, 1647 (*DR* 3:66); boyar, March 30, 1651 (*Ibid.*, p. 225); died, Sept. 12, 1654 (*DAI* 3:458).

*L'vov, Prince Vasilii Petrovich—okol'nichii, Sept. 8, 1647 (*DR* 3:74); last mention, April 2, 1657 (*DR* Dop. k 3:100); died, 1656/7 (*DRV* 20:112).

*Khitrovo, Bogdan Matveevich—okol'nichii, Nov. 27, 1647 (*DR* 3:74); boyar, between Nov. 7, 1666 and Sept. 3, 1667 (*DR* 3:655, 661); last mention, Feb. 29, 1680 (Bogoiavlenskii, *Sud'i*, p. 44); died, March 27, 1680 (Lobanov-Rostovskii, *Rus. rod. kniga* 2:318).

*Romodanovskii, Prince Ivan Ivanovich—okol'nichii, Nov. 27, 1647 (*DR* 3:74); boyar, April 1, 1657 (*DR* Dop. k 3:98); last mention, 1671/2 (BS 10:1r); buried, March 20, 1675 (*Mosk. nekropol'* 3:40) [The date of death, 1670/1, given in *DRV* 20:122 appears to be a mistake.].

*Pronskii, Prince Mikhail Petrovich—boyar, Dec. 25, 1647 (*DR* 3:78); died, Sept. 12, 1654 (*DAI* 3:458).

1648

*Miloslavskii, Il'ia Danilovich—okol'nichii, Jan. 17, 1648 (*DR* 3:86); boyar, Feb. 2, 1648 (*Ibid.*, p. 87); died, May 19, 1688 (BS 1:1v).

*Miloslavskii, Ivan Andreevich—okol'nichii, Feb. 12, 1648 (*DR* 3:87); boyar, March 1, 1657 (*DR* Dop. k 3:92); last mention, Jan. 26, 1663 (Bogoiavlenskii, *Sud'i*, p. 225); died, March 15, 1663 (Lobanov-Rostovskii, *Rus. rod. kniga* 1:383).

*Dolgorukii, Prince Iurii Alekseevich—boyar, Sept. 25, 1648 (*DR* 3:108); died, May 15, 1682 (*DAI* 10:23-25).

*Narbekov, Bogdan Fedorovich—dumnyi dvorianin, Oct. 22, 1648 (*RIB* 10:419); last mention, May, 1654 (*DR* 3:414); died, 1654/5 (*DRV* 20:110).

*Pushkin, Stepan Gavrilovich—okol'nichii, Dec. 25, 1648 (*DR* 3:110); died, soon after May 5, 1656 (*DR* Dop. k 3:41).

1649

*Zaborovskii, Semen Ivanovich—dumnyi d'iak, Feb. 2, 1649 (*DR* 3:113) [The date of appointment, 1654/5, in *DRV* 20:111 appears to be erroneous.]; dumnyi dvorianin, by July, 1664 (Sb. mosk. st. 357, sb. 2:5v); okol'nichii, June 18, 1677 (BK 7:47v; BS 14:226v); boyar, July 20, 1680; died, 1680/1 (BK 7:30v).

*Lobanov-Rostovskii, Prince Ivan Ivanovich—okol'nichii, March 25, 1649

(*DR* 3:116); boyar, Jan. 7, 1661 (*Ibid.*, p. 249); last mention, March 2, 1663 (Bogoiavlenskii, *Sud'i*, p. 185); died, April 17, 1664 (*Mosk. nekropol'* 2:179).

*Khovanskii, Prince Ivan Nikitich—boyar, April 1, 1649 (*DR* 3:117); last mention, April 18, 1656 (*DR* Dop. k 3:31); died, 1675 (P. V. Dolgorukov, *Rossiiskaia rodoslovnaia kniga* 1:281).

*Buturlin, Timofei Fedorovich—okol'nichii, April 1, 1649 (*DR* 3:117); died, 1650/1 (*Ibid.*, p. 268).

*Khilkov, Prince Ivan Andreevich—okol'nichii, May 6 or 7, 1649 (*RIB* 10:456; *DR* 3:118); boyar, Feb. 20, 1655 (*Ibid.*, p. 458); last mention, 1676/7 (BS 14:469v); buried, August 30, 1677 (*Mosk. nekropol'* 3:274).

*Buturlin, Fedor Vasil'evich—okol'nichii, Sept. 8, 1649 (*DR* 3:134); last mention, 1671/2 (BS 10:2r); died, Jan. 4, 1673 (*DRV* 20:124).

*Choglokov, Vasilii Aleksandrovich—okol'nichii, Dec. 25, 1649 (*DR* 3:145); last mention, Feb. 12, 1667 (*DAI* 6:231); died, 1666/7 (*DRV* 20:119).

1650

*Buturlin, Vasilii Vasil'evich—okol'nichii, March 17, 1650 (*DR* 3:151); boyar, March 17, 1652 (*Ibid.*, p. 299; Sb. mosk. st. 245:2v); died, December, 1655 (*DR* Dop. k 3:19).

*Sokovnin, Prokopii Fedorovich—okol'nichii, March 17, 1650 (*DR* 3:151); last mention, May 12, 1655 (Bogoiavlenskii, *Sud'i*, p. 210); died, 1661/2 (*DRV* 20:116).

*Rtishchev, Mikhail Alekseevich—striapchii s kliuchem, by Sept. 8, 1645 (*DR* 3:13); postel'nichii, Sept. 8, 1646 (*Ibid.*, p. 47); okol'nichii, August 6, 1650 (*DR* 3:181); last mention in service, June 27, 1652 (Bogoiavlenskii, *Sud'i*, p. 90); tonsured, 1652 (N. N. Kashkin, *Rodoslovnye razvedki* 1:377); buried, Dec. 3, 1677 (*Mosk. nekropol'* 3:44).

1651

*Khvorostinin, Prince Fedor Iur'evich—okol'nichii, March 17, 1651 (*DR* 3:224); boyar, Jan. 12, 1653 (*Ibid.*, p. 338; Sb. mosk. st. 1133:1v); last mention, July 30, 1655 (*DR* 3:485); buried, Dec. 22, 1655 (*Mosk. nekropol'* 3:271).

*Obolenskii, Prince Venedikt Andreevich—okol'nichii, last mention, March 17, 1651 (*DR* 3:224-225).

*Streshnev, Semen Luk'ianovich—kravchii, Sept. 28, 1645 (BK 4:18r); okol'nichii, March 30, 1651 (*DR* 3:226); boyar, March 11, 1655 (*Ibid.*, p. 460; *AMG* 2:399); last mention, June 30, 1666 (Bogoiavlenskii, *Sud'i*, p. 200); died, 1665/6 (*DRV* 20:118).

*Dolgorukii, Prince Dmitrii Alekseevich—okol'nichii, April 1, 1651 (*DR* 3:227); boyar, March 19, 1671 (*Ibid.*, p. 880; BS 8:2v); died, Nov. 7, 1673 (*Letopis' dvinskaia*, p. 34).

*Lopukhin, Larion Dmitrievich—dumnyi d'iak, April 11, 1651 (*DR* 3:236-237) [The date of appointment, 1654/5, given in *DRV* 20:111 appears to be an error.]; dumnyi dvorianin, March 17, 1667 (Sb. mosk. st. 1152:2v); died, July 29, 1677 (BS 14:277v).

*Kondyrev, Zhdan Vasil'evich—iasel'nichii, 1646/7 (*DRV* 20:105); dumnyi dvorianin, by April 16, 1651 (*DR* 3:243); okol'nichii, March 11, 1655 (*Ibid.*, p. 460); last mention, July 27, 1663 (*DR* Dop. k 3:389); died, 1666/7 (*DRV* 20:119).

*Kurakin, Prince Grigorii Semenovich—boyar, Nov. 8, 1651 (*DR* 3:285; Sb. mosk. st. 245:1v); died, March 1682 (BS 21:1v).

1652

*Pronskii, Prince Ivan Petrovich—boyar, March 17, 1652 (*DR* 3:299; Sb. mosk. st. 245:lv); died, Dec. 19, 1683 (BS 23:1v).

*L'vov, Prince Semen Petrovich—okol'nichii, April 18, 1652 (*DR* 3:306); died as prisoner of war, July, 1659 (Solov'ev, *Istoriia* 6:50-51).

*Golovin, Petr Petrovich—okol'nichii, July 17, 1652 (*DR* 3:322); last mention, Jan. 29, 1654 (*Ibid.*, p. 398); died, 1653/4 (*DRV* 20:109).

Ianov, Vasilii Fedorovich—dumnyi dvorianin, Oct. 1, 1652 (Sb. mosk. st. 1133:2v); last mention, May, 1654 (*DR* 3:414); died, April 6, 1657 (*Mosk. nekropol'* 3:406).

*Ziuzin, Nikita Alekseevich—okol'nichii, Nov. 8, 1652 (*DR* 3:332-333); boyar, April 3, 1653 (*Ibid.*, p. 347); last mention in service, May 6, 1661 (*Ibid.* Dop. k 3:263); exiled, December, 1664 or early 1665 (*RBS* 6:583-584).

1653

*Dolgorukii, Prince Petr Alekseevich—okol'nichii, Feb. 2, 1653 (*DR* 3:339); died, Feb. 8, 1669 (*DRV* 19:323).

*Sheremetev, Vasilii Borisovich—boyar, May 21, 1653 (*DR* 3:352); taken prisoner of war, Oct. 26, 1660 (*AMG* 3:488; Barsukov, *Rod Sheremetevykh* 5:445-449); died, April 24, 1682 (A. V. Barsukov, *Rodoslovie Sheremetevykh*, p. 9; BS 21:1v).

*Ivanov, Almaz—dumnyi d'iak, Sept. 28, 1653 (*DR* 3:369); pechatnik, March 17, 1667 (Sb. mosk. st. 1152:2v); died, April 27, 1669 (*DRV* 20:120).

*Alfer'ev, Ivan Vasil'evich—okol'nichii, Oct. 4, 1653 (*DR* 3:372); died, 1654/5 (*Ibid.*, p. 456).

*Kolychev, Aleksei Dmitrievich—okol'nichii, Nov. 13, 1653 (*DR* 3:379); last mention, August 6, 1659 (*DR* Dop. k 3:194); died, 1660/1 (*DRV* 20:115) or 1665 (M. L. Bode-Kolychev, *Boiarskii rod Kolychevykh*, p. 179).

*Troekurov, Prince Boris Ivanovich—okol'nichii, Nov. 21, 1653 (*DR* 3:381); boyar, April 11, 1673 (BK 6:31v); last mention, October, 1673 (*DR* 3:904); died, Jan. 17 or 18, 1674 (*DRV* 20:125; *Rus. pr. nekropol'* 1:870).

1654

*Pronchishchev, Afanasii Osipovich—dumnyi dvorianin, Feb. 2, 1654 (*DR* 3:399); died, Dec. 30, 1670 (BS 8:4v).

*Streshnev, Ivan Fedorovich bol'shoi—okol'nichii, March 17, 1654 (*DR* 3:403); boyar, June 18, 1676 (BS 14:3v); died, March 17, 1684 (BS 23:1r).

*Izmailov, Semen Artem'evich—okol'nichii, Sept. 8, 1654 (*DR* 3:454); last mention, 1671/2 (BS 10:2r); died, Jan. 7, 1674 (*DRV* 20:125).

1655

*Shcherbatov, Prince Timofei Ivanovich—okol'nichii, March 4, 1655 (*DR* 3:459); last mention, October, 1661 (*AI* 4:309); died, 1661/2 (Sb. mosk. st. 342, sb. 1:5v).

*Velikogo-Gagin, Prince Daniil Stepanovich—okol'nichii, March 4, 1655 (*DR* 3:459); died, August 14, 1675 (*Ibid.*, p. 1630).

*Urusov, Prince Semen Andreevich—kravchii, Jan. 15, 1641 (Sb. mosk. st. 166:19v); dismissed, 1644/5 (*DRV* 20:101); boyar, March 11, 1655 (*DR* 3:459; *AMG* 2:399); last mention, July 13, 1656 (*DR* Dop. k 3:60); died, 1656/7 (*DRV* 20:112).

*Buturlin, Andrei Vasil'evich—okol'nichii, March 11, 1655 (*DR* 3:460); died, 1675/6 (BS 14:4v).

*Eropkin, Ivan Fedorovich—dumnyi dvorianin, March 17, 1655 (*DR* 3:463); last mention, Jan. 1, 1660 (*DR* Dop. k 3:210; *AMG* 3:2-15); died, 1665/6 (*DRV* 20:118).

*Dolgorukii, Prince Fedor Fedorovich—okol'nichii, April 3, 1655 (*DR* 3:469); last mention, August 31, 1663 (*DR* 3:390); died, 1663/4 (*DRV* 20:117).

*Odoevskii, Prince Fedor Nikitich—boyar, April 15, 1655 (*DR* 3:470); buried, July 18, 1656 (*Mosk. nekropol'* 2:365).

*Elizarov, Prokofii Kuz'mich—dumnyi dvorianin, May 26, 1655 (*DR* 3:478); died, July, 1677 (BS 14:227v).

*Baklanovskii, Ivan Ivanovich—dumnyi dvorianin, August 15, 1655 (*DR* 3:487); last mention, Oct. 26, 1679 (*Ibid.* 4:703).

*Streshnev, Ivan Fedorovich men'shii—okol'nichii, Sept. 8, 1655 (*DR* Dop. k 3:7); last mention, Jan. 12, 1663 (*Ibid.*, p. 364).

1656

*Rtishchev, Fedor Mikhailovich—postel'nichii, August 11, 1650 (*DR* 3:182); okol'nichii, Jan. 12, 1656 (*DR* Dop. k 3:21); last mention, 1671/2 (BS 10:2r); died, July 21, 1673 (*DRV* 20:124).

*Romodanovskii, Prince Grigorii Grigor'evich—okol'nichii, April 29, 1656 (*DR* Dop. k 3:33); boyar, July 10, 1665 (BK 5:9v); died, May 15, 1682 (*DAI* 10:23-25).

*Boborykin, Nikita Mikhailovich—okol'nichii, May 17, 1656 (*DR* Dop. k 3:44); died, April, 1682 (BS 21:6v).

*Sheremetev, Petr Vasil'evich bol'shoi—boyar, Dec. 6, 1656 (*DR* Dop. k 3:85); died, April 29, 1690 (BK 10:1v).

*Streshnev, Rodion Matveevich—okol'nichii, Dec. 6, 1656 (*DR* Dop. k 3:85); boyar, June 18, 1676 (BK 7:24r; BS 14:3v); died, July 10, 1687 (*Mosk. nekropol'* 3:165).

*Prozorovskii, Prince Ivan Semenovich—boyar, Dec. 21, 1656 (*DR* Dop. k 3:87); died, June 22 or 24, 1670 (*DRV* 20:121; Solov'ev, *Istoriia* 6:304).

1657

*Eropkin, Vasilii Mikhailovich—okol'nichii, Jan. 1, 1657 (*DR* Dop. k 3:88); last mention, Oct. 27, 1666 (Bogoiavlenskii, *Sud'i*, p. 211); died, 1666/7 (*DRV* 20:119).

*Cherkasskii, Prince Grigorii Suncheleevich—boyar, Feb. 5, 1657 (*DR* Dop. k 3:89; Sb. mosk. st. 1140, sb. 1:1v); died, Oct. 14 or 15, 1672 (BK 6:26r; *DAI* 6:260).

*Volynskii, Vasilii Semenovich—okol'nichii, Nov. 27, 1657 (*DR* Dop. k 3:112); boyar, June 22, 1676 (BK 7:26v; BS 14:3r); died, September, 1682 (BK 7:38r).

1658

*Lobanov-Rostovskii, Prince Nikita Ivanovich—okol'nichii, Jan. 12, 1658 (*DR* Dop. k 3:115); died, 1657/8 (BK 5:33r).

*Pozharskii, Prince Ivan Dmitrievich—okol'nichii, April 4, 1658 (*DR* Dop. k 3:126); died, Feb. 15, 1668 (BS 1:3v).

*Ordin-Nashchokin, Afanasii Lavrent'evich—dumnyi dvorianin, April 23, 1658 (BK 5:20r); okol'nichii, by Feb. 18, 1665 (*RIB* 11:162); boyar, Feb. 2, 1667 (BK 5:9r); tonsured, 1671/2 (BS 10:2v); died, 1680 (Lobanov-Rostovskii, *Rus. rod. kniga* 2:52).

*Saltykov, Petr Mikhailovich—kravchii, by July 28, 1647 (*DR* 3:64); boyar, Nov. 27, 1658 (*DR* Dop. k 3:158); died, July 5, 1690 (BK 10:1r).

1659

*Volynskii, Mikhail Semenovich—okol'nichii, Feb. 2, 1659 (*DR* Dop. k 3:167); died, Jan. 25, 1669 (*DRV* 20:120).

*Repnin, Prince Ivan Borisovich—boyar, Feb. 3, 1659 (*DR* Dop. k 3:169); last mention, May 10, 1697 (Bogoiavlenskii, *Sud'i*, p. 162); died, June 5, 1697 (Vlas'ev, *Potomstvo* 1, pt. 2, p. 425).

*Khovanskii, Prince Ivan Andreevich—boyar, March 27, 1659 (*DR* Dop. k 3:179); executed, Sept. 17, 1682 (*DAI* 10:32; BK 7:19r).

*Matiushkin, Ivan Pavlovich—dumnyi dvorianin, 1653/4 (*DRV* 20:110) or by April 26, 1659 (*AMG* 3:658) [The evidence in Bogoiavlenskii, *Sud'i*, p. 26 and BK 5:20v suggests that the latter date is more likely.]; okol'nichii, Oct. 12, 1676 (BK 7:44r; BS 14:255v); buried, March 12, 1678 (*Mosk. nekropol'* 2:239).

*Anichkov, Grigorii Mikhailovich—dumnyi dvorianin, April 14, 1659 (*DR* Dop. k 3:182); last mention, Jan. 29, 1675 (*DR* 3:1198); died, 1675/6 (BS 13:4r) [The date of death, 1670/1, given in *DRV* 20:122 appears to be an error.].

1660

*Kurakin, Prince Fedor Fedorovich—boyar, Feb. 23, 1660 (*DR* Dop. k 3:216); died, Jan. 1, 1684 (BS 23:1v).

*Shcherbatov, Prince Osip Ivanovich—okol'nichii, May 2, 1660 (*DR* Dop. k 3:225); last mention, March 22, 1666 (*Letopis' dvinskaia*, p. 28); died, 1666/7 (*DRV* 20:119).

*Miloslavskii, Ivan Mikhailovich—okol'nichii, Sept. 1, 1660 (*DR* Dop. k 3:241); boyar, June 27, 1676 (BK 7:26v; BS 14:3r); died, July 26, 1685 (BS 24:1r).

1661

*Miloslavskii, Fedor Iakovlevich—okol'nichii, June 30, 1661 (*DR* Dop. k 3:276); last mention, Sept. 13, 1663 (*AMG* 3:545); died, 1664/5 (*DRV* 20:117).

*Sukin, Osip Ivanovich—okol'nichii, August 18, 1661 (*DR* Dop. k 3:283); died, May 4, 1669 (BS 3:3v).
*Boriatinskii, Prince Ivan Petrovich—born, 1615 (Vlas'ev, *Potomstvo* 1, pt. 2, p. 76); okol'nichii, Sept. 15, 1661 (*DR* Dop. k 3:288); boyar, August 15, 1676 (BK 7:26r; BS 14:3r); tonsured, 1688/9 (BK 10:4v; BS 28:1r); died, July 1, 1701 (Vlas'ev, *Potomstvo* 1, pt. 2, p. 78).
*Pronchishchev, Ivan Afanas'evich—dumnyi dvorianin, Sept. 15, 1661 (*DR* Dop. k 3:290); okol'nichii, Oct. 22, 1677 (BK 7:49v; BS 15:5v); died, 1686/7 (BK 10:24v).

1662

*Leont'ev, Zamiatnia Fedorovich—dumnyi dvorianin, April 5 or 6, 1662 (*DR* Dop. k 3:328; Zap. kn. mosk. st. 12:127v); last mention, Oct. 10, 1669 (*DAI* 6:231); died, March 14, 1670 (*DRV* 20:121).
*Chaadaev, Ivan Ivanovich—dumnyi dvorianin, April 9 or 11, 1662 (Zap. kn. mosk. st. 12:127r; *DR* Dop. k 3:330); okol'nichii, Oct. 21, 1677 (BK 7:49v); buried, Jan. 1, 1696 (*Mosk. nekropol'* 3:300).

1663

*Odoevskii, Prince Iakov Nikitich—boyar, August 16, 1663 (BK 5:7r); buried, August 9, 1697 (*Mosk. nekropol'* 2:365).
*Boriatinskii, Prince Iurii Nikitich—okol'nichii, Sept. 27, 1663 (Sb. mosk. st. 355, sb. 3:7v); boyar, Feb. 7, 1671 (*DR* 3:586; BS 8:2v); died, Jan. 7, 1685 (BS 24:1r).

1664

*Vorotynskii, Prince Ivan Alekseevich—boyar, Feb. 12, 1664 (BK 5:7r); died, July 24, 1679 (Vlas'ev, *Potomstvo* 1, pt. 1, p. 59).
*Golitsyn, Prince Aleksei Andreevich—boyar, Feb. 14, 1664 (*AMG* 3:552; BK 5:7r); died, March 9, 1694 (BS 35:425v).
*L'vov, Prince Nikita Iakovlevich—okol'nichii, by March, 1664 (Sb. mosk. st. 360, sb. 1:3v); last mention in service, August 4, 1668 (*DR* 3:827); tonsured, March 5, 1669 (*DRV* 20:121); died, March 29, 1684 (*Rus. pr. nekropol'* 1:501).
*Nashchokin, Grigorii Borisovich—dumnyi dvorianin, by March, 1664 (Sb. mosk. st. 360, sb. 1:4v); last mention, April 27, 1667 (Bogoiavlenskii, *Sud'i*, p. 225); died, October, 1677 (BS 15:6v).
*Bashmakov, Dementii Minich—dumnyi d'iak, April 17, 1664 (BK 5:23r);

dumnyi dvorianin, April 15, 1684 (BK 7:76r; BS 23:18v); died, Sept. 10, 1705 (*Mosk. nekropol'* 1:90).
*Khitrovo, Iakov Timofeevich—dumnyi dvorianin, Sept. 15, 1664 (BK 5:22v); died, 1675/6 or later (BS 14:8v).

1665

*Romodanovskii, Prince Iurii Ivanovich—boyar, July 10, 1665 (BK 5:9v); died, Feb. 20, 1683 (BS 22:1r).
*Karaulov, Grigorii Stepanovich—dumnyi d'iak, by August 18, 1665 (*DR* 3:590); dumnyi dvorianin, Dec. 25, 1677 (BK 7:70v; BS 15:6r); last mention, as okol'nichii, 1690/1 (BS 32:11v); buried, Oct. 23, 1691 (*Mosk. nekropol'* 2:18).
*Briukhovetskii, Ivan Martinovich—boyar, Oct. 22, 1665 (*DR* 3:595; BK 5:9r); demoted, 1667/8 (*DRV* 20:120); died, June, 1668 (Solov'ev, *Istoriia* 6:374).
*Durov, Aleksandr Stepanovich—dumnyi d'iak, Oct. 29, 1665 (*DR* 3:597); last mention, March 6, 1671 (Bogoiavlenskii, *Sud'i*, p. 201); died, 1670/1 (*DRV* 20:122).

1666

*Miloslavskii, Ivan Bogdanovich—okol'nichii, 1664/5 (*DRV* 20:118) or by May 21, 1666 (*DR* 3:619); demoted, August 29, 1666 (Sb. mosk. st. 379, sb. 1:3v); boyar, Jan. 9, 1671 (BS 8:2v); last mention, Sept. 21, 1680 (*DR* 4:177); died, 1681 (Lobanov-Rostovskii, *Rus. rod. kniga* 1:383).
*Khitrovo, Ivan Bogdanovich—dumnyi dvorianin, May 24, 1666 (*DR* 3:623); okol'nichii, Sept. 1, 1674 (*Ibid.*, p. 976; BK 6:39r); boyar, June 20 or 22, 1676 (BK 7:40r; BS 14:3r); buried, March 13, 1684 (*Mosk. nekropol'* 3:276).

1667

*Nashchokin, Bogdan Ivanovich—dumnyi dvorianin, Feb. 2, 1667 (BK 5:22r) or Feb. 12, 1667 (Sb. mosk. st. 1152:2v); died, 1682/3 or later (BS 22:10v).
*Dokhturov, Gerasim Semenovich—dumnyi d'iak, March 17, 1667 (Sb. mosk. st. 1152:2v); died, Jan. 31, 1676 (BS 14:10v).
*Golosov, Luk'ian Timofeevich—dumnyi d'iak, March 17, 1667 (Sb. mosk. st. 1152:2v); dumnyi dvorianin, July 26 or 28, 1682 (BK 7:74v, 80r); died, 1682/3 (BS 21:317v; 22:11v).

1668

*Rzhevskii, Ivan Ivanovich—dumnyi dvorianin, Nov. 10, 1668 (BK 6:45r); okol'nichii, March 4, 1677 (BK 7:46r; BS 14:226v); died, 1677/8 (BK 7:46r).

*Tolstoi, Andrei Vasil'evich—dumnyi dvorianin, Nov. 10, 1668 (BK 6:45r); okol'nichii, June 25 or 27, 1682 (BK 7:52r; BS 21:8v); last mention, 1697/8 (BS 42:5v).

1669

*Kozlovskii, Prince Grigorii Afanas'evich—okol'nichii, Jan. 19, 1669 (BS 3:3v); boyar, August 31, 1682 (BK 7:34r); died, Nov. 15, 1701 (*Mosk. nekropol'* 2:60).

*Rtishchev, Grigorii Ivanovich—striapchii s kliuchem, August 15, 1650 (*DR* 3:182); postel'nichii, May 12, 1656 (*DR* 3:40); dumnyi dvorianin, April 13, 1669 (BK 6:45r); last mention, Jan. 22, 1671 (*DR* 3:876); died, 1671 (*DRV* 20:122; Kashkin, *Rodoslovnye razvedki* 1:353).

*Ivanov, Larion—dumnyi d'iak, Oct. 2, 1669 (BS 5:4r); died, May 15, 1682 (*DAI* 10:23-25).

1670

*Nesterov, Afanasii Ivanovich—dumnyi dvorianin, by Jan. 14, 1670 (*DAI* 6:232-235); died, January, 1677 (BS 14:227r).

*Sokovnin, Fedor Prokof'evich—dumnyi dvorianin, April 17, 1670 (BK 6:46v; BS 5:4r); okol'nichii, August 15, 1677 (BK 7:48v; BS 14:226v); boyar, June 29, 1682 (BK 7:34v; BS 21:4v); exiled, March 9, 1697 (BS 41:2v).

Leont'ev, Fedor Ivanovich—dumnyi dvorianin, July 20, 1670 (BK 6:46v; BS 5:12v); okol'nichii, May 5, 1682 (BS 21:7r); died, Nov. 24, 1685 (BS 24:466v).

*Titov, Semen Stepanovich—dumnyi d'iak, July 20, 1670 (BK 6:51r; BS 5:4r); died, March 29, 1676 (BS 14:10v).

*Shcherbatov, Prince Konstantin Osipovich—okol'nichii, August 3, 1670 (BK 6:37r; BS 5:3v); boyar, June 29, 1682 (BK 7:34v; BS 21:4v); died, Sept. 24, 1697 (BS 42:1r).

*Skuratov, Petr Dmitrievich—okol'nichii, Sept. 29, 1670 (BK 6:38v; BS 8:3r); died, 1686/7 (BS 10:23v).

*Khitrovo, Ivan Sevast'ianovich bol'shoi—dumnyi dvorianin, Oct. 7, 1670 (BK 6:46r; BS 8:5v); okol'nichii, May 5, 1676 (BS 14:5v); tonsured and died, 1696/7 or later (BS 41:5v).

*Volkonskii, Prince Vasilii Bogdanovich—okol'nichii, Nov. 27, 1670 (BK 6:38r; BS 8:3r); died, April 15, 1675 (Vlas'ev, *Potomstvo* 1, pt. 3, p. 354).

*Matveev, Artemon Sergeevich—dumnyi dvorianin, Nov. 27, 1670 (BK 6:46r; BS 8:5v); okol'nichii, May 30, 1672 (BK 6:38r; BS 10:3v); boyar, Oct. 8, 1674 (*DR* 3:1070); exiled, 1676 (*DRV* 20:130); died, May 15, 1682 (*DAI* 10:23-25).

*Solovtsov, Iakov Pavlovich—dumnyi dvorianin, Nov. 27, 1670 (BK 6:47v; BS 8:5v); last mention, 1671/2 (BS 10:4r); died, August 14, 1674 (*Mosk. nekropol'* 3:139).

1671

*Dolgorukii, Prince Mikhail Iur'evich—boyar, Feb. 7, 1671 (*DR* 3:879; BS 8:2v); died, May 15, 1682 (*DAI* 10:23-25).

*Naryshkin, Kirill Poluektovich—dumnyi dvorianin, Feb. 7, 1671 (*DR* 3:879; BS 8:5v); okol'nichii, May 30, 1672 (*DR* Dop. k 3:465; BS 10:3v); boyar, Nov. 27, 1672 (BK 6:31v; *DR* 3:897); died, April 30, 1691 (BS 32:1v).

*Poltev, Semen Fedorovich—dumnyi dvorianin, April 23, 1671 (BK 6:47v; BS 8:5v); died, May, 1682 (BS 21:10v).

*Khitrovo, Aleksandr Sevast'ianovich—dumnyi dvorianin, August 16, 1671 (BK 6:47r; BS 8:5v); okol'nichii, June 18, 1676 (BK 7:42v; BS 14:5v); died, August 20, 1686 (BK 10:23v).

Bogdanov, Grigorii Karpovich—dumnyi d'iak, Nov. 12, 1671 (BK 6:52v; BS 10:5v); exiled to Siberia, May 19, 1682 (*DAI* 10:23-25); died, 1686/7 or later (BS 26:11r).

1672

*Lopukhin, Avram Nikitich—dumnyi dvorianin, May 30, 1672 (*DR* Dop. k 3:465; BS 10:4r); tonsured, 1681/2-1682/3 (BS 21:10v); died, August 2, 1685 (Dolgorukov, *Ros. rod. kniga* 2:57).

*Naryshkin, Fedor Poluektovich—dumnyi dvorianin, May 30, 1672 (*DR* Dop. k 3:465; BS 10:4r); last mention, 1675/6 (BS 14:8r); died, Dec. 15, 1676 (Lobanov-Rostovskii, *Rus. rod. kniga* 2:6).

*Matiushkin, Afanasii Ivanovich—lovchii, November, 1652 (Sb. mosk. st. 1131, sb. 4:8v); iasel'nichii, 1653/4 (*DRV* 20:110); dumnyi dvorianin, June 2, 1672 (BK 6:48r; BS 10:4r); died, May, 1676 (BS 14:8r).

*Mikhailov, Fedor—dumnyi d'iak, August 14, 1672 (BS 10:5v); last mention, 1678/9 (BS 16:8v).

*Trubetskoi, Prince Iurii Petrovich—boyar, Nov. 27, 1672 (BK 6:31v;

DR 3:897); died, June 12, 1679 (Dolgorukov, *Ros. rod. kniga* 1:321; BK 7:22v).

1673

*Panin, Vasilii Nikitich—dumnyi dvorianin, March 14, 1673 (BK 6:48r); last mention, Oct. 12, 1674 (*DR* 3:1078); died, 1674/5 (*DRV* 20:126).

1674

*Dolgorukii, Prince Vladimir Dmitrievich—okol'nichii, August 29, 1674 (BK 6:39v); boyar, Oct. 22, 1676 (BK 7:27v; BS 14:223v); died, July 12, 1701 (Vlas'ev, *Potomstvo* 1, pt. 3, p. 48).

*Pushkin, Matvei Stepanovich—okol'nichii, August 18, 1674 (BK 6:39v); boyar, Sept. 25, 1682 (BK 7:35v; BS 22:20r); demoted and exiled, March 9, 1697 (BS 41:2v).

1676

*Zheliabuzhskii, Ivan Afanas'evich—iasel'nichii, Oct. 30, 1663 (Sb. mosk. st. 359, sb. 1:65v); dumnyi dvorianin, April 14, 1676 (BK 7:65v; BS 14:8r); okol'nichii, Oct. 22, 1683 (BK 7:56v; BS 23:11v); died, after 1709 (BS 35:8r).

*Polianskii, Daniil Leont'evich—dumnyi d'iak, April 14, 1676 (BK 7:82v; BS 14:10r); died, April 22, 1702 (BS 46:7r).

Buturlin, Ivan Vasil'evich—okol'nichii, April 16, 1676 (BK 7:41v; BS 14:5v); boyar, May 9, 1677 (BK 7:28v; BS 14:223r); died, Oct. 12, 1697 (BS 42:1v).

*Golokhvastov, Vasilii Iakovlevich—dumnyi dvorianin, April 16, 1676 (BK 7:65r; BS 14:9v); died, Dec. 14, 1678 (BS 16:6r).

*Sobakin, Grigorii Nikiforovich—okol'nichii, April 23, 1676 (BK 7:41r; BS 14:5v); boyar, Dec. 3, 1681 (BK 7:31r; BS 21:3v); died, July 29, 1689 (BK 10:6r; BS 28:2v).

*Ladyzhenskii, Fedor Abrosimovich—dumnyi dvorianin, April 23, 1676 (BK 7:65r; BS 14:9v); died, Oct. 6, 1676 (BK 14:227r; *Rus. pr. nekropol'* 1:491).

*Troekurov, Prince Ivan Borisovich—okol'nichii, April 30, 1676 (BK 7:41v; BS 14:5v); boyar, Feb. 25, 1677 (BK 7:27r; BS 14:223r); died, Nov. 25, 1703 (BS 49:1v).

*Kamynin, Ivan Bogdanovich—dumnyi dvorianin, April 30, 1676 (BK 7:66v; BS 14:9v); buried, Jan. 18, 1678 (*Mosk. nekropol'* 2:12).

*Golitsyn, Prince Vasilii Vasil'evich—boyar, May 4, 1676 (BK 7:23v; BS 14:2r); exiled, Oct. 12, 1689 (BS 31:1r).

Semenov, Vasilii Grigor'evich—dumnyi d'iak, May 4, 1676 (BK 7:82r; BS 14:10r); died, Nov. 7, 1693 (BS 35:440v).

*Matiushkin, Petr Ivanovich—dumnyi dvorianin, May 5, 1676 (BS 14:9v); okol'nichii, Oct. 12, 1676 (BK 7:44r; BS 14:225v); boyar, Jan. 2, 1683 (BK 7:35r; BS 21:21v); last mention, 1690/1 (BS 32:3v); buried, Dec. 8, 1691 (Mosk. nekropol' 2:240).

Iushkov, Boris Gavrilovich—dumnyi dvorianin, May 6 or 7, 1676 (BK 7:66r; BS 14:9r); okol'nichii, Oct. 22, 1676 (BK 7:45v; BS 14:225r); boyar, June 26, 1682 (BS 21:4v); still alive, 1713 (BS 60:4v).

*Urusov, Prince Petr Semenovich—kravchii, Nov. 27, 1658 (DR Dop. k 3:158); boyar, May 7, 1676 (BK 7:23r; BS 14:2r); died, 1686/7 or later (BS 26:1r).

*Poltev, Fedor Alekseevich—striapchii s kliuchem, 1655/6 (DRV 20:112); postel'nichii, 1668/9 (Ibid., p. 120); dumnyi dvorianin, May 21 or 24, 1676 (BK 7:66r; BS 14:9r); died, 1675/6 (DRV 20:129) or 1678/9 (BS 16:6r).

*Kondyrev, Ivan Timofeevich—iasel'nichii, 1675/6 (DRV 20:131); dumnyi dvorianin, June 7, 1676 (BK 7:67v; BS 14:9r); okol'nichii, June 8, 1677 (BK 7:47v; BS 14:226v); boyar, June 27, 1682 (BK 7:33r; BS 21:4v); died, 1688/9 (BK 10:8v).

*Odoevskii, Prince Iurii Mikhailovich—boyar, June 8, 1676 (BK 7:24v; BS 14:2r); died, April 15, 1707 (Vlas'ev, Potomstvo 1, pt. 1, p. 85).

*Prozorovskii, Prince Petr Ivanovich—boyar, June 8, 1676 (BK 7:24v; BS 14:3v); still alive, 1713 (BS 60:4v).

Zykov, Afanasii Tikhonovich—dumnyi d'iak, June 8, 1676 (BK 7:82r; BS 14:11v); dumnyi dvorianin, July 28, 1682 (BK 7:74r); died, 1683/4 or later (BS 23:17v).

*Morozov, Mikhail Ivanovich—boyar, June 18, 1676 (BK 7:24r; BS 14:3v); died, March, 1678 (BS 15:2v).

*Golitsyn, Prince Mikhail Andreevich—boyar, June 20, 1676 (BK 7:25v; BS 14:3v); died, Sept. 25, 1687 (BK 10:3r).

*Lobanov-Rostovskii, Prince Aleksandr Ivanovich—okol'nichii, June 20, 1676 (BK 7:42r; BS 14:5r); died, Sept. 26, 1676 (BS 14:5r).

*Narbekov, Afanasii Samoilovich—kaznachei, 1662/3 (Sb. mosk. st. 1102, sb. 3:4v); okol'nichii, June 20, 1676; died, July 16, 1680 (BK 7:42r).

*Khovanskii, Prince Semen Andreevich—boyar, June 22, 1676 (BK 7:25; BS 14:3r); buried, Dec. 4, 1695 (Mosk. nekropol' 3:283).

Miloslavskii, Matvei Bogdanovich—okol'nichii, June 22 or 24, 1676 (BK 7:43v; BS 14:5r); boyar, June 25, 1682 (BK 7:33v; BS 21:4v); exiled to estate, February, 1697 (BS 41:1r); last mention, 1705 (BS 52:1r).

Golokhvastov, Iov Demidovich—dumnyi dvorianin, July 10, 1676 (BK 7:67v; BS 14:9r); okol'nichii, Feb. 28, 1690 (BK 10:37v; BS 31:11r); died, 1692/3 (BS 35:432r).

*Golitsyn, Prince Ivan Andreevich—boyar, August 15, 1676 (BK 7:26r; BS 14:3r); died, before 1681/2 (BS 16:2r; 21:1-2).

Khlopov, Kirill Osipovich—dumnyi dvorianin, Sept. 3, 1676 (BK 7:68v); okol'nichii, March 5, 1682 (BK 7:52v; BS 21:7r); boyar, July 10, 1690 (BK 10:15v; BS 31:4r); buried, March 18, 1691 (*Mosk. nekropol'* 3:278).

*Sobakin, Vasilii Nikiforovich—dumnyi dvorianin, 1675/6 (*DRV* 20:131); okol'nichii, Oct. 1, 1676 (BK 7:44v; BS 14:225v); died, April 29, 1677 (BS 14:471r).

Golovin, Aleksei Petrovich—okol'nichii, Nov. 5, 1676 (BK 7:45r; BS 14:225r); boyar, May 8, 1684 (BK 7:35r; BS 23:4v); died, May 16, 1690 (BS 31:3v).

Kondyrev, Petr Timofeevich—dumnyi dvorianin, Nov. 12, 1676 (BK 7:68r) or Jan. 7, 1677 (BS 14:228r); okol'nichii, July 10, 1677 (BK 7:47r; BS 14:226v); boyar, March 25, 1691 (BK 10:16r; BS 32:4v); last mention, 1697/8 (BS 42:2r).

Kondyrev, Semen Timofeevich—dumnyi dvorianin, Nov. 12, 1676 (BK 7:68r; BS 14:228v); okol'nichii, Nov. 22, 1677 (BK 7:49r; BS 15:5v); died, April 12, 1682 (BS 21:6r).

Golovin, Mikhail Petrovich—okol'nichii, Nov. 19, 1676 (BK 7:45r; BS 14:225r); boyar, August 29, 1682 (BK 7:34r; BS 21:4r); died, August 5, 1695 (*Mosk. nekropol'* 1:308).

1677

Cherkasskii, Prince Mikhail Alegukovich—boyar, Jan. 6, 1677 (BK 7:27v; BS 14:223v); last mention, 1711 (BS 58:1v); still alive, 1713 (*Mosk. nekropol'* 3:312).

Chirikov, Il'ia Ivanovich—okol'nichii, Jan. 6, 1677 (BK 7:46v; BS 14:225r); last mention, May 22, 1680 (Bogoiavlenskii, *Sud'i*, pp. 28, 39).

L'vov, Prince Stepan Fedorovich—okol'nichii, Jan. 6, 1677 (BK 7:46v; BS 14:225r); died, 1692/3 or later (BS 35:8v).

Kirillov, Averkii Stepanovich—dumnyi d'iak, Jan. 6, 1677 (BK 7:83v; BS 14:229r); died, May 16, 1682 (*DAI* 10:23-25).

Dashkov, Vasilii Iakovlevich—dumnyi dvorianin, Jan. 14, 1677 (BK 7:69v); died, between 1678/9 and 1681/2 (BS 16:6r; 21:1-8).

Romodanovskii, Prince Fedor Grigor'evich—boyar, March 7, 1677 (BK 7:27r; BS 14:223r); buried, Jan. 14, 1689 (*Mosk. nekropol'* 3:40).

Likharev, Ivan Petrovich—dumnyi dvorianin, March 27, 1677 (BK 7:69v; BS 14:228r); last mention, May 19, 1682 (*PSRL* 31:175).

Piatogo, Parfenii Iakovlevich—dumnyi d'iak, May 24, 1677 (BK 7:83v; BS 14:229r); dumnyi dvorianin, July, 1682 (BK 7:74v; BS 21:11r); died, 1683/4 or later (BS 23:17v).

Khovanskii, Prince Petr Ivanovich—boyar, June 18, 1677 (BK 7:28v; BS 14:223r); still alive, 1713 (BS 60:4v).

Kondyrev, Ivan Petrovich—dumnyi dvorianin, June 18, 1677 (BK 7:69r; BS 14:223r); died, 1686/7 or later (BS 26:8r).

Chirikov, Andrei Ivanovich—okol'nichii, July 10, 1677 (BK 7:47r; BS 14:226v); died, April 23, 1689 (BS 28:6v).

Gorokhov, Ivan Savinovich—dumnyi d'iak, July 25, 1677 (BK 7:83r; BS 14:230v); died, 1686/7 or later (BS 26:11r).

Volynskii, Iakov Semenovich—okol'nichii, last mention, August 15, 1677 (BK 7:48v; BS 14:226v).

Sheremetev, Petr Vasil'evich men'shii—boyar, Nov. 22, 1677 (BK 7:29v); died, April 24, 1697 (Barsukov, *Rodoslovie Sheremetevykh*, p. 9).

Romodanovskii, Prince Mikhail Grigor'evich—boyar, Dec. 25, 1677 (BK 7:29v; BS 15:3r); died, 1711 or later (BS 58:1v).

1678

Savelov, Timofei Petrovich—dumnyi dvorianin, Feb. 1, 1678 (BK 7:70v); okol'nichii, Oct. 22, 1689 (BK 10:36v; BS 31:10r); last mention, 1697/8 (BS 42:5r); died, March 15, 1699 (*LIRO* 38:15).

Zmeev, Venedikt Andreevich—dumnyi dvorianin, Feb. 10, 1678 (BK 7:70v; BS 15:6r); okol'nichii, June 25, 1682 (BK 7:52v; BS 21:8v); died, 1696/7 (BS 41:5v).

Rzhevskii, Aleksei Ivanovich—dumnyi dvorianin, August 17, 1678 (BK 7:70r; BS 15:6r); okol'nichii, Jan. 6, 1683 (BK 7:55v; BK 22:7r); died, 1689/90 (BS 31:9v).

Urusov, Prince Nikita Semenovich—boyar, Dec. 1, 1678 (BK 7:29r; BS 16:3v); buried, February, 1692 (*Mosk. nekropol'* 3:244).

Boriatinskii, Prince Daniil Afanas'evich—okol'nichii, Dec. 1, 1678 (BK 7:50v); boyar, Oct. 12, 1687 (BK 10:11r; BS 27:3r); died, 1696 (Vlas'ev, *Potomstvo* 1, pt. 2, 63).

1679

Streshnev, Nikita Konstantinovich—okol'nichii, June 12, 1679 (*DR* 4:83; BK 7:50v); boyar, May 3 or 7, 1682 (BK 7:32r; BS 21:4v); died, Dec. 6, 1702 (*Mosk. nekropol'* 3:165).

Polibin, Bogdan Fedorovich—dumnyi dvorianin, June 12, 1679 (*DR* 4:83;

BK 7:70r); okol'nichii, June 27, 1682 (BK 7:52r; BS 21:8v); died, 1697/8 or later (BS 42:5v).

1680

Iakovlev, Bogdan Vasil'evich—dumnyi dvorianin, March 1, 1680 (BK 7:71v); died, 1692/3 or later (BS 35:436v).

*Odoevskii, Prince Vasilii Fedorovich—kravchii s putem, 1675/6 (*DRV* 20:130); boyar, May 9, 1680 (BK 7:30v); died, Dec. 14, 1686 (BS 26:2v).

Akinfov, Nikita Ivanovich—dumnyi dvorianin, July 23, 1680 (BK 7:71v); okol'nichii, March 31, 1689 (BK 10:35v; BS 28:8r); still alive, 1713 (BS 60:5v).

Zaborovskii, Sergei Matveevich—dumnyi dvorianin, August 15, 1680 (*DR* 4:173; BK 7:71r); died, 1692/3 or later (BS 35:436v).

*Iazykov, Ivan Maksimovich—postel'nichii, 1675/6 (*DRV* 20:131); okol'-nichii, August 16, 1680 (*DR* 4:174; BK 7:59v); boyar, May 8, 1681 (BK 7:31v, 50r); died, May 15, 1682 (*DAI* 10:23-25).

Urusov, Prince Fedor Semenovich—boyar, Sept. 1, 1680 (BK 7:30r); buried, April 18, 1694 (*Mosk. nekropol'* 3:244).

Prozorovskii, Prince Petr Semenovich men'shii—boyar, Oct. 26, 1680 (BK 7:30r); buried, Jan. 3, 1691 (*Mosk. nekropol'* 2:466).

Nepliuev, Leontii Romanovich—dumnyi dvorianin, Oct. 26, 1680 (BK 7:71r); okol'nichii, Jan. 1, 1683 (BK 7:54r; BS 22:7r); boyar, Dec. 21, 1688 (DR 4:424-425; BK 10:12v); demoted and exiled, Oct. 12, 1689 (BS 31:3v).

Lykov, Prince Mikhail Ivanovich—born, July 13, 1640 (M. I. Semevskii, *Russkaia rodoslovnaia kniga* 1:9); okol'nichii, Nov. 27, 1680 (BK 7:50r); boyar, June 26, 1682 (BK 7:33v; BS 21:4v); died, Feb. 14, 1701 (*DRV* 19:356).

Korkodinov, Prince Ivan Mikhailovich—okol'nichii, Dec. 21, 1680 (BK 7:51v); boyar, July 10, 1691 (BK 10:17v; BS 32:4r); died, March 21, 1694 (BS 35:427r).

1681

Volynskii, Ivan Fedorovich—okol'nichii, Jan. 23, 1681 (BK 7:51v); boyar, Sept. 1, 1682 (BK 7:35v; BS 22:20r); died, 1696/7 or later (BS 41:2v).

Urusov, Prince Iurii Semenovich—boyar, Feb. 13, 1681 (BK 7:31v); still alive, 1713 (BS 60:4v).

Narbekov, Vasilii Savich—dumnyi dvorianin, Feb. 13, 1681 (BK 7:72v); okol'nichii, June 26, 1682 (BK 7:52r; BS 21:8v); died, 1705 or later (BS 52:3v).

Tolochanov, Semen Fedorovich—dumnyi dvorianin, Feb. 13, 1681 (BK 7:72v); okol'nichii, Jan. 26, 1683 (BK 7:58v; BS 22:8r); died, 1708 or later (BS 55:4v).

Ukraintsev, Emel'ian Ignat'evich—dumnyi d'iak, Feb. 27, 1681 (BK 7:83r); died, 1708 or later (BS 55:8v).

Iazykov, Pavel Petrovich—okol'nichii, Sept. 4, 1681 (BK 7:58v; BS 21:7v); died, 1682/3 or later (BS 21:313v).

Boborykin, Roman Fedorovich—okol'nichii, Sept. 5, 1681; died, Feb. 23, 1682 (BK 7:51r; BS 21:7r).

Gorchakov, Prince Boris Vasil'evich—okol'nichii, Nov. 21, 1681 (BK 7:51r; BS 21:7r); buried, Dec. 23, 1695 (*Mosk. nekropol'* 1:323).

Buturlin, Boris Vasil'evich—okol'nichii, Nov. 24, 1681 (BS 21:7r); boyar, August 29, 1682 (BK 7:34r; BS 21:4r); died, June 16, 1694 (BS 35:426r).

Romodanovskii, Prince Andrei Grigor'evich—boyar, Dec. 25, 1681 (BK 7:31r; BS 21:3r); died, May 4, 1686 (BS 24:463r).

Tiapkin, Vasilii Mikhailovich—dumnyi dvorianin, Dec. 25, 1681 (BK 7:72v; BS 21:11v); last mention, May 26, 1682 (*DAI* 10:31).

1682

Kurakin, Prince Ivan Grigor'evich—kravchii s putem, May 8, 1676 (BK 7:37v); boyar, Feb. 23, 1682, last mention (BK 7:32v, 57v; BS 21:3r); died, Sept. 15, 1682 (Dolgorukov, *Ros. rod. kniga* 1:315).

Cherkasskii, Prince Mikhail Iakovlevich—boyar, Feb. 26, 1682 (BK 7:32v; BS 21:3r); died, 1712 (BS 58:1v).

Prozorovskii, Prince Boris Ivanovich—boyar, Feb. 26, 1682 (BK 7:32r; BS 21:3r); still alive, 1713 (BS 60:4r).

Khilkov, Prince Iakov Vasil'evich—okol'nichii, March 5, 1682 (BK 7:51r; BS 21:7r); died, May 14, 1691 (BS 32:6v).

Narbekov, Fedor Savich—dumnyi dvorianin, March 5, 1682 (BK 7:72r; BS 21:11v); okol'nichii, July 25, 1691 (BK 10:39r; BS 32:9r); last mention, 1697/8 (BS 42:6v).

Lovchikov, Ivan Bogdanovich—dumnyi dvorianin, March 7, 1682 (BK 7:72r; BS 21:11v); died, October, 1692 (BS 35:14v).

Shein, Aleksei Semenovich—boyar, April 9, 1682 (BK 7:32r; BS 21:3r); last mention, 1699/1700 (Bogoiavlenskii, *Sud'i*, p. 138); died, Feb. 12, 1700 (*Mosk. nekropol'* 3:339).

Khrushchov, Fedor Grigor'evich men'shii—dumnyi dvorianin, April 9, 1682 (BK 7:72r; BS 21:11v); still alive, 1713 (BS 60:6v).

Naryshkin, Ivan Kirillovich—boyar, May 7, 1682 (BK 7:32r; BS 21:4v); died, May 17, 1682 (*DAI* 10:23-25).

Khovanskii, Prince Andrei Ivanovich—boyar, June 24 or 25, 1682 (*DAI* 10:38; BS 21:4v); executed, Sept. 17, 1682 (*DAI* 10:32; BS 21:4r).

Pleshcheev, Mikhail L'vovich—boyar, June 25, 1682 (*DAI* 10:38; BK 7:33v); died, Oct. 26, 1683 (BS 23:3v).

Miloslavskii, Larion Semenovich—okol'nichii, June 25, 1682 (BK 7:52v; BS 21:8v); boyar, March 31, 1689 (BK 10:13v; BS 28:4v); last mention, 1697/8 (BS 42:2v).

Khitrovo, Petr Savich—dumnyi dvorianin, June 25, 1682 (BS 21:11v); still alive, 1713 (BS 60:6v).

Pushechnikov, Vasilii Lavrent'evich—dumnyi dvorianin, June 25, 1682 (BK 7:73v; BS 21:11v); tonsured, 1709 or later (BS 56:7v).

Sheremetev, Boris Petrovich—born, April 25, 1652 (Barsukov, *Rod Sheremetevykh* 5:239); boyar, June 26, 1682 (BK 7:33v; BS 21:4v); still alive, 1713 (BS 60:4v).

Streshnev, Tikhon Nikitich—okol'nichii, June 26, 1682 (BK 7:52r; BS 21:8v); boyar, April 15, 1688 (BK 10:12v; BS 27:4v); senator, 1711 (BS 58:1r); died, Jan. 15, 1719 (*RBS* 19:593).

Khitrovo, Avram Ivanovich—dumnyi dvorianin, June 26, 1682 (BK 7:73r; BS 21:11r); last mention, 1697/8 (BS 42:8v); died, 1698 (Lobanov-Rostovskii, *Rus. rod. kniga* 2:320).

Zmeev, Vasilii Semenovich—dumnyi dvorianin, June 26, 1682 (BK 7:73v; BS 21:11r); still alive, 1713 (BS 60:6v).

Golitsyn, Prince Andrei Ivanovich—boyar, June 27, 1682 (BK 7:33r; BS 21:4v); died, 1703 or later (BS 49:1r).

Saltykov, Aleksei Petrovich—boyar, June 27, 1682 (BK 7:33r; BS 21:4v); still alive, 1713 (BS 60:4v).

Sunbulov, Maksim Isaevich—dumnyi dvorianin, June 27, 1682 (BK 7:73r; BS 21:11r); tonsured, 1696/7 or later (BS 41:8v).

Sukhotin, Ivan Ivanovich—dumnyi dvorianin, June 27, 1682 (BK 7:73r; BS 21:11r); died, 1686/7 or later (BS 26:9r).

Prozorovskii, Prince Vasilii Petrovich bol'shoi—boyar, June 29, 1682 (BK 7:33r; BS 21:4v); died, Nov. 24, 1687 (BS 27:3v).

Pushkin, Ivan Fedorovich—okol'nichii, June 29, 1682 (BK 7:53v; BS 21:8v); last mention, 1697/8 (BS 42:5v).

Izvol'skii, Vikula Fedorovich—dumnyi dvorianin, June 29, 1682 (BK 7:74v; BS 21:11r); died, August 3, 1697 (BS 41:8v).

Khitrovo, Nikita Savich—dumnyi dvorianin, June 29, 1682 (BK 7:73r; BS 21:11r); still alive, 1713 (BS 60:6v).

Miasnoi, Vasilii Danilovich—dumnyi dvorianin, June 29, 1682 (BK 7:74v; BS 21:11r); died, 1691/2 (BK 10:47r).

Sokovnin, Aleksei Prokof'evich—dumnyi dvorianin, June 29, 1682 (BS

21:11r); okol'nichii, July 28, 1682 (BS 21:8v); executed, March 4, 1697 (BS 41:5v).

Khovanskii, Prince Petr Ivanovich II—boyar, July 8, 1682 (BK 7:34v; BS 21:4r); last mention, 1694/5 (BS 36:2v).

Shaklovityi, Fedor Leont'evich—dumnyi d'iak, July 23, 1682 (BK 7:84v; BS 21:12r); dumnyi dvorianin, Jan. 26, 1688 (BS 27:13v); okol'nichii, March 21, 1689 (BK 10:34v); executed, Oct. 12, 1689 (BS 31:10v).

Mertvogo, Mikhail Stepanovich—dumnyi dvorianin, July 28, 1682 (BK 7:74r; BS 21:11r); died, 1682/3 (BS 22:11v).

Ogarev, Postnik Grigor'evich—dumnyi dvorianin, July 28, 1682 (BK 7:74v); died, 1702-1703 or later (BS 46:5r).

Khovanskii, Prince Ivan Ivanovich—boyar, August 29, 1682 (BK 7:34v; BS 21:4r); last mention, 1697/8 (BS 42:2v).

Izmailov, Matvei Petrovich—okol'nichii, Sept. 1, 1682 (BK 7:53r; BS 22:6r); died, Nov. 5, 1693 (BS 35:431r).

Musin-Pushkin, Ivan Alekseevich—okol'nichii, Sept. 1, 1682 (BK 7:53r; BS 22:7v); boyar, Sept. 9, 1698 (DR 4:1085-1086); senator, 1711 (BS 58:2v).

Sheremetev, Fedor Petrovich—boyar, Sept. 21, 1682 (BK 7:35v; BS 22:20r); still alive, 1713 (BS 60:4v).

Shakhovskoi, Prince Fedor Ivanovich—okol'nichii, Sept. 25, 1682 (BK 7:54v; BS 22:7v); died, 1707 or later (BS 53:4v).

Shcherbatov, Prince Dmitrii Nefed'evich—okol'nichii, Sept. 25, 1682 (BK 7:54v; BS 22:7v); died, 1708 or later (BS 55:4v).

Zotov, Nikita Moiseevich—dumnyi d'iak, Nov. 1, 1682 (BK 7:84v; BS 22:14v); dumnyi dvorianin, by 1702-1703 (BS 46:6v).

Buturlin, Ivan Fedorovich—okol'nichii, Nov. 21, 1682 (BK 7:54v; BS 22:7v); died, 1687/8 (BK 10:27v).

Obolenskii, Prince Matvei Venediktovich—okol'nichii, Nov. 24, 1682 (BK 7:54r; BS 22:7v); died, Nov. 16, 1687 (Mosk. nekropol' 2:356).

Astaf'ev, Pavel Mikhailovich—dumnyi d'iak, November, 1682 (BK 7:84r; BS 22:14r); died, 1687/8 (BK 10:62v).

Volkonskii, Prince Fedul Fedorovich—okol'nichii, Dec. 24, 1682 (BK 7:54r; BS 22:7r); died, May 11, 1707 (Vlas'ev, Potomstvo 1, pt. 3, p. 353).

Zykov, Fedor Andreevich—dumnyi dvorianin, Dec. 25, 1682 (BS 22:18r); last mention, April 7, 1699 (DR 4:1098).

1683

Tarbeev, Vasilii Nikitich—dumnyi dvorianin, Jan. 1, 1683 (BS 22:18r); last mention, 1690/1 (BS 32:11r).

Khotetovskii, Prince Ivan Stepanovich—okol'nichii, Jan. 12, 1683 (BK 7:55v; BS 22:7r); still alive, 1713 (BS 60:5v).

Zykov, Fedor Tikhonovich—dumnyi dvorianin, Jan. 12, 1683 (BS 22:18r); okol'nichii, Feb. 28, 1690 (BK 10:37r; BS 31:11r); last mention, Oct. 16, 1698 (Bogoiavlenskii, Sud'i, p. 209).

Dashkov, Andrei Iakovlevich—dumnyi dvorianin, Jan. 26, 1683 (DR 4:196; BS 22:18r); died, between 1697/8 and 1702 (BS 42:8v; 46:1-10).

Pavlov, Rodion Mikhailovich—dumnyi dvorianin, by April 13, 1683 (DR 4:212); okol'nichii, Feb. 28, 1690 (BK 10:37r; BS 31:11r); buried, April 23, 1695 (Mosk. nekropol' 2:391).

Priimkov-Rostovskii, Prince Nikita Ivanovich—okol'nichii, April 22, 1683 (BS 21:314v; BK 7:55r); boyar, Feb. 10, 1689 (BK 10:12r; BS 28:3r); last mention, 1690/1 (AI 5:349; BS 32:3v).

Lovchikov, Stepan Bogdanovich—dumnyi dvorianin, April 22, 1683 (BS 21:317r); died, 1710 or later (BS 57:5r).

Zvenigorodskii, Prince Semen Iur'evich—okol'nichii, May 13, 1683 (DR 4:215; BK 7:55r); died, March 19, 1690 (BS 31:9v).

Polibin, Artemii Fedorovich—dumnyi dvorianin, July 25, 1683 (DR 4:229; BS 21:317r); died, 1694/5 or later (BS 36:360r).

Lyzlov, Ivan Fedorovich—dumnyi dvorianin, August 15, 1683 (BS 21:317r); died, August 17, 1684 (BS 23:17r).

*Likhachev, Aleksei Timofeevich—striapchii s kliuchem, 1675/6 (DRV 20:131); okol'nichii, August 19, 1683 (DR 4:235; BK 7:55r); still alive, 1713 (BS 60:5v).

Likhachev, Mikhail Timofeevich—dumnyi dvorianin, August 19, 1683 (DR 4:235; BS 21:317r); okol'nichii, August 16, 1686 (BK 10:30v; BS 24:467r); last mention, 1705 (BS 52:3v).

Nikiforov, Protasii Ivanovich—dumnyi d'iak, August 19, 1683 (DR 4:235; BK 7:84r); died, 1711 or later (BS 58:8v).

Telepnev, Ivan Stepanovich—dumnyi dvorianin, Sept. 2, 1683 (BK 7:76v; BS 23:17r); died, 1686/7 or later (BS 26:10v).

Panin, Ivan Ivanovich—dumnyi dvorianin, Sept. 17, 1683 (BK 7:76v; BS 23:17r); died, March 9, 1702 (BS 46:5r).

Lopukhin, Petr Avramovich men'shii—dumnyi dvorianin, Oct. 22, 1683 (BK 7:76r; BS 23:17r); okol'nichii, Jan. 8, 1688 (BK 10:31r); boyar, Feb. 19, 1690 (BK 10:14v; BS 31:4v); died, 1698 (RBS 20:686).

1684

Saltykov, Fedor Petrovich—boyar, Feb. 10, 1684 (DR 4:270; BK 7:35r); died, Feb. 2, 1697 (Dolgorukov, Ros. rod. kniga 2:72).

Tatishchev, Mikhail Iur'evich—born, 1620 (S. S. Tatishchev, Rod Ta-

tishchevykh. 1400-1900, p. 34); dumnyi dvorianin, April 1, 1684 (BK 7:76r; BS 23:11v); okol'nichii, August 29, 1684 (BK 7:56v; BS 23:11v); boyar, Feb. 2, 1691 (BK 10:16v; BS 32:4v); last mention, 1697/8 (BS 42:2r); died, April 17, 1701 (*Mosk. nekropol'* 3:192).

Zhirovogo-Zasekin, Prince Vasilii Fedorovich—okol'nichii, May 8, 1684 (BS 23:11v); last mention, Jan. 31, 1695 (Bogoiavlenskii, *Sud'i*, p. 208); buried, July 5, 1695 (*Mosk. nekropol'* 1:448).

Tatishchev, Ivan Mikhailovich bol'shoi—dumnyi dvorianin, August 29, 1684 (BK 7:76r; BS 23:18v); okol'nichii, March 21, 1689; died, April 25, 1689 (BK 10:34v; BS 28:8r).

Glebov, Mikhail Ivanovich—dumnyi dvorianin, Sept. 2, 1684 (BK 7:77v; BS 24:12v); okol'nichii, Dec. 21, 1689 (BK 10:36r; BS 31:11v); still alive, 1713 (BS 60:5r).

Narbekov, Stepan Savich—dumnyi dvorianin, Sept. 2, 1684 (BK 7:77v; BS 24:12v); still alive, 1713 (BS 60:6v).

Potemkin, Petr Ivanovich—dumnyi dvorianin, Nov. 16 or 17, 1684 (BK 7:77r; BS 24:12v); okol'nichii, June 29, 1692 (BK 11:38v); last mention, 1697/8 (BS 42:6v).

1685

Somov, Parfenii Pavlovich—dumnyi dvorianin, Feb. 2, 1685 (BK 7:77r; BS 24:12v); died, 1684/5-1685/6 or later (BS 24:470r).

Iakovlev, Kirill Aristarkhovich—dumnyi dvorianin, March 1, 1685 (BS 24:12r); died, 1686/7 (BK 10:51v).

Kolupaev, Mikhail Petrovich—dumnyi dvorianin, March 1, 1685 (BK 7:78v; BS 24:12r); okol'nichii, Feb. 19, 1690 (BK 10:37v; BS 31:11v); buried, Sept. 19, 1694 (*Mosk. nekropol'* 2:71).

Pronchishchev, Petr Ivanovich—dumnyi dvorianin, March 1, 1685 (BK 7:78v; BS 24:12r); last mention, 1697/8 (BS 42:8r); died, 1700 (Lobanov-Rostovskii, *Rus. rod. kniga* 2:138).

Golitsyn, Prince Ivan Ivanovich bol'shoi—boyar, April 19, 1685 (*DR* 4:345-346; BK 7:36v); died, June 8, 1686 (BK 10:10r).

Dashkov, Prince Ivan Ivanovich—okol'nichii, April 19, 1685 (*DR* 4:346; BK 7:56r); died, 1686/7 or later (BS 26:139v).

Volkonskii, Prince Fedor L'vovich—okol'nichii, Nov. 27, 1685 (BK 10:29r; BS 24:467r); died, 1697/8 or later (BS 42:5r).

Golovin, Fedor Alekseevich—okol'nichii, Dec. 25, 1685 (BK 10:29r; BS 24:467r); boyar, Oct. 22, 1691 (BK 11:29v); last mention, 1705 (BS 52:2v); died, August 20, 1706 (Dolgorukov, *Ros. rod. kniga* 3:108).

1686

Pushkin, Iakov Stepanovich—okol'nichii, Jan. 12, 1686 (BK 10:30v; BS 24:467r); boyar, Oct. 22, 1690 (BK 10:16v; BS 32:4v); last mention, exiled, 1697/8 (BS 42:2r).

Tarbeev, Grigorii Fedorovich—dumnyi dvorianin, Jan. 12, 1686 (BK 7:78v; BS 24:470r); died, 1689/90 or later (BS 31:15r).

Golitsyn, Prince Aleksei Vasil'evich—boyar, Oct. 22, 1686 (BK 10:11v; BS 26:3r); demoted and exiled, Oct. 12, 1689 (BS 31:3v).

1687

Leont'ev, Ivan Iur'evich—dumnyi dvorianin, Feb. 20, 1687 (BK 10:52v; BS 26:10r); okol'nichii, Oct. 12, 1687 (BK 10:31v; BS 27:9v); died, 1696/7 or later (BS 41:5r).

Almazov, Semen Erofeevich—dumnyi dvorianin, March 30, 1687 (BK 10:52v; BS 26:10r); died, 1687/8 (BK 10:52v).

L'vov, Prince Mikhail Nikitich—okol'nichii, June 29, 1687 (BK 10:30r; BS 26:7v); boyar, June 29, 1692 (BK 11:29r); died, 1704 or later (BS 51:2v).

Leont'ev, Andrei Ivanovich—dumnyi dvorianin, June 29, 1687 (BK 10:52r; BS 26:10r); okol'nichii, Jan. 25, 1690 (BK 10:36r; BS 31:11v); died, 1704 or later (BS 51:4r).

Shepelev, Agei Alekseevich—okol'nichii and dumnyi general, Oct. 13, 1687; died, 1687/8 (BK 10:31v; BS 27:9v).

Sobakin, Mikhail Vasil'evich—okol'nichii, Oct. 14, 1687 (BK 10:31v; BS 27:9v); still alive, 1713 (BS 60:5v).

1688

Kosogov, Grigorii Ivanovich—dumnyi dvorianin, Jan. 8, 1688 (BK 10:53v; BS 27:13v); died, 1692/3 or later (BS 35:437v).

Nepliuev, Semen Protas'evich—dumnyi dvorianin, Jan. 12, 1688 (BK 10:53v; BS 27:13v); still alive, 1713 (BS 60:6v).

L'vov, Prince Petr Lukich—okol'nichii, Feb. 26, 1688 (BK 10:31r; BS 27:9r); still alive, 1713 (BS 60:5v).

Naryshkin, Lev Kirillovich—boyar, April 8, 1688 (BK 10:11r; BS 27:4v); died, Jan. 28, 1705 (*Mosk. nekropol'* 2:317).

Saltykov, Petr Petrovich—boyar, April 15, 1688 (BK 10:11r; BS 27:4v); last mention, 1697/8 (BS 42:2v); died, 1700 (Dolgorukov, *Ros. rod. kniga* 2:72).

Matiushkin, Ivan Afanas'evich—okol'nichii, June 29, 1688 (BK 10:32v; BS 27:9r); buried, Dec. 30, 1695 (*Mosk. nekropol'* 2:239).

Naryshkin, Matvei Filimonovich—okol'nichii, June 29, 1688 (*DR* 4:386; BK 10:32v); boyar, June 29, 1690; died, 1691/2 (BK 10:14r).

Iazykov, Semen Ivanovich—dumnyi dvorianin, June 29, 1688 (*DR* 4:386; BK 10:53r); okol'nichii, March 25, 1697 (BS 41:6r); last mention, 1697/8 (BS 42:6v); still alive, 1713 (*Mosk. nekropol'* 3:400).

Savelov, Ivan Petrovich men'shii—dumnyi dvorianin, June 29, 1688 (*DR* 4:386; BK 10:53r); tonsured, 1697/8 (BS 42:8r).

Larionov, Ivan Semenovich—dumnyi dvorianin, August 17, 1688 (BK 10:53r; BS 27:13v); died, 1703 or later (BS 49:7r).

Naryshkin, Kondratii Fomich—okol'nichii, August 27, 1688 (BK 10:32v; BS 27:9r); boyar, April 15, 1691 (BK 10:16r; BS 32:4r); died, Sept. 7, 1697 (BS 42:2r).

Savelov, Pavel Petrovich—dumnyi dvorianin, August 29, 1688 (BK 10:54v; BS 27:13v); okol'nichii, Dec. 21, 1688 (BK 10:33v; BS 28:8v); tonsured, March 3, 1693 (BS 35:9v); died, June 12, 1709 (*Rus. pr. nekropol'* 1:760).

Ivanov, Avtamon Ivanovich—dumnyi d'iak, August 29, 1688 (BK 10:62r; BS 27:13r); died, Nov. 14, 1709 (BS 56:8r).

1689

Naryshkin, Grigorii Filimonovich—okol'nichii, Jan. 6, 1689 (BK 10:33v; BS 28:8v); boyar, March 17, 1692 (BK 11:29r); died, July 16, 1695 (BS 36:3r).

Lopukhin, Fedor Avramovich—okol'nichii, Jan. 28, 1689 (BK 10:33r; BS 28:8v); boyar, June 29, 1689 (BK 10:13v; BS 28:4r); died, March 21, 1713 (*Mosk. nekropol'* 2:188).

Golovkin, Ivan Semenovich—okol'nichii, Feb. 7, 1689 (BK 10:33r; BS 28:8r); boyar, Nov. 10, 1691 (BK 11:29v); died, 1694/5 or later (BS 36:3r).

Lopukhin, Petr Avramovich bol'shoi—okol'nichii, Feb. 7, 1689 (BK 10:33r; BS 28:8r); boyar, Feb. 28, 1690 (BK 10:14r; BS 31:4v); died under torture, Jan. 24-25, 1695 (*RBS* 10:686; I. A. Zheliabuzhskii, *Zapiski Zheliabuzhskago s 1682 po 2 iiulia 1709*, p. 40).

Poltev, Semen Erofeevich—dumnyi dvorianin, Feb. 7, 1689 (BK 10:54r; BS 28:13v); okol'nichii, March 25, 1689; died, June 6, 1689 (BK 10:35v; BS:28:8r).

Lopukhin, Vasilii Avramovich—okol'nichii, March 17, 1689 (BK 10:34v; BS 28:8r); boyar, Nov. 10, 1691 (BK 11:29v); died, June 9, 1697 (*Mosk. nekropol'* 2:187).

Saltykov, Stepan Ivanovich—boyar, March 21, 1689 (BK 10:12r; BS 28:4v); died, 1707 or later (BS 53:1r).

Golovin, Ivan Ivanovich—okol'nichii, March 24, 1689 (BK 10:34r; BS 28:8r); last mention, 1697/8 (BS 42:5r); died, July 12, 1700 (Dolgorukov, *Ros. rod. kniga* 3:108).

Streshnev, Dmitrii Iakovlevich—okol'nichii, March 24, 1689 (BK 10:34r; BS 28:8r); died, Dec. 9, 1692 (BS 35:9v).

Saltykov, Iurii Ivanovich—boyar, March 25, 1689 (BK 10:12r; BS 28:4v); died, 1694/5 (BS 36:351r).

Samarin (or Kvashnin-Samarin), Kir'iak Ivanovich—okol'nichii, March 25, 1689 (BK 10:41v; BS 28:8r); tonsured, March 16, 1698 (BS 42:5r).

Chaplygin, Ivan Petrovich—dumnyi dvorianin, March 25, 1689 (BK 10:54r; BS 28:13r); died, 1704 or later (BS 51:7v).

Kirillov, Iakov Averkievich—dumnyi d'iak, March 25, 1689 (BK 10:62r; BS 28:15v); tonsured, 1692/3 or later (BS 35:19v); died, Sept. 3, 1695 (*Mosk. nekropol'* 1:512-513).

Apraksin, Petr Matveevich—okol'nichii, June 29, 1689 (BK 10:35r; BS 28:9v); boyar, Jan. 22, 1710 (BS 57:2r); still alive, 1713 (BS 60:4r).

Naryshkin, Ivan Ivanovich—okol'nichii, June 29, 1689 (*DR* 4:454; BK 10:35v); buried, Feb. 17, 1693 (*Mosk. nekropol'* 2:316).

Derevnin, Gavriil Fedorovich—dumnyi d'iak, June 29, 1689 (BK 10:63v; BS 28:15r); still alive, 1713 (BS 60:6r).

Domnin, Liubim Alfer'evich—dumnyi d'iak, June 30, 1689 (BK 10:63v; BS 28:15r); died, November, 1712 (BS 58:8v).

Ukhtomskii, Prince Ivan Iur'evich—okol'nichii, Nov. 3, 1689 (*DR* 4:504; BK 10:36v); last mention, 1690/1 (BS 32:8v).

Iazykov, Ivan Andreevich—dumnyi dvorianin, Dec. 21, 1689 (*DR* 4:512; BK 10:55v); last mention, September, 1690 (*AI* 5:349); died, 1690/1 (BS 32:12r).

1690

Voznitsyn, Prokofii Bogdanovich—dumnyi d'iak, Jan. 11, 1690 (BK 10:63r; BS 31:19r); died, Feb. 4, 1702 (BS 46:7v).

Naryshkin, Martem'ian Kirillovich—boyar, Feb. 19, 1690 (*DR* 4:529; BK 10:14v); died, March 3, 1697 (BS 41:2r).

Alad'in, Zamiatnia Fedorovich—dumnyi dvorianin, Feb. 23, 1690 (*DR* 4:532; BK 10:55v); died, March 29, 1693 (BS 35:15v).

Golitsyn, Prince Boris Alekseevich—boyar, Feb. 28, 1690 (BK 10:14r, 22v; BS 31:4v); still alive, 1713 (BS 60:4r).

Zasekin, Prince Ivan Nikitich—okol'nichii, March 2, 1690 (*DR* 4:537; BK 10:38v); died, June 26, 1693 (BS 35:10v).

Likharev, Boris Ivanovich—dumnyi dvorianin, March 2, 1690 (*DR* 4:537; BK 10:55v); still alive, 1713 (BS 60:6v).

Chemodanov, Fedor Ivanovich—dumnyi dvorianin, March 25, 1690 (*DR* 4:543; BK 10:55r); last mention, 1697/8 (BS 42:8r).

Shakhovskoi, Prince Perfilii Ivanovich—okol'nichii, June 29, 1690 (BK 10:38r; BS 31:12v); died, March 10, 1696 (BS 36:356v).

Streshnev, Vasilii Fedorovich—okol'nichii, June 29, 1690 (BK 10:38v; BS 31:11r); died, August 22, 1703 (BS 49:4r).

Suponev, Grigorii Semenovich—dumnyi dvorianin, June 29, 1690 (BK 10:55r; BS 31:16r); died, 1704 or later (BS 51:7v).

Prozorovskii, Prince Aleksei Petrovich—boyar, July 10, 1690 (*DR* 4:565; BK 10:15v); died, 1705 or later (BS 52:1r).

Koltovskii, Semen Semenovich—okol'nichii, July 10, 1690 (BK 10:39r; BS 32:9v); last mention, Oct. 18, 1691 (*DR* 4:613); buried, April 1, 1692 (*Mosk. nekropol'* 2:71).

Tugarinov, Mitrofan Petrovich—dumnyi d'iak, July 10, 1690 (BK 10:63r; BS 31:19r); last mention, 1697/8 (BS 42:11v).

Prozorovskii, Prince Andrei Petrovich men'shii—boyar, August 29, 1690 (*DR* 4:602; BK 10:15v); still alive, 1713 (BS 60:4r).

1691

Bukhvostov, Vasilii Borisovich—dumnyi dvorianin, Jan. 18, 1691 (BK 10:56v; BS 32:13v); okol'nichii, August 28, 1698 (BS 42:6r); died, 1704 or later (BS 51:5v).

Boriatinskii, Prince Fedor Iur'evich—okol'nichii, Feb. 1, 1691 (BK 10:39v; BS 32:9v); died, June 16, 1696 (BS 36:356v).

Verderevskii, Vasilii Petrovich—dumnyi dvorianin, Feb. 1, 1691 (BK 10:56v; BS 32:13v); died, 1694/5 or later (BS 36:361v).

Naryshkin, Vasilii Fedorovich—okol'nichii, March 17, 1691 (BK 10:39v; BS 32:9v); boyar, June 29, 1691 (BK 10:17v; BS 32:4r); last mention, 1697/8 (BS 42:2r); died, 1702 (Lobanov-Rostovskii, *Rus. rod. kniga* 2:7).

Saltykov, Petr Samoilovich—boyar, April 5, 1691 (BK 10:16r; BS 32:4r); still alive, 1713 (BS 60:4r).

Protas'ev, Aleksandr Petrovich—dumnyi dvorianin, July 3, 1691 (BK 10:59r; BS 32:13v); okol'nichii, July 25, 1691 (BK 10:39r; BS 32:9r); last mention, 1697/8 (BS 42:6v).

Volkonskii-Chermnyi, Prince Vladimir Ivanovich—okol'nichii, Oct. 22, 1691 (*DR* 4:620; BK 11:37v); died, 1694/5 or later (BS 36:356r).

Vlas'ev, Ivan Astaf'evich—dumnyi dvorianin, Oct. 22, 1691 (BK 11:44v); died, 1710 or later (BS 57:6v).

Leont'ev, Vasilii Iur'evich—okol'nichii, Nov. 10, 1691 (BK 11:37r); died, June 17, 1697 (BS 41:6v).

Prokof'ev, Mikhail Prokof'evich—dumnyi d'iak, Nov. 10, 1691 (BK 11:47v); last mention, 1697/8 (BS 42:11v).

1692

Iushkov, Timofei Borisovich—okol'nichii, March 17, 1692 (*DR* 4:659; BK 11:37r); buried, Dec. 17, 1695 (*Mosk. nekropol'* 3:397).

Tsykler, Ivan Eliseevich—dumnyi dvorianin, March 17, 1692 (*DR* 4:659; BK 11:44v); executed, March 4, 1697 (BS 41:9v).

Ershov, Vasilii Semenovich—dumnyi d'iak, March 3, 1692 (BK 11:47v); died, 1712 or later (BS 58:8v; 60:1-10).

Olovennikov, Perfilii Fedorovich—dumnyi d'iak, March 31, 1692 (*DR* 4:676; BK 11:47v); died, 1694/5 or later (BS 36:364r).

Matveev, Andrei Artamonovich—born, August 15, 1666 (Semevskii, *Rus. rod. kniga* 1:56); okol'nichii, April 2, 1692 (BK 11:37r); still alive, 1713 (BS 60:5r).

Trubetskoi, Prince Ivan Iur'evich—boyar, April 3, 1692 (*DR* 4:678; BK 11:29r); still alive, 1713 (BS 60:4r).

Shchepin, Ivan Ivanovich—dumnyi dvorianin, June 29, 1692 (BK 11:44v); died, 1710 or later (BS 57:6v).

1693

Golovlenkov, Fedor Ivanovich—dumnyi dvorianin, Jan. 26, 1693 (*DR* 4:754; BK 11:44r); died, 1704 or later (BS 51:7r).

Zhirovogo-Zasekin, Prince Mikhail Fedorovich—okol'nichii, Feb. 2, 1693 (BK 11:38v; BS 35:10r); died, 1707 or later (BS 53:4r).

Golovin, Petr Alekseevich—okol'nichii, Feb. 3, 1693 (*DR* 4:758-759; BK 11:38v); died, Nov. 17, 1694 (BS 36:7v).

Volkonskii, Prince Mikhail Andreevich—okol'nichii, Feb. 3, 1693 (*DR* 4:758-759; BK 11:38r); died, May 16, 1709 (Vlas'ev, *Potomstvo* 1, pt. 3, p. 382).

Shcherbatov, Prince Iurii Fedorovich—okol'nichii, Feb. 19, 1693 (*DR* 4:763; BK 11:38r); still alive, 1713 (BS 60:5r).

Prozorovskii, Prince Nikita Petrovich men'shii—boyar, Feb. 26, 1693 (*DR* 4:768; BK 11:30v); died, 1703 or later (BS 49:2r).

Choglokov, Timofei Vasil'evich—okol'nichii, Feb. 26, 1693 (*DR* 4:768; BK 11:38r); died, 1710 or later (BS 57:4r).

1695

Vinius, Andrei Andreevich—dumnyi d'iak, March 24, 1695 (BS 36:12r); still alive, 1713 (BS 60:6r).

1696

L'vov, Prince Petr Grigor'evich—okol'nichii, August 15, 1696 (BS 36:357v); last mention, 1705 (BS 52:3r).

1697

Dolgorukii, Prince Iakov Fedorovich—boyar, July 20, 1697 (BS 41:3r); senator, 1711 (BS 58:2v); died, June 20, 1720 (Vlas'ev, *Potomstvo* 1, pt. 3, p. 38).

1702?

Islen'ev, Ivan Ivanovich—dumnyi dvorianin, by 1702-1703 (BS 46:6v); died, 1703 or later (BS 49:7r).

1710

Shakhovskoi, Prince Iurii Fedorovich—boyar, April 12, 1710 (BS 57:2r); still alive, 1713 (BS 60:4r).

Patrikeev, Kuz'ma Khrisanfovich—okol'nichii, April 12, 1710 (BS 57:4r); still alive, 1713 (BS 60:5r).

Buturlin, Petr Vasil'evich—dumnyi dvorianin, April 12, 1710 (BS 57:6v); okol'nichii, April 20, 1712 (BS 58:4r); still alive, 1713 (BS 60:5r).

1711

Ushakov, Prokofii Afanas'evich—dumnyi dvorianin, Jan. 14, 1711 (BS 58:6r); still alive, 1713 (BS 60:6r).

Iushkov, Aleksei Aleksandrovich—okol'nichii, Nov. 4, 1711 (BK 11:39v; BS 58:4r); still alive, 1713 (BS 60:5r).

1712

Turgenev, Semen Iakovlevich—dumnyi dvorianin, Jan. 21, 1712 (BS 58:6r); still alive, 1713 (BS 60:6r).

Buturlin, Petr Ivanovich—boyar, April 20, 1712 (BS 58:2v); still alive, 1713 (BS 60:4r).

Shakhovskoi, Prince Mikhail Fedorovich—okol'nichii, April 20, 1712 (BS 58:4r); still alive, 1713 (BS 60:5r).

Zhirovogo-Zasekin, Prince Nikita Mikhailovich—okol'nichii, April 20, 1712 (BS 58:4r); still alive, 1713 (BS 60:5r).

APPENDIX C

The Boyar Duma in the
Seventeenth Century: Controversies

In recent decades, historians of Russia have paid little attention to the role of the Boyar Duma in the governing of the Muscovite state. Recent Soviet textbooks, for example, describe Muscovite institutions briefly as background to a more detailed treatment of social, economic, and political problems. Moreover, their description of the Duma repeats many of the views of V. O. Kliuchevskii in his magisterial work, *Boiarskaia duma drevnei Rusi*, first published in 1882. In a chapter of *Ocherki istorii SSSR. Period feodalizma. XVII v.*, three of the most distinguished historians of their generation—K. V. Bazilevich, S. K. Bogoiavlenskii, and N. S. Chaev—described the Duma as a "governmental organ of estate-representative monarchy" which assisted the tsar. In their opinion, it acted as the "highest institution of control in the state" and as the highest judicial instance whose decisions on ambiguous or difficult cases had the force of law, and it played an important role in the conduct of diplomacy. At the same time, the monarch could issue decrees without the Duma's participation and, within certain customary limits, determined who joined its ranks. Moreover, over the course of the seventeenth century, the Duma, as a whole, gradually lost its importance, and smaller bodies, made up of a few of its members, emerged to take over some of its functions.[1]

In many respects, the Soviet scholars did a remarkably good job of summarizing Kliuchevskii's views. The task was not easy. *Boiarskaia duma* is a long, complex, and, at times, very ambiguous book that deals with many distinct subjects. On one level, the work charts the history of the boyars as an elite group of royal servitors. Since, in Muscovite Russia, men usually reached high rank through a combination of distinguished family background and loyal service to the monarch, Kliuchevskii necessarily ventured into both social and administrative history. In these areas, his conclusions still stand up well, although later historians have modified some detailed points.

On another level, Kliuchevskii's book deals with constitutional issues.

He tried to determine the precise legal rights of the Duma as a body and its role in making and enforcing the laws of the realm. Three problems made the attempt a hazardous undertaking. First, the very nature of the search meant the imposition of nineteenth-century categories on the slippery reality of earlier times. Pre-modern governments often proceeded on the basis of custom and precedent rather than by general legal definitions or precise constitutional arrangements. To a degree, then, Kliuchevskii looked for a system where there probably was none. Secondly, his search for abstract constitutional norms tended to obscure the degree to which institutions change over the course of time. The royal council in England, for example, changed continuously in size and function under the Tudors and early Stuarts.[2] Given the turbulent history of Muscovite Russia, it is entirely likely that the institutional arrangements of the tsars' government were in a similar state of flux. At times, Kliuchevskii was acutely sensitive to the changing composition of the administrative elite and its institutional setting; on other occasions, he ignored chronological distinctions and used fragments of evidence from the fifteenth and seventeenth centuries as though they were interchangeable. Finally, the evidence at his disposal was ambiguous and of limited value. We have no records of the proceedings of the Duma. Instead, we, like Kliuchevskii, must work with the testimony of a few contemporary observers, notably Giles Fletcher and Grigorii Kotoshikhin, procedural norms in the law codes of 1550 and 1649, and the legal formulae in which chancery clerks phrased innumerable governmental decrees and legal decisions.

Marshalling this scattered evidence, Kliuchevskii argued that the Boyar Duma was the "fly-wheel that set the whole mechanism of government in motion. Moreover, in large measure, it constituted that mechanism, legislated, regulated all relations, and answered questions directed to the government."[3] The Duma advised the tsar, issued decrees (*prigovory*), supervised the administrative chanceries, decided appeals and other difficult judicial cases, and played an important role in the conduct of foreign policy. Indeed, as Kliuchevskii argued in considerable detail, the Duma as an institution had a central part in the legislative process of the Muscovite state.

Not all of his contemporaries accepted his views. V.I. Sergeevich, the distinguished historian of law, offered a trenchant critique of Kliuchevskii's work in two of his textbooks.[4] Sergeevich offered many objections to *Boiarskaia duma*, some profound and some petty. For our purposes, three have the greatest significance. First, Sergeevich argued that the Boyar Duma was not a "regular institution (*postoiannoe uchrezhdenie*)." Its size and composition changed continually. This observation is obviously true, but its significance is hard to determine. After all, governmental institutions can change in size or function without ceasing to be institutions. Moreover, there was nothing vague about the composition of the Duma at any particular moment; contemporaries knew perfectly well how many men held each of its ranks.

Secondly—and far more important—the Duma formed only one part of a whole network of relationships between the tsar and his leading subjects. To begin with, Sergeevich argued, the tsar did not have to consult with any of his servitors. As he rightly pointed out, many of the official decrees of the Muscovite state took the form of ukazes issued by the sovereign alone. Moreover, if the ruler engaged in formal consultations with his subjects, he was not obliged to work with the Duma as such; he might deal with the ecclesiastical hierarchy, a small group of boyars, the whole Duma, or an even larger group of clergy and laity, such as the zemskii sobor. In short, the Duma did not have a regular and clearly defined role in the formulation and administration of royal policy.

Finally, Sergeevich claimed, the stipulations of the law codes of 1550 and 1649 and the other fragments of evidence implying that the boyars had a regular judicial function referred, not to the Duma, but to a completely different institution—the Raspravnaia Palata. Although the first unequivocal evidence of the latter's existence dates from 1681, Sergeevich was convinced that it first took shape in the reign of Ivan IV and, after disappearing momentarily, became a regular part of the Muscovite judicial system in the seventeenth century.[5] Unlike the Boyar Duma, the Raspravnaia Palata was a real institution with clearly defined membership, procedures, and legal prerogatives which the rest of the royal administration had to respect. Most later historians have not accepted these arguments of Sergeevich because they are obviously circular and rest on as strained a reading of the evidence as Kliuchevskii ever perpetrated.

Despite its shortcomings, however, Sergeevich's critique made two valid central points. First, Kliuchevskii made the Duma's part in the political and administrative system far greater and its procedures far more systematic than his evidence warranted. Secondly, the Duma owed its position in the apparatus of government to tradition and custom, not to any constitutional guarantees. The tsar might or might not consult it, depending on the issue in question and on the broader political circumstances of the time.

What is the contemporary reader to conclude from these debates of long ago and from the scattered evidence that inspired them? Let us begin with the obvious. Long before the Muscovite monarchy took shape under Ivan III, there were boyars, prominent servitors in the prince's entourage ready to advise him or help him to lead his troops and to administer his domain. Gradually, before the end of the sixteenth century, the government created three additional ranks—okol'nichii, dumnyi dvorianin, and dumnyi d'iak—to honor royal advisers and favorites of less distinguished social origins. Moreover, although the phrase "Boyar Duma (*boiarskaia duma*)" appears only once in a document of the Muscovite period—in garbled form in Giles Fletcher's work first published in 1591—native documents refer frequently either to the boyars collectively ("*boiare*") or to a "*duma*."[6] Thus, without question, there were boyars who had a collective, as well as an individual, identity.

Secondly, it was in the interest of the tsars and their advisers to consult—or, at least, appear to consult—their leading subjects on important matters. The royal government attempted to govern a huge territory with a small corps of administrators. Like other pre-modern governments, it depended, in part, on its ability to convince its subjects to obey since it could not always force them to do so. For this reason, the rulers of Muscovy regularly went through the motions of consulting their leading subjects, thereby making them share responsibility for official policy. Time and again, the language of official enactments reflected this custom. To cite only one dramatic example, Aleksei Mikhailovich "consulted" with the church hierarchy and the members of the Boyar Duma before issuing the Law Code of 1649. Many of the decrees of the seventeenth century refer to the boyars' collective participation in their formulation in phrases such as the familiar, "the Sovereign ordered and the boyars decreed (*Gosudar' ukazal i boiare prigovorili*)."[7]

The system of consultation was extremely flexible and varied from one reign to the next, depending on the personal qualities of the monarch and the level of development of the administrative system of the realm. To my knowledge, no one has made a systematic study of the official enactments of the Muscovite state in order to trace the ebb and flow of the Duma's role in the royal administration. Indeed, in their concern to document general constitutional norms or their absence, Kliuchevskii and Sergeevich both tended to gloss over these changes over time. A preliminary survey of the most accessible legal sources suggests a working hypothesis—that it was precisely the weakest regimes whose leaders tried hardest to buttress their legitimacy by stressing that the tsar and his inner circle established policy in consultation with the leading spokesmen of society. Certainly, at first glance, references to the participation of the Boyar Duma in decision-making seem much more frequent in the reign of Mikhail Romanov and after 1676 than under the relatively stable and self-confident regime of Aleksei. Firmer conclusions must, however, await further study.

Sources from different decades of the seventeenth century clearly indicate the manner in which the Boyar Duma met. Boyars and other Duma members who happened to be in Moscow met at particular times in one of the chambers of the great palace in the Kremlin, where they sat in order of rank.[8] Indeed, over the course of the century, the time of Duma meetings, the agenda, and the procedures for conducting business were defined more and more precisely.[9] Such interesting details, however, tell us little about the Duma's real part in determining governmental policy.

Did the Boyar Duma as such really make decisions on matters of policy? Did the initiative on important questions come from within the Duma or from outside? Once a question was raised, did the boyars really discuss it or simply give their formal assent to decisions already made elsewhere? The state of the sources makes these vital questions particularly difficult to answer. Kotoshikhin's testimony, although jaundiced, may well be correct in essence. Under Tsar Aleksei, he claimed, initiative came from the ruler himself. The tsar ordered the boyars to discuss a particular issue, and, in fact, some of them would do so intelligently while others sat in stunned silence. It was the responsibility of the dumnye d'iaki to keep records of the decisions made.[10] The clear implication, then, is that the tsar and a small inner circle of advisers and favorites initiated policy and ultimately decided the most important matters of state. That is not to say, however, that decisions were made in isolation from the Duma; in the seventeenth century, members of the ruler's inner circle almost invariably joined its ranks.

Bureaucratic chanceries also presented questions for the boyars' consideration. As the general provisions of the law codes and many specific decrees make clear, the prikazy sent the Duma cases that they could not deal with on their own.[11] Somehow or other, the Duma rendered a decision and sent it back to the appropriate chancery for implementation. Here, too, the presence of the heads of many chanceries among the Duma's members provided a personal link with the lower echelons of the royal administration.

We are confronted, then, with an apparent paradox. As we have noted, the bureaucracy and the Duma itself grew rapidly in size over the course of the seventeenth century. This change had several important consequences. As the bureaucracy increased in complexity and sophistication, it presumably had less need of a higher instance to supervise its operations and to fill the gaps in its store of precedents. That was just as well since, as the Duma expanded, it was less and less likely to serve as an effective body directing the operations of government. Ironically, then, just at the time when official decrees defined the Duma's competence and procedures more and more precisely, it was less and less capable of functioning as a unit. Instead, a minority of its members—the leading royal advisers and chancery officials—made important decisions with the formal consent of the whole.

While the details are sketchy, the general direction of the Duma's evolution seems clear. Over the course of the seventeenth century, it changed from a comparatively small group of influential courtiers and officials to an increasingly "regular institution" in Sergeevich's sense. At the same time, however, the real power to make and implement decisions lay in the hands of small groups of powerful men within its ranks.

NOTES

INTRODUCTION

1. N. P. Zagoskin, *Istoriia prava moskovskago gosudarstva* 2:15, 36, 106. Zagoskin's brief study of the Duma is still the most balanced and sensible treatment of the subject.

2. See, especially, V. O. Kliuchevskii, *Boiarskaia duma drevnei Rusi* and V. I. Sergeevich, *Drevnosti russkago prava* 2:384-453, 463-501 and his *Lektsii i izsledovaniia po drevnei istorii russkago prava*, pp. 196-210. For a discussion of their debate on the Duma and its impact on more recent scholarship, see Appendix C.

3. Zagoskin, *Istoriia* 2:36, 117-118.

4. C. Wright Mills, *The Power Elite* popularized the term.

5. The main source on the composition of the ecclesiastical hierarchy in premodern Russia is P. Stroev, *Spiski ierarkhov i nastoiatelei monastyrei rossiiskoi tserkvi*.

6. Lawrence Stone, "Prosopography."

7. Muriel Atkin, now of George Washington University, and James J. Kenney, St. Mary's College, Maryland. I am eternally grateful for their efforts.

8. Robert O. Crummey, "Court Spectacles in Seventeenth-Century Russia: Illusion and Reality."

CHAPTER I

1. Kliuchevskii, *Boiarskaia duma*, p. 15.

2. *Ibid.*, pp. 531-532; Vladimir Dal', *Tolkovyi slovar' zhivogo velikorusskago iazyka* (4 vols., St. Petersburg-Moscow, 1912) 1:297. The Russian roots are *boi* (battle) and *bol'* (pain or concern).

3. The term "boiarskaia duma" was not used by Russians in the seventeenth century or earlier (Kliuchevskii, *Boiarskaia duma*, p. 532).

4. M. A. D'iakonov, *Ocherki obshchestvennago i gosudarstvennago stroia drevnei Rusi*, p. 278. The word *okol'nichii* is clearly related to *okolo* (around) and is therefore a logical designation for those who accompany their lord.

5. A. A. Zimin, "Sostav Boiarskoi dumy v XV-XVI vekakh," p. 79; M. F. Vladimirskii-Budanov, *Obzor istorii russkago prava*, p. 162.

6. See S. B. Veselovskii, *Issledovaniia po istorii klassa sluzhilykh zemlevla-del'tsev.*

7. See Gustave Alef, "The Crisis of the Muscovite Aristocracy: a Factor in the Growth of Monarchical Power" and his "Reflections on the Boiar Duma in the Reign of Ivan III."

8. Soviet scholars have recently published a great deal of useful material on the boyar elite in the sixteenth century. There is as yet no systematic interpretative study of the boyars based on these sources and compilations. Fortunately, Ann M. Kleimola is now working on just such a study. See, for example, her article, "The Changing Face of the Muscovite Aristocracy. The 16th Century: Sources of Weakness."

9. Sergeevich, *Drevnosti* 1:437.

10. Any choice of terms, other than a literal translation of Muscovite juridical terminology, automatically introduces a subjective element into the discussion. To give one example, Richard Hellie in *Enserfment and Military Change in Muscovy* refers to the members of the Duma as part of the "upper service class." Hellie's choice of words serves him well but seems inappropriate in the present context for several reasons. Apart from its literary awkwardness, the term tends to exaggerate the degree to which service to the state dominated the lives of Russian high nobles and, by extension, virtually excludes significant comparison of Russia and western European society in our period. While not without its pitfalls, the word "aristocracy" permits us to stress the boyars' success in maintaining their power over time and to compare their position to that of their western European counterparts.

11. The literature on the *oprichnina* is extensive, and much of the recent work is of high quality. See, in particular, A. A. Zimin, *Oprichnina Ivana Groznogo*; R. G. Skrynnikov, *Nachalo oprichniny* and *Oprichnyi terror.* For a discussion of the recent Soviet literature, see Robert O. Crummey, "Ivan the Terrible."

12. For a trenchant discussion of the historiography of the oprichnina and a powerful statement of the latter position, see S. B. Veselovskii, *Issledovaniia po istorii oprichniny.*

13. The classic work on the Time of Troubles is still S. F. Platonov, *Ocherki po istorii Smuty v moskovskom gosudarstve XVI-XVII vv. The Time of Troubles* is a useful English translation of Platonov's *Smutnoe vremia*, a later summary of his masterpiece.

14. See E. V. Stashevskii, *Smolenskaia voina 1632-1634. Organizatsiia i sostoianie moskovskoi armii* (Kiev, 1919). On the diplomatic background to the war, see O. L. Vainshtein, *Rossiia i tridtsatiletnaia voina* (Moscow, 1947).

15. *Ocherki istorii SSSR. Period feodalizma. XVII v.*, pp. 480-518; A. N. Mal'tsev, *Rossiia i Belorussiia v seredine XVII veka.*

16. Hellie, *Enserfment*, pp. 174-180; A. A. Novosel'skii, *Bor'ba moskovskogo gosudarstva s tatarami v pervoi polovine XVII veka*; A. I. Iakovlev, *Zasechnaia cherta moskovskago gosudarstva v XVII v.* (Moscow, 1916).

17. *Ocherki istorii SSSR. XVII v.*, pp. 518-541. S. M. Solov'ev, *Istoriia Rossii s drevneishikh vremen*, bks. 5-7, is still an indispensable source of information

on the political and diplomatic history of seventeenth-century Russia. On Russo-Turkish relations, see N. A. Smirnov, *Rossiia i Turtsiia v XVI-XVII vv.*

18. For a provocative general discussion of military change in early modern Europe and its economic and social impact, see Michael Roberts, "The Military Revolution, 1560-1660" and Geoffrey Parker, "The 'Military Revolution,' 1560-1660—a Myth?"

19. Hellie, *Enserfment*, pp. 271-272; P. N. Miliukov, *Gosudarstvennoe khoziaistvo Rossii v pervoi chetverti XVIII stoletiia i reforma Petra Velikago*, p. 52.

20. Hellie, *Enserfment*, pp. 167-225; A. V. Chernov, *Vooruzhennye sily russkogo gosudarstva v XV-XVII vv.*, pp. 133-155.

21. Miliukov, *Gosudarstvennoe khoziaistvo*, p. 54.

22. V. O. Kliuchevsky, *A Course in Russian History. The Seventeenth Century*, still the best survey of Russian history in the seventeenth century, makes the point with particular eloquence in chap. 11. See also Miliukov, *Gosudarstvennoe khoziaistvo*, pp. 58-91.

23. N. F. Demidova, "Biurokratizatsiia gosudarstvennogo apparata absoliutizma v XVII-XVIII vv.," pp. 214-217.

24. S. K. Bogoiavlenskii, *Prikaznye sud'i XVII veka*.

25. For a fresh and positive assessment of the seventeenth-century bureaucracy, see Borivoj Plavsic, "Seventeenth-Century Chanceries and Their Staffs."

26. Note, for example, the government's ability to identify and destroy leading religious dissidents throughout the country. See Robert O. Crummey, *The Old Believers and the World of Antichrist*, chaps. 2 and 3, and V. G. Druzhinin, *Raskol na Donu v kontse XVII veka* (St. Petersburg, 1889).

27. For a particularly good discussion of the enserfment of the peasantry, see Hellie, *Enserfment*, pt. 2. See also Jerome Blum, *Lord and Peasant in Russia from the Ninth to the Nineteenth Century* (Princeton, 1961), chap. 14.

28. The literature on peasant revolts and the Razin uprising, in particular, is enormous. See *Ocherki istorii SSSR. XVII v.*, pp. 277-312; I. V. Stepanov, *Krest'ianskaia voina v Rossii v 1670-1671 gg.*; Paul Avrich, *Russian Rebels 1600-1800*, chap. 2.

29. See *Ocherki istorii SSSR. XVII v.*, pp. 224-264, 325-336; P. P. Smirnov, *Posadskie liudi i ikh klassovaia bor'ba do serediny XVII veka*; V. I. Buganov, *Moskovskoe vosstanie 1662 g.* and his *Moskovskie vosstaniia kontsa XVII v.* There is a very large literature on urban revolts in the seventeenth century that includes monographs and articles on the uprisings in a number of provincial towns.

30. For a summary economic history of the Muscovite period, see P. I. Lyashchenko, *History of the National Economy of Russia to the 1917 Revolution*, pp. 179-228.

31. See R.E.F. Smith's excellent study, *Peasant Farming in Muscovy*.

32. See, for example, Paul Bushkovitch's stimulating new book, *The Merchants of Moscow, 1580-1650*.

33. See the essays of Samuel H. Baron, especially "Who were the *Gosti*?" and "The Weber Thesis and the Failure of Capitalist Development in 'Early Modern' Russia," *JfGO* 18 (1970):321-336.

34. Baron, "*Gosti*," pp. 20-21 and "Weber Thesis," p. 322. For a translation of one of the petitions, see Richard Hellie, ed., *Readings for Introduction to Russian Civilization: Muscovite Society*, pp. 66-91.

35. Michael Cherniavsky, "The Old Believers and the New Religion," *Slavic Review* 25 (1966):1-39, here p. 10.

36. Kliuchevsky, *Seventeenth Century*, chaps. 14 and 15; Crummey, *Old Believers*; Cherniavsky, "Old Believers"; Serge Zenkovsky, *Russkoe staroobriadchestvo*; N. F. Kapterev, *Patriarkh Nikon i Tsar' Aleksei Mikhailovich*.

37. See, for example, *PRP* 5:201-207, 217-220, 237, 390-391; 6:40-41. To my knowledge, no scholar has made a statistical study of the incidence of "constitutional" terminology in Muscovite Russia. Such an undertaking might well prove to be an exercise in futility.

On the meeting place of the Duma, see Kliuchevskii, *Boiarskaia duma*, pp. 408-409.

38. *PRP* 4:260; 6:77. See also N. P. Eroshkin, *Istoriia gosudarstvennykh uchrezhdenii dorevoliutsionnoi Rossii*, pp. 33-35, 52-53, 63-64.

39. P. I. Ivanov, *Alfavitnyi ukazatel' familii i lits, upominaemykh v boiarskikh knigakh*.

40. G. Kotoshikhin, *O Rossii v tsarstvovanie Alekseia Mikhailovicha*, pp. 23-27; Benjamin Philip Uroff, "Grigorii Karpovich Kotoshikhin. On Russia in the Reign of Alexis Mikhailovich. An Annotated Translation," pp. 65-66.

41. Robert O. Crummey, "Peter and the Boiar Aristocracy, 1689-1700," pp. 276-278.

42. On the regency government, see C. Bickford O'Brien, *Russia under Two Tsars, 1682-1689*.

43. The most important sources on the changing composition of the Duma are the so-called "Sheremetev list," published as "Posluzhnoi spisok starinnykh boiar i dvoretskikh, okol'nichikh i nekotorykh drugikh pridvornykh chinov s 6970 po 7184 (to est' s 1462 po 1676) god . . ."; *DR*; *KR*; BK; BS; Sb. mosk. st.: Zap. kn. mosk. st. 12.

For an analysis of the "boiarskie knigi" and "boiarskie spiski" as sources, see A. A. Vostokov, "Boiarskie knigi kak material dlia istorii vysshego russkago sluzhilago sosloviia"; M. P. Lukichev, "Boiarskie knigi XVII v."; idem, "Obzor boiarskikh knig XVII v."; S. P. Mordovina and A. L. Stanislavskii, "Boiarskie spiski kontsa XVI-nachala XVII v. kak istoricheskii istochnik"; idem, *Boiarskie spiski poslednei chetverti XVI-nachala XVII v. i rospis' russkogo voiska 1604 g. Ukazatel' sostava Gosudareva dvora po fondu Razriadnogo prikaza* and Stanislavskii's "Boiarskie spiski v deloproizvodstve Razriadnogo prikaza."

Also Bogoiavlenskii, *Sud'i*; S. B. Veselovskii, *D'iaki i pod'iachie XV-XVII v.*; N. P. Likhachev, *Razriadnye d'iaki XVI veka*; Zimin, "Sostav"; A. V. Barsukov, *Spiski gorodovykh voevod i drugikh lits voevodskago upravleniia moskovskago gosudarstva XVII stoletiia*; *AMG*; *AAE*; *AI*; *DAI*; *RIB*, vols. 9, 10 and 11; *DRV*, vol. 19; *Sinbirskii sbornik*, vol. 1 (hereafter cited as *Sin. sb.*); A. A. Titov, ed., *Letopis' dvinskaia*; "Utverzhdennaia gramota ob izbranii na moskovskoe gosudarstvo Mikhaila Fedorovicha Romanova" (hereafter cited as "Ut. gramota"); So-lov'ev, *Istoriia*, and Platonov, *Ocherki*.

The most important genealogical and biographical sources are *RBS; RK*; P. V. Dolgorukov, *Rossiiskaia rodoslovnaia kniga*; A. B. Lobanov-Rostovskii, *Russkaia rodoslovnaia kniga*; G. A. Vlas'ev, *Potomstvo Riurika*; L. M. Savelov, *Opyt rodoslovnago slovaria russkogo drevniago dvorianstva. Rodoslovnye zapisi*; M. I. Semevskii, *Russkaia rodoslovnaia kniga*; A. V. Barsukov, *Rod Sheremetevykh* and *Rodoslovie Sheremetevykh*; M. L. Bode-Kolychev, *Boiarskii rod Kolyche-vykh*; P. M. Raevskii, *Rod tsaria, tsareven i kniazei Shuiskikh*; S. S. Tatishchev, *Rod Tatishchevykh. 1400-1900*; E. E. Trubetskaia, *Skazaniia o rode kniazei Tru-betskikh; Mosk. nekropol'; Rus. pr. nekropol'*.

44. Zimin, "Sostav," p. 82.

45. Kliuchevskii, *Boiarskaia duma*, chap. 23.

46. Between 1613 and 1689, only eleven Duma members ended their careers in disgrace. Five of them were executed—M. B. Shein and A. V. Izmailov in 1634, Princes I. A. and A. I. Khovanskii in 1682, and F. L. Shaklovityi in 1689. Another six apparently died of natural causes; Prince I. V. Golitsyn in 1624 (*DR* 1:642), N. N. Novokshchenov in 1619/20 (Veselovskii, *D'iaki*, p. 376), N. A. Ziuzin at the end of 1664 or early in 1665 (*RBS* 6:583-584), G. K. Bogdanov in 1682 (*DAI* 10:23-25), and Prince V. V. Golitsyn and L. R. Nepliuev in 1689 (BS 31:1r and 3v). Four more fell into disfavor but were soon restored to grace— B. M. Saltykov (*DR* 1:845-846), I. T. Gramotin (*RIB* 9:438), Prince S. V. Pro-zorovskii (Sb. mosk. st. 51, sb. 3:2v), and I. B. Miloslavskii (Sb. mosk. st. 379, sb. 1:3v).

47. *DR* 3:113; Sb. mosk. st. 357, sb. 2:5v; BK 7:30v, 47v; BS 14:226v.

48. Kotoshikhin, p. 23; Kliuchevskii, *Boiarskaia duma*, pp. 392-394.

49. S. F. Platonov, "Moskovskoe pravitel'stvo pri pervykh Romanovykh," p. 342.

50. Platonov, *Time of Troubles*, p. 167.

51. E. V. Stashevskii, *Ocherki po istorii tsarstvovaniia Mikhaila Fedorovicha*, pp. 57-59, 77-79, 92, 197.

52. Kliuchevskii, *Boiarskaia duma*, pp. 224-228, 387-406; *Seventeenth Cen-tury*, p. 227.

53. This point has been argued in detail in Robert O. Crummey, "The Origins of the Noble Official: the Boiar Elite, 1613-1689," pp. 50-55. See pp. 69-71.

54. Robert O. Crummey, "The Reconstitution of the Boiar Aristocracy, 1613-1645," pp. 191-197. The figures in "Noble Official," table 1, are more authori-tative than those in "Reconstitution," table 1, because the former are based on more extensive archival research and more subtle statistical categories.

55. *Ibid.*, pp. 199-200.

56. Lawrence Stone, *The Crisis of the Aristocracy, 1558-1641*, p. 23.

57. On the general problem of restorations, see Robert Kann, *The Problem of Restoration: a Study in Comparative Political History*.

58. See, for example, Robert O. Crummey, "Court Groupings and Politics in Russia, 1645-1649."

59. Material on the official careers of Duma members is found in many sources, particularly those mentioned in note 43. In addition, on diplomacy, see *PDS* and N. I. Bantysh-Kamenskii, *Obzor vneshnikh snoshenii Rossii (po 1800 god)*.

60. Brenda Meehan-Waters, *Autocracy and Aristocracy: the Russian Service Elite of 1730* and her article "The Muscovite Noble Origins of the Russians in the Generalitet of 1730."

61. Crummey, "Noble Official," p. 65.

62. *Ibid*., pp. 59-61. Since we know the dates of birth of very few seventeenth-century statesmen, I have followed the custom of the period and assumed that future Duma members performed their first recorded service assignment at the age of fifteen. See S. V. Rozhdestvenskii, *Sluzhiloe zemlevladenie v moskovskom gosudarstve XVI veka*, pp. 297-298 and Kliuchevskii, *Boiarskaia duma*, p. 392.

63. Kotoshikhin, *O Rossii*, p. 23; Uroff, "On Russia," p. 65; Kliuchevskii, *Boiarskaia duma*, pp. 393-394n.

64. On the mean age of new Duma members, see p. 37.

65. The seventeen families are the Vorotynskiis, Odoevskiis, Morozovs, Pronskiis, Golitsyns, Kurakins, Mstislavskiis, Romanovs, Bakhteiarov-, Lobanov-, Temkin-Rostovskiis, Nagois, Saltykovs, Troekurovs, Trubetskois, Sheins, and Shuiskiis.

These conclusions are based on the data in the records of service and the genealogies listed in note 43. Our list of first- and second-class boyar families agrees, in large measure, with Kotoshikhin's list as amended by Kliuchevskii.

66. Up until 1676, the most members of any one family to hold Duma rank simultaneously was five. The Streshnevs, royal in-laws, established the record in the mid-1650s, and the Khitrovos, parvenu favorites, tied it in the early 1670s. The L'vovs, Miloslavskiis, Romodanovskiis, and Sheremetevs had four Duma members at one time, and nine additional families had three. The calculations are based on the data in Appendix B.

67. For example, the Romodanovskiis and Khilkovs.

68. Lawrence Stone, "The Inflation of Honors, 1558-1641," pp. 59-65.

69. See, for example, the complaints of representatives of the lower nobility in ' 1642 and 1648 in *SGGD* 3:378-400 and P. P. Smirnov, ed., "Chelobitnye dvorian i detei boiarskikh vsekh gorodov v pervoi polovine XVII v.," p. 53.

70. Solov'ev, *Istoriia* 7:248-249; M. Ia. Volkov, "Ob otmene mestnichestva v Rossii," pp. 63-66.

71. Kotoshikhin, *O Rossii*, p. 24; Uroff, "On Russia," p. 67.

72. *DR*, 3:1109, 1111; Sergeevich, *Drevnosti* 2:413-414.

73. *DR* 4:187-188; Sergeevich, *Drevnosti* 2:438-453; Kliuchevskii, *Boiarskaia duma*, pp. 433-438.

74. *DR* 4:357, 364, 390, 430, 446, 460, 465-466.

75. For example, *DR* 3:1623-1624. On the *blizhnie boiare* in the sixteenth century, see Zimin, "Sostav," pp. 80-81.

76. Kliuchevskii, *Boiarskaia duma*, pp. 495-496; Volkov, "Ob otmene." The text of the reform project is published in E. Zamyslovskii, *Tsarstvovanie Fedora Alekseevicha* 1:xxxiv-xxxv.

77. Robert O. Crummey, "Reflections on Mestnichestvo in the 17th Century."

CHAPTER II

1. N. P. Pavlov-Sil'vanskii, *Sochineniia*, vol. 1, chap. 4; V. B. El'iashevich, *Istoriia prava pozemel'noi sobstvennosti v Rossii*, vol. 1, chap. 10; Rozhdestvenskii, *Sluzhiloe zemlevladenie*, chap. 3.

2. Pavlov-Sil'vanskii, *Sochineniia* 1:90-91; El'iashevich, *Istoriia* 2:30-32; Rozhdestvenskii, *Sluzhiloe zemlevladenie*, pp. 145-147; Zimin, *Reformy*, pp. 437-439.

3. See, for example, the excellent discussion in Stone, *Crisis*, chap. 8.

4. Hans-Joachim Torke, "Adel und Staat vor Peter dem Grossen (1649-1689)"; Hellie, *Enserfment*, pp. 213-216.

5. Smirnov, "Chelobitnye dvorian"; Hellie, *Enserfment*, pp. 129-136.

6. S. B. Veselovskii, *Feodal'noe zemlevladenie v severo-vostochnoi Rusi*, vol. 1, chaps. 3 and 8; Alef, "Crisis."

7. Lloyd E. Berry and Robert O. Crummey, eds., *Rude & Barbarous Kingdom*, p. 145.

8. The literature on *mestnichestvo* is vast. See, in particular, A. I. Markevich, *O mestnichestve. Russkaia istoriografiia v otnoshenii k mestnichestvu* and his *Istoriia mestnichestva v moskovskom gosudarstve v XV-XVII veke*; S. O. Shmidt, "Mestnichestvo i absoliutizm (postanovka voprosa)," *Stanovlenie rossiiskogo samoderzhavstva*, pp. 262-307.

9. *DR* 1:539-543, 561-562.

10. See, for example, the essays in *Russian Officialdom* and Alef, "Reflections."

11. I have been unable to make a systematic study of literacy in the boyar elite in the seventeenth century. In a world increasingly dominated by bureaucratic routine, it was, I suspect, very difficult to conduct government business or to manage a household entirely by relying on literate subordinates.

12. Brenda Meehan-Waters, "Social and Career Characteristics of the Administrative Elite, 1689-1761," p. 105.

13. Plavsic, "Seventeenth-century Chanceries," pp. 27-41.

14. The main sources on the official careers of members of the boyar elite are listed in chapter I, notes 43 and 59.

15. Crummey, "Noble Official," pp. 59-63.

16. Solov'ev, *Istoriia* 7:249.

17. *BK* 10:31v; *DR* Dop. k 3:285, 992; *KR* 2:1052, 1193; *AMG* 3:170, 179-180, 242-244; Solov'ev, *Istoriia* 7:210; *RIB* 11:100, 394; Volkov, "Ob otmene," pp. 65-67; A. A. Novosel'skii, "Praviashchie gruppy v sluzhilom "gorode" XVII v."

18. Crummey, "Noble Official," pp. 63-65; *AMG* 2:283; 3:507; N. Novikov, ed., *Istoriia o nevinnom zatochenii blizhniago boiarina Artemona Sergeevicha Matveeva*, p. 389. It is risky to attribute the rise of Matveev or any other seventeenth-century statesman to a single cause. In the early decades of his career, he carried out a number of diplomatic missions to the Ukraine—probably a job that required a military man—and apparently enjoyed the personal favor of the tsar.

19. Chernov, *Vooruzhennye sily*, pp. 164-165; Buganov, *Moskovskie vosstaniia*, pp. 68-78; Hellie, *Enserfment*, pp. 161-165, 202-208.

228 NOTES TO CHAPTER I

20. Crummey, "Noble Official," p. 65.

21. See N. N. Danilov's comments in his "V. V. Golicyn bis zum Staatsstreich vom Mai 1682," pp. 10-11, 31.

22. *DR* 2:317, 409; Samuel H. Baron, ed., *The Travels of Olearius in 17th Century Russia*, pp. 203-204 (hereafter cited as Olearius, *Travels*).

23. Bogoiavlenskii, *Sud'i*, pp. 119-131, 144-149.

24. *Ibid.*, pp. 18-20, 26, 31-35, 78, 83, 91, 93-94, 120-122, 128-130, 138, 145-148, 165-166, 197-198, 200, 210, 223.

25. *Ibid.*, pp. 28, 35-36; Veselovskii, *D'iaki*, p. 233.

26. Kotoshikhin, *O Rossii*, pp. 85-86; Uroff, "On Russia," pp. 163-165; I. Ia. Gurliand, *Prikaz Velikago gosudaria tainykh del*; A. I. Zaozerskii, *Tsar' Aleksei Mikhailovich v svoem khoziaistve*.

27. Bogoiavlenskii, *Sud'i*, pp. 197-198; Gurliand, *Prikaz*, pp. 117-120; Zaozerskii, *Tsar'*, pp. 82-85.

28. Bogoiavlenskii, *Sud'i*, pp. 166-168.

29. A. I. Zaozerskii, *Tsarskaia votchina XVII v.*, p. 75; Solov'ev, *Istoriia* 7:294, 299, 390, 451-463; *PDS* 6:489-490; *Rozysknyia dela o Fedore Shaklovitom i ego soobshchenikakh* 1:265-274.

30. Crummey, "Noble Official," p. 66.

31. Bogoiavlenskii, *Sud'i*, p. 121.

32. *Ibid.*, pp. 24-26.

33. S. A. Belokurov, "O Posol'skom prikaze."

34. Kotoshikhin, *O Rossii*, pp. 40-71, 86-88; Uroff, "On Russia," pp. 93-141, 165-167.

35. *DR* 1:299; 2:380-381.

36. BK 5:21v, 22r; 7:26r, 72v; *DR Dop. k* 3:247, 279; *PDS* 5:1201; Solov'ev, *Istoriia* 6:76-78, 173-180; 7:226-229.

37. See Garrett Mattingly, *Renaissance Diplomacy*.

38. *DR* 3:908; Solov'ev, *Istoriia* 6:505, 508-523; 7:181, 216-222; Belokurov, "O Posol'skom prikaze," p. 65.

39. The sources on Ordin-Nashchokin's career are very extensive. The outline can be reconstructed from *DR*; *AMG*; *PDS*; and Solov'ev, *Istoriia*. There is a brilliant characterization of Nashchokin in Kliuchevsky, *Seventeenth Century*, chap. 17. I. V. Galaktionov and E. V. Chistiakova, *A. L. Ordin-Nashchokin, russkii diplomat XVII v.* is a helpful popular biography. For his early career and his relations with Dubrovskii, see pp. 17-35. On his early diplomatic missions, see also I. V. Galaktionov, ed., *Ranniaia perepiska A. L. Ordina-Nashchokina (1642-1645 gg.)*.

40. BS 8:5v; 10:3v; *AMG* 2:283, 420; 3:507; Bogoiavlenskii, *Sud'i*, pp. 85, 130; Solov'ev, *Istoriia* 6:16-17, 421, 607-608; *Istoriia Matveeva*, pp. 390-391.

41. Crummey, "Reconstitution," p. 209.

42. *DR* 3:124, 413, 456; *DAI* 3:458; A. Iakovlev, *Kholopstvo i kholopy v moskovskom gosudarstve XVII v.*, pp. 513-516.

43. This figure differs from the one in the text of "Noble Official," p. 68. The correct figure appears in tables 9 and 10 of the same article. The classification of

chancery officials who performed other forms of service, usually diplomatic, accounts for the difference.

44. Crummey, "Noble Official," pp. 67-69.

45. I. Andreevskii, *O namestnikakh, voevodakh i gubernatorakh*, pp. 35-39; A. D. Gradovskii, *Istoriia mestnago upravleniia v Rossii*, pp. 381-391.

46. Robert O. Crummey, "Crown and Boiars under Fedor Ivanovich and Michael Romanov," pp. 553-556.

47. Chernov, *Vooruzhennye sily*, pp. 169-170; Hellie, *Enserfment*, p. 213; Novosel'skii, *Bor'ba*, pp. 371-372.

48. Crummey, "Crown and Boiars," pp. 557-558; Smirnov, *Posadskie liudi* 1:404-405.

49. N. N. Danilov, "Vasilij Vasil'evič Golicyn (1682-1714)," pp. 560-561; "Zapiski de-la Nevilla o Moskovii, 1689 g.," p. 444 (hereafter cited as Neuville, "Zapiski").

50. *DR* 3:408, 411, 412, 416, 419, 422, 427, 429, 434-435, 439, 450, 455, 461, 465, 478; Dop. k 3:8-9, 15, 36, 105, 130, 212, 218-219, 235, 254, 329, 346, 370, and many references in *AMG*.

51. *DR* 3:412-420.

52. *DR* Dop. k 3:35, 40, 50, 55, 79, 103, 109-110, 174, 177-178.

53. *DR* 3:151-152.

54. *DR* 3:872, 880-881; *DAI* 6:59.

55. Crummey, "Crown and Boiars," p. 557; *AMG* 2:567-568, 604, 734-735.

56. Crummey, "Crown and Boiars," pp. 558-559.

57. The three were Prince F. A. Khilkov, T. F. Buturlin, and Prince I. P. Pronskii (*DR* 3:30, 56, 59, 91, 117, 121, 299; *AMG* 2:150-151, 264).

58. *AMG* 2:274, 623-626, 631; 3:20, 28, 88, 288, 573-574; *DR* 3:843.

59. Solov'ev, *Istoriia* 7:209-215; *Ocherki istorii SSSR. XVII v.*, pp. 524-529; Patrick Gordon, *Passages from the Diary of General Patrick Gordon of Auchleucheries in the Years 1635-1699*, pp. 106-107.

60. *KR* 2:1054 (V. A. Zmeev), 1068 (K. A. Iakovlev).

61. Barsukov, *Rod Sheremetevykh* 5:90; "Puteshestvie v Moskoviiu Barona Augustina Maierberga i Goratsiia Vil'gel'ma Kal'vuchchi, poslov Imperatora Leopol'da k Tsariu i Velikomu Kniaziu Alekseiu Mikhailovichu v 1661 gody," p. 43. Tsar Aleksei bitterly criticized Prince I. I. Lobanov-Rostovskii for his recklessness in attacking the town of Mstislavl' in a manner that needlessly cost the lives of many of his men (*Zapiski otdeleniia russkoi i slavianskoi arkheologii Imperatorskago russkago arkheologicheskago obshchestva* 2:742-749. Hereafter cited as *ZORSA*).

62. Gordon, *Passages*, pp. 106-107; Solov'ev, *Istoriia* 6:620; *Ocherki istorii SSSR. XVII v.*, pp. 513-514; G. Luk'ianov, ed., "Chastnaia perepiska kn. Petra Ivanovicha Khovanskago, ego sem'i i rodstvennikov," p. 320.

63. Shmidt, *Stanovlenie*, pp. 262-307; Crummey, "Reflections," pp. 275-281.

64. See Gordon's comments on the difficulty of training a Russian officer of much lower rank (*Passages*, p. 53).

65. Crummey, "Peter," pp. 284-287; Meehan-Waters, *Autocracy*, pp. 161-163.

66. On Russia's "undergoverned provinces" in a later period, see S. F. Starr, *Decentralization and Self-Government in Russia, 1830-1870* (Princeton, 1972), chap. 1.

67. Barsukov, *Spiski*, pp. 8-12, 63-66, 86-89, 101-104, 152-156, 183-187, 209-211, 235-242; Crummey, "Crown and Boiars," pp. 559-560.

68. Crummey, "Crown and Boiars," pp. 560-561. The general comments are based on combining the data from Barsukov, *Spiski* and the other sources listed in chapter 1, notes 43 and 59.

69. Rzhevskii served as governor of Eniseisk in Siberia before his promotion to the Duma and in Ustiug Velikii in the European north in the early 1670s while a dumnyi dvorianin (*DR* Dop. k 3:170, 898; Barsukov, *Spiski*, pp. 73, 261).

70. At various times, Khilkov served two terms in Pskov and one each in occupied Dorpat in Livonia between 1656 and 1658 and in two important provincial centers within Russia—Tobol'sk and Astrakhan' (*DR* 3:460, 933; Dop. k 3:169; *AMG* 2:573-574; *AI* 4:327, 364; *DAI* 4:98, 185, 345; 5:170; Barsukov, *Spiski*, pp. 11, 185-186, 239, 278).

71. Barsukov, *Spiski*, pp. 155-156.

72. *Rude & Barbarous Kingdom*, p. 150.

73. Prince P. I. Rybin-Pronskii, 1639-1645/6 (Barsukov, *Spiski*, p. 237).

74. For a good example, see Iakovlev, *Kholopstvo*, pp. 533-555.

75. *ZORSA* 2:659-681.

76. *AI* 4:346-347.

77. For example, *DAI* 3:249; Barsukov, *Rod Sheremetevykh* 3:426-427.

78. See the comments of E. D. Stashevskii, *Zemlevladenie moskovskago dvorianstva v pervoi polovine XVII veka*, p. 33. I am grateful for the help of Brian Davies of the University of Chicago on this point. His dissertation will be a major contribution to our understanding of the Muscovite provincial administration in the seventeenth century.

79. For other cases of official corruption in the provinces, see *AMG* 3:2-15; *ChOIDR*, 1887, no. 3, pp. 8-9; "Chastnaia perepiska," pp. 370-372; Solov'ev, *Istoriia* 6:93; Barsukov, *Rod Sheremetevykh* 6:124-127; 7:101-103; M. M. Bogoslovskii, *Petr I. Materialy dlia biografii* 1:35; N. Ustrialov, *Istoriia tsarstvovaniia Petra Velikago* 2:465.

Provincial governors could wreak other kinds of havoc as well; in the early 1620s, Prince I. F. Khovanskii, the governor of Astrakhan', and his subordinates quarrelled so bitterly that the government dismissed and disgraced them all (*AI* 3:265).

80. *DRV* 20:61; *Sin. sb.*, pp. 86, 92-93, 96, 98, 105, 109-110, 114, 118, 122, 124, 126, 130, 133-134; *RK 1475*, pp. 187, 236, 244, 276, 278, 292, 308, 341, 343, 358, 360, 372, 388, 391, 397, 400, 413, 417, 420, 430, 439, 448, 459, 467, 471, 476, 497, 516; Bantysh-Kamenskii, *Obzor* 4:131; *RBS*.

81. *DR* 1:131, 144, 162-167, 197, 268, 307, 332, 439, 484, 522; 2:179, 187, 275, 366-367, 389, 627; *KR* 1:502, 1063; Bogoiavlenskii, *Sud'i*, pp. 62, 67-68, 81,

133, 139, 155, 159, 191, 218, 222-223; *Sin. sb.*, pp. 128, 149; Vlas'ev, *Potomstvo* 1, pt. 2, pp. 486-490; Smirnov, *Posadskie liudi* 1:404.

82. The published and archival sources that give the outline of Romodanovskii's career, although incomplete, suggest that he spent very little time in Moscow except for the years 1645-1650 in his youth and the four years between his retirement in 1678 and his death in the Moscow uprising of 1682. They do not account for his activities between mid-1664 and early 1668, when he may well have rested in Moscow or on one of his estates. Kurakin spent almost no extended periods in Moscow between 1637 and 1669, when he was allowed to retire to the court. By that time, he was apparently well over sixty. From the early 1650s, Khovanskii spent a great deal of time away from Moscow. He enjoyed a brief period of respite in the 1660s, when he was head of the Post Chancery. Even then, however, he sometimes had to leave the capital on brief assignments. He spent the years 1669-1681 almost continually in the field, a fact that probably explains his political isolation in the crisis of 1682.

83. Solov'ev, *Istoriia* 7:482.

84. Dolgorukii led armies against the Poles in the years 1654-1656 and 1658-1661 and against the Razin revolt in 1670-1671. In between, he remained in Moscow as head of the Artillery Chancery and later of the Kazan' Office. Except for one brief military assignment in 1674, he remained at court for the last eleven years of his life until he too died at the hands of the rebels in 1682. At the height of his career, Trubetskoi also served in many capacities. Between 1646 and 1662, he was nominal head of the Kazan' Office, but left Moscow on a number of military and diplomatic assignments, particularly in the mid- and late 1650s.

85. Matveev left Moscow a number of times on brief diplomatic and military assignments in the years between 1646 and 1660. During the 1660s he remained in the capital as one of the commanders of the garrison and in 1669 took over the Little Russia Chancery, the first of a portfolio of bureaucratic offices that formed the foundation of his power as head of the government from 1671 to 1676. Similarly, Khitrovo left Moscow relatively briefly in the late 1640s and 1650s on military and diplomatic errands. After 1660, he never left the court, as far as we know. Between assignments in the field, he held a wide variety of positions in the chanceries beginning in 1649.

86. Crummey, "Noble Official," p. 70.

87. Bogoiavlenskii, *Sud'i*, pp. 170-178. Pronskii, Odoevskii and Morozov later became boyars.

88. *Ibid.*, pp. 144-149. In 1689, T. N. Streshnev became director and remained in that position until 1700.

89. *Ibid.*, pp. 129-131.

90. *Ibid.*, pp. 197-198; Zaozerskii, *Tsar'*, pp. 79-107.

91. See, for example, the remarks of Korb and Neuville on E. I. Ukraintsev (*ChOIDR*, 1863, no. 3, p. 317; "Zapiski," p. 432).

92. Bogoiavlenskii, *Sud'i*, pp. 166-168.

93. *RBS* 4:16-18; Veselovskii, *D'iaki*, p. 113; Savelov, *Opyt* 2:159-160; Li-

khachev, *Razriadnye d'iaki*, pp. 185-186. In 1646, Gavrenev owned estates with 797 peasant households.

94. Olearius, *Travels*, p. 209; *DAI* 10:23-25.

95. See *Rozysknyia dela* 1:1-504.

96. Bogoiavlenskii, *Sud'i*, pp. 130-131; Solov'ev, *Istoriia* 7:461-462; Ustrialov, *Istoriia* 2:79-80.

97. G. S. Dokhturov, L. A. Domnin, A. S. Durov, F. K. Elizarov, I. S. Gorokhov, I. K. Griazev, G. S. Karaulov, L. D. Lopukhin, T. Iu. Lugovskii, and E. I. Ukraintsev all served briefly with the army at some point in their careers. When a bureaucrat took up the sword, the results could be disastrous if we can believe Neuville's nasty comments about Ukraintsev ("Zapiski," pp. 244-245).

98. Meehan-Waters, "Characteristics," pp. 89-105.

99. Bogoiavlenskii, *Sud'i*, pp. 34-35, 44.

100. *Ibid.*, pp. 20, 91, 178.

101. *Ibid.*, pp. 13-14, 24-25, 54-55, 120, 164-165; Smirnov, *Posadskie liudi* 1:370.

102. Bogoiavlenskii, *Sud'i*, pp. 14, 25, 55, 89, 165, 213.

103. *Ibid.*, pp. 15-16, 39, 58-59, 84-85, 95, 119, 130-131, 137-138.

104. *Ibid.*, pp. 44-45, 64-65, 136-137, 167, 195-196, 201-202; *DR* 2:368; 3:3, 45, 872, 941; Dop. k 3:132, 192, 223; *AMG* 2:612-616; 3:119, 163-171; *DAI* 10:23-25.

105. Bogoiavlenskii, *Sud'i*, pp. 19-21, 44, 48, 53, 82-84, 90-91, 97-98, 157-158, 163, 178-180, 215, 219; I. Kozlovskii, *F. M. Rtishchev*, pp. 28-69. Grigorii Gavrilovich Pushkin's career presents an earlier example of essentially the same pattern (Crummey, "Reconstitution," p. 205). Pushkin, however, performed vital functions in other spheres, especially diplomacy.

106. See, for example, A. Iakovlev, *Prikaz sbora ratnykh liudei*, pp. 122-160.

107. Iakovlev, *Kholopstvo*, p. 561. The decree of April 30, 1680, ordering the chanceries to use only the director's name in their documentation, encouraged this assumption (*PSZ* 2:264).

108. Iakovlev stresses that the noble directors of the Prikaz sbora ratnykh liudei linked it directly to the tsar and to his inner circle of advisers (*Prikaz*, p. 159).

109. Meehan-Waters, "Characteristics," pp. 80-84, 89-94.

110. See, for example, Walter M. Pintner's comments in "The Evolution of Civil Officialdom, 1755-1855," pp. 215-224.

111. Belokurov, "O Posol'skom prikaze," pp. 42-47; Galaktionov and Chistiakova, pp. 63-129.

112. *DR* 2:278, 732; 3:285, 556, 560; Dop. k 3:17, 128, 132, 171, 247, 279, 289-291, 359, 380, 662, 880, 886; 4:68, 171, 357, 643; *AMG* 3:441; *DAI* 9:156; *AAE* 4:429; *PDS* 3:135; 5:392-393, 426-427, 557-558, 730-748, 932, 1159-1164; 6:1030-1031, 1049-1055, 1493, 1533, 1595, 1598-1599; 7:1277-1278; *PSRL* 31:170; Solov'ev, *Istoriia* 5:581-582; 7:502-504; K. I. Iakubov, ed., "Rossiia i Shvetsiia v pervoi polovine XVII veka," p. 93. Like A. S. Matveev, Chaadaev began his

career as a soldier and his diplomatic activities probably grew out of his long experience in the Ukraine.

113. Kotoshikhin, *O Rossii*, pp. 41-42; Uroff, "On Russia," pp. 93-94.

114. Bantysh-Kamenskii, *Obzor* 1:17-34, 101-123, 173-190, 214-235; 3:114-160; 4:78-85, 145-204; Smirnov, *Rossiia i Turtsiia*, vol. 2; Uroff, "On Russia," pp. 394-395.

115. To mention only one of innumerable examples, the delegates to the meeting with ambassadors from Sweden in 1661—Prince I. S. Prozorovskii, Prince I. P. Boriatinskii, and I. A. Pronchishchev—were known as the governors of Tver', Riazhsk, and Elat'ma respectively (*DR* Dop. k 3:247). Dumnye d'iaki did not receive honorary titles, but once a chancery official won promotion to dumnyi dvorianin he received one for use in diplomacy. I. A. Gavrenev, for example, became known as governor of Kashin (*ibid.*, p. 118). The same man usually used the same honorary title throughout his career; Ordin–Nashchokin remained governor of Shatsk, for instance (*ibid.*, pp. 174, 678).

116. See Smirnov, *Rossiia i Turtsiia*, vol. 2.

117. Bantysh-Kamenskii, *Obzor* 3:114-160; 4:145-204. The figures leave out resident ambassadors in Poland. On the individuals mentioned, *DR* 2:744; 3:67, 140, 320, 591; Dop. k 3:44, 61, 95, 131, 211, 310, 408, 689, 935, 989, 1103-1104; *AMG* 2:509-510, 534; 3:29-30, 279, 567; *AI* 4:266; *PDS* 4:339, 522; 5:90; 6:1594-1595; Solov'ev, *Istoriia* 5:558-564; 6:41-45, 185; Barsukov, *Rod Sheremetevykh* 3:344; 4:318. See also the references in note 112.

118. *DR* 2:424-428; 3:538, 560, 932; Dop. k 3:14-15, 95, 117-118, 129, 135, 179, 191, 269, 298, 315-322, 395; *PDS* 4:78, 115; 5:89, 681; *AI* 3:333; Solov'ev, *Istoriia* 6:506-508.

119. Belokurov's remarks, based on sixteenth-century sources, do not apply completely to the seventeenth ("O Posol'skom prikaze," p. 14). The appointment of negotiators was not entirely random in the latter period.

120. *DR* Dop. k 3:118, 129, 179; Bantysh-Kamenskii, *Obzor* 1:229-230.

121. *DR* Dop. k 3:14-15, 269, 293; *PDS* 4:78.

122. Heinz E. Ellersieck, "Russia under Aleksei Mikhailovich and Fedor Alekseevich, 1645-1682: the Scandinavian Sources," pp. 290-291.

123. See Roy Strong, *Splendor at Court: Renaissance Spectacle and the Theatre of Power* (Boston, 1973). Strong's bibliography provides an excellent introduction to the extensive literature on court ceremonies and festivals in sixteenth- and seventeenth-century western Europe.

124. See Crummey, "Court Spectacles."

125. For a thoughtful sociological study of Versailles, see Norbert Elias, *Die höfische Gesellschaft*. The literature on Louis XIV's court is vast.

126. For a detailed description of Tsar Aleksei Mikhailovich's daily routine, see I. Zabelin, *Domashnii byt russkikh tsarei v XVI i XVII st.*, pp. 367-376. See also the comments of Paul of Aleppo, an ecclesiastical visitor to Aleksei's court in W. Palmer, *The Patriarch and The Tsar* 2:100-102, 107, 136-137.

127. The basic reference work on the Russian hierarchy is Stroev, *Spiski*.

128. Ioakim was patriarch from 1674 to 1690; his three younger brothers re-

ceived Duma rank in 1678, 1688, and 1689 respectively (BK 7:70v; 10:53r, 54v; V. Berkh, *Tsarstvovanie Tsaria Feodora Alekseevicha*, pt. 2, p. 3; L. M. Savelov, *Rod dvorian Savelovykh*, pp. 27-28).

129. Kliuchevsky makes the point with particular eloquence in *Seventeenth Century*.

130. One example of the danger of exaggerating the thoroughness and completeness of the reforms of the seventeenth century can be seen in the collection of essays on Peter I in *Canadian/American Slavic Studies* 8 (1974). While the individual essays took eminently defensible positions, for the most part, the cumulative effect of the symposium, in my view, reduces Peter and his reforms to insignificance. Once again, I suspect, eager young revisionists replaced the exaggerations of earlier generations with their own.

CHAPTER III

1. Roger M. Keesing, *Kin Groups and Social Structure*, p. 31. A lineage is "a unilineal descent group whose members trace their descent from a known ancestor and know the genealogical connections to that ancestor." Clans are unilineal descent groups whose members do not know the genealogical connections to their presumed common ancestor.

2. *RK*; M. E. Bychkova, *Rodoslovnye knigi XVI-XVII vv. kak istoricheskii istochnik*, p. 4. The Great Velvet Book subdivides some large non-titled clans which I am treating as a single unit. In particular, the official register distinguishes between several different sub-families of Kolychevs and Pleshcheevs. As the text makes clear and other sources confirm, these divisions date from the sixteenth century. In these cases, the official court registers of the seventeenth century often ignore these distinctions, usually referring, for example, to A. D. Nemiatyi-Kolychev simply as Kolychev. For the sake of convenience, I have followed the latter practice. See *RK* 1:298-308; 2:103-114; the references to members of these clans in *RK 1475*; and *DR* 3:379; Dop. k 3:42, 50.

3. *RK* 1:338-346; Dolgorukov, *Ros. rod. kniga* 2:151-159.

4. Semevskii, *Rus. rod. kniga* 3:3-15.

5. *RK* 1:182-185; 2:124-126; Vlas'ev, *Potomstvo* 1, pt. 1, pp. 68-87; Barsukov, *Rodoslovie*.

6. *RK* 2:216-217; Lobanov-Rostovskii, *Rus. rod. kniga* 2:216-217.

7. See Appendix B, pp. 178-214. On the Pushkins, see Veselovskii's imaginative essay in *Issledovaniia po istorii zemlevladel'tsev*, pp. 39-139.

8. Veselovskii, *Issledovaniia po istorii oprichniny*, pp. 397-400, 427-430; *RK* 1:276-308; 2:103-114; Dolgorukov, *Ros. rod. kniga* 4:136-144, 173-182.

9. Veselovskii, *Issledovaniia po istorii oprichniny*, pp. 414-417, 441-442; *RK* 1:259-267; Lobanov-Rostovskii, *Rus. rod. kniga* 1:396-399; Dolgorukov, *Ros. rod. kniga* 2:69-73.

10. Veselovskii, *Issledovaniia po istorii oprichniny*, p. 433; *RK* 1:218-219; Vlas'ev, *Potomstvo* 1, pt. 2, pp. 414-425.

11. *RK* 1:68-72; Dolgorukov, *Ros. rod. kniga* 1:234-235. The Polish branch of the clan survived through the eighteenth century.

12. The impact of these catastrophes on the Russian nobility should be investigated. As part of this study, I tried to substantiate a hypothesis that the heavy losses in the Polish Wars, particularly the Russian defeats at Konotop and Chudnovo, destroyed the flower of the traditional military nobility and helped to open the way for the many social outsiders who rose to Duma rank in the latter half of the century. Unfortunately, Soviet archives yielded almost no material on this subject.

13. These statements are based on comparing the records of noble service in the sources listed in chapter I, note 43, especially *DR; KR* and *AMG*, with the genealogical materials listed in the same note.

14. Information on seventeenth-century noble marriages comes from the genealogical sources listed in chapter I, note 43 unless otherwise indicated.

15. The genealogies of these clans are found respectively in P. N. Petrov, *Istoriia rodov russkago dvorianstva*, pp. 16-17 and L. M. Savelov, "Kniazia Pozharskie," facing p. 88; K. B. *Opyt istoricheskago rodosloviia Izmailovykh*, pp. 1-22; N. P. Likhachev, *Genealogicheskaia istoriia odnoi pomeshchich'ei biblioteki*, facing p. 16; GBL, f. 178, no. 734:179r.

16. Nancy Shields Kollmann, for example, proceeds on this assumption in her stimulating dissertation, "Kinship and Politics: the Origin and Evolution of the Muscovite Boyar Elite in the Fifteenth Century."

17. *DR* 1:990-991; 3:303.

18. *Ibid*. 1:539-543; Zap. kn. mosk. st. 12:203v-r; Markevich, *O mestnichestve*, pp. 387-388. See also Markevich, *Istoriia*, pp. 426-427, 457.

19. Crummey, "Noble Official," pp. 54-55. The figures are drawn from the data in table 2, adjusted to include only boyars and okol'nichie.

20. The diagram and the idea behind it come from Maurice Zeitlin and Richard Earl Ratcliff, "Research Methods for the Analysis of the Internal Structure of the Dominant Classes: the Case of Landlords and Capitalists in Chile," p. 27. I am grateful to my colleague Arnold J. Bauer for this reference.

21. Crummey, "Noble Official," pp. 50-51, 55-57. The figures come from table 3.

22. This figure results from comparing the data in table 3 with information on the social origin of Duma members.

23. Lobanov-Rostovskii, *Rus. rod. kniga* 1:368. The date of the marriage is not recorded. In all probability, it took place long before Matiushkin became a dumnyi dvorianin, probably in 1654 (*DRV* 20:110). He began his recorded service in 1625 (*DR* 1:742). The first sign that he was destined for greater things came in 1634, when he became second highest officer of the Great Treasury. He retained the same position until 1661/2, serving under a succession of royal favorites (Bogoiavlenskii, *Sud'i*, pp. 24-26). By the time he first received this assignment, his—and the tsar's—father-in-law, L. S. Streshnev, had been a Duma member for four years and a boyar for several months (*DR* 2:108, 365).

24. S. M. Solov'ev, *Istoriia otnoshenii mezhdu russkimi kniaz'iami riurikova doma*, pp. 26-30. Solov'ev suggests that this particular pattern appeared because, in many large families, the oldest nephew was probably older than his third

uncle. This particular formulation was used in judging the relative seniority of a clan's members in order to settle precedence disputes (Markevich, *Istoriia*, pp. 409-419).

25. Shields Kollmann, "Kinship," pp. 55-62.

26. The material on genealogies comes from the sources listed in chapter 1, note 43 and in the bibliography under "Genealogy."

Among the princes who were newcomers to the boyar elite, the proportion who were the senior representatives of their clans when they entered the Duma is almost exactly the same as for all aristocrats.

27. When we subject the most prominent non-titled parvenu clans—those who had at least three Duma members in our period—to the same test, we discover that 44 percent of their representatives in the boyar elite were the senior members of their clans at the time of their promotions.

28. *Opyt istoricheskago rodosloviia dvorian i grafov Matiushkinykh*, pp. 1-13; N. N. Kashkin, *Rodoslovnye razvedki* 1:284-309.

29. Lobanov-Rostovskii, *Rus. rod. kniga* 2:5-7; *RK* 2:72-76.

30. Crummey, "Reconstitution," pp. 192-195. See above pp. 24-27.

31. Seven of the twelve new aristocratic boyars were the senior members of their families. They were Prince I. F. Troekurov, Prince A. V. Sitskii, Prince F. I. Lykov, Prince D. I. Dolgorukii, Prince A. V. Khilkov, L. I. Dalmatov-Karpov, and Prince S. V. Prozorovskii. For the genealogies, see *RK* 1:116-117 (Troekurov), 172-174 (Prozorovskii), 225-226 (Lykov), 228-233 (Dolgorukii); 2:77-79 (Khilkov); Lobanov-Rostovskii, *Rus. rod. kniga* 2:216-217 (Sitskii); Savelov, *Opyt* 3:13 (Dolmatov-Karpov), 84 (Dolgorukii).

32. Thirteen of the sixteen aristocratic new boyars occupied the senior position in their clans. They were B. I. and G. I. Morozov, Princes I. A. and A. A. Golitsyn, I. P. and V. P. Sheremetev, Princes P. A. and B. A. Repnin, Prince A. F. Litvinov-Mosal'skii, N. D. and M. A. Veliaminov, Prince Iu. A. Sitskii, and Prince N. I. Odoevskii. For the genealogies, see note 4 and *RK* 1:36-40 (Golitsyn), 218-219 (Repnin), 249-257 (Veliaminov), 259-267 (Morozov), 327-328 (Litvinov-Mosal'skii); Lobanov-Rostovskii, *Rus. rod. kniga* 1:396-399 (Morozov).

33. For the genealogies, see *RK* 1:181-182 (Vorotynskii), 2:103-114 (Kolychev); Dolgorukov, *Ros. rod. kniga* 1:69-71; Vlas'ev, *Potomstvo* 1, pt. 1, pp. 584-625 (Zvenigorodskii); pt. 2, pp. 251-282 (Obolenskii).

34. For the genealogies not mentioned in earlier notes, see *RK* 1:36-42 (Kurakin), 57-60 (Pronskii).

35. For the genealogy of the Khovanskiis, see *RK* 1:31-35. The fact that many aristocratic families, including those which tended to observe the rules of seniority, had several members each in the Duma in the years 1676-1689 may help to explain why 60 percent of the new aristocratic boyars of that period were the eldest representatives of their clans at the time of their promotion.

36. The data on marriages come from the genealogical sources cited in earlier footnotes and in V. and G. Kholmogorov, "Istoricheskie materialy o tserkvakh i selakh XVII-XVIII st."

When the genealogies do not record the individual's date of birth, I have sometimes made an educated guess by assuming that he first performed official service at the age of 15. Dates of marriages and of dowries have rarely been preserved in the published materials and, when they are available, the individuals involved are often obscure figures about whom we know almost nothing else. In most cases for which we can make the calculation, men first married in their late teens or early twenties, women in their teens. To mention only individual examples, V. P. Sheremetev and T. V. Sobakina were both 16 when they married in 1684 (Barsukov, *Rod Sheremetevykh* 7:416); M. F. Rtishchev was 17 when he married P. S. Vasil'chikova in 1679 (Kashkin, *Rodoslovnye razvedki* 1:381; *Moskovskaia delovaia i bytovaia pis'mennost' XVII veka*, p 188); when P. N. Kaftyreva married Prince M. A. Golitsyn in 1663, she was 18 and he 23 (S. Serchevskii, *Zapiski o rode kniazei Golitsynykh*, p. 213). In the most dramatic case I found, Prince N. I. Repnin was a widower at 18! (Vlas'ev, *Potomstvo* 1, pt. 2, pp. 426-428).

37. *ES* 1:420. I have not yet found so remarkable an example of fertility among the boyar clans, largely, I suspect, because genealogies often left out the names of daughters. In many family trees, women's names begin to appear frequently only in the last decades of the seventeenth century.

38. This assumption is based on the behavior of the royal families of Muscovy and isolated clear examples from the boyar elite, such as the marriages of the Morozov brothers in 1648 and 1649. In a significant number of cases, Duma members' widows remarried.

39. Lawrence Stone, "The Rise of the Nuclear Family in Early Modern England: The Patriarchal Stage," p. 48.

40. See, for example, the wills of Princess M. P. Volkonskaia, Princess E. F. Odoevskaia, Prince V. T. Dolgorukii, and Prince N. I. Odoevskii published respectively in E. G. Volkonskaia, *Rod kniazei Volkonskikh*, pp. 173-188; Barsukov, *Rod Sheremetevykh* 7:341-348; *Izvestiia RGO* 2:17-25; 4:379-391. In all four cases, men played the decisive role in disposing of their wives' dowries. Odoevskaia was bound by the provisions of her late husband's will, while Volkonskaia gave her husband, who was still alive, considerable latitude in adjusting the terms of her testament should she die before him. At least one upper-class woman of the seventeenth century—Ol'ga Vasil'evna Godunova, née Ziuzina—took the initiative in disposing of her dower estates in her will dated 1625. Her independent attitude may have arisen from her position as a widow and a nun and from her determination to provide for the Chudov Monastery where she intended to be buried (*ChOIDR*, 1868, no. 4, pp. 1-5).

41. Barsukov, *Rod Sheremetevykh* 7:414-415.

42. Likhachev, *Razriadnye d'iaki*, pp. 183-186.

43. See, for example, Fedor Griboedov, *Istoriia o tsariakh i velikikh kniaz'iakh zemli russkoi*. Vol. 121 of *Pamiatniki drevnei pis'mennosti* (St. Petersburg, 1896), p. 37; I. M. Kudriavtsev, ed., *Artakserksovo deistvo*, p. 126.

44. Ivan IV's second wife, Mariia Temriukovna, was a Cherkasskii. Ivan's ill-fated son of the same name married E. I. Sheremeteva (Barsukov, *Rod Sheremetevykh* 7:413).

45. Markevich, *Istoriia*, pp. 541-542; Crummey, "Reflections," p. 277.

46. Kozlovskii, *Rtishchev*, chaps. 3-4; *ChOIDR*, 1874, no. 1, pp. 169-170.

47. Solov'ev, *Istoriia* 6:47, 394-396; *AI* 4:262-263; A. I. Zaozerskii, *Tsarskaia votchina*, pp. 283-284; Kapterev, *Patriarkh i Tsar'* 1:38-47, 59-71.

48. Lobanov-Rostovskii, *Rus. rod. kniga* 1:119, 339; 2:295; Dolgorukov, *Ros. rod. kniga* 1:286; 4:412-413; Semevskii, *Rus. rod. kniga* 1:9; N. Miatlev, "Rodoslovnyia zametki," pp. 3-5.

49. Lobanov-Rostovskii, *Rus. rod. kniga* 1:383-384; 2:109; Vlas'ev, *Potomstvo* 1, pt. 1, pp. 87-88; pt. 3, p. 31; Semevskii, *Rus. rod. kniga* 1:231; *RBS* 23:179.

50. Lobanov-Rostovskii, *Rus. rod. kniga* 2:6-8; Dolgorukov, *Ros. rod. kniga* 2:39; Semevskii, *Rus. rod. kniga* 2:240; *DR* 3:1056; Vlas'ev, *Potomstvo* 1, pt. 2, p. 494; *ChOIDR*, 1886, no. 3, p. 103.

51. Apart from the examples we have discussed in the text, N. P. Likhachev has identified five sixteenth-century examples of marriage alliances between princely families and chancery officials. In all cases, a male aristocrat married the daughter of a d'iak ("Rodstvennyia sviazi kniazheskikh familii s sem'iami d'iakov").

52. See note 44. The Odoevskiis belonged to the group, thanks to a connection with the old ruling family. It was not a propitious one, to be sure; a Princess Odoevskaia married Ivan IV's cousin, Vladimir Andreevich of Staritsa, in 1555 and perished with him in 1569. Prince Boris Kanbulatovich Cherkasskii married an aunt of the future tsar, Mikhail Romanov, and gave his daughter in marriage to F. I. Sheremetev, a union that lasted into our period (Vlas'ev, *Potomstvo* 1, pt. 1, p. 73; Dolgorukov, *Ros. rod. kniga* 2:37; Barsukov, *Rod Sheremetevykh* 7:413).

53. Barsukov, *Rod Sheremetevykh* 3:406-407; 7:416; Vlas'ev, *Potomstvo* 1, pt. 1, pp. 83, 87.

54. Barsukov, *Rod Sheremetevykh* 7:415-416; Vlas'ev, *Potomstvo* 1, pt. 1, pp. 86, 88; N. F. Ikonnikov, *NdR, la noblesse de Russie* D:463.

55. Vlas'ev, *Potomstvo* 1, pt. 1, p. 79; Barsukov, *Rod Sheremetevykh* 7:414; Lobanov-Rostovskii, *Rus. rod. kniga* 2:217, 328, 338.

56. Kashkin, *Rodoslovnyia razvedki* 1:369-374; Kozlovskii, *Rtishchev*, pp. 138-139. The Miloslavskiis may have had another entrée into the court. According to Vlas'ev's genealogical compilation, the new tsaritsa's sister, Irina, had been married to Prince D. A. Dolgorukii before her untimely death in 1645 (*Potomstvo* 1, pt. 3, p. 31).

57. Vlas'ev, *Potomstvo* 1, pt. 1, pp. 76-90.

58. Dolgorukov, *Ros. rod. kniga* 1:285-287; Ikonnikov, *NdR* D:457-469. See also note 54.

59. Barsukov, *Rod Sheremetevykh* 3:421; 7:413-416; Dolgorukov, *Ros. rod. kniga* 1:55; Lobanov-Rostovskii, *Rus. rod. kniga* 1:115; 2:3; Vlas'ev, *Potomstvo* 1, pt. 1, p. 79; *Izvestiia RGO* 1:7-8; Likhachev, *Razriadnye d'iaki*, pp. 183-184; *RBS* 23:179, 203, 229. The Sheremetevs' marriages are an excellent example of the inconsistencies in the published genealogies. Several reference works confidently give us the names of Sheremetev wives, whose maiden names are un-

known according to Barsukov, the official historian of the clan (*Rod Sheremete-vykh* 6:112).

60. Vlas'ev, *Potomstvo* 1, pt. 2, pp. 484-496.

61. *Ibid.* 1, pt. 3, pp. 334-386; Savelov, *Opyt* 2:159-160; *ChOIDR*, 1911, no. 3, p. 161.

62. Lobanov-Rostovskii, *Rus. rod. kniga* 2:6-8.

63. *Ibid.* 2:318-321; Ikonnikov, *NdR* D:462; GBL, f. 178, no. 3284:39v.

64. Kashkin, *Rodoslovnyia razvedki* 1:367, 406; Vlas'ev, *Potomstvo* 1, pt. 1, p. 86.

65. *Ibid.* 1, pt. 1, pp. 453-495; pt. 3, pp. 14-73; *ChOIDR*, 1889, no. 1, p. 58.

CHAPTER IV

1. S. N. Eisenstadt, *The Political Systems of Empires*, pp. 215-216.

2. For an illuminating discussion of court parties in the reign of Catherine II, see David L. Ransel, *The Politics of Catherinian Russia: the Panin Party*. See also Ransel's article, "Bureaucracy and Patronage: the View from an Eighteenth-Century Russian Letter-Writer."

3. Lawrence Stone is fond of an example from English history that illustrates our problem beautifully. Recent research has shown that Charles I was a distant cousin of John Hampden! (Stone, "Rise of the Nuclear Family," p. 17).

4. On the "general crisis of the seventeenth century," see Trevor Aston, ed., *Crisis in Europe, 1560-1660*.

5. The best general accounts of the crisis of 1648 are *Ocherki istorii SSSR. XVII v.*, pp. 222-249, and Smirnov, *Posadskie liudi* 2:5-248.

Among the most valuable Russian contemporary accounts are *Pskovskie letopisi* 2:288-289; S. F. Platonov, "Novyi istochnik dlia istorii moskovskikh volnenii 1648 g."; *idem*, "Moskovskiia volneniia 1648 goda"; V. I. Buganov, "Opisanie moskovskogo vostaniia 1648 g. v Arkhivskom sbornike."

Among foreign sources, the dispatches of the Swedish resident in Moscow, Karl Pommerening, and the travel account of Olearius stand out. See Iakubov, "Rossiia i Shvetsiia," pp. 417-433, and Olearius, *Travels*, pp. 203-214. See also Leo Loewenson, "The Moscow Rising of 1648," which includes the text of a seventeenth-century English translation of the "Leiden brochure."

K. V. Bazilevich and S. A. Piontkovskii, eds., *Gorodskie vosstaniia v moskovskom gosudarstve XVII v.*, contains a variety of source material. For a useful discussion of the Russian narrative sources, see E. V. Chistiakova, "Letopisnye zapisi o narodnykh dvizheniiakh serediny XVII v." and Buganov, "Zapiski sovremennika o moskovskikh vosstaniiakh 1648 i 1662 godov."

A. Zertsalov published chancery materials containing information on the 1648 revolts in "O miatezhakh v gorode Moskve i v sele Kolomenskom 1648, 1662 i 1771 gg." and "K istorii moskovskago miatezha 1648 g."

The classic monographic study of the revolt is S. V. Bakhrushin, "Moskovskoe vosstanie 1648 g.," *Nauchnye trudy* 2:46-91.

6. On this question, see Robert O. Crummey, "Court Groupings and Politics in Russia, 1645-1649."

7. Iakubov, "Rossiia," pp. 424-427; Olearius, *Travels*, pp. 203-210; *Gorodskie vosstaniia*, pp. 73-77; Buganov, "Opisanie," p. 228.

8. Crummey, "Court Groupings," pp. 212-217.

9. These statements are based on data in the sources listed in chapter I, note 43.

10. While this comment may strike the reader as a case of underlining the obvious, historians of Muscovite Russia sometimes ignore this possibility when discussing the political allegiance of prominent courtiers. Smirnov's treatment of Prince N. I. Odoevskii serves as an example. In an early monograph, he suggested that Odoevskii was Cherkasskii's ally; in a later work, however, he assigned him to Morozov's grouping. The author fails to consider that so prominent a figure might have belonged to neither faction. Yet, I suspect, it was precisely his skill as a "trimmer" that kept Odoevskii safe from dangerous political entanglements during his long career and brought him through the crises of 1648 and 1682 (Smirnov, *Posadskie liudi* 2:170 as compared with p. 22 and the same author's *Pravitel'stvo B. I. Morozova i vosstanie v Moskve 1648 g.*, pp. 57, 61).

11. At that time, he became the head of the Zemskii Prikaz (Bogoiavlenskii, *Sud'i*, p. 47).

12. Solov'ev, *Istoriia* 5:483-484.

13. *DAI* 3:149, 189, 225, 243; *DR* 3:95; Bogoiavlenskii, *Sud'i*, p. 219; Vlas'ev, *Potomstvo* 1, pt. 3, p. 344; Smirnov, *Posadskie liudi* 2:205; *RIB* 10:419; Lobanov-Rostovskii, *Rus. rod. kniga* 1:383.

14. Crummey, "Court Groupings," pp. 207-212.

15. Iakubov, "Rossiia," p. 419; Olearius, *Travels*, p. 205.

16. Ivan Petrovich Sheremetev's second wife was Princess Marfa Vasil'evna Volkonskaia. Their marriage took place in 1634 and probably lasted until Ivan Petrovich took monastic vows shortly before his death in the summer of 1647. The Sheremetevs' ties dated from Fedor Ivanovich Sheremetev's marriage to Princess Irina Borisovna Cherkasskaia. Apparently Sheremetev was a widower when he made his will in 1645. A few years later, Nikita Ivanovich married Dar'ia Stepanovna Pushkina, a kinswoman of Morozov's ally. Since the groom's name first appears in the service registers under the year 1651, the marriage probably took place in the middle or late 1650s. Prince Iakov Kudenetovich Cherkasskii, Morozov's rival, was married to a sister or daughter of Prince Semen Vasil'evich Prozorovskii, and Mikhail Ivanovich Morozov later married Prozorovskii's daughter, Domna. The younger Morozov probably married a few years after 1648 since his name first appears in the service records for that year (Vlas'ev, *Potomstvo* 1, pt. 3, p. 354; *Mosk. nekropol'* 3:349; Barsukov, *Rod Sheremetevykh* 3:192, 495-510; 7:442, 444; Dolgorukov, *Ros. rod. kniga* 2:38; Smirnov, *Posadskie liudi* 2:204; Lobanov-Rostovskii, *Rus. rod. kniga* 1:399; *DR* 3:81).

17. Once again, the most useful brief account of the crisis is found in *Ocherki istorii SSSR. XVII v.*, pp. 325-336. For a full and useful modern account, see Buganov, *Moskovskie vosstaniia*.

The most important Russian narrative sources on the crisis are Sil'vestr Medvedev, "Sozertsanie kratkoe let 7190, 91 i 92, v nikh zhe chto sodeiasia vo grazhdanstve," and the accounts of A. A. Matveev, P. N. Krekshin, and I. A. Zhe-liabuzhskii in *Zapiski russkikh liudei. Sobytiia vremen Petra Velikago.* See also M. N. Tikhomirov, "Zametki zemskogo d'iachka vtoroi poloviny XVII v." *Vosstanie v Moskve 1682 goda. Sbornik dokumentov* is a very valuable collection of sources, a number of which were previously unpublished. Solov'ev published important materials in *Istoriia* 7:320-348.

Among the most valuable contemporary foreign accounts are the dispatches of the Danish ambassador, Butenant von Rosenbusch published in Ustrialov, *Istoriia* 1:330-346, and the letters of the Dutch ambassador, van Keller, found in The Hague in the Algemeen Rijksarchief. Staten-General. Lias-Rusland, 7365. See also the Polish reports published in A. Theiner, ed., *Documents historiques relatifs aux règnes d'Alexis Michaélowitch, Féodor III et Pierre le Grand, Czar de Russie,* pp. 239-243.

There is a large body of secondary literature on 1682. See, in particular, Solov'ev, *Istoriia* 7:261-302; S. K. Bogoiavlenskii's stimulating article, "Khovanshchina," and A. Shtraukh's interesting but doctrinaire monograph, *Streletskii bunt 1682 g.* See also Bogoslovskii, *Petr I* 1:37-48. N. I. Pavlenko published a trenchant review of Buganov's book, "Ob otsenke streletskogo vosstaniia 1682 g. (Po povodu monografii V. I. Buganova "Moskovskie vosstaniia kontsa XVII v.")." For an account of the crisis in English, see O'Brien, *Russia,* pp. 14-39.

18. Matveev, *Zapiski,* p. 6. Matveev completed his work in 1716 at the earliest (Buganov, *Moskovskie vosstaniia,* p. 25).

19. See Veselovskii's helpful comments on the complex choices facing the tsar's courtiers in the apparent succession crisis of 1553 (*Issledovaniia po istorii oprichniny,* pp. 281-283).

On the patriarch's role in arranging Peter's accession to the throne, see Medvedev, "Sozertsanie kratkoe," pp. 43-45; *DRV* 7:376-384; and *Ocherki istorii SSSR. XVII v.,* p. 326.

20. *DAI* 10:23-25; TsGADA, f. 210, Stolbtsy prikaznogo stola 1152:111v-118v; Solov'ev, *Istoriia* 7:268, 275; N. P. Likhachev, "K voprosu o podpisiakh dumnykh liudei na postanovleniiakh Boiarskoi dumy," pp. 56-57; Bogoiavlenskii, "Khovanshchina," pp. 188-189; Buganov, *Moskovskie vosstaniia,* pp. 150-152.

21. Matveev, *Zapiski,* pp. 12, 18-19; Bogoiavlenskii, "Khovanshchina," p. 187; Buganov, *Moskovskie vosstaniia,* pp. 133-142; Shtraukh, pp. 21-24.

22. Pavlenko makes this questionable suggestion in "Ob otsenke," p. 93.

23. Medvedev quotes the document justifying the actions of the strel'tsy ("Sozertsanie kratkoe," pp. 68-75). See also Buganov, *Moskovskie vosstaniia,* pp. 155-156.

24. Rosenbusch's testimony in Ustrialov, *Istoriia* 1:336; Matveev, *Zapiski,* pp. 25-26; Bogoiavlenskii, "Khovanshchina," p. 187; Buganov, *Moskovskie vosstaniia,* pp. 153-154.

25. Bogoiavlenskii, *Sud'i,* p. 167.

26. Matveev, *Zapiski,* pp. 19-22.

27. *Ibid.,* pp. 6-19.

28. BK 7:73r.

29. Matveev, *Zapiski*, p. 41; Buganov, *Moskovskie vosstaniia*, pp. 195, 254-255.

30. For a list of the new Duma members, see Appendix B, pp. 204-205. Bogoiavlenskii analyzes the changes in the leadership of the chanceries in "Khovanshchina," pp. 189-193.

31. Bogoiavlenskii, *Sud'i*, pp. 44, 57, 65, 87, 124, 151, 161, 174, 187, 226.

32. The political role of the Khitrovo clan is hard to trace. The main figure of the family, Bogdan Matveevich, was apparently an enemy of A. S. Matveev and the Naryshkins (*Istoriia Matveeva*, pp. 350-351). Contemporary Scandinavian observers, however, reported a struggle for power between Khitrovo and the Miloslavskiis in the early years of Fedor's reign (Ellersieck, "Russia," pp. 313-316). Both of these statements may well be true. It is entirely possible that Khitrovo made an alliance with the Miloslavskiis to destroy Matveev's career, then turned against his erstwhile collaborators.

It is equally unclear why the Khitrovos remained prominent in 1682 since Bogdan Matveevich had died two years earlier (Lobanov-Rostovskii, *Rus. rod. kniga* 2:318). Apart from the memory of earlier alliances, the clan had two other links to the Miloslavskii camp. Bogdan Matveevich's widow, Mar'ia Ivanovna, a strong-willed woman, had close ties to the royal family and lived until 1693 or later (*Istoriia Matveeva*, p. 351; *DR* 4:799). Moreover, at about this time, Aleksandr Sevast'ianovich Khitrovo married Domna Semenovna, née Prozorovskaia, the widow of M. I. Morozov, who died in 1678 (GBL, f. 178, no. 3284:95r; BS 15:2v). As we shall see, the Miloslavskiis had close ties of marriage with the Prozorovskiis.

33. Bogoiavlenskii, "Khovanshchina," pp. 190-191; 208; Buganov, *Moskovskie vosstaniia*, p. 257.

34. A. A. Matveev identified Rzhevskii, Polibin, V. S. Narbekov, and Prince P. L. L'vov as partisans of Sophia and Golitsyn who were exiled in 1689 for this allegiance (*Zapiski*, pp. 57-58).

35. See the exchanges of letters between Ukraintsev, in Moscow, and Golitsyn, in the country with the royal family, in July of 1682 (*Vosstanie v Moskve 1682 goda*, pp. 60-69). It is also possible that F. L. Shaklovityi became an ally of Golitsyn in 1682; he was raised to the rank of dumnyi d'iak on July 23 of that year and soon performed vital missions for the regency government (BK 7:84v; Solov'ev, *Istoriia* 7:294, 299).

36. It should be noted that, in discussing the groupings of 1648, we have not included any individuals simply because they were close relatives of identifiable faction members. If we had added extra Morozovs and Pushkins to the Morozov group, it would have been about the same size as the factions of 1682.

37. Medvedev, "Sozertsanie kratkoe," pp. 97-98; Bogoiavlenskii, "Khovanshchina," pp. 215-218.

38. *Ibid.*, p. 205.

39. BK 7:52v; 10:24v; *PDS* 6:1030, 1054, 1082-1083; Bantysh-Kamenskii, *Obzor* 3:153, 158.

40. The court registers record only brief appearances in Moscow and its suburbs in 1674, 1678 and 1679 (*DR* 3:920-933; 4:51, 66, 120).

41. Ustrialov, *Istoriia* 2:97-98; Solov'ev, *Istoriia* 7:391-392, 451.

42. Ustrialov, *Istoriia* 2:79-80, 96-97; Solov'ev, *Istoriia* 7:61-62; Neuville, "Zapiski," pp. 255-257, 448-449; Matveev, *Zapiski*, pp. 57-58.

43. P. N. Miliukov, *Ocherki po istorii russkoi kul'tury* 3:163-166. Miliukov sharply contrasts the cultural style and interests of Prince V. V. Golitsyn and the young Peter. See also E. A. Belov, "Moskovskie smuty v kontse XVII veka," p. 355.

44. Lobanov-Rostovskii, *Rus. rod. kniga* 1:383.

45. BK 7:33r, 73v; Lobanov-Rostovskii, *Rus. rod. kniga* 2:6-7; Semevskii, *Rus. rod. kniga* 1:240.

46. Bogoiavlenskii, "Khovanshchina," pp. 214-215.

47. *Vosstanie v Moskve 1682 goda*, pp. 110-111; *AAE* 4:368-369; Zheliabuzhskii, *Zapiski*, p. 5.

48. Matveev, *Zapiski*, p. 43; Buganov, *Moskovskie vosstaniia*, pp. 265-268.

49. The literature on Nikon is very extensive. See, in particular, I. Shusherin, *Zhitie Sviateishago Patriarkha Nikona*; Kapterev, *Patriarkh i Tsar'*; N. Gibbenet, *Istoricheskoe izsledovanie dela Patriarkha Nikona*; Palmer, *Patriarch and Tsar*; and *Delo o Patriarkhe Nikone*.

On Nashchokin, see Galaktionov and Chistiakova and V. S. Ikonnikov, "Blizhnii boiarin Afanasii Lavrent'evich Ordin-Nashchokin, odin iz predshestvennikov petrovskoi reformy." See also Solov'ev, *Istoriia* 6:361, 397-398. Kliuchevsky painted a fine verbal portrait of Nashchokin in *Seventeenth Century*, pp. 359-378.

50. Ellersieck, "Russia," pp. 281-282.

51. *Ibid.*, pp. 283-287; Paul of Aleppo's comments in Palmer, *Patriarch and Tsar* 2:165-166; Mayerberg's remarks in *ChOIDR*, 1874, no. 1, pp. 170-171; Kapterev, *Patriarkh i Tsar'* 2:136-141; Solov'ev, *Istoriia* 6:197-199; *Ocherki istorii SSSR. XVII v.*, pp. 354-356; Kliuchevskii, *Boiarskaia duma*, pp. 431-432.

52. For the lists of the courtiers left in charge of the court in Moscow when the tsar went to the front, see *DR* 3:413, 461.

53. The main sources on Nikon's relations with the boyars are his replies to the questions of S. L. Streshnev, composed in about 1662-1663 (Palmer, *Patriarch and Tsar*, vol. 1; *Ocherki istorii SSSR. XVII v.*, p. 358), and the records of the tsar's attempts to negotiate with him after the break between them in 1658. Some undated letters of Nikon to Ziuzin are published in *ZORSA* 2:581-590.

54. *PSZ* 1:602-603 (no. 365); Gibbenet, *Istoricheskoe izsledovanie* 1:101; 2:114-140, 493-495, 598-602, 746-759; *Delo o Nikone*, pp. 181-210; Bogoiavlenskii, *Sud'i*, p. 106; Solov'ev, *Istoriia* 6:249-252; D. I. Ilovaiskii, *Istoriia Rossii* 5:307.

55. Gibbenet, *Istoricheskoe izsledovanie* 2:750-757; Solov'ev, *Istoriia* 6:249-252.

56. Gibbenet suggests that, in spite of his denial of complicity in the Ziuzin affair, Nashchokin may have been a secret sympathizer of Nikon (*Istoricheskoe izsledovanie* 2:139-140). I suspect that Nashchokin's attitude was similar to that of Rtishchev.

57. Kozlovskii, *Rtishchev*, pp. 35, 74, 90-91; Kashkin, *Rodoslovnye razvedki* 1:437-438. Scandinavian observers hinted that Rtishchev and Nikon may have quarreled in 1655, when the former returned to Moscow from the front (Ellersieck, "Russia," pp. 285-286). The "life" of Morozova, the martyr for Old Belief, identifies M. A. Rtishchev as a supporter of Nikon (Kashkin, *Rodoslovnye razvedki* 1:379). His relationship to the patriarch was probably similar to that of his son.

58. Gibbenet, *Istoricheskoe izsledovanie* 1:26-28, 178-179; Palmer, *Patriarch and Tsar* 3:40; 4:118-119; Solov'ev, *Istoriia* 6:211-212.

59. Palmer, *Patriarch and Tsar* 1:154-172, 354-355; Solov'ev, *Istoriia* 6:227-230, 262; Kapterev, *Patriarkh i Tsar'* 2:196-197; Iu. Arsen'ev, "Blizhnii boiarin kniaz' Nikita Ivanovich Odoevskoi i ego perepiska s galitskoi votchinoi (1650-1684)," pp. 15-16.

60. Palmer, *Patriarch and Tsar* 1:16; Solov'ev, *Istoriia* 6:254.

61. Gibbenet, *Istoricheskoe izsledovanie* 2:505-518, 609-610; Solov'ev, *Istoriia* 6:224-226, 231-235, 621; Barsukov, *Rod Sheremetevykh* 6:217-222; Ilovaiskii, *Istoriia* 5:460.

Dolgorukii's relationship with Nikon is hard to determine. In addition to the reports of a rift between the two, the sources also contain hints that, at the time of his break with the tsar, Nikon regarded Dolgorukii as his only friend at court (Solov'ev, *Istoriia* 6:215-217).

62. *Delo o Nikone*, p. 112.

63. The list of those who dealt with Nikon on the government's behalf or participated in the investigation of his conduct includes I. I. Baklanovskii, D. M. Bashmakov, P. K. Elizarov, A. Ivanov, L. Ivanov, L. D. Lopukhin, A. I. Matiushkin, A. S. Matveev, M. S. Pushkin, Prince Iu. I. Romodanovskii, P. M. Saltykov, R. M. Streshnev, and Prince A. N. Trubetskoi. Dolgorukii and Odoevskii also dealt with Nikon as the tsar's agents (*DR* 3:1289; Dop. k 3:363, 371, 388; Solov'ev, *Istoriia* 6:212-214, 218-220, 223-224, 231-236, 246-248, 277-278; Barsukov, *Rod Sheremetevykh* 7:221; Arsen'ev, "Blizhnii boiarin," pp. 15-16; Palmer, *Patriarch and Tsar* 4:235; Gibbenet, *Istoricheskoe izsledovanie* 1:27-28).

64. Kapterev, *Patriarkh i Tsar'* 2:141. Some Duma members may well have exacerbated the hostility between Nikon and Aleksei Mikhailovich by distorting the messages which they conveyed. This seems to have been the case, for example, with Prince Iu. I. Romodanovskii (Solov'ev, *Istoriia* 6:212).

65. Galaktionov, *Ranniaia perepiska*, pp. 9, 13, 31, 86; Galaktionov and Chistiakova, pp. 30-32.

66. Solov'ev, *Istoriia* 6:174.

67. *Ibid.*, p. 395.

68. Galaktionov, *Ranniaia perepiska*, p. 56.

69. Ellersieck, "Russia," pp. 290-292, 297-299; Solov'ev, *Istoriia* 6:394-396; Barsukov, *Rod Sheremetevykh* 6:536; Ikonnikov, "Blizhnii boiarin," pp. 287-289; C. Bickford O'Brien, "Muscovite Prikaz Administration of the Seventeenth Century, the Quality of Leadership," p. 231.

70. Solov'ev, *Istoriia* 6:394-401; Kliuchevsky, *Seventeenth Century*, pp. 363-365.

71. *AMG* 3:597; *DAI* 5:26-27; Solov'ev, *Istoriia* 6:64-69, 619; Ellersieck, "Russia," p. 290; Ikonnikov, "Blizhnii boiarin," pp. 38-39, 57-58.

72. Galaktionov and Chistiakova, p. 65. Certainly Nashchokin thought that Odoevskii looked down on him and tried to undercut his position (*RBS* 12:287).

73. Ikonnikov, "Blizhnii boiarin," pp. 288-289; Solov'ev, *Istoriia* 6:165, 621; Galaktionov and Chistiakova, p. 85; *RBS* 12:287; Ellersieck, "Russia," p. 290.

74. The best single source on Matveev's career is *Istoriia Matveeva*, his apologia. The secondary literature is extensive but generally of poor quality. The best of several pre-revolutionary biographies is L. Shchepot'ev, *Blizhnii boiarin Artamon Sergeevich Matveev kak kul'turnyi politicheskii deiatel' XVII veka*. The only recent study of note is T. V. Starostina, "Ob opale A. S. Matveeva v sviazi s sysknym delom 1676-1677 gg. o khranenie zagovornykh pisem."

75. *Istoriia Matveeva*, pp. 187-189, 348-351, 356-357; Ellersieck, "Russia," pp. 301-303; Solov'ev, *Istoriia* 7:186-187.

76. *Istoriia Matveeva*, pp. 350-351; Samuel Collins, *The Present State of Russia*, pp. 120-121; Mayerberg's comments in *ChOIDR*, 1873, no. 3, p. 74; *Rodoslovnaia kniga roda Khitrovo*, pp. 43-44; Solov'ev, *Istoriia* 6:621; 7:186; Barsukov, *Rod Sheremetevykh* 8:205.

77. In the early stages of his career, Khitrovo occasionally left Moscow to serve in the field. The last occasion was in 1656 (*DR* 3:413, 483-485; Dop. k 3:55). Thereafter he served exclusively at court in chanceries closely connected to the royal household, particularly the Great Court, which he headed from 1664 to 1678 (Bogoiavlenskii, *Sud'i*, pp. 19-21, 53, 97-98, 157-158, 178-180, 219). Collins, who did not like him, called him the "whispering favorite" (*Present State*, p. 121).

78. Ransel, "Bureaucracy and Patronage," pp. 154-155, 162-163, 171, 177.

79. "Chastnaia perepiska." The Golitsyn letters are published in several collections: *Moskovskaia pis'mennost'*, pp. 16-35; *Vosstanie v Moskve 1682 goda*, pp. 60-69; "Pis'ma k Kniaziu Vasil'iu Vasil'evichu Golitsynu"; "Boiarin Kniaz' Vasilii Vasil'evich Golitsyn. Gramotki k nemu ot rodnykh v 1677 g."; "Kniaz' Vasilii Vasil'evich Golitsyn. Pis'ma k kniaziu raznykh lits v 1677 g."; "Kniaz' Vasilii Vasil'evich Golitsyn. Pis'ma k nemu Boeva, Baklanovskago i Leont'eva v 1677 g."; Ustrialov, *Istoriia* 1:346-382. V. G. Semenov's letters to Golitsyn are published in *Vremennik OIDR* 4:65-66; 5:11.

80. *Vremennik OIDR* 6:36. It is unclear whether she wrote the letters herself or dictated them to a scribe. The letters have a very personal tone and may well come from her own hand.

81. The Golitsyn correspondence contains a number of letters of this type. For examples, see *Vremennik OIDR* 8:52, 54; 10:48, 51. F. Narbekov used particularly flowery and obsequious language in his letter (*ibid*. 8:53). The practice of writing such letters which "mean next to nothing" was apparently still common at the end of the eighteenth century (Ransel, "Bureaucracy and Patronage," p. 170, n. 43).

Letters of this type remind one of Petr Ivanovich Bobchinsky's request to the supposed Inspector General—that, when back in St. Petersburg, he tell "senators and admirals and the like" and even the emperor simply that "in such and such a town lives a man called Petr Ivanovich Bobchinsky" (N. Gogol, *The Government Inspector*, adapted by Peter Raby [Minneapolis, 1972], p. 83).

82. *ZORSA* 2:712-713. See also the reference to Prince D. M. Pozharskii as patron in Stashevskii, *Zemlevladenie*, p. 29.

83. Prince I. Odoevskii, for example, asked Golitsyn to look with favor on one of the men under his command (*Vremennik OIDR* 13:29). The Odoevskiis and Golitsyns were related by marriage (*AMG* 2:386-387). A similar connection seems to have led the well-known courtier and landlord, A. I. Bezobrazov, to turn to T. N. Streshnev (A. A. Novosel'skii, *Votchinnik i ego khoziaistvo v XVII veke*, p. 9).

84. K. O. Khlopov and I. I. Chaadaev turned to their allies, the Khovanskiis, for support ("Chastnaia perepiska," pp. 366-367, 371-372).

85. Bezobrazov seems to have held the same expectations of V. G. Semenov, the great chancery official whom he cultivated assiduously (Novosel'skii, *Votchinnik*, pp. 9-12).

86. *Vremennik OIDR* 6:38-39, 44-45; 10:29, 48, 50, 56; 13:29-30.

87. See, for example, *Moskovskaia pis'mennost'*, p. 17; *Russkaia starina* 74:356-359.

88. "Chastnaia perepiska," pp. 326-327; *Vremennik OIDR* 10:45.

89. "Chastnaia perepiska," pp. 346-347; Buganov, *Moskovskie vosstaniia*, pp. 102, 104, 120.

90. M. N. Tikhomirov, *Pskovskoe vosstanie 1650. Iz istorii klassovoi bor'by v russkom gorode XVII v.*, p. 5; Kashkin, *Rodoslovnye razvedki* 1:365-381, 410; *Rodoslovnaia kniga Khitrovo* 1:16-48.

91. Ellersieck, "Russia," p. 313. On several occasions, Ivanov served in chanceries headed by Khitrovo (Bogoiavlenskii, *Sud'i*, pp. 90-91, 97, 163).

92. *RIB* 10:419; Lobanov-Rostovskii, *Rus. rod. kniga* 1:383.

93. *RBS* 12:294-295.

94. "Chastnaia perepiska," p. 304.

95. *Istoriia Matveeva*, pp. 210-332. When he fell into disgrace, A. I. Bezobrazov behaved the same way—to no avail (Novosel'skii, *Votchinnik*, pp. 28-29).

CHAPTER V

1. The summary lists of Duma members' landholdings are to be found as follows:

1613—A. P. Barsukov, ed., "Dokladnaia vypiska 121 (1613) goda o votchinakh i pomest'iakh."

1638—A. I. Iakovlev, "Sluzhiloe zemlevladenie po dannym Prikaza sbora ratnykh liudei (1638 g.)"

1647—S. V. Rozhdestvenskii, "Rospis' zemel'nykh vladenii moskovskago boiarstva 1647-8 goda."

1653—N. Nikol'skii, *Kirillo-Belozerskii Monastyr' i ego ustroistvo do vtoroi chetverti XVII v.* 1, app. 1, pp. xxvi-xxxiii.

1678—A. A. Novosel'skii, "Rospis' krest'ianskikh dvorov, nakhodivshikhsia vo vladenii vysshego dukhovenstva, monastyrei i dumnykh liudei po perepisnym knigam 1678 g."

1696—S. I. Elagin, *Istoriia russkago flota. Period azovskii. Prilozheniia*, pt. 1, pp. 181-202.

The partial list for 1670 is Sb. mosk. st. 447, sb. 3, supplemented by figures in other Stolbtsy moskovskogo stola and Boiarskie spiski of the late 1660s and early 1670s.

It should be noted that I have used Iakovlev's 1638 figures as adjusted by Ia. E. Vodarskii in his article, "Praviashchaia gruppa svetskikh feodalov v Rossii v XVII v."

The lists of 1638, 1647, 1678, and 1696 come from the archives of the central chanceries in Moscow. All were compiled from governmental land cadastres as part of the bureaucracy's efforts to keep up-to-date records of the economic resources of the tsar's servitors and, in some cases, of the church as well. Chancery clerks prepared the list of 1638, for example, as part of the mobilization of the army to meet the threat of invasion by the Crimean Tatars. The list of 1653 is likewise a compilation of data from the cadastres; in this case, however, the document was preserved in the archive of the St. Cyril Monastery of Beloozero. Once the 1638 list is adjusted, as Vodarskii did, the data in all five documents are fully comparable.

The list for 1613 came to light among the papers of the Office of Secret Affairs. Apparently it was compiled as part of the new Romanov government's efforts to sort out conflicting claims to ownership of land resulting from the chaotic conditions of the Time of Troubles. It is the only one of the lists that measures estates by their area, rather than by their population. What I have grandly called the list of 1670 is my compilation of data from the margins of a number of documents in the files of the Military Records Office. The data are obviously incomplete and are useful only for rough comparison of the relative wealth in land of particular individuals and families.

2. Barsukov, "Dokladnaia vypiska," pp. 1-2. In the sixteenth and seventeenth centuries, a chetvert' of land was equal to about 4.1 acres.

3. Novosel'skii, "Rospis'," pp. 123, 139.

4. *PRP* 6:202-205, 223-228.

5. *Ibid.*, p. 173.

6. Kotoshikhin, *O Rossii*, pp. 96-97; Uroff, "On Russia," pp. 183-184; BK; *AMG* 1:138-147.

7. E. I. Kamentseva and N. N. Ustiugov, *Russkaia metrologiia*, pp. 143-160; Iu. A. Tikhonov, *Pomeshchich'i krest'iane v Rossii*, pp. 106-107.

8. *Ibid.*, pp. 107-113.

9. *Ibid.*, p. 297.

10. I. Zabelin, "Bol'shoi boiarin v svoem votchinnom khoziaistve (XVIIyi vek)," p. 14; A. I. Zaozerskii, "Boiarskii dvor," p. 101; Zabelin, *Domashnii byt russkikh tsarei*, p. 414.

11. Tikhonov, *Pomeshchich'i krest'iane*, pp. 110-111.

12. *Rozysknyia dela* 3:195, 227-230.

13. Novosel'skii, *Votchinnik*, p. 25.

14. *Ibid.*, p. 24; Zaozerskii, "Boiarskii dvor," p. 95; Barsukov, *Rod Shereme-tevykh* 3:517.

15. Kotoshikhin, p. 97; Miliukov, *Gosudarstvennoe khoziaistvo*, p. 49, argues that lesser servitors, at least, received their salaries only at irregular intervals.

16. For example, *AMG* 2:18-19, 167, 174-175, 177-178, 203, 238, 269-270.

17. Barsukov, "Dokladnaia vypiska"; Crummey, "Reconstitution," pp. 201-203.

18. Iakovlev, "Sluzhiloe zemlevladenie," as corrected by Vodarskii, "Pravia-shchaia gruppa," pp. 85-104.

19. The figures for 1638 are exceptional in this regard; the dumnye dvoriane and dumnye d'iaki together owned an average of 376 peasant households and the okol'nichie a mean of 218 households. The main reason for this anomalous result is the presence of the powerful and wealthy chancery official, I. T. Gramotin, in the former group. It should be noted that, in this case, I have used Iakovlev's figures without adjustment.

20. Hellie, *Enserfment*, p. 127.

21. Crummey, "Reconstitution," pp. 202-203. In 1613, the future Duma members owned 2,190 chetverti or about 9,000 acres of land on the average and those who would not reach the Duma 1,170 chetverti or about 4,800 acres.

22. A. M. Gnevushev, "Zemlevladenie i sel'skoe khoziaistvo v moskovskom gosudarstve XVI-XVII vv.," p. 290.

23. Barsukov, "Dokladnaia vypiska"; *Akty, otnosiashchiesia k istorii zapadnoi Rossii* 4:376, 382 (grants to A. V. Izmailov).

24. Iu. V. Got'e, *Zamoskovnyi krai v XVII veke*, pp. 206-223; Gnevushev, "Zemlevladenie," pp. 290-292.

25. D. I. Petrikeev, *Krupnoe krepostnoe khoziaistvo XVII v.*, pp. 17-35.

26. Rozhdestvenskii, "Rospis'," pp. 196-198.

27. Novosel'skii, "Rospis'," p. 128.

28. Prince I. A. Khilkov, Prince N. S. Urusov, N. K. Streshnev, A. I. Rzhevskii, I. Gorokhov.

29. See Novosel'skii, *Bor'ba*.

30. E. V. Stashevskii, *K istorii kolonizatsii Iuga*; Hellie, *Enserfment*, pp. 113-114. On A. I. Bezobrazov as an owner of southern lands, see Novosel'skii, *Votchinnik*, pp. 43-48.

31. The tables are based on data from the sources listed in note 1 of this chapter.

32. Bogoiavlenskii, "Khovanshchina," pp. 214-215.

33. Prince D. M. Pozharskii, Prince Iu. A. Dolgorukii, Prince I. A. Khovanskii II.

34. Veselovskii, *Feodal'noe zemlevladenie* 1:165-202.

35. *PRP* 6:208, 242-243, 263; El'iashevich, *Istoriia* 2:156-165.

36. Barsukov, *Rod Sheremetevykh*, vols. 1 and 2.

37. *Ibid.* 1:81, 454; 2:486-506.

38. Zimin, *Reformy*, pp. 366-371. Zimin argues that the policy could not be

implemented for lack of available land; most other writers on the subject believe that the reform was actually carried out.

39. Iu. A. Tikhonov, "Podmoskovnye imeniia russkoi aristokratii vo vtoroi polovine XVII-nachale XVIII v."; for references to particular estates and manor houses, see M. A. Il'in, *Podmoskov'e.*

40. Barsukov, *Rod Sheremetevykh* 1:449-465.

41. *Ibid.* 2:62, 227-228, 300.

42. *Ibid.* 2:364-366.

43. Rozhdestvenskii, "Rospis'," pp. 199-200, 207-208, 224. The text gives the total holdings of I. P. Sheremetev as 339 households, but the figures for his individual properties add up to 331.

44. *Ibid.*, pp. 194-196.

45. Barsukov, *Rod Sheremetevykh* 3:319-336, 495-510; on the definition of "*rodovye votchiny*," see Veselovskii, *Feodal'noe zemlevladenie* 1:18-20.

46. Barsukov, *Rod Sheremetevykh* 3:319-336, 495-510. By the time of his death, all of Sheremetev's estates were votchinas, either inherited or purchased.

47. Arsen'ev, "Blizhnii boiarin," pp. 24-25.

48. Vlas'ev, *Potomstvo* 1, pt. 1, pp. 68-71.

49. Barsukov, "Dokladnaia vypiska," p. 14.

50. Rozhdestvenskii, "Rospis'," pp. 205-207.

51. TsGADA, f. 1209, no. 264:505v-509v.

52. *Izvestiia RGO* 4:379-391.

53. Novosel'skii, "Rospis'," pp. 122-123.

54. *Izvestiia RGO* 4:379-391.

55. Barsukov, *Rod Sheremetevykh* 1:450-465. As far as I know, Prince Ia. N. Odoevskii's will has not been published.

56. Veselovskii, *Issledovaniia po istorii oprichniny*, pp. 296-298.

57. Belokurov, *Snosheniia* 1:1-5; TsGADA, f. 181, no. 176: 323-324.

58. Rozhdestvenskii, *Sluzhiloe zemlevladenie*, p. 216.

59. Barsukov, "Dokladnaia vypiska," p. 5.

60. *LIRO* 12:17-24; TsGADA, f. 1209, no. 264:72v-75v; no. 686:59v-60r. All of Cherkasskii's estates were votchinas.

61. *LIRO* 12:19.

62. Barsukov, *Rod Sheremetevykh* 3:501-502.

63. *LIRO* 12:23.

64. Rozhdestvenskii, "Rospis'," pp. 215-217.

65. Suleshev's will is published in *LIRO* 18:21-30. See K. I. Arsen'ev, "Vyshiia pravitel'stvennyia litsa vremen Tsaria Mikhaila Feodorovicha," p. 12, and, on Pavlovo, Nizhnii-Novgorod region, Rozhdestvenskii, "Rospis'," p. 216.

66. Elagin, *Istoriia* 1:184.

67. Ancestral estates were defined as those that had remained in the possession of a family for more than one generation (Veselovskii, *Sluzhiloe zemlevladenie* 1:20).

68. Petrikeev, *Khoziaistvo*; Zabelin, "Bol'shoi boiarin"; Novosel'skii, *Votchinnik*; Arsen'ev, "Blizhnii boiarin"; Zaozerskii, "Boiarskii dvor"; E. I. Zaozerskaia,

"Iz istorii feodal'noi votchiny i polozhenie krest'ian v pervoi polovine XVII veka"; *Akty khoziaistva boiarina B. I. Morozova; Khoziaistvo krupnogo feodala semnadtsatogo veka.*

69. At the height of his fortune, Morozov owned about 9,100 households; Bezobrazov owned at most 239 (Petrikeev, p. 33; Novosel'skii, *Votchinnik*, pp. 30-31).

70. Novosel'skii, *Votchinnik*, pp. 7-9; *Rozysknyia dela* 2:81-94.

71. Petrikeev, *Khoziaistvo*, pp. 54-81; Zabelin, "Bol'shoi boiarin," pp. 16-19, 501-509; Novosel'skii, *Votchinnik*, pp. 50-90; Zaozerskaia, "Iz istorii," pp. 49-50.

72. *Akty khoziaistva* 1:153.

73. Zaozerskaia, "Iz istorii," pp. 48-49.

74. Novosel'skii, *Votchinnik*, p. 87; on problems with a non-Russian steward, see Zabelin, "Bol'shoi boiarin," p. 499.

75. *Akty khoziaistva* 1:151.

76. *ChOIDR*, 1873, no. 4, pp. 114, 167-168; A. A. Zimin, "Khoziaistvennyi god v s. Pavlovskom (seredina XVII v.)," p. 67; Petrikeev, *Khoziaistvo*, p. 159.

77. For example, *Akty khoziaistva* 1:138, 176.

78. Arsen'ev, "Blizhnii boiarin," pp. 32-34, 38-40, 51.

79. Novosel'skii, *Votchinnik*, pp. 82-83.

80. Zabelin, "Bol'shoi boiarin," pp. 27-28.

81. Petrikeev, *Khoziaistvo*, pp. 144-145; Zabelin, "Bol'shoi boiarin," pp. 27-28, 32-38; Novosel'skii, *Votchinnik*, pp. 149-159; Arsen'ev, "Blizhnii boiarin," p. 32; Zimin, "Khoziaistvennyi god," pp. 70-71; Zaozerskii, "Boiarskii dvor," pp. 103-105; Zaozerskaia, "Iz istorii," p. 60.

82. Zaozerskii, "Boiarskii dvor," p. 103.

83. Zabelin, "Bol'shoi boiarin," p. 37.

84. *Ibid.*, p. 41.

85. Novosel'skii, *Votchinnik*, p. 116.

86. *Ibid.*, pp. 140-142.

87. Petrikeev, *Khoziaistvo*, pp. 135-137.

88. Novosel'skii, *Votchinnik*, pp. 133-135.

89. Petrikeev, *Khoziaistvo*, p. 84.

90. Zaozerskaia, "Iz istorii," p. 52.

91. Novosel'skii, *Votchinnik*, pp. 158-159.

92. Petrikeev, *Khoziaistvo*, p. 88.

93. Novosel'skii, *Votchinnik*, pp. 160-161, 182; Tikhonov, *Pomeshchich'i krest'iane*, p. 31.

94. Petrikeev, *Khoziaistvo*, p. 145; Novosel'skii, *Votchinnik*, p. 160. Cf. Tikhonov, *Pomeshchich'i krest'iane*, pp. 288-289. The figures for Morozov's and Bezobrazov's estates fall within the range of indices that Tikhonov compiled for all of central Russia in the same period.

95. Zaozerskaia, "Iz istorii," pp. 54-56.

96. Arsen'ev, "Blizhnii boiarin," p. 31; Rozhdestvenskii, "Rospis'," p. 207.

97. Zaozerskii, "Boiarskii dvor," p. 105.

98. Petrikeev, *Khoziaistvo*, p. 146.

99. *Akty khoziaistva* 2:91; Arsen'ev, "Blizhnii boiarin," pp. 65-67, 83-90, 96.

100. Arsen'ev, "Blizhnii boiarin," p. 96.

101. Zabelin, "Bol'shoi boiarin," pp. 44-45.

102. *Ibid.*, pp. 45-47; Zimin, "Khoziaistvennyi god," p. 77; *Khoziaistvo feodala* 1:67-68.

103. Petrikeev, *Khoziaistvo*, p. 113.

104. Kozlovskii, *Rtishchev*, pp. 118-120.

105. Petrikeev, *Khoziaistvo*, p. 123.

106. *Ibid.*, pp. 120-121; P. F. Bakanov, "Tovarnoe proizvodstvo v feodal'noi votchine XVII veka," pp. 97-100.

107. Petrikeev, *Khoziaistvo*, p. 182.

108. *Ibid.*, p. 120.

109. *Ibid.*, p. 124.

110. *Ibid.*, pp. 126-130; Zabelin, "Bol'shoi boiarin," p. 485; Bakanov, "Tovarnoe proizvodstvo," p. 95.

111. On similar attitudes in the eighteenth century, see Michael Confino, *Domaines et seigneurs en Russie vers la fin du XVIIIe siècle*, pp. 104-105.

112. Petrikeev, *Khoziaistvo*, pp. 94-95.

113. Cf. Confino, *Domaines et seigneurs*, pp. 156-159.

114. Zaozerskii, *Tsar'*, pp. 115-139.

115. *Akty khoziaistva* 2:63-72; Petrikeev, *Khoziaistvo*, pp. 148-150.

116. Zabelin, "Bol'shoi boiarin," p. 13.

117. Zaozerskii, "Boiarskii dvor," pp. 96, 108.

118. Zaozerskaia, "Iz istorii," pp. 58-59.

119. Zaozerskii, "Boiarskii dvor," p. 93.

120. *Ibid.*, pp. 97, 106; Arsen'ev, "Blizhnii boiarin," pp. 38-40.

121. *Akty khoziaistva* 1:140; 2:80-81; Petrikeev, *Khoziaistvo*, pp. 133-134; Zabelin, "Bol'shoi boiarin," p. 478.

CHAPTER VI

1. *Pervye p'esy russkogo teatra*, pp. 31-39.

2. Kotoshikhin, *O Rossii*, p. 46; Uroff, "On Russia," p. 101.

3. On mestnichestvo, see the works listed in chapter II, note 8; Volkov, "Ob otmene"; and A. Savin, "Mestnichestvo pri dvore Liudovika XIV."

4. *DR* 1:383-384, 573, 867-869; Markevich, *O mestnichestve*, pp. 485-486, 505.

5. *DR* 1:641-642; 2:273; Dop. k 3:274.

6. *DR* 1:97, 506-507. Such a painless solution was rarely available in the seventeenth century.

7. *DR* 2:444-445; Dop. k 3:98-100.

8. Crummey, "Reflections," p. 279; Markevich, *Istoriia*, pp. 471, 521-525.

9. M. Ia. Volkov states that the "boyar elite (*znat'*)" opposed the reform but presents no evidence to support his claim ("Ob otmene," p. 65).

10. *AMG* 1:111, 655-657; 3:97-98.

11. *Vremennik OIDR* 7:75; *Moskovskaia pis'mennost'*, pp. 18-19.

12. For example, *AMG* 3:322, 325, 548. Prince I. A. Khovanskii referred to

himself, for instance, as "Ivashka Khovanskii." When corresponding with individual boyars, the tsar used the full name, including the patronymic.

13. The most abusive of well-documented seventeenth-century landlords, A. I. Bezobrazov, was, strictly speaking, not a member of the Duma; some men who were may well have rivalled him in the use of invective. Prince N. I. Odoevskii sometimes treated his underlings very sternly, and even B. I. Morozov, a relatively polite and reasonable lord, reacted with great severity when he heard that a sharecropper on one of his estates had insulted him while on a drunken spree. Morozov treated the unfortunate offender almost as though he had committed lese majesty against the tsar himself (Novosel'skii, *Votchinnik*, pp. 82-83; Arsen'ev, "Blizhnii boiarin," p. 51; *Akty khoziaistva* 1:128-129; *Ocherki istorii SSSR. XVII v.*, pp. 309-311).

14. F. I. Miller, *Izvestie o dvorianakh rossiiskikh*, pp. 309-312.

15. For example, *DR* 1:379; 2:381, 471; 3:204, 405-406, 880-881; Dop. k 3:34, 48-49, 284-285; *AMG* 1:491; 3:97, 137; *PDS* 6:1593-1594, 1598-1599, 1606; Vlas'ev, *Potomstvo* 1, pt. 3, p. 48.

16. For outstanding examples, see *Treasures from the Kremlin*, pp. 61, 69, 158, 163; *Istoriia russkogo iskusstva* 4:557.

17. "Rospis' vsiakim veshcham, den'gam i zapasam, chto ostalos' po smerti Nikity Ivanovicha Romanova i dachi po nem na pomni dushi," pp. 75-85, 116, 122-128; "Opis' vydelennomu nasledstvu Kniazhne Lykovoi posle diadi 'eia Streshneva," pp. 18-20; *Rozysknyia dela* 4:5-8, 557-562; Zaozerskii, "Boiarskii dvor," p. 94.

18. For example, *DRV* 15:219-229; *ChOIDR*, 1874, no. 1, pp. 1-11; 1896, no. 3, p. 32.

19. *ZORSA* 2:702-706.

20. *DR* 3:486, 810, 872; Dop. k 3:150, 155, 158, 208, 262, 342; *Vremennik OIDR* 5:11.

21. *ZORSA* 2:751; see Nannerl O. Keohane, *Philosophy and the State in France: the Renaissance to the Enlightenment*, p. 18.

22. Olearius, *Travels*, p. 99.

23. Apart from Olearius' account, the best contemporary description is found in Mayerberg's work, *ChOIDR*, 1874, no. 1, pp. 186-188. For composite descriptions of the ceremony, see Zabelin, *Domashnii byt russkikh tsarei*, pp. 406-417; V. Savva, *Moskovskie tsari i vizantiiskie vasilevsy*, pp. 165-174; G. Ostrogorsky, "Zum Stratordienst des Herrschers in der Byzantinisch-Slavischen Welt," p. 194.

24. Zabelin, *Domashnii byt russkikh tsarei*, pp. 367-376; Kliuchevskii, *Boiarskaia duma*, pp. 406-409; *Rude & Barbarous Kingdom*, pp. 236-239.

25. Zabelin, *Domashnii byt russkikh tsarei*, pp. 376-435.

26. *PSZ* 2:641 (no. 1095).

27. See Crummey, "Court Spectacles." I based my argument on the following representations of the ceremony: Olearius, *Travels*, the fourth plate between pages 150 and 151; the drawing of the same scene in the *Albom Maierberga*.

Vidy i bytovye kartiny Rossii XVII veka; Jacob Ulfeldt, *Hodoeporicon Rutheni-cum*, plates 2 and 3; and *Poslaniia Ivana Groznogo*, plate facing p. 332.

28. Iakov Reitenfel's, "Skazaniia Svetleishemu Gertzogu Toskanskomu Koz'me Tret'emu o Moskovii," p. 87.

29. *Rude & Barbarous Kingdom*, pp. 25-27, 54-55.

30. For example, Olearius, *Travels*, p. 65. Olearius describes a dinner of dishes from the tsar's table served to the ambassadors in their own quarters.

31. For the elaborate ritual of a wedding banquet, see Kotoshikhin, *O Rossii*, pp. 8-9; Uroff, "On Russia," pp. 41-44.

32. Kotoshikhin, *O Rossii*, pp. 29-31; Uroff, "On Russia," pp. 74-75; Zabelin, *Domashnii byt russkikh tsarei*, pp. 277-282.

33. J. Tazbir, "Privilegirovannoe soslovie feodal'noi Pol'shi," p. 164. As far as I know, Duma members and other prominent courtiers dressed in essentially the same way on ceremonial occasions.

34. Olearius, *Travels*, p. 60; *Vremennik OIDR* 6:40; 13:31. If a Golitsyn had to borrow a robe from the government, less favored courtiers surely had to do likewise!

35. Zabelin, *Domashnii byt russkikh tsarei*, p. 371.

36. Note the comments of Paul of Aleppo, an Eastern Orthodox visitor to Aleksei's court, on the rigor of the tsar's devotions. Paul remarked that leading courtiers nicknamed the ruler "the young monk" (Palmer, *Patriarch and Tsar* 2:100-102, 107, 137, 178-182).

37. *Vremennik OIDR* 13:31.

38. Kotoshikhin, *O Rossii*, pp. 32-35; Uroff, "On Russia," pp. 80-85; I. Zabelin, *Domashnii byt russkikh tsarits v XVI i XVII st.*, pp. 494-505.

39. Olearius, *Travels*, p. 220.

40. Collins, *Present State*, p. 62; *Istoriia Moskvy* 1, supplement, maps of the Moscow Kremlin in 1605 and 1675-1680.

41. *RBS* 19:580-581; *AI* 5:39-40; *Istoriia Moskvy* 1:643.

42. Barsukov, *Rod Sheremetevykh* 7:18-19.

43. *Rozysknyia dela* 4:1-186; Zabelin, *Domashnii byt russkikh tsarei*, pp. 549-566; Danilov, "Golicyn," p. 579. N. I. Romanov owned five houses in the city (Zaozerskaia, "Iz istorii," p. 59).

44. "Iz istorii Moskvy (Opis' g. Moskvy posle pozhara 10 aprelia 1629 g.)"; *Istoriia Moskvy* 1, supplement, map of the western section of the Belyi Gorod in 1629.

45. *Ibid.*, map of the eastern section of the Belyi Gorod in 1631.

46. Olearius, *Travels*, p. 155.

47. *Istoriia Moskvy* 1:505, illustration of the house of V. I. Sheremetev; M. G. Rabinovich, *O drevnei Moskvy*, pp. 231-234; *Istoriia russkogo iskusstva* 4:82-83.

48. *Ibid.*, p. 160. Compare the illustration of a sixteenth-century house in Rabinovich, p. 231 with the seventeenth-century examples reproduced in *Istoriia Moskvy* and *Istoriia russkogo iskusstva* vol. 4. On private chapels, see Kotoshikhin, *O Rossii*, p. 147; Uroff, "On Russia," p. 266.

49. There are extensive descriptions of Golitsyn's house and its furnishings in Zabelin, *Domashnii byt russkikh tsarei*, pp. 549-566; *Rozysknyia dela* 4:1-162. See the picture of the facade in *Istoriia russkogo iskusstva* 4:226. For a description of the house and an elaborate project for its restoration, written in the early 1920s, see Grabar', *O russkoi arkhitekture*, pp. 367-371. Despite Grabar' 's best efforts, the Moscow city authorities demolished the Golitsyn mansion, by then partially restored, at the beginning of the 1930s (*ibid.*, p. 419).

50. S. K. Bogoiavlenskii, *Nauchnoe nasledie. O Moskve XVII veka*, pp. 221-232. For a helpful discussion of Muscovite architectural terminology, see pp. 192-220.

51. *Istoriia russkogo iskusstva* 4:82-83, 160. Compare the illustration of the rebuilt Kirillov house on p. 83 with the drawing of the building in its seventeenth-century form in *Istoriia Moskvy* 1:511.

52. *Istoriia russkogo iskusstva* 4:228-229.

53. Olearius, *Travels*, p. 159.

54. *Istoriia Moskvy* 1:452. See also Kotoshikhin, *O Rossii*, pp. 157-158; Uroff, "On Russia," p. 283.

55. Zaozerskii, "Boiarskii dvor," pp. 95-96.

56. *PDS* 6:488.

57. For example, *DR* 2:207.

58. Zaozerskii, "Boiarskii dvor," p. 96.

59. Elias, *Gesellschaft*, p. 141. The author contrasts the attitudes of Louis XIV's courtiers with those of our own day.

60. Tazbir, "Privilegirovannoe soslovie," p. 161; Olearius, *Travels*, p. 220.

61. Kotoshikhin, *O Rossii*, pp. 147-149; Uroff, "On Russia," pp. 266-268; Olearius, *Travels*, pp. 158-159; *ChOIDR*, 1906, no. 3, pp. 154-156.

62. *PDS* 5:438-441.

63. For example, Olearius, *Travels*, p. 294. Mayerberg made very favorable comments about Ordin-Nashchokin as a host (*ChOIDR*, 1873, no. 3, p. 37).

64. Olearius, *Travels*, p. 158.

65. Tikhonov, "Podmoskovnye imeniia," p. 136.

66. Barsukov, *Rod Sheremetevykh* 6:491-492.

67. Novosel'skii, *Votchinnik*, pp. 33-37.

68. *PRP* 6:202. The Code also sets limits for servitors of lower rank. Oddly enough, the article in question does not mention dumnye dvoriane.

69. Data on the boyars' lands in the Moscow district come from the sources mentioned in chapter I, note 43; the Kholmogorovs' collection of materials; Tikhonov, "Podmoskovnye imeniia"; Zaozerskii, *Tsarskaia votchina*; Stashevskii, *Zemlevladenie*; Sb. mosk st. 447 and 775; TsGADA, f. 1209, nos. 264, 686 and 9809.

70. Novosel'skii, "Rospis'," pp. 122-148. Only 13 Duma members owned land in the Zvenigorod district, and, of these, all but two also owned land in the Moscow uezd.

71. The boyars, okol'nichie, dumnye dvoriane, and dumnye d'iaki owned an average of 46.7, 10.9, 17.1, and 18.8 peasant households respectively.

72. Novosel'skii, "Rospis'," pp. 122, 124.

73. Tikhonov, "Podmoskovnye imeniia," pp. 146-152; *Rozysknyia dela* 4:341-400, 413-456.

74. *Istoriia Moskvy* 1:523-524.

75. *ChOIDR*, 1886, no. 1, pp. 120-121; 1888, no. 4, p. 99; 1889, no. 1, pp. 31, 90; 1892, no. 1, pp. 110, 177-178; 1896, no. 4, pp. 35-36, 74; 1901, no. 1, p. 44; 1911, no. 3, pp. 189, 201, 215-216, 263, 266, 360.

76. *Istoriia Moskvy* 1:523-524.

77. See the map in the supplement to *Istoriia Moskvy*, vol. 1.

78. *Ibid.*, p. 524.

79. Tikhonov, "Podmoskovnye imeniia," pp. 139, 146-147.

80. *Ibid.*, pp. 149, 152.

81. A. P. Gudzinskaia and N. G. Mikhailova, "Graficheskie materialy kak istochnik po istorii arkhitektury pomeshchich'ei i krest'ianskoi usadeb v Rossii XVII v."; M. A. Anikst and V. S. Turchin, *V okrestnostiakh Moskvy. Iz istorii russkoi usadebnoi kul'tury XVII-XIX vekov*, plate 5. It is unclear which Nikol'-skoe is depicted. In the Moscow district alone, there were several villages of that name. For an illustration of the Kolomenskoe palace, see Anikst and Turchin, plate 3.

82. See the lavish illustrations in Anikst and Turchin.

83. Zimin, "Khoziaistvennyi god," p. 66; Petrikeev, *Khoziaistvo*, p. 46; Zabelin, "Bol'shoi boiarin," pp. 44-45.

84. *ChOIDR*, 1905, no. 3, p. 88; Zabelin, "Bol'shoi boiarin," p. 44; Olearius, *Travels*, p. 101.

85. Palmer, *Patriarch and Tsar* 2:136; Barsukov, *Rod Sheremetevykh* 4:240-241.

86. Olearius, *Travels*, pp. 233-242, 249-258, 269-277.

87. *ChOIDR*, 1896, no. 3, p. 32.

88. Kozlovskii, *Rtishchev*, pp. 155-168.

89. Solov'ev, *Istoriia* 6:404-405.

90. *Vremennik OIDR* 8:51.

91. "Chastnaia perepiska," p. 309.

92. I have found a total of 42 Duma members who entered monasteries at some point in their lives. Information on monastic professions comes from the sources listed in chapter I, note 43; P. Kazanskii, *Rodoslovnaia Golovinykh, vladel'tsev sela Novospasskago*; Raevskii, *Rod Shuiskikh*; Iu. M. Eksin, "Dmitrii Pozharskii"; I. G. Spasskii, "Moskovskaia matematicheskaia rukopisnaia kniga serediny XVII v. i ee pervyi vladelets," p. 70.

93. Ivanov, *Alfavitnyi ukazatel'*, p. 344; Kashkin, *Rodoslovnye razvedki* 1:377; *Rus. pr. nekropol'* 1:767.

94. Vlas'ev, *Potomstvo*, pt. 3, p. 29. On this custom, see Olearius, *Travels*, p. 274.

95. *DAI* 10:23-25. The available evidence does not permit broad generalizations about the frequency of religious professions among boyar women. Given

the importance of marriage to boyar clans, it is likely that relatively few of their female members became nuns, at least until late in life.

96. *Izvestiia RGO* 4:379-380.

97. *Ibid.*, pp. 380-381.

98. *LIRO* 12:17; 18:23; *Izvestiia RGO* 2:21-22; Barsukov, *Rod Sheremetevykh* 3:496-497; 7:19.

99. *Ibid.* 3:511.

100. *LIRO* 6-7:26; Eksin, "Pozharskii," p. 119.

101. N. Miatlev, "K rodosloviiu kniazei Mstislavskikh," p. 301.

102. Volkonskaia, p. 174. The great chancery official I. T. Gramotin also made a bequest of land (Veselovskii, *D'iaki*, pp. 129-130). For other examples, see *ChOIDR*, 1907, no. 1, pp. 28-29 (the will of A. A. Nagoi) and V. V. Passek, *Istoricheskoe opisanie moskovskago Simonova monastyria*, p. 144 (grants of Prince Iu. E. Suleshov and an "exchange" of Prince Ia. N. Odoevskii as well as grants of the Mstislavskiis).

103. *PRP* 6:257-258.

104. *Prilozhenie k rodoslovnoi knige roda Khitrovo*, pp. 236-286.

105. *Ibid.*, pp. 274-279.

106. *LIRO* 12:17-24; Barsukov, *Rod Sheremetevykh* 7:10; *Vkladnaia kniga moskovskago Novospasskago monastyria*, pp. 28-31; Arkhimandrit Iakinf, *Kratkoe istoricheskoe opisanie moskovskago stavropigal'nago pervoklasnago Novospaskago [sic] monastyria . . .* , pp. 82-90. See also A. I. Ivanov, "*Kormovaia kniga*" *Koliazina monastyria* and *Vkladnyia i kormovyia knigi rostovskago Borisoglebskago monastyria v XV, XVI, XVII i XVIII stoletiiakh.*

107. "Chastnaia perepiska," p. 357; *Prilozhenie k rodoslovnoi Khitrovo*, p. 212.

108. *RBS* 2:544. The Kamynins apparently had close ties with the Svenskii Monastery in the same district. See V. Arsen'ev, ed., "Vkladnaia kniga brianskago Svenskago monastyria," pp. 392-413.

109. See the materials collected by the Kholmogorovs, cited in chapter III, note 36.

110. *ChOIDR*, 1885, no. 4, pp. 121, 125-126, 131.

111. Novosel'skii, *Votchinnik*, pp. 19-20. In spite of his many unpleasant qualities, Bezobrazov practiced his religion diligently and built two churches on his estates. He even spent some of his own money to pay the salaries of icon painters and a choirmaster.

112. Il'in, *Podmoskov'e*, pp. 75, 137, 163, 255-256; *Istoriia russkogo iskusstva* 4:256-259, 260 n. 1.

113. *RBS* 14:246; Eksin, "Pozharskii," p. 118; *Istoriia russkogo iskusstva* 4:134-135, 142.

114. N. P. Rozanov, "Opisanie moskovskikh tserkvei uchinennoe Moskovskoiu konsistorieiu v 1817 godu, s pokazaniam, kogda tserkvi postroeny i ot chego imeiut nazvanie svoei mestnosti," p. 83; see also Arkhimandrit Grigorii, "O domovykh tserkvakh Moskovskoi eparkhii."

115. *Istoriia Moskvy* 1:505.

116. Bogoiavlenskii, *Nauchnoe nasledie*, p. 231. See the illustration in *Istoriia russkogo iskusstva* 4:269.

117. Olearius, *Travels*, p. 377.

118. Kozlovskii, *Rtishchev*, p. 168.

119. "Chastnaia perepiska," pp. 457-458.

120. *Vremennik OIDR* 7:72.

121. Zabelin, "Bol'shoi boiarin," pp. 495-496.

122. *Ibid.*, pp. 17, 494-495; Arsen'ev, "Blizhnii boiarin," p. 53. A. I. Sobolevskii estimated that, in the seventeenth century, virtually all parish priests were literate. See his *Obrazovannost' Moskovskoi Rusi XIV-XVII vekov*, p. 5.

123. Zenkovsky, *Russkoe staroobriadchestvo*, pp. 267-269; Kozlovskii, *Rtishchev*, p. 160.

124. Among Duma members, there were no significant differences in men's religious practices. Chancery officials were as devout as aristocrats, if not more so.

125. Zenkovsky, *Staroobriadchestvo*, pp. 137-138.

126. See Kliuchevsky, *Seventeenth Century*, pp. 275-301; S. F. Platonov, *Moscow and the West*, chaps. 2 and 3; Miliukov, *Ocherki* 3, chap. 4.

127. See K. V. Kharlampovich, *Malorossiiskoe vliianie na velikorusskuiu tserkovnuiu zhizn'*.

128. See N. F. Kapterev, *Kharakter otnoshenii Rossii k pravoslavnomu vostoku v XVI i XVII stoletiiakh* and his *Patriarkh i Tsar'*.

129. Kliuchevsky, *Seventeenth Century*, pp. 302-303; Solov'ev, *Istoriia* 5:491-492.

130. Platonov, *Moscow and the West*, pp. 62-70, 85-88; Edward L. Keenan, *The Kurbskii-Groznyi Apocrypha: the Seventeenth-Century Genesis of the "Correspondence" Attributed to Prince A. M. Kurbskii and Tsar Ivan IV*.

131. Kliuchevsky, *Seventeenth Century*, pp. 342-353.

132. For a stimulating recent discussion of the court theater, see A. N. Robinson, *Bor'ba idei v russkoi literature XVII veka*, chap. 2 and his "Pervyi russkii teatr kak iavlenie evropeiskoi kul'tury," *Novye cherti v russkoi literature i iskusstve (XVII-nachalo XVIII v.)*, pp. 8-27.

133. Zaozerskaia, "Iz istorii," p. 64.

134. Olearius, *Travels*, p. 130. Olearius does not explain how he did so.

135. TsGADA, f. 396, no. 594. The document itself has no heading and later archivists have labelled it with the name I. D. Mstislavskii, evidently an error since no such person appears in the service records of the period.

136. Solov'ev, *Istoriia* 7:181.

137. On Ordin-Nashchokin, see Kliuchevsky, *Seventeenth Century*, pp. 359-378; Galaktionov and Chistiakova; Ikonnikov, "Blizhnii boiarin." It is a pity that C. Bickford O'Brien did not live to finish his projected biography of Nashchokin.

138. For samples of such news digests, see *Vesti-kuranty. 1600-1639 gg.* (Moscow, 1972) and *Vesti-kuranty. 1642-1644 gg.* (Moscow, 1976). Daniel Clarke Waugh is preparing a study of literary contacts and the flow of information between Russia and central Europe, with particular emphasis on the *kuranty*.

139. E. V. Chistiakova, *Sotsial'no-ekonomicheskie vzgliady A. L. Ordin-Na-shchokina*, pp. 34, 41-43.

140. *Istoriia russkogo iskusstva* 4:358, 536; V. Nikol'skii, "Boiarin Khitrovo. Iz istorii drevnerusskogo sobiratel'stva"; M. I. Slukhovskii, *Bibliotechnoe delo v Rossii do XVIII veka*, p. 104; V. Trutovskii, "Boiarin i oruzhnichii Bogdan Matveevich Khitrovo i moskovskaia Oruzheinaia palata."

141. Kozlovskii, *Rtishchev*, pp. 77-79; Kashkin, *Rodoslovnye razvedki* 1:413-416, 423; Kliuchevsky, *Seventeenth Century*, pp. 353-358.

142. Kozlovskii, *Rtishchev*, pp. 157-158.

143. Kharlampovich, *Vliianie*, pp. 125-137.

144. Kashkin, *Rodoslovnye razvedki* 1:415.

145. Platonov, *Moscow and the West*, pp. 104-105.

146. S. P. Luppov, *Kniga v Rossii v XVII veke*, pp. 113-114.

147. There is a great deal of published material on Matveev, most of it old and unsatisfactory. See chapter IV, note 74.

148. "Opis' imushchestva boiarina Artemona Sergeevicha Matveeva."

149. N. M. Moleva, "Muzyka i zrelishcha v Rossii XVII stoletiia," p. 152.

150. I. M. Kudriavtsev, "Izdatel'skaia" deiatel'nost' Posol'skogo prikaza (K istorii russkoi rukopisnoi knigi vo vtoroi polovine XVII veka)," pp. 181-182, 185-186, 194-195. On Spafari, see I. N. Mikhailovskii, *Vazhneishie trudy Nikolaia Spafariia (1672-1677)* (Kiev, 1897).

151. Luppov, *Kniga v XVII veke*, pp. 102-107; S. A. Belokurov, *O biblioteke moskovskikh gosudarei v XVI stoletii*, pp. 69-74.

152. Kliuchevsky, *Seventeenth Century*, pp. 379-384; Platonov, *Moscow and the West*, pp. 113-114.

153. Danilov, "Golicyn," p. 4.

154. Volkov, "Ob otmene," pp. 55-56; Danilov, "Golicyn," pp. 540-543.

155. *Ibid.*, pp. 575-577.

156. *Ocherki russkoi kul'tury XVII veka* 2:199; Lindsey A. J. Hughes, "Western European Graphic Material as a Source for Moscow Baroque Architecture," p. 439.

157. Luppov, *Kniga v XVII veke*, pp. 107-110; *Rozysknyia dela* 4:9, 30-33, 55-58, 99, 160, 215.

158. Danilov, "Golicyn," p. 577.

CONCLUSIONS

1. See Ping-ti Ho, *The Ladder of Success in Imperial China: Aspects of Social Mobility, 1368-1911*.

2. Daniel Matuszewski's long-awaited study compares the Muscovite and Ottoman systems in far greater detail.

3. See Halil Inalcik, *The Ottoman Empire. The Classical Age, 1300-1600*; S. J. Shaw, *Between Old and New: the Ottoman Empire under Sultan Selim III, 1789-1807*.

4. For a fine comparative treatment of European societies in the early modern period, see Perry Anderson, *Lineages of the Absolutist State*. See also Stone,

Crisis; H. R. Trevor-Roper, *The Gentry, 1540-1640*; Davis Bitton, *The French Nobility in Crisis, 1560-1640*; Guy Chaussinand-Nogaret, *La noblesse au XVIIIe siècle: de la feodalité aux lumières.*

5. Anderson, *Lineages*, part 2, chs. 1, 2, 6; Otto Hintze, *The Historical Essays of Otto Hintze*, pp. 43-58.

6. See A. Giesztor, S. Kieniewicz, E. Rostworowski, J. Tazbir, and H. Wereszycki, *History of Poland*, chs. 8 and 9; J. Tazbir, ed., *Polska XVII wieku. Państwo, społeczeństwo, kultura*; W. Czapliński and J. Długosz, *Życie codzienne magnaterii polskiej w XVII wieku.*

7. For a brilliant review of the recent Polish literature on serfdom and its economic implications, see Andrzej Kamiński, "Neo-Serfdom in Poland-Lithuania." Recent studies place less emphasis than earlier works on the international grain trade with western Europe as the motive force behind the development of the economy of the nobles' estates and of serfdom. See also Andrzej Wyczański, *Studia nad folwarkiem szlacheckim w Polsce w latach 1500-1580.*

8. In his new book, *The Origins of Autocracy: Ivan the Terrible in Russian History*, pp. 20-21, Alexander Yanov suggests that, in these terms, the Russian high nobility had unique qualities for a relatively short time at best. The combination of compulsory service and an aristocratic social standing and way of life lasted, he suggests, only until 1762, when the government freed the nobles from the necessity to serve. The legal meaning of this decree is not in dispute. Its practical significance is less clear, however. If, for reasons of tradition or economic necessity, most Russian nobles continued to perform official service, their lives still displayed the same features as those of their predecessors in the seventeenth century.

APPENDIX C

1. *Ocherki istorii SSSR. XVII v.*, pp. 348-353.

2. G. R. Elton, ed., *The Tudor Constitution. Documents and Commentary* (Cambridge, 1960), pp. 87-93; F. G. Marcham, *A Constitutional History of Modern England, 1485 to the Present* (New York, Evanston and London, 1960), pp. 25-26, 30-32, 105, 112-113.

3. Kliuchevskii, *Boiarskaia duma*, p. 1.

4. Sergeevich, *Drevnosti* 2:384-453, 463-501 and *Lektsii*, pp. 196-210.

5. Sergeevich, *Drevnosti* 2:439-452; *Lektsii*, pp. 207-210; *DR* 4:187.

6. *Rude & Barbarous Kingdom*, p. 153.

7. For example, *PSZ* 2, nos. 633, 634, 644, 860, 1116, 1170; *PRP* 5:237.

8. *AI* 3:304 (no. 167); *PRP* 5:205-206; Kotoshikhin, *O Rossii*, pp. 24-25; Olearius, *Travels*, p. 221. The testimony of these sources differs on the precise times and places of the Duma's meetings.

9. *PSZ* 1:828, 984; 2:4 (nos. 460, 582, 621).

10. Kotoshikhin, pp. 24-25.

11. For example, *PRP* 5:203-206.

BIBLIOGRAPHY[1]

ARCHIVAL SOURCES

Arkhiv Akademii nauk SSSR. Moscow.
> fund 620 (S. B. Veselovskii), nos. 21, 34, 35, 38, 40, 42, 47, 48, 49, 50, 51.

Gosudarstvennaia biblioteka imeni V. I. Lenina. Rukopisnyi otdel. Moscow. (Cited as GBL).
> fund 29 (Sobranie Beliaeva), nos. 104, 107.
> fund 178 (Muzeinoe sobranie), nos. 734, 3284.

TsGADA.
> fund 181, no. 176.
> fund 210 (Razriadnyi prikaz), BK, BS, Bezglavnye stolbtsy, nos. 4, 45, 65, 221, Knigi moskovskogo stola, nos. 60, 96, 125, 144, 177, Sb. mosk. st., nos. 25, 28, 32, 51, 111, 131, 154, 165, 166, 182, 202, 216, 245, 342, 355, 357, 359, 360, 379, 447, 775, 1066, 1102, 1103, 1131, 1133, 1140, 1152, 1161, Stolbtsy prikaznogo stola, no. 1152, Zap. kn. mosk. st., no. 12.
> fund 396 (Oruzheinaia palata), nos. 594, 674.
> fund 1209 (Pomestnyi prikaz), nos. 264, 686, 9809.

Algemeen Rijksarchief. The Hague.
> Staten-General. Lias-Rusland, no. 7365.

Svenska Riksarkivet. Stockholm.
> Muscovitica 39.

PRINTED SOURCES

Primary Sources

Akty iuridicheskie. St. Petersburg, 1838.
Akty khoziaistva boiarina B. I. Morozova. 2 vols. Moscow-Leningrad, 1929.

---

[1] For additional entries, see Abbreviations.

Akty otnosiashchiesia k istorii iuzhnoi i zapadnoi Rossii. 15 vols. St. Petersburg, 1861-1892.

Akty otnosiashchiesia k istorii zapadnoi Rossii. 5 vols. St. Petersburg, 1846-1855.

Arkhiv kniazia F. A. Kurakina. 8 vols. St. Petersburg, 1890-1899.

Albom Maierberga. Vidy i bytovye kartiny Rossii XVII veka. Moscow, 1903.

Arsen'ev, V., ed. "Vkladnaia kniga brianskago Svenskago monastyria." *Izvestiia RGO* 4:392-433.

Baron, Samuel H., ed. *The Travels of Olearius in 17th Century Russia*. Stanford, 1967.

Barsukov, A. P., ed. "Dokladnaia vypiska 121 (1613) goda o votchinakh i pomest'iakh." *ChOIDR*, 1895, no. 1, pp. 1-24.

Bartenev, P., ed. *Sobranie pisem Tsaria Alekseia Mikhailovicha*. Moscow, 1856.

Bazilevich, K. V., and Piontkovskii, S. A., eds. *Gorodskie vosstaniia v moskovskom gosudarstve XVII v*. Moscow-Leningrad, 1936.

Belokurov, S. A., ed. "Dneval'nyia zapiski Prikaza tainykh del, 7165-7183 gg." *ChOIDR*, 1908, no. 1, pp. 1-224; no. 2, pp. 255-346.

Berkh, V. N., ed. *Sistematicheskie spiski boiaram, okol'nichim i dumnym dvorianam s 1468 goda do unichtozheniia sikh chinov*. St. Petersburg, 1833.

Berry, Lloyd E., and Crummey, Robert O., eds. *Rude & Barbarous Kingdom*. Madison, Milwaukee and London, 1968.

"Boiarin Kniaz' Vasilii Vasil'evich Golitsyn. Gramotki k nemu ot rodnykh v 1677 g." *Russkaia starina* 74 (1892):353-366.

Buganov, V. I., ed. "Opisanie moskovskogo vosstaniia 1648 g. v Arkhivskom sbornike." *Istoricheskii arkhiv*, 1957, no. 4, pp. 227-230.

"Chelobitnaia na okol'nichago i voevodu Mikh. Sem. Volynskago "nemilostivogo na monastyri gonitelia, smertnogo chasu zabytelia, bezstrashno iavna grabitelia, nepravednogo sud'iu i mzdoimtsa". 177 g." *ChOIDR*, 1887, no. 3, pp. 8-9.

Collins, Samuel. *The Present State of Russia*. London, 1671.

Delo o Patriarkhe Nikone. St. Petersburg, 1897.

Demidov, I. M., ed. "Rodoslovnyia zapisi Spaso-raevskoi pustyni XVII veka." *LIRO* 33-34 (1913):19-27.

"Dukhovnoe zaveshchanie A. A. Nagogo v 1617 g." *ChOIDR*, 1907, no. 1, pp. 28-29.

Elagin, S. I. *Istoriia russkago flota. Period azovskii. Prilozheniia*. Pt. 1. St. Petersburg, 1864.

Esipov, G. V., ed. *Sbornik o Petre Velikom*. Moscow, 1872.

The Eyewitness Chronicle (Letopys samovydtsia). Vol. 7 of *Harvard Series in Ukrainian Studies*. Cambridge, Mass., 1972.

Galaktionov, I. V., ed. *Ranniaia perepiska A. L. Ordina-Nashchokina (1642-1645 gg.)*. Saratov, 1968.

Golitsyn, N. N., ed. *Materialy dlia polnoi rodoslovnoi rospisi kniazei Golitsynykh*. Kiev, 1880.

———. *Ukazatel' imen lichnykh upominaemykh v Dvortsovykh razriadakh*. St. Petersburg, 1912.

Golokhvastov, Dmitrii, ed. "Akty, otnosiashchiesia do roda dvorian Golokhvastovykh." *ChOIDR*, 1847-1848, no. 3, pp. 49-87; no. 4, pp. 79-118; no. 5, pp. 73-140.

Gordon, Patrick. *Passages from the Diary of General Patrick Gordon of Auchleuchries in the Years 1635-1699*. London, 1968.

"Gramota Tsaria Alekseia Mikhailovicha A. L. Ordinu-Nashchokinu o pozhalovanii ego v dumnye dvoriane." *ChOIDR*, 1896, no. 3, p. 32.

Grigorii, Arkhimandrit, ed. "Dukhovnaia zheny Alekseia Ivanovicha Godunova, Ol'gi Vasil'evny, urozhdennoi Zuzinoi [sic], 1625 goda." *ChOIDR*, 1868, no. 4, pp. 1-5.

Hellie, Richard, ed. *Readings for Introduction to Russian Civilization: Muscovite Society*. Chicago, 1967.

Iakovlev, A. I., ed. "Sluzhiloe zemlevladenie po dannym Prikaza sbora ratnykh liudei (1638 g.)." In *Sergeiu Fedorovichu Platonovu. Ucheniki, druz'ia i pochitateli. Sbornik statei, posviashchennykh S. F. Platonovu*, pp. 450-453. St. Petersburg, 1911.

Iakubov, K. I., ed. "Rossiia i Shvetsiia v pervoi polovine XVII veka." *ChOIDR*, 1897, no. 3, pp. 1-240; no. 4, pp. 241-288; 1898, no. 1, pp. 289-494.

Ivanov, A. I., ed. *"Kormovaia kniga" Koliazina monastyria*. Tver', 1892.

Ivanov, P. I. *Alfavitnyi ukazatel' familii i lits, upominaemykh v boiarskikh knigakh*. Moscow, 1853.

"Iz arkhiva Tainykh del." *Starina i novizna* 15:34-179.

"Iz istorii Moskvy (Opis' g. Moskvy posle pozhara 10 aprelia 1629 g.)," ed. V. Lebedev. *Krasnyi arkhiv* 101(1940):197-227.

Kashkin, N. N., ed. "Stolptsy kniazei Cherkasskikh." *Izvestiia RGO* 2:1-16.

Keep, John, ed. "Mutiny in Moscow, 1682: a Contemporary Account." *Canadian Slavonic Papers* 23(1981):410-442.

Khoziaistvo krupnogo feodala semnadtsatogo veka. 2 vols. Leningrad, 1933-1936.

Kholmogorov, V. and G., eds. "Istoricheskie materialy o tserkvakh i selakh XVII-XVIII st." *Chteniia v Obshchestve liubitelei dukhovnago prosveshcheniia* 1880; 1882; 1886; *ChOIDR*, 1885, no. 3, pp. 1-80;

no. 4, pp. 81-167; 1886, no. 1, pp. 1-80; no. 3, pp. 81-160; no. 4, pp. 161-229; 1888, no. 4, pp. 1-169; 1889, no. 1, pp. 1-166; 1892, no. 1, pp. i-viii, 1-244; 1896, no. 4, pp. i-vi, 1-94; 1897, no. 1, pp. 95-188; 1901, no. 1, pp. i-vii, 1-160; no. 2, pp. 161-284; 1901, no. 4, pp. i-viii, 1-122; 1911, no. 3, pp. 123-336; 1913, no. 2, pp. 337-380.

"Kniaz' Vasilii Vasil'evich Golitsyn. Pis'ma k kniaziu raznykh lits v 1677 g." *Russkaia starina* 57(1888):735-738.

"Kniaz' Vasilii Vasil'evich Golitsyn. Pis'ma k nemu Boeva, Baklanovskago i Leont'eva v 1677 g." *Russkaia starina* 63(1889):129-132.

Kotoshikhin, G. *O Rossii v tsarstvovanie Alekseia Mikhailovicha.* St. Petersburg, 1906.

Krest'ianskaia voina pod rukovodstvom Stepana Razina. 3 vols. Moscow, 1954-1962.

Kudriavtsev, I. M., ed. *Artakserksovo deistvo.* Moscow-Leningrad, 1957.

Leach, Catherine S., ed. *Memoirs of the Polish Baroque: the Writings of Jan Chryzostom Pasek, a Squire of the Commonwealth of Poland and Lithuania.* Berkeley, 1976.

Likhachev, N. P., ed. "Dokumenty o kniaz'iakh Sitskikh: II. Sudnoe votchinnoe delo stol'nika Kniazia Iuriia Andreevicha Sitskago o nasledstve posle Kniazia Petra Vladimirovicha Bakhteiarova-Rostovskago." *Izvestiia RGO* 3:222-352.

Likhachev, N. P., and Miatlev, N. V., eds. *Tysiachnaia kniga 7059-1550 goda.* Orel, 1911.

Loewenson, Leo. "The Moscow Rising of 1648." *Slavonic and East European Review* 32(1948):146-156.

Luk'ianov, G., ed. "Chastnaia perepiska Kn. Petra Ivanovicha Khovanskago, ego sem'i i rodstvennikov." *Starina i novizna* 10(1905):283-462.

Massa, I. *Kratkoe izvestie o Moskovii v nachale XVII v.* Moscow, 1937.

Materialy dlia istorii russkago dvorianstva. 3 vols. St. Petersburg, 1885.

Medvedev, Sil'vestr. "Sozertsanie kratkoe let 7190, 91 i 92, v nikh zhe chto sodeiasia vo grazhdanstve." *ChOIDR,* 1894, no. 4, pp. iii-lii, 1-198.

Miliukov, P. N., ed. *Drevneishaia razriadnaia kniga offitsial'noi redaktsii (po 1565 g.).* Moscow, 1901.

Moskovskaia delovaia i bytovaia pis'mennost' XVII veka. Moscow, 1968.

Nikol'skii, N. *Kirillo-belozerskii monastyr' i ego ustroistvo do vtoroi chetverti XVII v.* Vol. 1. St. Petersburg, 1896.

Novikov, N., ed. *Istoriia o nevinnom zatochenii blizhniago boiarina Artemona Sergeevicha Matveeva.* St. Petersburg, 1776.

Novombergskii, N., ed. *Slovo i delo gosudarevy*. Vol. 14 of *Zapiski Moskovskago Arkheologicheskago Instituta*. Moscow, 1911.

Novosel'skii, A. A., ed. *Razriadnyi prikaz (nachalo XVI v.-1711 g.). Opis'
stolbtsov dopolnitel'nogo otdela arkhivnogo fonda no. 210.* Moscow,
1950.

———. "Rospis' krest'ianskikh dvorov, nakhodivshikhsia vo vladenii
vyshego dukhovenstva, monastyrei i dumnykh liudei po perepisnym
knigam 1678 g." *Istoricheskii arkhiv* 4(1949):88-149.

"O ssylke Voina Nashchokina v Kirillov monastyr'." *ChOIDR*, 1885, no.
2, pp. 2-3.

"Opis' imushchestva boiarina Artemona Sergeevicha Matveeva." *Ch-
OIDR*, 1900, no. 2, pp. 9-21.

"Opis' vydelennomu nasledstvu Kniazhne Lykovoi posle diadi eia Streshneva." *Vremennik OIDR* 5(1850):18-26.

Palmer, W., ed. *The Patriarch and the Tsar*. 6 vols. London, 1871-1876.

*Pamiatniki russkogo narodno-razgovornogo iazyka XVII stoletiia (Iz fonda
A. I. Bezobrazova)*. Moscow, 1965.

"Pervoe votsarenie Petra Velikago." *DRV* 7:372-402.

Pervye p'esy russkogo teatra. Eds. O. A. Derzhavina, A. S. Demin, and
A. N. Robinson. Moscow, 1972.

"Piat' sgovornykh riadnykh zapisei XVII v. i nachala XVIII vv." *Ch-
OIDR*, 1901, no. 2, pp. 1-7.

Pis'ma i bumagi Imperatora Petra Velikogo. 12 vols. in 19. St. Petersburg-Petrograd, 1887-1918; Moscow-Leningrad, 1946-1977.

"Pis'ma k Kniaziu Vasil'iu Vasil'evichu Golitsynu." *Vremennik OIDR*
6(1850):36-48;   7(1850):69-76;   8(1850):51-54;   10(1851):29-56;
13(1852):25-36.

"Pis'ma K. Vasil'ia Vasil'evicha Golitsyna k dumnomu d'iaku Razriadnago
prikaza Vasil'iu Grigor'evichu Semenovu." *Vremennik OIDR* 5:11.

"Pis'mo okol'nichago Bogdana Matveevicha Khitrovo k boiarinu Borisu
Ivanovichu Morozovu (1654 goda)." *Vremennik OIDR* 1:16.

Platonov, S. F., ed. "Novyi istochnik dlia istorii moskovskikh volnenii
1648 g." *ChOIDR*, 1893, no. 1, pp. 1-19.

Popov, A. N. *Izbornik slavianskikh i russkikh sochinenii i statei, vnesen-
nykh v khronografy russkoi redaktsii*. Moscow, 1869.

Poslaniia Ivana Groznogo. Moscow-Leningrad, 1951.

"Posluzhnoi spisok starinnykh boiar i dvoretskikh, okol'nichikh i nekotorykh drugikh pridvornykh chinov s 6970 po 7184 (to est' s 1462 po
1676) god . . ." *DRV* 20:1-131.

*Povsiadnevnykh dvortsovykh vremen Gosudarei, Tsarei i Velikikh Kni-
azei Mikhaila Feodorovicha i Alekseia Mikhailovicha, zapisok*. 2 parts.
Moscow, 1769.

Prilozhenie k rodoslovnoi knige roda Khitrovo. St. Petersburg, 1867.

"Proekt ustava o sluzhebnom starshinstve boiar, okol'nichikh i dumnykh liudei po tridtsati chetyrem stepeniam, sostavlennyi pri Tsare Feodore Alekseeviche." In *Arkhiv istoriko-iuridicheskikh svedenii, otnosiashchikhsia do Rossii,* ed. N. Kachalov, bk. 1, pp. 21-44. St. Petersburg, 1876.

Pskovskie letopisi. Ed. A. N. Nasonov. Vol. 2. Moscow, 1955.

"Puteshestvie v Moskoviiu Barona Augustina Maierberga i Goratsiia Vil'gel'ma Kal'vuchchi, poslov Imperatora Leopol'da k Tsariu i Velikomu Kniaziu Alekseiu Mikhailovichu v 1661 godu." Transl. A. N. Shemiakin. *ChOIDR* 1873, no. 3, pp. i-vii, 1-104; no. 4, pp. 105-168; 1874, no. 1, pp. 169-216.

Raptschinsky, B., ed. "Bescheiden betreffende het Gezantschap van Koenraad van Klenck naar Moscovie in 1675-1676." *Bijdragen en Mededeelingen van het Historisch Genootschap* 59(1938):83-190.

Razriadnaia kniga 1475-1605. 1 vol. in 3 parts. Moscow, 1977-1978.

Razriadnaia kniga 1559-1605. Moscow, 1974.

Reitenfel's, Iakov. "Skazaniia Svetleishemu Gertsogu Toskanskomu Koz'me Tret'emu o Moskovii." Transl. A. Stankevich. *ChOIDR,* 1905, no. 3, pp. iii-x, 1-128; 1906, no. 3, pp. 129-228.

"Riadnaia zapis' Eleny Alekseevny Ziuzinoi (zheny Kniazia Dmitriia Mamstriukovicha Cherkasskago)." *Izvestiia RGO* 3:97-99.

"Riadnaia zapis' o zhenit'be Kniazhny Solomonidy Semenovny Tatevoi i Kniazia Iuriia Andreevicha Zvenigorodskago, 1626 g." *LIRO* 25-26(1911):25-27.

Roginskii, Z. I. *Poezdka gontsa Gerasima Semenovicha Dokhturova v Angliiu v 1645-1646 gg.* Iaroslavl', 1959.

"Rospis' vsiakim veshcham, den'gam i zapasam, chto ostalos' po smerti boiarina Nikity Ivanovicha Romanova i dachi po nem na pomni dushi." *ChOIDR,* 1887, no. 3, pp. 1-128.

Rozhdestvenskii, S. V. "Rospis' zemel'nykh vladenii moskovskago boiarstva 1647-8 goda." *Drevnosti. Trudy Arkheograficheskoi komissii Imp. arkheologicheskago obshchestva* 3(1913):193-238.

Rozysknyia dela o Fedore Shaklovitom i ego soobshchnikakh. 4 vols. St. Petersburg, 1884-1893.

Ruskii vremianik sirech' letopisets, soderzhashchii rossiiskuiu istoriiu ot 6370 (862) do 7189 (1681) leta, razdelennyi na dve chasti. 2 vols. in 1. Moscow, 1820.

Russkii istoricheskii sbornik. 7 vols. Moscow, 1837-1844.

Sbornik gramot Kollegii ekonomii. 2 vols. Petrograd-Leningrad, 1922-1929.

Sbornik kniazia Khilkova. St. Petersburg, 1879.

Shchukin, P. I. *Sbornik starinnykh bumag, khraniashchikhsia v Muzee P. I. Shchukina.* 10 vols. Moscow, 1896-1902.

Shusherin, I. *Zhitie Sviateishago Patriarkha Nikona.* St. Petersburg, 1817.

Sinbirskii sbornik. Vol. 1. Moscow, 1844.

Smirnov, M. I. "Feodal'nye vladeniia pereslavskikh i inogorodnykh monastyrei v Pereslavl'-Zalesskom uezde XIV-XVIII st." In *Proshloe pereslavskoi derevni.* Vol. 12 of *Trudy Pereslavl'-Zalesskogo istoriko-khudozhestvennogo i kraevednogo muzeia.* Pereslavl'-Zalesskii, 1929.

Smirnov, P. P., ed. "Chelobitnye dvorian i detei boiarskikh vsekh gorodov v pervoi polovine XVII v." *ChOIDR,* 1915, no. 3, pp. 1-73.

"Sobstvennoruchnoe pis'mo dumnago razriadnago d'iaka Vasil'ia Grigor'-evicha Semenova k kniaziu Vasil'iu Vasil'evichu Golitsynu." *Vremennik OIDR* 4:65-66.

Spisok pogrebennykh v Troitskoi sergievoi lavre ot osnovaniia onoi do 1880 goda. Moscow, 1880.

Storozhev, V. N. "Materialy dlia istorii russkago dvorianstva." *ChOIDR,* 1909, no. 3, pp. 1-222.

Struminsky, Bohdan; Rowland, Daniel; and Kasinec, Edward. "Two Seventeenth-Century Russian Charters in the Newberry Library, Chicago." *Slavonic and East European Studies* 60(1982):591-611.

"Tainoe pis'mo Af. Ordina-Nashchokina Tsariu Alekseiu Mikhailovichu." *ChOIDR,* 1896, no. 4, pp. 6-7.

Theiner, A., ed. *Documents historiques relatifs aux règnes d'Alexis Michaélowitch, Féodor III et Pierre le Grand, Czars de Russie.* Rome, 1859.

Tikhomirov, M. N. "Zametki zemskogo d'iachka vtoroi poloviny XVII v." *Istoricheskii arkhiv* 2(1939):93-100.

Titov, A. A., ed. *Letopis' dvinskaia.* Moscow, 1889.

Ulfeldt, Jacob. *Hodoeporicon Ruthenicum.* Frankfurt, 1608.

Uroff, Benjamin Philip. "Grigorii Karpovich Kotoshikhin. On Russia in the Reign of Alexis Mikhailovich. An Annotated Translation." 2 vols. Ph.D. dissertation, Columbia University, 1970.

"Utverzhdennaia gramota ob izbranii na moskovskoe gosudarstvo Mikhaila Fedorovicha Romanova." *ChOIDR,* 1906, no. 3, pp. 1-110.

Vkladnaia kniga moskovskago Novospasskago monastyria. Vol. 39 of *Pamiatniki drevnei pis'mennosti i iskusstva.* St. Petersburg, 1883.

Vkladnaia kniga nizhegorodskago Pecherskago monastyria. Ed. A. A. Titov. Moscow, 1898.

Vkladnyia i kormovyia knigi rostovskago Borisoglebskago monastyria v XV, XVI, XVII i XVIII stoletiiakh. Ed. A. A. Titov. Iaroslavl', 1881.

Vodarskii, Ia. E., and Pavlenko, P. P., eds. "Svodnye dannye 1678 g. o

kolichestve podatnykh dvorov po perepisi v evropeiskoi Rossii."
Sovetskie arkhivy, 1971, no. 6, pp. 64-88.

Vosstanie v Moskve 1682 goda. Sbornik dokumentov. Moscow, 1976.

Zabelin, I., ed. "Knigi vo ves' god v stol estvy podavat' (Dopolnenie k
Domostroiu blagoveshchenskago popa Sil'vestra)." *Vremennik OIDR*
6(1850):i-vi, 7-44.

──────. "Svedeniia o podlinnom Ulozhenii Tsaria Alekseia Mikhailovicha." *Arkhiv istoriko-iuridicheskikh svedenii, otnosiashchikhsia do
Rossii*, bk. 1, pp. 4-14.

*Zapiski Otdeleniia russkoi i slavianskoi arkheologii Imperatorskago rus-
skago arkheologicheskago obshchestva*. Vol. 2. St. Petersburg, 1861.

Zapiski russkikh liudei. Sobytiia vremen Petra Velikago. St. Petersburg,
1841.

"Zapiski de-la Nevilla o Moskovii, 1689 g." Transl. A. I. Braudo. *Russkaia starina* 71:419-450; 72:241-281.

"Zapisnyia knigi moskovskago stola." *RIB* 9:385-576.

"Zapisnyia knigi moskovskago stola 1636-1663 g." Vols. 10 and 11 of *RIB*.

Zertsalov, A., ed. "K istorii moskovskago miatezha 1648 g." *ChOIDR*,
1893, no. 3, pp. 1-12.

──────. "O miatezhakh v gorode Moskve i v sele Kolomenskom 1648,
1662 i 1771 gg." *ChOIDR*, 1890, no. 3, pp. 1-440.

Zheliabuzhskii, I. A. *Zapiski Zheliabuzhskago s 1682 po 2 iiulia 1709*.
St. Petersburg, 1840.

"Zhiletskoe zemlevladenie v 1632 godu." Vols. 31 and 32 of *LIRO*.

Genealogy

Barsukov, A. V. *Rod Sheremetevykh*. 8 vols. St. Petersburg, 1881-1904.

──────. *Rodoslovie Sheremetevykh*. St. Petersburg, 1904.

Bode-Kolychev, M. L. *Boiarskii rod Kolychevykh*. Moscow, 1886.

Brandenburg, N. E. *Rod kniazei Mosal'skikh (XIV-XIX st.)*. St. Petersburg, 1892.

Bychkova, M. E. *Rodoslovnye knigi XVI-XVII vv*. Moscow, 1975.

Chelishchev, N. A. *Sbornik materialov dlia istorii roda Chelishchevykh*.
St. Petersburg, 1893.

Chernopiatov, V. I. *Rod Ladyzhenskikh*. Moscow, n.d.

Dolgorukov, P. V. *Rossiiskaia rodoslovnaia kniga*. 4 vols. St. Petersburg, 1854-1857.

──────. *Skazaniia o rode kniazei Dolgorukovykh*. St. Petersburg, 1840.

Dolgorukov, V., ed. *Dolgorukovy i Dolgorukie-Argushinskie*. St. Petersburg, 1869.

El'chaninov, I. N. *Materialy dlia genealogii Iaroslavskogo dvorianstva.* 2 vols. Iaroslavl', 1913.

Golitsyn, N. N. *Materialy dlia polnoi rodoslovnoi rospisi kniazei Golitsynykh.* Kiev, 1880.

―――. *Rod kniazei Golitsynykh.* St. Petersburg, 1892.

Iablochkov, M. T. *Dvorianskoe soslovie Tul'skoi gubernii.* Vols. 7-9. Tula, 1904.

Ikonnikov, N. F. *NdR, la noblesse de Russie.* 2nd. ed. 25 vols. Paris, 1957-1966.

"Iz sobraniia aktov kniazei Khovanskikh." *ChOIDR,* 1913, no. 4, pp. 20-39.

K. B. *Opyt istoricheskago rodosloviia Izmailovykh.* St. Petersburg, 1841.

Kashkin, N. N. *Rodoslovnye razvedki.* 2 vols. St. Petersburg, 1912-1913.

Kazanskii, P. *Rodoslovnaia Golovinykh, vladel'tsev sela Novospasskago.* Moscow, 1847.

Kobeko, D. F. *Rodoslovnyia zametki o nekotorykh deiateliakh Smutnago vremeni.* St. Petersburg, 1908.

―――. *Sheremetevy i kniaz'ia Urusovy.* St. Petersburg, 1900.

Leont'ev, D. N. *Materialy dlia rodosloviia dvorian Leont'evykh i Petrovo-Solovykh.* Kazan', 1881.

Likhachev, N. P. *Genealogicheskaia istoriia odnoi pomeshchich'ei biblioteki.* St. Petersburg, 1913.

―――. *Novoe rodoslovie kniazei Golitsynykh.* St. Petersburg, 1893.

―――. "Rodstvennyia sviazi kniazheskikh familii s sem'iami d'iakov." *Izvestiia RGO* 1:114-119.

Liubimov, S. *Opyt istoricheskikh rodoslovii.* Petrograd, 1915.

Lobanov-Rostovskii, A. B. *Russkaia rodoslovnaia kniga.* 2 vols. St. Petersburg, 1895.

Miatlev, N. "K rodosloviiu kniazei Mstislavskikh." In *Sbornik statei posviashchennykh L. M. Savelovu,* pp. 300-317. Moscow, 1915.

―――. "Rodoslovnyia zametki." *LIRO* 25-26(1911):3-16.

Miatlev, N. and Kobeko, D. "O pervoi zhene boiarina Gleba Morozova." *Izvestiia RGO* 2:85-88.

Miller, F. I. *Izvestie o dvorianakh rossiiskikh.* St. Petersburg, 1790.

Novitskii, V. I. *Vybornoe i bol'shoe dvorianstvo XVI-XVII vekov.* Kiev, 1915.

Novye rodoslovnye knigi XVI v. Vol. 2 of *Redkie istochniki po istorii Rossii.* Moscow, 1977.

Obshchii gerbovnik dvorianskikh rodov Vserossiiskoi imperii. 10 vols. St. Petersburg, 1797-1836.

Opyt istoricheskago rodosloviia dvorian i grafov Matiushkinykh. St. Petersburg, 1841.

Petrov, P. N. *Istoriia rodov russkago dvorianstva.* St. Petersburg, 1886.

Pleshko, N. D. *Kniaz'ia Obolenskie, rodoslovie.* New York, 1959.

Popov, P. N., ed. *Istoriia rodov russkago dvorianstva.* Vol. 1. St. Petersburg, 1886.

Raevskii, P. M. *Rod tsaria, tsareven i kniazei Shuiskikh.* Paris, 1957.

Rodoslovnaia kniga roda Khitrovo. Vol. 1. St. Petersburg, 1866.

"Rodoslovnaia kniga velikogo rossiiskago gosudarstva velikikh kniazei . . ." *Vremennik OIDR* 10(1851):i-viii, 1-286.

Rummel', V. V., and Golubtsov, V. V. *Rodoslovnyi sbornik russkikh dvorianskikh familii.* 2 vols. St. Petersburg, 1886-1887.

Savelov, D. "Vekovaia nespravedlivost'." In *Sbornik statei posviashchennykh L. M. Savelovu,* pp. 81-94. Moscow, 1915.

Savelov, L. M. "Kniazia Pozharskie." *LIRO* 6-7(1906):1-88.

──────. *Kniazia Shcherbatovy po Beloozeru v XVII veke.* n.p., n.d.

──────. *Lektsii po russkoi genealogii.* Moscow, 1908.

──────. *Materialy dlia istorii roda dvorian Savelovykh.* 2 vols. Moscow, 1894-1896.

──────. *Opyt rodoslovnago slovaria russkago drevniago dvorianstva. Rodoslovnye zapisi.* 3 vols. Moscow, 1906-1909.

──────. *Rod dvorian Savelovykh.* Moscow, 1895.

──────. *Russkoe drevnee dvorianstvo. Materialy dlia rodoslovnago slovaria.* Athens, 1933.

──────. "Savelkovy i Savelovy XV-XX vv.: rodoslovie." *LIRO* 37-38 (1914):appendix.

Semevskii, M. I. *Russkaia rodoslovnaia kniga.* 2 vols. St. Petersburg, 1873-1878.

Serchevskii, S. *Zapiski o rode kniazei Golitsynykh.* St. Petersburg, 1853.

Sheremetev, P. "O kniaz'iakh Khovanskikh." *LIRO* 13-14(1908):3-164.

Tatishchev, S. S. *Rod Tatishchevykh. 1400-1900.* St. Petersburg, 1900.

Trubetskaia, E. E. *Skazaniia o rode kniazei Trubetskikh.* Moscow, 1891.

Vlas'ev, G. A. *Potomstvo Riurika.* 2 vols. in 4. St. Petersburg-Petrograd, 1906-1918.

──────. *Rod dvorian Glebovykh.* Moscow, 1911.

Volkonskaia, E. G. *Rod kniazei Volkonskikh.* St. Petersburg, 1900.

Zapiski o rodie kniazei Golitsynykh. St. Petersburg, 1853.

Monographs

Abramovich, G. V. *Pomestnaia sistema i pomestnoe khoziaistvo v Rossii v poslednei chetverti XV i v XVI v.* (Abstract of a doctoral dissertation). Leningrad, 1975.

Absoliutizm v Rossii, XVII-XVIII vv. Ed. N. M. Druzhinin. Moscow, 1964.

Anderson, Perry. *Lineages of the Absolutist State.* London, 1974.

Andreevskii, I. *O namestnikakh, voevodakh i gubernatorakh.* St. Petersburg, 1864.

Anikst, M. A., and Turchin, V. S. *V okrestnostiakh Moskvy. Iz istorii russkoi usadebnoi kul'tury XVII-XIX vekov.* Moscow, 1979.

Aristov, N. *Moskovskie smuty v pravlenie Tsarevny Sofii Alekseevny.* Warsaw, 1871.

Aston, Trevor, ed. *Crisis in Europe 1560-1660.* Garden City, N.Y., 1967.

Avrich, Paul. *Russian Rebels 1600-1800.* New York, 1972.

Bakhrushin, S. V. *Nauchnye trudy.* 4 vols. in 5. Moscow, 1952-1959.

Bantysh-Kamenskii, N. I. *Obzor vneshnikh snoshenii Rossii (po 1800 god).* 4 vols. Moscow, 1894-1902.

Barsukov, A. V. *Spiski gorodovykh voevod i drugikh lits voevodskago upravleniia moskovskago gosudarstva XVII stoletiia.* St. Petersburg, 1902.

Bazilevich, K. V. *Denezhnaia reforma Alekseia Mikhailovicha i vosstanie v Moskve v 1662 g.* Moscow-Leningrad, 1936.

Belokurov, S. A. *O biblioteke moskovskikh gosudarei v XVI veke.* Moscow, 1898.

———. "O Posol'skom prikaze." *ChOIDR,* 1906, no. 3, pp. 1-170.

———. *Snosheniia Rossii s Kavkazom.* Vol. 1 (1578-1613). Moscow, 1889.

Berkh, V. *Tsarstvovanie Tsaria Feodora Alekseevicha.* 2 parts. St. Petersburg, 1835.

Bitton, Davis. *The French Nobility in Crisis, 1560-1640.* Stanford, 1969.

Blum, Jerome. *Lord and Peasant in Russia from the Ninth to the Nineteenth Century.* Princeton, 1961.

Bogoiavlenskii, S. K. *Nauchnoe nasledie. O Moskve XVII veka.* Moscow, 1980.

———. *Prikaznye sud'i XVII veka.* Moscow-Leningrad, 1946.

Bogoslovskii, M. M. *Petr I. Materialy dlia biografii.* 5 vols. Moscow, 1940-1948.

Brown, Peter Bowman. "Early Modern Bureaucracy: the Evolution of the Chancellery System from Ivan III to Peter the Great, 1478-1717." Ph.D. dissertation, University of Chicago, 1978.

Buganov, V. I. *Moskovskoe vosstanie 1662 g.* Moscow, 1964.

———. *Moskovskie vosstaniia kontsa XVII v.* Moscow, 1969.

———. "Razriadnye knigi poslednei chetverti XV-1-oi poloviny XVII vv. kak istoricheskii istochnik." Candidate's dissertation, Moskovskii gosudarstvennyi istoriko-arkhivnyi institut, 1954.

Buganov, V. I. *Razriadnye knigi poslednei chetverti XV-nachala XVII v.* Moscow, 1962.

Bushkovitch, Paul. *The Merchants of Moscow, 1580-1650.* New York, 1980.

Chaussinand-Nogaret, Guy. *La noblesse au XVIII siècle: de la feodalité aux lumières.* Paris, 1976.

Chernov, A. V. *Vooruzhennye sily russkogo gosudarstva v XVI-XVII vv.* Moscow, 1954.

Chernykh, P. Ia. *Iazyk Ulozheniia 1649 goda.* Moscow, 1953.

Chicherin, B. N. *Oblastnyia uchrezhdeniia Rossii v XVII veke.* Moscow, 1856.

Chistiakova, E. V. *Sotsial'no-ekonomicheskie vzgliady A. L. Ordin-Nashchokina.* Voronezh, 1950.

Confino, Michael. *Domaines et seigneurs en Russie vers la fin du XVIIIe siècle.* Paris, 1963.

Crummey, Robert O. *The Old Believers and the World of Antichrist: the Vyg Community and the Russian State, 1694-1855.* Madison, Milwaukee and London, 1970.

Czapliński, Władysław and Długosz, Józef. *Życie codzienne magnaterii polskiej w XVII wieku.* Warsaw, 1976.

D'iakonov, M. A. *Ocherki obshchestvennago i gosudarstvennago stroia drevnei Rusi.* St. Petersburg, 1908.

Dvorianstvo i krepostnoi stroi Rossii XVI-XVIII vv.: Sbornik statei posviashchennyi pamiati Alekseia Andreevicha Novosel'skogo. Ed. N. I. Pavlenko. Moscow, 1975.

Eisenstadt, S. N. *The Political System of Empires.* New York, 1969.

Elias, Norbert. *Die höfische Gesellschaft.* Neuwied and Berlin, 1969.

El'iashevich, V. B. *Istoriia prava pozemel'noi sobstvennosti v Rossii.* 2 vols. Paris, 1948-1951.

Ellersieck, Heinz E. "Russia under Aleksei Mikhailovich and Feodor Alekseevich, 1645-1682: the Scandinavian Sources." Ph.D. dissertation, UCLA, 1955.

Eroshkin, N. P. *Istoriia gosudarstvennykh uchrezhdenii dorevoliutsionnoi Rossii.* Moscow, 1968.

Galaktionov, I. V., and Chistiakova, E. V. *A. L. Ordin-Nashchokin, russkii diplomat XVII v.* Moscow, 1961.

Gibbenet, N. *Istoricheskoe izsledovanie dela Patriarkha Nikona.* 2 vols. St. Petersburg, 1882-1884.

Giesztor, Aleksander; Kieniewicz, Stefan; Rostworowski, Emanuel; Tazbir, Janusz; and Wereszycki, Henryk. *History of Poland.* 2nd. ed. Warsaw, 1979.

Gorskii, A. V. *Istoricheskoe opisanie Sviato-troitskiia sergievy lavry.* Moscow, 1890.

Got'e, Iu. V. *Zamoskovnyi krai v XVII veke.* Moscow, 1937.

Goubert, Pierre. *The Ancien Regime: French Society, 1600-1750.* New York, 1974.

Grabar', I. *O russkoi arkhitekture.* Moscow, 1969.

Gradovskii, A. D. *Istoriia mestnago upravleniia v Rossii.* Vol. 2 of *Sobranie sochinenii.* 9 vols. St. Petersburg, 1899-1904.

Gurliand, I. Ia. *Prikaz velikago gosudaria tainykh del.* Iaroslavl', 1902.

Heers, Jacques. *Family Clans in the Middle Ages.* Amsterdam, New York, Oxford, 1977.

Hellie, Richard. *Enserfment and Military Change in Muscovy.* Chicago and London, 1971.

Hintze, Otto. *The Historical Essays of Otto Hintze.* Ed. Felix Gilbert. New York, 1975.

Ho, Ping-ti. *The Ladder of Success in Imperial China: Aspects of Social Mobility, 1368-1911.* New York, 1962.

Iakinf, Arkhimandrit. *Kratkoe istoricheskoe opisanie moskovskago stavropigal'nago pervoklasnago Novospaskago [sic] monastyria . . .* Moscow, 1802.

Iakovlev, A. *Kholopstvo i kholopy v moskovskom gosudarstve XVII v.* Vol. 1. Moscow-Leningrad, 1943.

———. *Prikaz sbora ratnykh liudei.* Vol. 46 of *Uchenyia zapiski Moskovskago universiteta. Otdel istoriko-filologicheskii.* Moscow, 1917.

Il'in, M. A. *Podmoskov'e.* Moscow, 1965.

Ilovaiskii, D. I. *Istoriia Rossii.* 5 vols. in 6. Moscow, 1876-1905.

Inalcik, Halil. *The Ottoman Empire. The Classical Age, 1300-1600.* London, 1973.

Istoricheskoe opisanie moskovskago Spaso-Andronikova monastyria. Moscow, 1865.

Istoriia Moskvy. 6 vols. in 7. Moscow, 1952-1959.

Istoriia russkogo iskusstva. Ed. I. E. Grabar' et al. 13 vols. in 16. Moscow, 1953-1969.

Kamentseva, E. I., and Ustiugov, N. V. *Russkaia metrologiia.* Moscow, 1965.

Kann, Robert A. *The Problem of Restoration: a Study in Comparative Political History.* Berkeley and Los Angeles, 1968.

Kapterev, N. F. *Kharakter otnoshenii Rossii k pravoslavnomu vostoku v XVI i XVII stoletiiakh.* Sergiev Posad, 1914.

———. *Patriarkh Nikon i Tsar' Aleksei Mikhailovich.* 2 vols. Sergiev Posad, 1909-1912.

Keenan, Edward L. *The Kurbskii-Groznyi Apocrypha: the Seventeenth-*

Century Genesis of the "Correspondence" Attributed to Prince A. M. Kurbskii and Tsar Ivan IV. Cambridge, Mass., 1971.

Keesing, Roger M. *Kin Groups and Social Structure.* New York, 1975.

Kent, Francis William. *Household and Lineage in Renaissance Florence.* Princeton, 1977.

Keohane, Nannerl O. *Philosophy and the State in France: the Renaissance to the Enlightenment.* Princeton, 1980.

Kharlampovich, K. V. *Malorossiiskoe vliianie na velikorusskuiu tserkovnuiu zhizn'.* Vol. 1. Kazan', 1914.

Kliuchevskii, V. O. *Boiarskaia duma drevnei Rusi.* Moscow, 1909.

———. *A Course in Russian History: the Seventeenth Century.* Chicago, 1968.

———. *Sochineniia.* 8 vols. Moscow, 1956-1959.

Kopreeva, T. N. *Russko-pol'skie otnosheniia vo vtoroi polovine XVII veka* (Dissertation abstract). Leningrad, 1952.

Kozlovskii, I. *F. M. Rtishchev.* Kiev, 1906.

Lantzeff, G. V. *Siberia in the Seventeenth Century.* Berkeley and Los Angeles, 1943.

Laslett, Peter, ed. *Household and Family in Past Time.* Cambridge, 1972.

Leonid, Arkhimandrit. *Istoricheskoe opisanie meshchevskago Georgievskago muzhskago obshchezhitel'nago monastyria.* Moscow, 1870.

Likhachev, N. P. *Razriadnye d'iaki XVI veka.* St. Petersburg, 1888.

Liubomirov, P. G. *Ocherk istorii Nizhegorodskogo opolcheniia.* Moscow, 1939.

Luppov, S. P. *Kniga v Rossii v XVII veke.* Leningrad, 1970.

Lyashchenko, P. I. *History of the National Economy of Russia to the 1917 Revolution.* New York, 1949.

Mal'tsev, A. N. *Rossiia i Belorussiia v seredine XVII veka.* Moscow, 1974.

Markevich, A. I. *Istoriia mestnichestva v moskovskom gosudarstve v XV-XVII v.* Odessa, 1888.

———. *O mestnichestve. Russkaia istoriografiia v otnoshenii k mestnichestvu.* Kiev, 1879.

Mattingly, Garrett. *Renaissance Diplomacy.* Baltimore, 1955.

Meehan-Waters, Brenda. *Autocracy and Aristocracy: the Russian Service Elite of 1730.* New Brunswick, N.J., 1982.

Miliukov, P. N. *Gosudarstvennoe khoziaistvo Rossii v pervoi chetverti XVIII stoletiia i reforma Petra Velikago.* St. Petersburg, 1892.

———. *Ocherki po istorii russkoi kul'tury.* 3 vols. Paris, 1930-1937.

Mills, C. Wright. *The Power Elite.* New York, 1956.

Novosel'skii, A. A. *Bor'ba moskovskogo gosudarstva s tatarami v pervoi polovine XVII veka.* Moscow-Leningrad, 1948.

————. *Votchinnik i ego khoziaistvo v XVII veke.* Moscow-Leningrad, 1929.

O'Brien, C. Bickford. *Russia under Two Tsars, 1682-1689: the Regency of Sophia Alekseevna.* Berkeley and Los Angeles, 1952.

Ocherkii istorii SSSR. Period feodalizma. XVII v. Moscow, 1955.

Ocherki russkoi kul'tury XVII veka. 2 parts. Moscow, 1979.

Ovchinnikova, E. S. *Portret v russkom iskusstve XVII veka.* Moscow, 1955.

Passek, V. V. *Istoricheskoe opisanie moskovskago Simonova monastyria.* Moscow, 1843.

Pavlov-Sil'vanskii, N. P. *Sochineniia.* 3 vols. St. Petersburg, 1909-1910.

Petrikeev, D. I. *Krupnoe krepostnoe khoziaistvo XVII v.* Leningrad, 1967.

Platonov, S. F. *Moskva i zapad.* Berlin, 1926. In English, *Moscow and the West.* Transl. Joseph L. Wieczynski. Hattiesburg, Miss., 1972.

————. *Ocherki po istorii Smuty v moskovskom gosudarstve XVI-XVII vv.* St. Petersburg, 1910.

————. *Smutnoe vremia.* Prague, 1924. In English, *The Time of Troubles.* Transl. J. T. Alexander. Lawrence, Kansas, 1970.

Pogodin, M. P. *Semnadtsat' pervykh let v zhizni Imperatora Petra Velikago, 1672-1689.* Moscow, 1875.

Pushkarev, Sergei G. *Dictionary of Russian Historical Terms from the Eleventh Century to 1917.* New Haven and London, 1970.

Ransel, David L. *The Politics of Catherinian Russia: the Panin Party.* New Haven, 1975.

Rabinovich, M. G. *O drevnei Moskve.* Moscow, 1964.

Robinson, A. N. *Bor'ba idei v russkoi literature XVII veka.* Moscow, 1974.

————. *Novye cherti v russkoi literature i iskusstve (XVII-nachalo XVIII v.).* Moscow, 1976.

Rozhdestvenskii, S. V. *Sluzhiloe zemlevladenie v moskovskom gosudarstve XVII veka.* St. Petersburg, 1897.

Russkoe gosudarstvo v XVII veke. Moscow, 1961.

Sakharov, L. *Istoricheskoe opisanie suzdal'skago pervoklassnago Spaso-Evfimieva monastyria.* Vladimir, 1878.

Savva, V. *Moskovskie tsari i vizantiiskie vasilevsy.* Kharkov, 1901.

Selifontov, N. N. *Ocherk sluzhebnoi deiatel'nosti i domashnei zhizni stol'nika i voevody XVII stoletiia, Vasiliia Aleksandrovicha Daudova.* St. Petersburg, 1871.

Sergeevich, V. I. *Drevnosti russkago prava.* 3 vols. St. Petersburg, 1903-1909.

Sergeevich, V. I. *Lektsii i izsledovaniia po drevnei istorii russkago prava.* St. Petersburg, 1899.

Shaw, S. J. *Between Old and New: the Ottoman Empire under Sultan Selim III, 1789-1807.* Cambridge, Mass., 1971.

Shchepot'ev, L. *Blizhnii boiarin Artamon Sergeevich Matveev kak kul'turnyi politicheskii deiatel' XVII veka.* St. Petersburg, 1906.

Shields Kollmann, Nancy. "Kinship and Politics: the Origin and Evolution of the Muscovite Boyar Elite in the Fifteenth Century." Ph.D. dissertation, Harvard University, 1980.

Shtraukh, A. *Streletskii bunt 1682 g.* Fasc. 1 of *Nauchnye trudy Industrial'no-pedagogicheskii institut imeni K. Libknekhta. Seriia sotsial'no-ekonomicheskaia.* Moscow, 1928.

Shmidt, S. O. *Stanovlenie rossiiskogo samoderzhavstva.* Moscow, 1973.

Skrynnikov, R. G. *Ivan Groznyi.* Moscow, 1975.

———. *Nachalo oprichniny.* Leningrad, 1966.

———. *Oprichnyi terror.* Leningrad, 1969.

Slukhovskii, M. I. *Bibliotechnoe delo v Rossii do XVIII veka.* Moscow, 1968.

Smirnov, N. A. *Rossiia i Turtsiia v XVI-XVII vv.* Vol. 94 of *Uchenye zapiski MGU.* Moscow, 1946.

Smirnov, P. P. *Posadskie liudi i ikh klassovaia bor'ba do serediny XVII veka.* 2 vols. Moscow-Leningrad, 1947-1948.

———. *Pravitel'stvo B. I. Morozova i vosstanie v Moskve 1648 g.* Fasc. 2 of series 3 of *Trudy Sredne-aziatskogo gosudarstvennogo universiteta.* Tashkent, 1929.

Smith, R.E.F. *Peasant Farming in Muscovy.* Cambridge, 1977.

Sobolevskii, A. I. *Obrazovannost' moskovskoi Rusi XIV-XVII vekov.* St. Petersburg, 1892.

Sofronenko, K. A. *Malorossiiskii prikaz russkogo gosudarstva vtoroi poloviny XVII i nachala XVIII veka.* Moscow, 1962.

Solov'ev, S. M. *Istoriia otnoshenii mezhdu russkimi kniaz'iami riurikova doma.* Moscow, 1847.

———. *Istoriia Rossii s drevneishikh vremen.* 29 vols. in 15 books. Moscow, 1959-1966.

Stashevskii, E. D. *K istorii kolonizatsii iuga.* Moscow, 1913.

———. *Ocherki po istorii tsarstvovaniia Mikhaila Fedorovicha.* Vol. 1. Kiev, 1913.

———. *Zemlevladenie moskovskago dvorianstva v pervoi polovine XVII veka.* Moscow, 1911.

Stone, Lawrence. *The Crisis of the Aristocracy 1558-1641.* London, Oxford, New York, 1967.

Stepanov, I. V. *Krest'ianskaia voina v Rossii v 1670-1671 gg*. Leningrad, 1966.

Stroev, P. *Spiski ierarkhov i nastoiatelei monastyrei rossiiskoi tserkvi*. St. Petersburg, 1877.

Suvorin, A. *Razskaz iz russkoi istorii: boiarin Matveev*. Moscow, 1864.

Tazbir, Janusz, ed. *Polska XVII wieku. Państwo, społeczeństwo, kultura*. Warsaw, 1969.

Tereshchenko, A. *Opyt obozreniia zhizni sanovnikov, upravliavshikh inostrannymi delami v Rossii*. Part 1. St. Petersburg, 1837.

Tikhomirov, M. N. *Pskovskoe vosstanie 1650. Iz istorii klassovoi bor'by v russkom gorode XVII v*. Moscow-Leningrad, 1935.

Tikhonov, Iu. A. *Pomeshchich'i krest'iane v Rossii*. Moscow, 1974.

Torke, Hans-Joachim. *Die Staatsbedingte Gesellschaft im Moskauer Reich*. Leiden, 1974.

Treasures from the Kremlin. New York, 1979. Catalogue of an exhibition from the State Museums of the Moscow Kremlin at the Metropolitan Museum of Art, New York, May 19-September 2, 1979 and the Grand Palais, Paris, October 12, 1979-January 7, 1980.

Trevor-Roper, H. R. *The Gentry, 1540-1640. Economic History Review Supplements*. No. 1. Cambridge, n.d.

Ustrialov, N. *Istoriia tsarstvovaniia Petra Velikago*. 5 vols. in 6. St. Petersburg, 1858-1863.

Veselovskii, S. B. *D'iaki i pod'iachie XV-XVII vv*. Moscow, 1975.

———. *Feodal'noe zemlevladenie v severo-vostochnoi Rusi*. Vol. 1. Moscow-Leningrad, 1947.

———. *Issledovaniia po istorii klassa sluzhilykh zemlevladel'tsev*. Moscow, 1969.

———. *Issledovaniia po istorii oprichniny*. Moscow, 1963.

———. *Soshnoe pis'mo*. 2 vols. Moscow, 1915-1916.

Wójcik, Zbigniew. *Traktat andruszowski 1667 roku i jego geneza*. Warsaw, 1959.

Wyczański, Andrzej. *Studia nad folwarkiem szlacheckim w Polsce w latach 1500-1580*. Warsaw, 1960.

Yanov, Alexander. *The Origins of Autocracy: Ivan the Terrible in Russian History*. Berkeley, Los Angeles and London, 1981.

Zabelin, I. *Domashnii byt russkikh tsarei v XVI i XVII st*. Moscow, 1895.

———. *Domashnii byt russkikh tsarits v XVI i XVII st*. Moscow, 1869.

Zagoskin, N. P. *Istoriia prava moskovskago gosudarstva*. 2 vols. Kazan', 1877-1879.

Zamyslovskii, E. *Tsarstvovanie Fedora Alekseevicha*. Part 1. St. Petersburg, 1871.

Zaozerskii, A. I. *Tsar' Aleksei Mikhailovich v svoem khoziaistve*. Vol. 135 of *Zapiski Istoriko-filologicheskago fakul'teta Imperatorskago petrogradskago universiteta*. Petrograd, 1917.

————. *Tsarskaia votchina XVII v*. Moscow, 1937.

Zenkovsky, Serge A. *Russkoe staroobriadchestvo. Dukhovnye dvizheniia semnadtsatogo veka*. Munich, 1970.

Zimin, A. A. *Oprichnina Ivana Groznogo*. Moscow, 1964.

————. *Reformy Ivana Groznogo*. Moscow, 1960.

Articles

Alef, Gustave. "The Crisis of the Muscovite Aristocracy: a Factor in the Growth of Monarchical Power." *FzOG* 15(1970):15-58.

————. "Das Erlöschen des Abzugsrechts der Moskauer Bojaren." *FzOG* 10(1965):7-74.

————. "Reflections on the Boiar Duma in the Reign of Ivan III." *Slavonic and East European Review* 45(1967):76-123.

Arsen'ev, Iu. "Blizhnii boiarin kniaz' Nikita Ivanovich Odoevskoi i ego perepiska s galitskoiu votchinoi (1650-1684)." *ChOIDR*, 1903, no. 2, pp. 3-129.

Arsen'ev, K. I. "Vyshiia pravitel'stvennyia litsa vremen Tsaria Mikhaila Feodorovicha." In *Uchenyia zapiski Vtorago otdeleniia Imperatorskoi akademii nauk*, bk. 4, pp. 1-40. St. Petersburg, 1858.

Arsen'ev, V. "Votchiny boiar Romanovykh v Aleksinskom uezde Tul'skoi gubernii." *LIRO* 37-38:20-22.

Bakanov, P. F. "Tovarnoe proizvodstvo v feodal'noi votchine XVII veka." *Voprosy istorii*, 1953, no. 5, pp. 94-102.

Bakhrushin, S. V. "Moskovskoe vosstanie 1648 g." In *Nauchnye trudy*, vol. 2, pp. 46-91. Moscow, 1954.

Baron, Samuel H. "Who were the *Gosti*?" *California Slavic Studies* 7(1973):1-40.

Belov, E. A. "Moskovskie smuty v kontse XVII veka." *ZhMNP*, 1887, no. 1, pp. 99-146; no. 2, pp. 319-366.

Bogoiavlenskii, S. K. "Khovanshchina." *Istoricheskie zapiski* 10(1941):180-221.

————. "Raspravnaia palata pri Boiarskoi dumy." In *Sbornik statei, posviashchennykh V. O. Kliuchevskomu*, pp. 409-426. Moscow, 1909.

Brückner, A. "Fürst W. W. Golizyn (1643-1714)." In *Beiträge zur Kulturgeschichte Russlands im XVII Jahrhundert*, pp. 279-354. Leipzig, 1887.

Buganov, V. I. " "Dvortsovye razriady" pervoi poloviny XVII v." In *Arkheograficheskii ezhegodnik za 1975 god*, pp. 252-258. Moscow, 1976.

————. " "Kantsler" predpetrovskoi pory." *Voprosy istorii*, 1971, no. 10, pp. 144-156.

————. " "Vrazhdotvornoe" mestnichestvo." *Voprosy istorii*, 1974, no. 11, pp. 118-133.

————. "Zapiski sovremennika o moskovskikh vosstaniiakh 1648 i 1662 godov." In *Arkheograficheskii ezhegodnik za 1958 g.*, pp. 99-114. Moscow, 1960.

Bychkova, M. E. "Iz istorii sozdaniia rodoslovnykh rospisei kontsa XVII v. i Barkhatnoi knigi." *Vspomogatel'nye istoricheskie distsipliny* 12(1981):90-109.

Chaianov, A. "Sobiratel'stvo v staroi Moskve. I. Sobraniia XVI i XVII veka." *Sredi kollektsionerov*, 1922, no. 1, pp. 26-29.

Chistiakova, E. V. "Letopisnye zapisi o narodnykh dvizheniiakh serediny XVII v." In *Problemy obshchestvenno-politicheskoi istorii Rossii i slavianskikh stran*, pp. 242-252. Moscow, 1963.

Crummey, Robert O. "Court Groupings and Politics in Russia, 1645-1649." *FzOG* 24(1978):203-221.

————. "Court Spectacles in Seventeenth-Century Russia: Illusion and Reality." Forthcoming in *Studies on the History and Culture of Medieval Russia*.

————. "Crown and Boiars under Fedor Ivanovich and Michael Romanov." *Canadian/American Slavic Studies* 6(1972):549-574.

————. "Ivan the Terrible." In *Windows on the Russian Past*, eds. Samuel H. Baron and Nancy W. Heer, pp. 57-74. Columbus, Ohio, 1977.

————. "The Origins of the Noble Official: the Boiar Elite, 1613-1689." In *Russian Officialdom: the Bureaucratization of Russian Society from the Seventeenth to the Twentieth Century*, eds. Walter M. Pintner and Don K. Rowney, pp. 46-75. Chapel Hill, N. C., 1980.

————. "Peter and the Boiar Aristocracy, 1689-1700." *Canadian/American Slavic Studies* 8(1974):274-287.

————. "The Reconstitution of the Boiar Aristocracy, 1613-1645." *FzOG* 18(1973):187-220.

————. "Reflections on Mestnichestvo in the 17th Century." *FzOG* 27(1980):269-281.

————. "Russian Absolutism and the Nobility." *Journal of Modern History* 49(1977):456-467.

[Danilov] N. N. "V. V. Golicyn bis zum Staatsstreich vom Mai 1682." *JfGO* 1(1936):1-33.

Danilov, N. N. "Vasilij Vasil'evič Golicyn (1682-1714)." *JfGO* 2(1937): 539-596.

Demidova, N. F. "Biurokratizatsiia gosudarstvennogo apparata absoliutizma v XVII-XVIII v." In *Absoliutizm v Rossii*, pp. 206-242. Moscow, 1964.

———. "Iz istorii zakliucheniia Nerchinskogo dogovora 1689." In *Rossiia v period reform Petra I*, ed. N. I. Pavlenko, pp. 289-310. Moscow, 1973.

Dewey, H. W. and Kleimola, A. M. "Suretyship and Collective Responsibility in Pre-Petrine Russia." *JfGO* 18(1970):337-354.

Dubinskaia, L. G. "Pomestnoe i votchinnoe zemlevladenie meshcherskogo kraia vo vtoroi polovine XVII v." In *Dvorianstvo i krepostnoi stroi v Rossii XVI-XVIII v.*, pp. 120-134. Moscow, 1975.

Eksin, Iu. M. "Dmitrii Pozharskii." *Voprosy istorii*, 1976, no. 8, pp. 107-119.

Elenev, N. A. "Stol'nik Potemkin i ego portrety." *Novik*, 1957, pp. 39-50.

Figarovskii, V. A. "Krest'ianskoe vosstanie 1614-1615 gg." *Istoricheskie zapiski* 73(1963):194-218.

Floria, B. N. "Evoliutsiia podatnogo immuniteta." *Istoriia SSSR*, 1972, no. 1, pp. 48-71.

Gnevushev, A. M. "Zemlevladenie i sel'skoe khoziaistvo v moskovskom gosudarstve XVI-XVII vv." In *Russkaia istoriia v ocherkakh i stat'iakh*, ed. M. V. Dovnar-Zapol'skii, vol. 3, pp. 267-311. Kiev, 1912.

Grekov, B. D. "Pomeshchich'e khoziaistvo v XVI-XVII vv. v Novgorodskoi oblasti." *Uchenye zapiski Instituta istorii RANIONa* 6(1928):75-109.

Grigorii, Arkhimandrit. "O domovykh tserkvakh Moskovskoi eparkhii." *ChOIDR*, 1876, no. 3, pp. 1-29.

Gudzinskaia, A. P. and Mikhailova, N. G. "Graficheskie materialy po istorii arkhitektury pomeshchich'ei i krest'ianskoi usadeb v Rossii XVII v." *Istoriia SSSR*, 1971, no. 5, pp. 214-227.

Gurliand, I. Ia. "Prikaz sysknykh del." In *Sbornik statei po istorii prava, posviashchennyi Mikhailu Flegontovichu Vladimirskomu-Budanovu*, pp. 87-109. Kiev, 1904.

Hughes, Diane. "Domestic Ideals and Social Behavior: Evidence from Medieval Genoa." In *The Family in History*, ed. Charles E. Rosenberg, pp. 115-143. Philadelphia, 1975.

Hughes, Lindsey A. J. "The 17th-century 'Renaissance' in Russia." *History Today* 30(February 1980):41-45.

———. "Western European Graphic Materials as a Source for Moscow Baroque Architecture." *Slavonic and East European Review* 55(1977):433-443.

Ikonnikov, V. S. "Blizhnii boiarin Afanasii Lavrent'evich Ordin-Nashchokin, odin iz predshestvennikov petrovskoi reformy." *Russkaia starina* 40:17-66, 273-308.

Kamiński, Andrzej. "Neo-Serfdom in Poland-Lithuania." *Slavic Review* 34(1975):253-268.

Keep, J.L.H. "The Decline of the Zemsky Sobor." *Slavonic and East European Review* 36(1957):100-122.

———. "The Muscovite Élite and the Approach to Pluralism." *Slavonic and East European Review* 48(1970):201-232.

———. "The Regime of Filaret (1619-1633)." *Slavonic and East European Review* 38(1960):334-360.

Kleimola, A. M. "Boris Godunov and the Politics of Mestnichestvo." *Slavonic and East European Review* 53(1975):355-370.

———. "The Changing Face of the Muscovite Aristocracy. The 16th Century: Sources of Weakness." *JfGO* 25(1977):481-493.

———. "Military Service and Elite Status in Muscovy in the Second Quarter of the Sixteenth Century." *Russian History* 7(1980):47-64.

Kobrin, V. B. "Sostav Oprichnogo dvora Ivana Groznogo." In *Arkheograficheskii ezhegodnik za 1959 god*, pp. 16-91. Moscow, 1960.

Kudriavtsev, I. M. " 'Izdatel'skaia" deiatel'nost' Posol'skogo prikaza (K istorii russkoi rukopisnoi knigi vo vtoroi polovine XVII veka)." *Kniga. Issledovaniia i materialy* 8(1963):179-244.

Likhachev, N. P. "K voprosu o podpisiakh dumnykh liudei na postanovleniiakh Boiarskoi dumy." *Letopis' zaniatii Arkheograficheskoi komissii* 17(1907):47-62.

———. "Rodstvennyia sviazi kniazheskikh familii s sem'iami d'iakov." *Izvestiia RGO* 1:114-119.

Lukichev, M. P. "Boiarskie knigi XVII v." *Sovetskie arkhivy*, 1980, no. 5, pp. 50-54.

———. "Istochniki boiarskikh knig XVII veka." In *Voprosy istochnikovedeniia i istoriografii istorii SSSR. Dooktiabr'skii period. Sbornik statei*, pp. 134-142. Moscow, 1981.

———. "Obzor boiarskikh knig XVII v." In *Arkheograficheskii ezhegodnik za 1979 god*, pp. 255-266. Moscow, 1981.

———. "Svedeniia o boiarskikh knigakh v arkhivnykh opisiakh XVII-XVIII vekov." In *Istochnikovedcheskie issledovaniia po istorii feodal'noi Rossii. Sbornik statei*, pp. 49-61. Moscow, 1981.

MacMullen, Ramsay. "Roman Elite Motivation: Three Questions." *Past and Present*, no. 88 (August 1980), pp. 3-15.

Malinovskii, A. "Boiarin, dvoretskoi i namestnik serpukhovskii, Artemon Sergeevich Matveev, nachal'nik gosudarstvennago Prikaza posol'skoi pechati." *Trudy i letopisi Obshchestva istorii i drevnostei rossiiskikh, uchrezhdennago pri Imperatorskom moskovskom universitete* 7(1837):57-67.

Matveev, P. "Opala i ssylka boiarina A. S. Matveeva." *Istoricheskii Vestnik* 89(1902):780-819.

282 BIBLIOGRAPHY

Meehan-Waters, Brenda. "The Muscovite Noble Origins of the Russians in the Generalitet of 1730." *Cahiers du monde russe et soviétique* 12(1971):28-75.

———. "Social and Career Characteristics of the Administrative Elite, 1689-1761." In *Russian Officialdom*, pp. 76-105.

Moleva, N. M. "Muzyka i zrelishcha v Rossii XVII stoletiia." *Voprosy istorii*, 1971, no. 11, pp. 143-154.

Mordovina, S. P. and Stanislavskii, A. L. "Boiarskie spiski kontsa XVI-nachala XVII v. kak istoricheskii istochnik." *Sovetskie arkhivy*, 1973, no. 2, 90-96.

———. "Sostav osobogo dvora Ivana IV v period "Velikogo kniazheniia" Simeona Bekbulatovicha." In *Arkheograficheskii ezhegodnik za 1976 god*, pp. 153-193. Moscow, 1977.

Mordovina, S. P. "Kharakter dvorianskogo predstavitel'stva na zemskom sobore 1598 goda." *Voprosy istorii*, 1971, no. 2, pp. 55-63.

———. "K istorii Utverzhdennoi gramoty 1598 g." In *Arkheograficheskii ezhegodnik za 1968 god*, pp. 127-141. Moscow, 1970.

Murav'eva, L. L. "Promyslovaia derevnia tsentral'noi Rossii v usloviiakh krepostnichestva (vtoraia polovina XVII v.)." In *Dvorianstvo i krepostnoi stroi v Rossii XVI-XVIII vv.*, pp. 108-119.

Nikol'skii, V. K. "Boiarin Khitrovo. Iz istorii drevnerusskogo sobiratel'-stva." *Sredi kollektsionerov*, 1922, no. 10, pp. 15-23.

———. " "Boiarskaia popytka" 1681 g." *Istoricheskie izvestiia*, 1917, no. 2, 57-87.

Novosel'skii, A. A. "Praviashchie gruppy v sluzhilom "gorode" XVII v." *Uchenye zapiski RANIONa* 5(1929):315-335.

O'Brien, C. Bickford. "Muscovite *Prikaz* Administration of the Seventeenth Century, the Quality of Leadership." *FzGO* 24:223-235.

———. "Russia and Eastern Europe: the Views of A. L. Ordin-Naščokin." *JfGO* 17(1969):369-379.

Ostrogorsky, G. "Das Projekt einer Rangtabelle aus der Zeit des Caren Fedor Alekseevič." *Jahrbücher für Kultur und Geschichte der Slaven* 9(1933):86-138.

———. "Zum Stratordienst des Herrschers in der Byzantinisch-Slavischen Welt." *Seminarium Kondakovianum* 7(1935):187-204.

Parker, Geoffrey. "The "Military Revolution," 1560-1660—a Myth?" *Journal of Modern History* 48(1976):195-214.

Pavlenko, N. I. "Ob otsenke streletskogo vosstaniia 1682 g. (Po povodu monografii V. I. Buganova "Moskovskie vosstaniia kontsa XVII v.")." *Istoriia SSSR*, 1971, no. 3, pp. 77-94.

Pintner, Walter M. "The Evolution of Civil Officialdom, 1755-1855." In *Russian Officialdom*, pp. 190-226.

Platonov, S. F. "Moskovskoe pravitel'stvo pri pervykh Romanovykh." In *Stat'i po russkoi istorii (1883-1912)*, pp. 339-406. St. Petersburg, 1912.

———. "Moskovskie volneniia 1648 goda." In *Stat'i po russkoi istorii (1883-1912)*, pp. 62-75.

Plavsic, Borivoj. "Seventeenth-century Chanceries and their Staffs." In *Russian Officialdom*, pp. 19-45.

Preobrazhenskii, A. A. "Ob evoliutsii feodal'noi zemel'noi sobstvennosti v Rossii XVII-nachala XIX veka." *Voprosy istorii*, 1977, no. 5, pp. 46-62.

Raeff, Marc. "The Bureaucratic Phenomena of Imperial Russia, 1700-1905." *American Historical Review* 84(1979):399-411.

Ransel, David L. "Bureaucracy and Patronage: the View from an Eighteenth-Century Russian Letter-Writer." In *The Rich, the Well-Born, and the Powerful*, ed. F. C. Jaher, pp. 154-178. Urbana, 1973.

Rexheuser, Rex. "Adelsbesitz und Heeresverfassung im Moskauer Staat des 17. Jahrhunderts." *JfGO* 11(1973):1-17.

Roberts, Michael. "The Military Revolution, 1560-1660." In *Essays in Swedish History*, pp. 195-225. Minneapolis, 1967.

Rotenberg, S. S. "Monarkhiia s Boiarskoi dumy." *Uchenye zapiski Moskovskogo pedagogicheskogo instituta im V. I. Lenina* 35, fasc. 2(1946), pp. 56-95.

Rozanov, N. P. "Opisanie moskovskikh tserkvei, uchinennoe Moskovskoiu konsistorieiu v 1817 godu, s pokazaniam, kogda tserkvi postroeny i ot chego imeiut nazvanie svoei mestnosti." *ChOIDR*, 1874, no. 4, pp. 78-121.

Savin, A. "Mestnichestvo pri dvore Liudovika XIV." In *Sbornik statei posviashchennykh V. O. Kliuchevskomu*, pp. 277-290.

Shmidt, S. O. "Mestnichestvo i absoliutizm (postanovka voprosa)." In *Absoliutizm v Rossii*, pp. 168-205.

Spasskii, I. G. "Moskovskaia matematicheskaia rukopisnaia kniga serediny XVII v. i ee pervyi vladelets." In *Arkheograficheskii ezhegodnik za 1979 god*, pp. 56-74. Moscow, 1981.

Stanislavskii, A. L. "Boiarskie spiski v deloproizvodstve Razriadnogo prikaza." In *Aktovoe istochnikovedenie*, pp. 123-152. Moscow, 1979.

———. "Opyt izucheniia boiarskikh spiskov kontsa XVI-nachala XVII v." *Istoriia SSSR*, 1971, no. 4, pp. 97-110.

Starostina, T. V. "Ob opale A. S. Matveeva v sviazi s sysknym delom 1676-1677 gg. o khranenie zagovornykh pisem." *Uchenye zapiski Karelo-finskogo gosudarstvennogo universiteta* 2(1947), fasc. 1 (Istoricheskie i filologicheskie nauki), pp. 44-89.

———. "Iz istorii antifeodal'nykh vystuplenii krest'ianstva Rossii v 70-e gody XVII v." *Uchenye zapiski Petrozavodskogo gosudarstvennogo universiteta* 11(1962) (Istoricheskie nauki):255-263.

Stone, Lawrence. "The Inflation of Honours, 1558-1641." *Past and Present*, no. 14 (November 1958), pp. 45-70.

———. "Prosopography." *Daedalus* 100(1971):46-79.

———. "The Rise of the Nuclear Family in Early Modern England: the Patriarchal Stage." In *The Family in History*, pp. 13-57.

Szeftel, Marc. "The History of Suretyship in Old Russian Law." *Sûretés personnelles: receuils de la Société Jean Bodin* 29(1971):841-866.

Tazbir, J. "Privilegirovannoe soslovie feodal'noi Pol'shi." *Voprosy istorii*, 1977, no. 12, pp. 159-167.

Tikhonov, Iu. A. "Feodal'naia renta v pomeshchich'ikh imeniiakh tsentral'noi Rossii v kontse XVII-pervoi chetverti XVIII v." In *Rossiia v period reform Petra I*, pp. 199-215.

———. "Otpisnye i otkaznye knigi Pomestnogo prikaza kak istochnik o boiarskikh i dvorianskikh vladeniiakh Moskovskogo uezda XVII-nachale XVIII v." In *Arkheograficheskii ezhegodnik za 1968*, pp. 142-153. Moscow, 1970.

———. "Podmoskovnye imeniia russkoi aristokratii vo vtoroi polovine XVII-nachale XVIII vv." In *Dvorianstvo i krepostnoi stroi v Rossii XVI-XVIII vv.*, pp. 135-158.

Torke, Hans-Joachim. "Adel und Staat vor Peter dem Grossen (1649-1689)." *FzOG* 27(1980):282-298.

Troitskii, S. M. "Khoziaistvo krupnogo sanovnika Rossii v pervoi chetverti XVIII v." In *Rossiia v period reform Petra I*, pp. 215-248.

———. "O skupke zemel' A. D. Menshikovym, A. V. Makarovym i I. A. i P. I. Musinymi-Pushkinami (Iz istorii krupnogo feodal'nogo zemlevladeniia v Rossii pervoi treti XVIII v.)." In *Voprosy agrarnoi istorii tsentra i severo-zapada RSFSR*, pp. 88-102. Smolensk, 1972.

Trutovskii, V. "Boiarin i oruzhnichii Bogdan Matveevich Khitrovo i moskovskaia Oruzheinaia palata." *Starye gody*, 1909, July-September, pp. 345-383.

Varga, Ilona. "Katonai szolgálat és a XVI-XVII századi orosz uralkodó osztály rétegzödése a besorolási prikáz dokumentumainak tükrében." *Acta universitatis szegediensis. Acta historica* 22(1966):45-55. Summary in French.

Vasilevskaia, E. A. "Terminologiia mestnichestva i rodstva." *Trudy Istoriko-arkhivnogo instituta* 2(1946):155-179.

Veselovskii, S. B. "Dve zametki o Boiarskoi dume." In *Sergeiu Fedorovichu Platonovu. Ucheniki, druz'ia i pochitateli. Sbornik statei, posviashchennykh S. F. Platonovu*, pp. 305-310.

Vodarskii, Ia. E. "Chislennost' naseleniia i kolichestvo pomestno-votchinnikh zemel' v XVII v. (po pistsovym i perepisnym knigam)." In *Ezhegodnik po agrarnoi istorii Vostochnoi Evropy 1964 god*, pp. 217-230. Kishinev, 1966.

————. "Praviashchaia gruppa svetskikh feodalov v Rossii v XVII v." In *Dvorianstvo i krepostnoi stroi Rossii XVI-XVIII vv.*, pp. 70-107.

Volkov, M. Ia. "Ob otmene mestnichestva v Rossii." *Istoriia SSSR*, 1977, no. 2, pp. 53-67.

Vostokov, A. A. "Boiarskie knigi kak material dlia istorii vysshego russkago sluzhilago sosloviia." In *Materialy dlia istorii russkago dvorianstva*, vol. 3, pp. 26-48. St. Petersburg, 1885.

Welke, Martin. "Russland in der deutschen Publizistik des 17. Jahrhunderts (1613-1689)." *FzOG* 23(1976):105-276.

Wójcik, Zbigniew. "Russian Endeavors for the Polish Crown in the Seventeenth Century." *Slavic Review* 41(1982):59-72.

Zabelin, I. "Bol'shoi boiarin v svoem votchinnom khoziaistve (XVIIyi vek)." *Vestnik Evropy*, 1871, no. 1, pp. 5-49; no. 2, pp. 465-514.

Zaozerskaia, E. I. "Iz istorii feodal'noi votchiny i polozhenie krest'ian v pervoi polovine XVII veka." *Materialy po istorii sel'skogo khoziaistva i krest'ianstva SSSR* 4(1960):39-66.

Zaozerskii, A. I. "Boiarskii dvor." *Russkii istoricheskii zhurnal* 7(1921):88-114.

Zeitlin, Maurice and Ratcliff, Richard Earl. "Research Methods for the Analysis of the Internal Structure of the Dominant Classes: the Case of Landlords and Capitalists in Chile." *Latin American Research Review* 10, no. 3 (1975), pp. 5-62.

Zernin, A. P. "Sud'ba mestnichestva, preimushchestvenno pri pervykh dvukh gosudariakh dinastii Romanovykh." In *Arkhiv istoriko-iuridicheskikh svedenii, otnosiashchikhsia do Rossii*, vol. 3, pp. 1-138.

Zertsalov, A. "Plan XVII veka chasti goroda Moskvy (ulitsy Maroseika i Il'inka i Krasnaia Ploshchad')." *ChOIDR*, 1896, no. 3, pp. 1-7.

Zimin, A. A. "Istochniki po istorii mestnichestva v XV-pervoi treti XVI v." In *Arkheograficheskii ezhegodnik za 1968 god*, pp. 109-118. Moscow, 1970.

————. "Khoziaistvennyi god v s. Pavlovskom (seredina XVII v.)." *Materialy po istorii sel'skogo khoziaistva i krest'ianstva SSSR* 6(1965):64-83.

————. "Sostav Boiarskoi dumy v XV-XVI vekakh." In *Arkheograficheskii ezhegodnik za 1957 god*, pp. 41-87. Moscow, 1958.

INDEX

Absolutism: in Russia and Prussia, 172

Adashev, Aleksei Fedorovich: former owner of I. V. Sheremetev's estate, 118

Akinfov, Nikita Ivanovich: as a Duma member, 202

Alad'in, Zamiatnia Fedorovich: as a Duma member, 210

Alcohol: consumption of, 146

Aleksei Mikhailovich, Tsar: attitude toward flight of A. L. Ordin-Nashchokin's son, 160; attitude toward precedence disputes, 137; became tsar, 83; character as a ruler, 77; children of, 75; conduct during the revolt of 1648, 84; cultural attitudes, 158-159; daily schedule, 141; decorum at the banquets of, 142; directs the Office of Secret Affairs, 40, 54; exiled B. I. Morozov, 84; friend of F. M. Rtishchev, 57; grants of land to Morozov, 112; guest at Morozov's country estate, 130; heirs of, 89; innovations on the estates of, 132; letter of consolation to N. I. Odoevskii, 139; love of falconry, 149-150; married Mariia Miloslavskaia, 78, 87; married Nataliia Naryshkina, 78, 101; military reforms under, 45; parody petition of, 104; patron of A. L. Ordin-Nashchokin, 77, 97, 100; of Patriarch Nikon, 20-21, 77, 97; of A. S. Matveev, 54, 97; of F. M. Rtishchev, 54, 99; of Morozov, 85, 88; of B. M. Khitrovo, 57; policy on appointments to the Duma, 27-29; policies on employment and promotion of servitors, 63-64; praise of Ordin-Nashchokin's piety, 105-151; piety of, 253 n. 36; promoted social upstarts,

69; promulgated the Code of 1649, 218; scolded V. B. Sheremetev for arrogance, 140; toured the military front, 37; traces of aristocratic revival under, 74; mentioned, 16, 46, 105, 109, 148, 164, 219

Alfer'ev, Ivan Vasil'evich: as a Duma member, 190

Almazov, Semen Erofeevich: as a Duma member, 208

Aman: character in the Play of Artaxerxes, 136

Ambassadors, reception of. See Reception of foreign ambassadors

Ancestral estates: of the Sheremetevs, 119

Andreev, Petr: parish priest, 155

Andreevskii Monastery: mentioned, 160

Andrusovo, Truce of: ended Russo-Polish War, 17; mentioned, 42

Anichkov, Grigorii Mikhailovich: as a Duma member, 193; chancery service of, 56

Anichkov, Ivan Mikhailovich: as a Duma member, 187

Apothecary Chancery: I. B. Cherkasskii in, 56; A. S. Matveev in, 56; provided access to the tsar's person, 56

Apraksins: as royal in-laws, 77

Apraksin, Petr Matveevich: as a Duma member, 210

Arbat Street, Moscow: mentioned, 144

Archangel: administrative center of the north, 49; mentioned, 104

Aristocracy: characteristics, 164; definition, 14, 65, 81

Armory: as an "academy of the applied arts," 160; I. M. Iazykov in, 57

INDEX

305

Telepnev, Ivan Stepanovich: as a Duma
member, 206
Temkin-Rostovskii, Prince Mikhail Mikhailovich: as a Duma member, 187; commander in the Thirteen Years' War, 46;
importance of lineage, 74
Theatre. See Court theatre
Tiapkin, Vasilii Mikhailovich: as a Duma
member, 203; client of A. L. Ordin-
Nashchokin, 105; cultural attitudes, 159;
resident ambassador in Poland, 42; role
in negotiating the Treaty of Bakhchisarai, 42
Tikhonov, Iu. A.: on the money rent
payed by central Russian peasants, 109
Titov, Semen Stepanovich: as a Duma
member, 196
Tiumen', cathedral in: mentioned, 155
Tolochanov, Semen Fedorovich: as a
Duma member, 203
Tobol'sk: administrative center of Siberia,
49; Archbishop of, 155; mentioned, 50-
51
Tolstoi, Andrei Vasil'evich: as a Duma
member, 196
Tolstois: longevity in high rank, 29; rose to
the boyar elite in the seventeenth century, 66
Tonsure: use of to destroy political rivals,
152
Trakhaniotov, Petr Tikhonovich: as a
Duma member, 187; lynched, 84, 86-87;
marriage ties to the Morozovs, Miloslav-
skiis and Pleshcheevs, 87; partisan of
B. I. Morozov, 85
Transfiguration, Church of the. See No-
vodevich'i Convent
Tret'iakov, Petr Alekseevich: as a Duma
member, 180
Troekurov, Princes: genealogical seniority
among, 74; landholdings, 115; marriage
ties to the Khitrovos, 81; to the Streshnevs, 78; placed all men in the Duma,
30
Troekurov, Prince Boris Ivanovich: as a
Duma member, 191; enemy of A. S.
Matveev, 102
Troekurov, Prince Ivan Borisovich: ally of
the Miloslavskiis? 94; as a Duma member, 198; landholdings, 114; Moscow
palace of, 145

Troekurov, Prince Ivan Fedorovich: as a
Duma member, 182
Troubles, Time of: events, 15-16; impact
on the Sheremetevs' landholdings, 118;
royal land grants during, 111; mentioned, 117, 119, 123, 154
Trubetskoi, Princes: landholdings, 115;
owned a palace in the Moscow Kremlin,
143; placed all men in the Duma, 30
Trubetskoi, Prince Aleksei Nikitich: as a
Duma member, 186; commander in the
Thirteen Years' War, 46; enemy of Ni-
kon? 100; negotiated with Hapsburg
diplomats, 60; partisan of B. I. Moro-
zov? 85; service in Moscow and the
provinces, 52
Trubetskoi, Prince Andrei Vasil'evich: as a
Duma member, 179
Trubetskoi, Prince Dmitrii Timofeevich: as
a Duma member, 178-179; landhold-
ings, 114
Trubetskoi, Prince Iurii Petrovich: as a
Duma member, 197-198; landholdings,
114; produced potash on his estates, 130
Trubetskoi, Prince Ivan Iur'evich: as a
Duma member, 212
Trubetskoi, Prince Timofei Romanovich:
pattern of service of, 52, 231 n. 84
Tsar's Workshop: I. M. Iazykov in, 57
Tsykler, Ivan Eliseevich: as a Duma mem-
ber, 212
Tudors: policies toward the aristocracy,
170
Tugarinov, Mitrofan Petrovich: as a Duma
member, 211
Tula: boyars rarely commanders in, 47
Turgenev, Semen Iakovlevich: as a Duma
member, 214
Turkey. See Ottoman Empire
Tushino: headquarters of the second False
Dmitrii, 15

Ubory: parish church at, 154
Ukhtomskii, Prince Ivan Iur'evich: as a
Duma member, 210
Ukraine: influence of scholars from, 157;
"left bank" of acquired by Russia, 17; lo-
cal power of the Polish magnates in, 173
Ukraintsev, Emel'ian Ignat'evich: as a
Duma member, 203; early chancery
service, 39; served under the regency

LIBRARY OF CONGRESS CATALOGING IN PUBLICATION DATA

Crummey, Robert O.
  Aristocrats and servitors.

  Bibliography: p.
  Includes index.
  1. Soviet Union—Politics and government—1613-1689.
  2. Soviet Union—Nobility—History—17th century.
  3. Elite (Social sciences)—Soviet Union. I. Title.
  II. Title: Boyar elite in Russia, 1613-1689.
  DK114.C78 1983   305.5'2'0947   83-3064
  ISBN 0-691-05389-8